THE ROYAL HORTICULTURAL SOCIETY

## PLANT ❧ GUIDES

# PERENNIALS

# THE ROYAL HORTICULTURAL SOCIETY
## PLANT ❦ GUIDES
# PERENNIALS

COVENT
GARDEN
BOOKS

# A DORLING KINDERSLEY BOOK

Produced for Dorling Kindersley by PAGE One
Cairn House, Elgiva Lane, Chesham, Buckinghamshire

EDITOR Helen Parker
DESIGNER Bob Gordon
MANAGING EDITOR Francis Ritter
MANAGING ART EDITOR Derek Coombes
PRODUCTION Adrian Gathercole
PICTURE RESEARCH Sharon Southren

This edition published in 1999 for Covent Garden Books

First published in Great Britain in 1996
by Dorling Kindersley Limited
9 Henrietta Street, London WC2E 8PS

2 4 6 8 10 9 7 5 3 1

Visit us on the World Wide Web at
http://www.dk.com

A CIP catalogue record for this book
is available from the British Library

ISBN 1-8718-5438-5

Colour reproduction by Colourscan, Singapore
Printed and bound by Star Standard Industries, Singapore

# CONTENTS

## SMALL

## CONTRIBUTORS

LINDEN HAWTHORNE
*Writer and supplier of all text*

MICHAEL UPWARD
*Perennials in the Garden, Catalogue
of Perennials, Guide to Perennial
Care, Daylilies, Michaelmas
Daisies, Penstemons, Peonies, Phlox*

LARRY BARLOW  *Chrysanthemums*
ERIC CATTERALL  *Begonias*
DIANA GRENFELL  *Hostas*
DAVID HITCHCOCK
*Carnations and Pinks*
HAZEL KEY  *Pelargoniums*
SIDNEY LINNEGAR  *Irises*
DAVID McCLINTOCK  *Grasses*
DIANA MILLER  *African Violets*
PHILIP SWINDELLS
*Primulas, Ferns*
JOHN THIRKELL  *Delphiniums*

# HOW TO USE THIS BOOK

THIS BOOK PROVIDES the ideal quick reference guide to selecting and identifying perennials for the garden.

The **Perennials in the Garden** section is a helpful introduction to perennials and gives advice on choosing a suitable plant for a particular site or purpose, such as for a border, container, or simply as a specimen.

To choose or identify a perennial, turn to the **Catalogue of Perennials**, where photographs are accompanied by concise plant descriptions and useful tips on cultivation and propagation. The entries are grouped by size, season of interest, as well as by colour (see the colour wheel below) to make selection easier.

For additional information on perennial cultivation, routine care and propagation, turn to the **Guide to Perennial Care**, where general advice on all aspects of caring for your perennials can be found.

At the end of the book, a useful two-page glossary explains key terms, and a comprehensive index of every perennial, its synonyms, and common names, together with a brief genus description, allows quick and easy access to the book by plant name.

### The colour wheel

All the perennials in the book are grouped according to the colour of their main feature of interest. They are always arranged in the same order, indicated by the colour wheel below, from white through reds and blues, to yellows and oranges. Variegated plants are categorized by the colour of their variegation, for example, white or yellow.

## THE SYMBOLS

The symbols below are used throughout the **Catalogue of Perennials** to indicate a plant's preferred growing conditions and hardiness. However, both the climate and soil conditions of your particular site should also be taken into account, as they may affect a plant's growth.

☼ Prefers full sun　　◊ Prefers well-drained soil

☼ Prefers partial shade　◊ Prefers moist soil

☀ Tolerates full shade　◆ Prefers wet soil

pH　Needs acid soil

❄　Half-hardy – can withstand temperatures down to 0°C (32°F)

❄ ❄　Frost hardy – can withstand temperatures down to -5°C (23°F)

❄ ❄ ❄　Fully hardy – can withstand temperatures down to -15°C (5°F)

♈　RHS Award of Garden Merit. The symbol indicates those perennials deemed by the Royal Horticultural Society to be of exceptional quality and reliability. They must be of good constitution and not susceptible to any pest or disease, as well as not requiring any highly specialized care.

## Perennial size categories

The perennials featured in the Catalogue of Perennials are divided according to the average height they attain. However, heights may vary from the ones given, according to site, growing conditions, climate and age.

The categories are as follows:
LARGE
Over 1.2m (4ft)
MEDIUM
60cm–1.2m (2–4ft)
SMALL
Up to 60cm (2ft)

# HOW TO USE THE CATALOGUE OF PERENNIALS

**HEADINGS**
Each chapter is subdivided into sections, according to the average size of the plants and their main season of interest.

The plant's *family name* appears here.

The plant's *common name(s)* appear here.

The plant's *botanical name* appears here.

**PLANT PORTRAITS**
The colour photographs show each plant's main features and colour (see the colour wheel on previous page).

**ENTRIES**
A brief plant description giving details of growing habit, flowers, fruits and leaves, followed by information on native habitat, tips on cultivation and propagation and a list of other botanical names.

**FEATURE PAGES**
Plant groups or genera of special interest to the gardener are presented on separate feature pages. A brief introduction giving general information on appearance, use, cultivation and propagation is followed by concise plant entries.

---

SMALL/Summer • 261

Asteraceae/Compositae | YELLOW OX-EYE

*BUPHTHALMUM SALICIFOLIUM*
*Habit* Upright, spreading. *Flowers* Daisy-like, borne singly on sturdy, leafy stems throughout summer. Clear yellow, with narrow, widely spaced ray florets around a darker yellow disc. *Leaves* Lance-shaped to linear-lance-shaped, toothed or entire. Mid-green.
• NATIVE HABITAT Damp, stony places, C. Europe.
• CULTIVATION Grow in moist, well-drained soil, in sun or light shade. May need staking. Spreads on fertile soils. Good for wild or cottage gardens.
• PROPAGATION Seed or division in spring or autumn.

☼ ◊
❄ ❄ ❄
HEIGHT 60cm (2ft)
SPREAD 1m (3ft)

Asteraceae/Compositae

*GAZANIA RIGENS* var. *UNIFLORA*
*Habit* Mat-forming. *Flowers* Daisy-like, with pointed, borne singly on short stems, in early summer. Yellow-orange or yellow ray florets around a yellow disc. *Leaves* Spoon-shaped or divided, smooth. Dark green above, silvery-white beneath.
• NATIVE HABITAT South Africa.
• CULTIVATION Tolerant of dry soils and salt-laden winds. Suitable for containers. Treat as an annual in cool areas. Grow in well-drained soil in a warm, sunny, sheltered site.
• PROPAGATION By seed or division in spring.

☼ ◊
❄
HEIGHT 23cm (9in)
SPREAD 20–30cm (8–12in)

Asteraceae/Compositae

*BIDENS FERULIFOLIA*
*Habit* Clump-forming, spreading, short-lived. *Flowers* Starry, 4cm (1½in) across, in profusion, from mid-spring to first frosts. Golden-yellow. *Leaves* Very finely divided, fennel-like. Fresh green.
• NATIVE HABITAT Grassland and waste ground in southern USA, Mexico, Guatemala.
• CULTIVATION Grow in sun, in well-drained soil. Good for a border, gravel plantings, hanging basket and other containers. May be grown as an annual.
• PROPAGATION Seed, division, or stem cuttings in spring.

☼ ◊
❄ ❄
HEIGHT 30cm (12in) or more
SPREAD 30cm (12in)

Crassulaceae

*SEDUM AIZOON* 'Euphorbioides'
*Habit* Clump-forming, rhizomatous. *Flowers* Small, star-shaped, borne in dense, slightly rounded heads, over long periods in summer. Dark yellow, opening from red buds. *Leaves* Fleshy, oblong-lance-shaped. Bluish-green.
• NATIVE HABITAT Species occurs on dry hills, in scrub and on rocky streambanks, in N. Asia.
• CULTIVATION Grow in fertile, moist but well-drained soil, in sun or light shade.
• PROPAGATION By division in spring or autumn.
• OTHER NAMES *S. aizoon* 'Aurantiacum'.

☼ ◊
❄ ❄ ❄
HEIGHT 45cm (18in)
SPREAD 45cm (18in)

---

FERNS • 299

## FERNS

Among the most popular of all foliage plants, ferns add texture and atmosphere to the house or garden, where they are particularly effective in settings by streams or in damp, shady corners. Hardy ferns are suitable for growing in woodland gardens, or in the open garden where they benefit from moist, neutral to alkaline conditions. Many of the smaller types are excellent for a shady rock garden. Tender tropical ferns are best cultivated indoors in a greenhouse or conservatory, or as house plants where they should be kept moist, but not waterlogged. Protection should be given from direct sunlight.
Ferns are raised mainly by spores but may be propagated by division or, in some species, by bulbils.

*PTERIS CRETICA ALBOLINEATA*
*Habit* Clump-forming. *Leaves* Evergreen or semi-evergreen, to 20cm (8in) long, forked or in linear segments. Pale green with a creamy-white central stripe.
• TIPS Grow in humus in cooler climates. Propagate by division in spring or spore in summer.
• HEIGHT 45cm (18in).
• SPREAD 30cm (12in).

*Pteris cretica albolineata*
✿ ◐
Min. 5°C (41°F).

*POLYPODIUM AUREUM* 'Mandaianum'
*Habit* Creeping. *Leaves* Evergreen, to 1m (3ft) long, deeply lobed, with orange sporangia beneath. Blue-green.
• TIPS Grow indoors in cooler climates. Divide in spring.
• OTHER NAMES *Phlebodium aureum* 'Mandaianum'.
• HEIGHT 1–1.5m (3–5ft).
• SPREAD 60cm (2ft).

*Polypodium aureum* 'Mandaianum'
✿ ◊
Min. 5°C (41°F).

*DRYOPTERIS FILIX-MAS*
*Habit* Arching. *Leaves* Deciduous or semi-evergreen, lance-shaped, arising like a shuttlecock from a crown of stout, brown scaly rhizomes. Mid-green.
• TIPS Grow in humus-rich soil in a shady border. Sow spores in summer or divide in spring or autumn.
• HEIGHT 1.2m (4ft).
• SPREAD 1m (3ft).

*Dryopteris filix-mas*
Male fern
✿ ◐ ❄ ❄ ❄ ❄    ♀

*DICKSONIA ANTARCTICA*
*Habit* Slow-growing, trunk-forming. *Leaves* Evergreen or semi-evergreen, to 3m (10ft) long, arching, divided into linear segments. Dark green, pale green when young.
• TIPS Needs filtered, moist and moderate humidity. Excellent for a cool conservatory. Propagate by spores in summer.
• HEIGHT 6m (20ft) or more.
• SPREAD 4m (12ft).

*Dicksonia antarctica*
Man fern, Soft tree fern
✿ ◐ ◐    ♀

*PLATYCERIUM BIFURCATUM*
*Habit* Epiphytic. *Leaves* Evergreen, with round, papery sterile fronds, and arching, forked, fertile fronds with a velvety-brown spore patch beneath. Grey-green.
• TIPS Grow indoors in cooler climates, on bark attached to a raft of moss. Needs high humidity.
• HEIGHT 1m (3ft).
• SPREAD 1m (3ft).

*Platycerium bifurcatum*
Common stag's-horn fern
✿ ◊
Min. 5°C (41°F).

---

**SYMBOLS**
The symbols indicate the sun, soil and temperature requirements (see THE SYMBOLS on previous page). Minimum temperatures are given for plants that cannot survive below 0°C (32°F).

**FEATURE PLANT DESCRIPTIONS**
As with the main Catalogue entries, a brief plant description is followed by useful tips on cultivation and propagation where these are not already given in the general introduction.

**SIZES**
The average height and spread of the plants are given, although these may vary according to site, growing conditions, climate and age.

# PERENNIALS IN THE GARDEN

PERENNIALS, PERHAPS MORE than any other group of plants, offer an infinitely rich palette of colour, form, fragrance and texture. There are perennials suitable for almost every area in the garden, however large or small, and whatever the mood or style.

Perennials are defined as non-woody plants that live for two or more years. Some, such as *Helleborus niger*, are evergreen, and so provide valuable winter interest. Most, however, are herbaceous, and die back in autumn. While this has the disadvantage of leaving bare beds in winter, many gardeners enjoy this seasonality, not least because the burgeoning new growth heralds the onset of spring.

With thoughtful selection, perennials can be used to create borders with a prolonged season of interest. They can be used in a mixed border with shrubs to give long-term structure, or with spring bulbs and long-flowering annuals to fill in during the quieter periods that precede and follow the glorious, if short-lived, mid-summer flush of bloom.

## Choosing perennials

All successful planting designs depend on thoroughly analyzing the site before carefully selecting plants to suit the conditions that exist in the garden. It is always preferable to select perennials that suit the soil type, climate and aspect than to struggle to keep plants alive in unsuitable conditions.

With their broad spectrum of colour and scent, perennials are obviously valued for their flowers. A number also have very attractive foliage, ranging from the emerald-green, neatly pleated leaves of *Veratrum* to the delicate tracery of *Dicentra*. The beauty of foliage nearly always outlasts that of the flowers, and the variety of textures and colours of leaves provides great potential for extending the season of interest – especially important in a smaller garden.

## Formal border

*This traditional formal border is laid out in broad, straight beds flanking a path of smooth, fresh green turf. There is a gentle graduation of height, both from front to back and along the long axis of the border.*

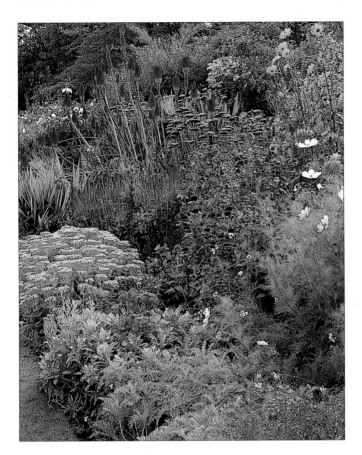

**Summer border**
*Here hot-coloured flowers are offset by the cooler greys of the foreground foliage, and low, rounded plants provide a horizontal foil to the strongly upright spikes of red-hot pokers* (Kniphofia).

Perennials range in height from the architectural grandeur of the cardoon (*Cynara cardunculus*), to the lowest of ground-covering plants, permitting infinite variations of form, perspective and composition. Their versatility can be applied to a range of planting themes and situations.

### Herbaceous border
The herbaceous border may be designed in a variety of styles to set or enhance the overall character and tone of the garden. Since late Victorian times, herbaceous borders have proved to be an enduringly popular means of displaying perennials. In traditional borders, the usually rectangular beds were flanked by smooth green lawns, often with a backdrop of warm brick or precision-cut hedging. The profusion of summer and autumn-flowering perennials was banked according to height and arranged in bold and distinct drifts to provide tones and contrast of colour, form and texture. These well-proven principles apply equally to more modern designs, even where space is limited and borders must be created on a more modest scale.

The ordered elegance of a traditional border suits a formal garden or, for a more contemporary style, an island bed set in a sea of turf, gravel or paving. The cottage garden relies on the deceptively random placement of fluid and informal drifts, set to spill over and disguise the hard lines and edges of paving.

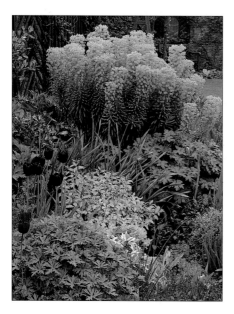

**Mixed border**
*Here the season of interest is extended beyond the mid-summer peak of the perennials by tulips in spring, and into autumn with the golden leaves of* Euphorbia.

## The mixed border

As its name suggests, the mixed border may contain a combination of small trees, shrubs, bulbs, annuals and biennials to complement the often short-lived beauty of perennial plants. This mixed planting is invaluable in small gardens, where empty beds in winter may appear tediously dominant. Mixed borders provide the greatest opportunity for creating year-round interest and imaginative plant associations, but need very careful planning if they are to ensure an attractive seasonal progression, especially in the duller months between autumn and spring.

While the volume of space given over to each type of plant will vary according to taste, the allocation of one-third to one-half of the space to the planting of shrubs offers the best potential for a varied design that provides year-round

interest. Use a mixture of evergreen and deciduous shrubs to impart structure and substance to the design, and consider carefully their habit, form, flowering and fruiting period. Bear in mind that their summer foliage will provide a foil and backdrop to the summer-flowering perennials. Shrubs with attractive, glossy foliage are usually preferable, but even those with dull summer leaves have a place. They can be used as a support for scrambling herbaceous plants such as *Clematis recta*.

In the early months of the year, the emerging foliage of the perennials can be enhanced and enlivened by a successional display of spring and early summer bulbs. A sequence that includes snowdrops, narcissus, *Muscari*, fritillaries and tulips, from the single earlies such as *Tulipa* 'Diana' to the single late-flowering tulips such as *T.* 'Queen of Night', will provide interest from late winter through to early summer. Later in the season, use summer-flowering bulbs such as *Allium sphaerocephalum* or *Galtonia candicans* to grow through and complement perennials in full bloom. Later still, sun-loving bulbs such as *Nerine bowdenii* and *Amaryllis belladonna*, prolong the display well into autumn.

Annuals and biennials also make useful contributions to the mixed border. They may be used as "fillers" until other plants reach their mature dimensions, and are indispensable when used to mask gaps left by perennials such as *Papaver orientale* that die back after flowering. Select annuals carefully; the vivid colours of many modern seed races can appear garish when set against perennials of soft and subtle colour.

## Designing beds and borders

When designing a planting scheme, the basic principles are essentially the same, whether planning a herbaceous border, island bed or mixed border. Considerations of height, mass, shape, and sequential interest, in combination with texture and colour are all variable factors that may be exploited to achieve particular design effects. It is also vital to research an individual plant's natural preferences in cultivation, and to choose plants that are suitable for the soil type, aspect and climate that exist in the garden. Imagination and personal taste will inevitably influence your planting schemes but there are a few basic guidelines to follow.

## General principles
It is important at the outset to decide on the preferred style of planting, since this provides a clear suggestion as to the size, shape and form of the beds to be planted. The choice of style will be dictated in part by personal taste and imagination, but it may also be guided by observation of the architectural style of the house and any existing hard landscaping in the garden, such as walls, steps and paving. A formally elegant and well-ordered style usually succeeds best when planted into a straight-edged and symmetrical border. A more relaxed and informal planting, with irregular drifts of plants, is more likely to succeed in borders with irregular, curved outlines.

## Informal planting
*The hard edges and lines of the steps are masked and softened here by an informal profusion of foliage and flowers set to spill gracefully over them. The bold sculptural forms of hostas and Carex elata 'Aurea' are used to add focus and a strong structural element to the scheme.*

The size of the border will vary, but as a guide, the larger the garden the bigger the border should be to maintain a sense of proportion and scale with the house and its surroundings. A width of 1.5m (5ft) is the minimum necessary to permit balanced grouping of plants and graduations of height and form; a width of 2.7m (9ft) lends much more versatility, where space permits.

When planning a planting scheme, consider the space required for individual plants at maturity and take into account their rate of growth, so that the smallest are not overwhelmed. Large clumps or drifts can be planted in extensive borders, but take care to plant smaller clumps in tiny gardens. Do not be afraid to make fine adjustments to the plan when setting it out.

**Contrasting foliage**
*The success of this sophisticated planting relies on strong contrasts of texture and form provided by the jagged foliage of* Rheum palmatum *(rear), the heart-shaped leaves of* Ligularia dentata *and the arching, strap-shaped leaves of an ornamental grass.*

## Height, form, texture and colour

Borders are generally planted up with the tallest plants at the back and the lowest at the front. The aim is to create undulating graduations of mass and height, from front to back and along the long axis of the border. In an island bed, taller plants are set along the central axis, with lower ones at the margins, to give tiered effects in which no one plant hides another. This rule, though, is not immutable, and the occasional use of taller plants with an airy habit at the border front can add great individuality to a design.

For greatest impact, small and medium plants are best massed in groups of one type, with taller, more substantial species used singly to form dynamic focus and counterpoint. Set out smaller plants in random blocks 3, 5 or 7 (depending on size) to form natural and irregular drifts of contrasting colour, form and texture.

Perennials range widely in habit from low, spreading forms that provide strong horizontal lines, through rounded mound-forming types to those with a narrowly upright silhouette that are used to give vertical emphasis. Juxtapose contrasting forms to create a composition in which strong horizontal and vertical elements

**Planting in drifts**
*Planting random and odd-numbered groups of plants, creates bold and irregular drifts of varying size, shape, and colour. Subtle graduations of height and texture along the long axis of the border creates a sense of perspective.*

are balanced by a mass of softer, rounded shapes, and use plants with a strong, spiky outline, like the red-hot pokers, to provide emphatic contrasts and dynamic diagonals.

Foliage constitutes the greatest mass in a border, and so has strong impact and great potential for contrast and harmony. Textural variety depends on both leaf shape and surface texture. Harmonize finely cut or delicate leaves with those of substantial size and simple outline, such as *Rheum palmatum*, and use matt or silky surface textures in contrast with glossy and light-reflecting leaves. Colour associations in a border may be daring and experimental or subtle and restrained.

Colour affects the mood of a planting scheme, perhaps more than any other factor. Monochromatic themes may appear simple to plan, but without carefully placed contrasts of small areas of strong and intense hues they can become monotonous. Soft pastels set against cool blue or intense violet creates restful and sophisticated effects, whereas hot shades of orange, yellow and rich red lend warmth and exuberance. When combining hot and cool shades, use foliage to separate blocks of strong or clashing colours. Plants with silver or grey leaves are useful in this respect, since their cool neutrals associate well with almost every colour of the spectrum.

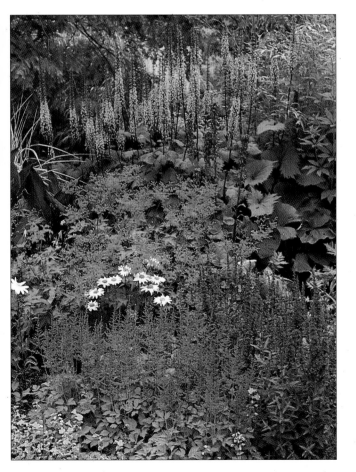

**Harmonizing textures**
*A tiered arrangement of plants with airy and feathery flowers, such as* Astilbe, Lythrum *and* Filipendula, *with the golden spires of* Ligularia stenocephala *in the background, forms a satisfying contrast of texture and form.*

# PLANTERS' GUIDE TO PERENNIALS

**FOR EXPOSED SITES**
*Anemone hupehensis*
*Centaurea hypoleuca* cvs
*Centranthus ruber*
*Kniphofia caulescens*
*Limonium latifolium*
*Phlomis russeliana*
*Phormium tenax*
*Sedum spectabile*
*Stachys byzantina*

**AIR POLLUTION-TOLERANT**
*Aquilegia vulgaris*
*Bergenia cordifolia*
*Euphorbia amygdaloides*
*Geranium endressii*
*Helleborus niger, H. orientalis*
*Hemerocallis* most
*Heuchera* most
*Hosta* most
*Lamium maculatum*
*Leucanthemum* x *superbum*
*Polemonium* most
*Polygonatum* some
*Pulmonaria* species
*Rudbeckia* most
*Sedum spectabile*
*Sisyrinchium striatum*
*Smilacina racemosa*
*Symphytum* most
*Thalictrum* most
*Tiarella* most
*Veronica gentianoides*

**FOR MOIST SHADE**
*Astilbe* most
*Astrantia major*
*Bergenia* all
*Brunnera macrophylla*
*Cimifuga simplex*
*Convallaria majalis*
*Gentiana asclepiadea*
*Hemerocallis*
*Hosta*
*Kirengeshoma palmata*
*Ligularia przewalskii*
*Peltiphyllum peltatum*
*Platycodon grandiflorus*

*Polygonum bistorta*
*Rodgersia* species
*Thalictrum* species
*Trilllium* species
*Veratrum* species

**FOR DRY SHADE**
*Acanthus mollis*
*Aconitum carmichaelii*
*Anemone hupehensis,*
   *A.* x *hybrida*
*Dicentra*
*Epimedium*
*Euphorbia amygdaloides*
*Geranium* some
*Helleborus orientalis*
*Tellima grandiflora*

**WINTER INTEREST**
*DECORATIVE FLOWERS*
*Bergenia* 'Ballawley',
   *B. cordifolia*
*Euphorbia amygdaloides*
   var. *robbiae*
*Helleborus argutifolius,*
   *H. niger*
*Pulmonaria* some
*DECORATIVE LEAVES*
*Bergenia* 'Ballawley',
   *B. cordifolia*
*Euphorbia amygdaloides*
   var. *robbiae*
*Helleborus argutifolius*
*Heuchera micrantha* 'Palace
   Purple'
*Lamium maculatum*
*Ophiopogon planiscapus*
   'Nigrescens'
*Phormium* cvs.
*Stachys byzantina*

**FRAGRANT FLOWERS**
*Centranthus ruber*
*Convallaria majalis*
*Cosmos atrosanguineus*
*Dianthus* many
*Erysimum* many
*Filipendula ulmaria*

*Hesperis matronalis*
*Nicotiana* many
*Paeonia lactiflora*
*Phlox paniculata*
*Primula* many

**ARCHITECTURAL PLANTS**
*Acanthus* most
*Angelica archangelica*
*Cortaderia selloana*
*Crambe cordifolia*
*Cynara cardunculus*
*Foeniculum vulgare*
*Gunnera manicata*
*Helleborus argutifolius*
*Hosta sieboldiana* var. *elegans*
*Phormium tenax*
*Rheum palmatum*
*Rodgersia* species

**FAST-GROWING PERENNIALS**
*Artemisia lactiflora*
*Campanula lactiflora*
*Centaurea macrocephala*
*Cephalaria gigantea*
*Crambe cordifolia*
*Cynara cardunculus*
*Ferula communis*
*Filipendula rubra*
*Galega* x *hartlandii*
*Gunnera manicata*
*Helianthus* most
*Kniphofia caulescens*
*Ligularia stenocephala*
*Phormium tenax*
*Rheum palmatum*
*Romneya coulteri*
*Salvia concertiflora*

# CATALOGUE OF
# PERENNIALS

| Onagraceae | WHITE ROSEBAY |
|---|---|

## *EPILOBIUM ANGUSTIFOLIUM ALBUM*

**Habit** Vigorous, upright, rhizomatous, spreading.
**Flowers** Small, 4-petalled, in long, open, erect spires, in late summer. White. **Leaves** Narrowly lance-shaped, wavy-edged. Dark green.
• NATIVE HABITAT Woodland edge, roadsides, waste ground, Europe, Asia, North America.
• CULTIVATION Grow in moist, well-drained soil, in sun or shade. Good for a wild garden.
• PROPAGATION By softwood cuttings of sideshoots in spring.
• OTHER NAMES *Chamaenerion angustifolium album.*

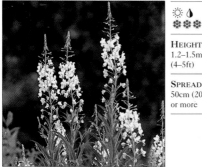

☼ ◐
❋ ❋ ❋

HEIGHT
1.2–1.5m
(4–5ft)

SPREAD
50cm (20in)
or more

| Solanaceae | FLOWERING TOBACCO |
|---|---|

## *NICOTIANA SYLVESTRIS* ♔

**Habit** Vigorous, upright, branching. **Flowers** Night-scented, tubular, produced in large, open clusters, in summer. White. **Leaves** Large, broadly elliptic, wrinkled. Blue-green.
• NATIVE HABITAT Argentina.
• CULTIVATION Tolerant of shade. Grow in any fertile, well-drained soil. The plant will perform best if planted in sheltered areas where the heavy fragrance can be appreciated. May also be grown as an annual.
• PROPAGATION By seed in spring.

☼ ◐
❋ ❋

HEIGHT
1.5m (5ft)
or more

SPREAD
75cm (30in)

| Papaveraceae | MATILIJA POPPY |
|---|---|

## *ROMNEYA COULTERI* ♔

**Habit** Vigorous, woody-based, rhizomatous.
**Flowers** Large, fragrant, with white, crêpe-textured petals around a boss of golden stamens, in late summer. **Leaves** Deeply divided. Blue-grey.
• NATIVE HABITAT Dry canyons in mountain foothills of California and Mexico.
• CULTIVATION Grow in a warm, sunny, sheltered site, in deep, well-drained soil. In cold areas, provide a dry mulch in winter. Resents transplanting.
• PROPAGATION By basal cuttings in early spring, by seed in autumn, or by root cuttings in winter.

☼ ◐
❋ ❋

HEIGHT
1.5–2m
(5–6ft)

SPREAD
2m (6ft)

| Brassicaceae/Cruciferae | |
|---|---|

## *CRAMBE CORDIFOLIA* ♔

**Habit** Vigorous, much-branched, with a woody rootstock. **Flowers** Small, fragrant, 4-petalled, in large, open, airy sprays, in summer. White. **Leaves** Large, lobed, heart-shaped, crinkled. Dark green.
• NATIVE HABITAT Open areas in stony soils, Caucasus mountains.
• CULTIVATION Tolerates semi-shade but flowers best in full sun. Grow in any well-drained soil. A beautiful specimen for a large border.
• PROPAGATION By division in spring, or by seed in autumn or spring.

☼ ◐
❋ ❋ ❋

HEIGHT
2m (6ft)

SPREAD
1.2m (4ft)
or more

| Apiaceae/Umbelliferae | |
|---|---|

## ERYNGIUM EBURNEUM

**Habit** Clump-forming. **Flowers** Small, rounded, thistle-like, on branched stems, in late summer. Green with white stamens. **Leaves** Evergreen, arching, sword-shaped, spined at the margin. Grey-green.
• NATIVE HABITAT Damp grasslands, South America.
• CULTIVATION Grow in fertile, moist but well-drained soil, in a warm, sunny site. Flowers dry well for winter arrangements; cut before fully open.
• PROPAGATION By seed in autumn, division in spring, or root cuttings in winter.

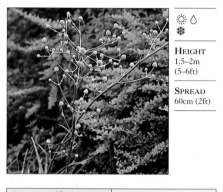

☼ ◊
❅

HEIGHT
1.5–2m
(5–6ft)

SPREAD
60cm (2ft)

| Asteraceae/Compositae | |
|---|---|

## ECHINOPS SPHAEROCEPHALUS

**Habit** Clump-forming. **Flowers** Tiny, in tight, globular heads borne on long, grey-white stems in late summer. Grey-white. **Leaves** Deeply divided, spiny. Grey-green above, white-downy beneath.
• NATIVE HABITAT Scrub, grasslands, from S. and C. Europe to Russia.
• CULTIVATION Grow in an open position in well-drained, not too fertile soil. Tolerates poor, dry soils.
• PROPAGATION By division or seed in autumn, or by root cuttings in winter.
• OTHER NAMES E. paniculatus.

☼ ◊
❅ ❅ ❅

HEIGHT
2m (6ft)

SPREAD
1m (3ft)

| Asphodelaceae/ Liliaceae | |
|---|---|

## EREMURUS HIMALAICUS

**Habit** Upright, with fleshy rhizomes. **Flowers** Small, shallowly cup-shaped, in long, dense spires, in early summer. White. **Leaves** Strap-shaped, smooth, in basal clumps. Mid-green.
• NATIVE HABITAT Dry, stony areas, Afghanistan, N.W. Himalayas.
• CULTIVATION Grow in a warm, sheltered site in well-drained, sandy soil. Rarely needs staking. Over winter protect crowns with a mulch of dry bracken.
• PROPAGATION By division in spring or early autumn, or by seed in autumn.

☼ ◊
❅ ❅

HEIGHT
2–2.5m
(6–8ft)

SPREAD
1m (3ft)

| Rosaceae | GOAT'S BEARD |
|---|---|

## ARUNCUS DIOICUS

**Habit** Clump-forming, rhizomatous. **Flowers** Tiny, carried in airy, branching, pyramidal plumes above the foliage, in mid-summer. Creamy-white. **Leaves** Large, long-stalked, divided into lance-shaped, toothed leaflets. Dark green.

• NATIVE HABITAT Damp, shady woods, and streambanks, often in mountainous areas, from W. and C. Europe, Caucasus, S. Russia, and E. North America.

• CULTIVATION Thrives in moist soils and tolerates semi-shade. Grow in any moderately fertile, moisture-retentive but well-drained soil. Suitable for the back of a herbaceous border, and in a wild or woodland garden. Makes a magnificent specimen for waterside plantings.

• PROPAGATION By seed in autumn, or division in spring or autumn.

• OTHER NAMES *A. plumosus, A. sylvester, Spiraea aruncus.*

HEIGHT
1.5m (5ft)

SPREAD
1m (3ft)

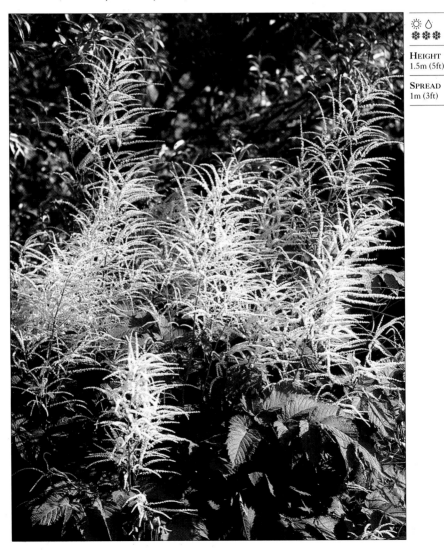

| Ranunculaceae | |
|---|---|

## CLEMATIS RECTA

**Habit** Upright, clump-forming. **Flowers** Sweetly scented, star-shaped, upright, borne in many-flowered terminal clusters in mid-summer. Milky-white. **Leaves** Divided into pointed, oval-lance-shaped segments. Dark blue-green or grey-green.
• NATIVE HABITAT  Scrub, on sunny hillsides, in S. and C. Europe, to Russia, and the Caucasus.
• CULTIVATION  Grow in fertile, well-drained soil in sun. Cut down old flowered stems in late winter.
• PROPAGATION  By seed in autumn, or division in spring.

☀ ◊
✿ ✿ ✿

HEIGHT
1.2–1.5m
(4–5ft)

SPREAD
1m (3ft)

| Papaveraceae | PLUME POPPY, TREE CELANDINE |
|---|---|

## MACLEAYA CORDATA  ♀

**Habit** Clump-forming, rhizomatous. **Flowers** Tiny, without petals, borne in dense, feathery, plume-like sprays in summer. Creamy-white. **Leaves** Large, rounded-heart-shaped, toothed and lobed, mostly basal. Grey to olive-green above, white beneath.
• NATIVE HABITAT  Grassland in China and Japan.
• CULTIVATION  Grow in moist but well-drained soil. Excellent at the back of a herbaceous border.
• PROPAGATION  By division in early spring, or root cuttings in winter.

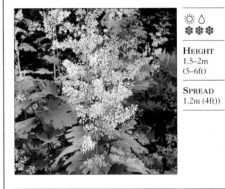

☀ ◊
✿ ✿ ✿

HEIGHT
1.5–2m
(5–6ft)

SPREAD
1.2m (4ft))

| Rosaceae | CANADIAN BURNET |
|---|---|

## SANGUISORBA CANADENSIS

**Habit** Clump-forming, rhizomatous. **Flowers** Tiny, in dense, slightly arching, bottle-brush spikes borne above the foliage in late summer. White. **Leaves** Divided, with 7–17 lance-shaped, toothed, leaflets, heart-shaped at the base. Mid-green.
• NATIVE HABITAT  Marshes, N.E. North America.
• CULTIVATION  Tolerates semi-shade. Grow in fertile, moist, well-drained soil. Good for woodland gardens and streambank or waterside plantings.
• PROPAGATION  By division in spring, or by seed in autumn.

☀ ◊
✿ ✿ ✿

HEIGHT
1.2–1.5m
(4–5ft)

SPREAD
0.6–1m
(2–3ft)

| Asteraceae/Compositae | WHITE MUGWORT |
|---|---|

## ARTEMISIA LACTIFLORA  ♀

**Habit** Vigorous, upright, clump-forming. **Flowers** Tiny, in large, open sprays, in summer. Creamy-yellow, opening from creamy-white buds. **Leaves** Divided into jagged-toothed segments. Dark green.
• NATIVE HABITAT  Scrub, open areas in forests, W. China.
• CULTIVATION  Tolerates partial shade. Grow in moisture-retentive, but well-drained soil. Needs unobtrusive staking. It makes a useful foliage plant as a backdrop for stronger colours.
• PROPAGATION  By division in spring or autumn.

☀ ◊
✿ ✿ ✿

HEIGHT
1.5–2m
(5–6ft)

SPREAD
0.6–1m
(2–3ft)

| Zingiberaceae | SHELL FLOWER, SHELL GINGER |
|---|---|

## *ALPINIA ZERUMBET*

**Habit** Clump-forming, with fleshy, ginger-scented rhizomes. **Flowers** Tubular, in drooping clusters, mainly in summer. White, with yellow lips, marked pink at the throat. **Leaves** Evergreen, lance-shaped with fringed margins, borne on reed-like stems.
• NATIVE HABITAT Tropical forest margins, E. Asia.
• CULTIVATION Grow as a house or conservatory plant in cool climates. Water freely and feed fortnightly when in growth. Needs high humidity.
• PROPAGATION Division in spring or early summer.
• OTHER NAMES *A. nutans, A. speciosa.*

☀ ◊

Min. 18°C
(64°F)

**HEIGHT**
3m (10ft)

**SPREAD**
1m (3ft)

| Papaveraceae | PLUME POPPY |
|---|---|

## *MACLEAYA MICROCARPA* 'Coral Plume'

**Habit** Clump-forming, rhizomatous. **Flowers** Tiny, borne in airy, branched plumes in summer. Rich pink-buff. **Leaves** Large, rounded, lobed, heart-shaped at base. Grey-green above, downy beneath.
• NATIVE HABITAT Garden origin.
• CULTIVATION Tolerates part-shade. Grow in any well-drained soil. May be invasive but can be confined by chopping through and removing the roots at the margins of the clump.
• PROPAGATION By division in early spring, or root cuttings in winter.

☀ ◊
❋ ❋ ❋

**HEIGHT**
2–2.5m
(6–8ft)

**SPREAD**
1–1.2m
(3–4ft)

| Asphodelaceae/ Liliaceae | |
|---|---|

## *EREMURUS ROBUSTUS*

**Habit** Upright, with fleshy rhizomes. **Flowers** Small, shallowly cup-shaped, in long, dense spires on stout stems, in summer. Pink. **Leaves** Strap-shaped, smooth, in basal clumps, dying back in summer. Mid-green.
• NATIVE HABITAT Dry, stony areas, C. Asia.
• CULTIVATION Grow in a warm, sheltered site in very well-drained, sandy soil. Needs staking. Mulch crowns in winter with dry bracken.
• PROPAGATION By division in spring or early autumn, or by seed in autumn.

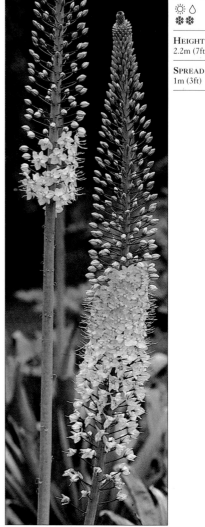

☀ ◊
❋ ❋

**HEIGHT**
2.2m (7ft)

**SPREAD**
1m (3ft)

| Malvaceae | |
|---|---|

## *LAVATERA CACHEMIRIANA*

**Habit** Short-lived, wiry-stemmed, woody-based.
**Flowers** Cup-shaped, with widely spaced, silky petals, notched at the tip, in summer. Clear pink.
**Leaves** Semi-evergreen, 3–5 lobed, rounded, heart-shaped at the base. Green, downy beneath.
• NATIVE HABITAT Meadows, W. Himalayas.
• CULTIVATION Tolerates part-shade. Grow in any fertile, well-drained soil.
• PROPAGATION By softwood cuttings in early spring or summer.
• OTHER NAMES *L. cachemirica*.

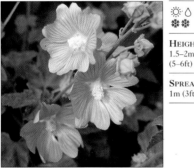

☀ ◊
❀ ❀

HEIGHT
1.5–2m
(5–6ft)

SPREAD
1m (3ft)

| Malvaceae | TREE LAVATERA |
|---|---|

## *LAVATERA* 'Kew Rose'

**Habit** Robust, woody-based, sub-shrubby.
**Flowers** Cup-shaped, with silky petals notched at the tip, borne on purple-tinted stems in summer. Clear deep pink with darker veining. **Leaves** Evergreen or semi-evergreen, 3–5 lobed, rounded, heart-shaped at base. Green, downy beneath.
• NATIVE HABITAT Garden origin.
• CULTIVATION Tolerates part-shade, but best in full sun. Grow in any fertile, well-drained soil.
• PROPAGATION By softwood cuttings in early spring or summer.

☀ ◊
❀ ❀

HEIGHT
1.5–2m
(5–6ft)
or more

SPREAD
1m (3ft)

| Ranunculaceae | |
|---|---|

## *THALICTRUM DELAVAYI* ♗
## 'Hewitt's Double'

**Habit** Dense, clump-forming. **Flowers** Tiny, double, nodding, borne in open, fluffy, terminal sprays in mid- to late summer. Lilac-pink.
**Leaves** Smooth, finely divided, resembling those of maidenhair fern. Mid-green.
• NATIVE HABITAT Garden origin.
• CULTIVATION Grow in cool, humus-rich, moist but well-drained, fertile soil, in sun or light, dappled shade. An elegant border perennial.
• PROPAGATION By division in spring.

☀ ◊
❀ ❀ ❀

HEIGHT
1.5–2m
(5–6ft)

SPREAD
60cm (2ft)

| Apiaceae/Umbelliferae | |
|---|---|

## *PIMPINELLA MAJOR* 'Rosea'

**Habit** Robust, clump-forming. **Flowers** Tiny, borne in small umbels on stout, upright stems, in mid-summer. Pink. **Leaves** Large, simply divided into toothed, almost heart-shaped segments. Dark green.
• NATIVE HABITAT Species occurs in scrub and grassland in Europe as far east as the Caucasus.
• CULTIVATION Grow in moist, fertile soil in sun or part-shade. Suitable for borders, wild gardens and wildflower borders.
• PROPAGATION By seed or division in early spring.

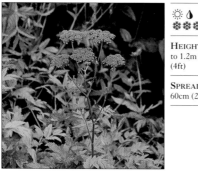

☼ ◑
✿ ✿ ✿

HEIGHT
to 1.2m
(4ft)

SPREAD
60cm (2ft)

| Rosaceae | |
|---|---|

## *FILIPENDULA PALMATA* 'Rubra'

**Habit** Vigorous, upright. **Flowers** Tiny, in feathery plumes, on long, branching stems, in mid-summer. Soft pink. **Leaves** Large, with 7–9 jaggedly cut, lobes. Dark green.
• NATIVE HABITAT Damp meadows, prairies, E. North America.
• CULTIVATION Grow in moist or wet soils, where it tolerates sun. It will rapidly colonize a boggy garden.
• PROPAGATION By seed in autumn, or by division in autumn or winter.
• OTHER NAMES *F. rubra.*

☼ ◑
✿ ✿ ✿

HEIGHT
2–2.5m
(6–8ft)

SPREAD
1.2m (4ft)

| Lamiaceae/Labiatae | |
|---|---|

## *SALVIA INVOLUCRATA*　　　　🏆

**Habit** Upright, woody-based, sub-shrubby. **Flowers** Large, 2-lipped, borne in dense spikes from late summer to autumn. Rose-crimson with pink bracts. **Leaves** Oval, long-pointed, heart-shaped at the base. Rich green.
• NATIVE HABITAT Mexico.
• CULTIVATION Grow in a warm, sunny, sheltered site, in any moderately fertile, well-drained soil.
• PROPAGATION By seed or softwood cuttings in mid-summer.

☼ ◊
✿

HEIGHT
1.2–1.5m
(4–5ft)

SPREAD
1m (3ft)

| Asclepiadaceae | SILK WEED |
|---|---|

## *ASCLEPIAS INCARNATA*

**Habit** Upright, many-branched, tuberous-rooted. **Flowers** Small, borne in dense, stout-stemmed clusters, over long periods in summer. Pink to pink-purple, occasionally white. **Leaves** Narrowly lance-shaped, slightly fleshy. Blue-green.
• NATIVE HABITAT Marshes, scrub and by pools and lakes, in North America.
• CULTIVATION Grow in fertile, humus-rich, moist but well-drained soil, in a sunny site. Good for a herbaceous border, or for waterside plantings.
• PROPAGATION By seed or division in spring.

☼ ◊
✿ ✿ ✿

HEIGHT
to 1.5m
(5ft)

SPREAD
60cm (2ft)

| Polygonaceae | |
|---|---|

## RHEUM PALMATUM 'Atrosanguineum'

**Habit** Clump-forming, with a stout rootstock.
**Flowers** Tiny, in large, fluffy plumes, borne on long, stout, branching stems in early summer. Crimson. **Leaves** Very large, lobed, deeply cut, glossy. Dark red-purple on emergence, later bluish-green.

• NATIVE HABITAT The species occurs in scrub, rocky areas and by streamsides in the mountains of W. China.
• CULTIVATION Grow in deep, fertile, moisture-retentive but well-drained soil, in sun or dappled shade. An annual mulch of organic matter is beneficial. Suitable for planting by streambanks (above water level), for large borders, and a very attractive addition to a woodland garden. It requires a generous allocation of space for best effect. A very handsome plant.
• PROPAGATION By division in spring.
• OTHER NAMES *R. palmatum* 'Atropurpureum'.

HEIGHT
2m (6ft)

SPREAD
2m (6ft)

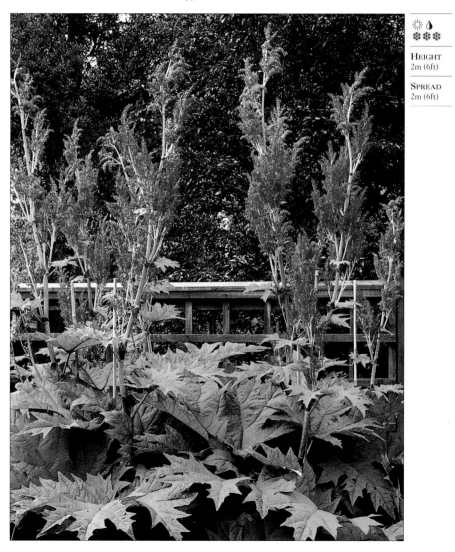

| Asteraceae/Compositae | |
|---|---|

## CIRSIUM RIVULARE ATROPURPUREUM

**Habit** Clump-forming, shortly rhizomatous.
**Flowers** Small, thistle-like, in clusters on long stems, in mid-summer. Deep crimson.
**Leaves** Narrow, deeply cut, with weak-spined margins, mostly in basal clumps.
• NATIVE HABITAT Species occurs in damp, usually acid meadows, in C. and S.W. Europe.
• CULTIVATION Prefers moist, well-drained, humus-rich, sandy soils. Will not tolerate waterlogged soil.
• PROPAGATION By division in spring, or basal shoots in summer.

☼ ◐
❄ ❄ ❄

HEIGHT
1.2m (4ft)
or more

SPREAD
60cm (2ft)

| Papaveraceae | SATIN POPPY |
|---|---|

## MECONOPSIS NAPAULENSIS

**Habit** Clump-forming, short-lived perennial or biennial. **Flowers** Large, drooping and poppy-like, satiny, borne in branched clusters on long, bristly stems in late spring and early summer. Red, purple or blue. **Leaves** Deeply divided. Pale green, clothed in stiff, bronze hairs.
• NATIVE HABITAT Himalayas, C. Nepal to S.W. China.
• CULTIVATION Grow in moist, humus-rich soils, in semi-shade or shade, in a cool, sheltered site.
• PROPAGATION By fresh seed in late summer.

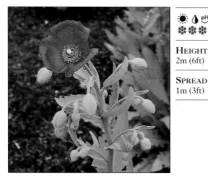

☼ ◐ pH
❄ ❄ ❄

HEIGHT
2m (6ft)

SPREAD
1m (3ft)

| Campanulaceae | |
|---|---|

## LOBELIA TUPA

**Habit** Clump-forming, with a tufted rootstock.
**Flowers** Large, 2-lipped, with 3 spreading lower lobes, borne in very long spikes in late summer. Bright brick-red. **Leaves** Large, lance-shaped, softly hairy, mostly basal. Bright green.
• NATIVE HABITAT Sandy, coastal hills, Chile.
• CULTIVATION Grow in fertile, sandy but humus-rich, very well-drained soil, in sun. Suitable for a warm, sunny border. Dislikes cold, wet conditions in winter.
• PROPAGATION By seed or division in spring.

☼ ◊
❄ ❄

HEIGHT
1.5–2m
(5–6ft)

SPREAD
1m (3ft)

| Melianthaceae | HONEYBUSH |
|---|---|

## MELIANTHUS MAJOR ♈

**Habit** Open-branched evergreen shrub, herbaceous in cool climates. **Flowers** Small, tubular, in terminal spikes, in summer. Blood-red. **Leaves** Evergreen or deciduous, to 45cm (18in) long, divided into 7–13 toothed, oval leaflets. Glaucous blue.
• NATIVE HABITAT Cape Province, South Africa.
• CULTIVATION Grow in fertile, well-drained soil in sun. Mulch in winter. Cut back top growth in spring. Excellent herbaceous foliage plant, in cool climates.
• PROPAGATION Seed in spring or semi-ripe cuttings in summer.

☼ ◊
❄ ❄

HEIGHT
2–3m
(6–10ft), to
1.2m (4ft)
in cool
climates

SPREAD
2–3m
(6–10ft)

| Apiaceae/Umbelliferae | PURPLE FENNEL |
|---|---|

## FOENICULUM VULGARE 'Purpureum'

**Habit** Upright, branching. **Flowers** Small, in large, flat umbels, in summer. Yellow. **Leaves** Aromatic, finely divided into slender filaments. Bronze-purple.
• NATIVE HABITAT Garden origin.
• CULTIVATION Grow in any well-drained soil in sun. Excellent for foliage contrast in a border, especially with silver- or golden-yellow-leaved plants. Dead-head to prevent seeding.
• PROPAGATION By seed in autumn. May self-seed.
• OTHER NAMES *F. vulgare* 'Bronze'.

☼ ◊
✿✿✿

HEIGHT
to 2m (6ft)

SPREAD
45cm (18in)

| Verbenaceae | PURPLE TOP |
|---|---|

## VERBENA BONARIENSIS

**Habit** Clump-forming. **Flowers** Tiny, in broad, flattened heads on slender, wiry stems, in summer and autumn. Bright blue-purple. **Leaves** Lance-shaped, serrated, wrinkled, in basal rosettes. Dark green.
• NATIVE HABITAT Damp grassland, South America.
• CULTIVATION Grow in any fertile soil. May self-seed where conditions suit.
• PROPAGATION By stem cuttings in late summer or autumn, or by seed in autumn or spring.
• OTHER NAMES *V. patagonica.*

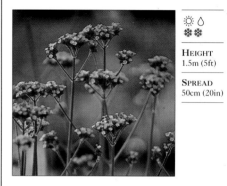

☼ ◊
✿✿

HEIGHT
1.5m (5ft)

SPREAD
50cm (20in)

| Melanthiaceae/ Liliaceae | BLACK FALSE HELLEBORE |
|---|---|

## VERATRUM NIGRUM  ♥

**Habit** Clump-forming, rhizomatous. **Flowers** Small, in dense, branched plumes, from late summer onwards. Chocolate-purple. **Leaves** Oval to narrowly oval, deeply pleated. Brilliant green.
• NATIVE HABITAT Sub-alpine meadows, S. Europe, Asia and Siberia.
• CULTIVATION Grow in deep, fertile soils in semi-shade, or part-day sun where soils are reliably moist. Provide shelter from wind. The rhizomes are toxic.
• PROPAGATION By division or seed in autumn.

◐ ◑
✿✿✿

HEIGHT
2m (6ft)

SPREAD
60cm (2ft)

| Asteraceae/Compositae | CARDOON |
|---|---|

## CYNARA CARDUNCULUS  ♥

**Habit** Clump-forming. **Flowers** Large, thistle-like, on stout, grey stems, in late summer. Purple. **Leaves** Arching, deeply divided, usually spiny, to 1m (3ft) long. Silver-grey.
• NATIVE HABITAT Rocky slopes, dry grasslands, S.W. Europe.
• CULTIVATION Tolerant of heavy clay soils. Grow in any deep, fertile soil. A stately plant for a large border. The flowers dry well if cut before fully open, and the blanched stems are edible.
• PROPAGATION By seed or division in spring.

☼ ◊
✿✿✿

HEIGHT
2m (6ft)

SPREAD
1m (3ft)

| Ranunculaceae | |
|---|---|

## *ACONITUM* 'Spark's Variety' ♈

***Habit*** Upright, tuberous-rooted. ***Flowers***
Large, hooded, with a hemispherical helmet,
borne on widely branching, rather flexuous
stems in mid- to late summer. Rich violet-blue.
***Leaves*** Deeply divided into 3 or 5 narrow,
glossy lobes. Dark green.
• NATIVE HABITAT Garden origin.
• CULTIVATION Grow in moist but well-drained,
fertile soil, in sun or part-shade. Divide every
2–3 years to maintain vigour. The roots are toxic.
• PROPAGATION By division in autumn.

☼ ◌
❄ ❄ ❄

HEIGHT
1.2m (4ft)

SPREAD
50cm (20in)

| Lamiaceae/Labiatae | |
|---|---|

## *SALVIA GUARANITICA* ♈

***Habit*** Upright, sub-shrubby. ***Flowers*** Tubular,
2-lipped, in branching spikes, in late summer and
autumn. Rich deep blue. ***Leaves*** Oval, pointed,
heart-shaped at the base. Dark green.
• NATIVE HABITAT Brazil.
• CULTIVATION Grow under glass in potting compost,
or outdoors in full sun, in a warm sheltered site, in
fertile, well-drained soil. Good for tubs or large pots
in a cool conservatory. May be grown as an annual.
• PROPAGATION By seed in spring or softwood
cuttings in summer.

☼ ◌
❄

HEIGHT
1.5m (5ft)

SPREAD
60cm (24in)

| Lamiaceae/Labiatae | BOG SAGE |
|---|---|

## *SALVIA ULIGINOSA* ♈

***Habit*** Upright, sub-shrubby. ***Flowers*** Tubular,
2-lipped, in long, branching spires, in late summer
and autumn. Clear deep blue. ***Leaves*** Oblong to
lance-shaped, saw-toothed. Mid-green.
• NATIVE HABITAT Brazil, Uruguay, Argentina.
• CULTIVATION Grow in fertile, moist but well-
drained soil, in full sun. Needs a warm, sheltered
site. Provide support. May also be grown in tubs
or large pots in a cool conservatory.
• PROPAGATION By seed in spring or softwood
cuttings in summer.

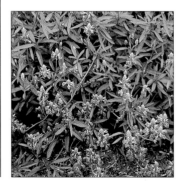

☼ ◌
❄

HEIGHT
2m (6ft)

SPREAD
45cm (18in)

| Campanulaceae | |
|---|---|

## *CAMPANULA LACTIFLORA* 'Prichard's Variety'

**Habit** Upright, slender-stemmed. **Flowers** Large, nodding, bell-shaped, in dense, leafy, branched heads, from early summer to autumn. Violet-blue. **Leaves** Narrowly oval, borne along the length of the stem. Mid-green.
• NATIVE HABITAT Garden origin.
• CULTIVATION Tolerates partial shade. Grow in any fertile, moisture-retentive soil. May need staking in windy situations. This is an excellent long-lasting perennial for planting in a herbaceous border or at the edge of a woodland garden in dappled sunshine. It performs a very useful function in providing a contrasting colour among the autumnal tints later in the season. Excellent as a cut flower.
• PROPAGATION By basal cuttings in early summer, or division in autumn or spring.

**HEIGHT**
75cm–1m
(30–36in)
or more

**SPREAD**
60cm (24in)

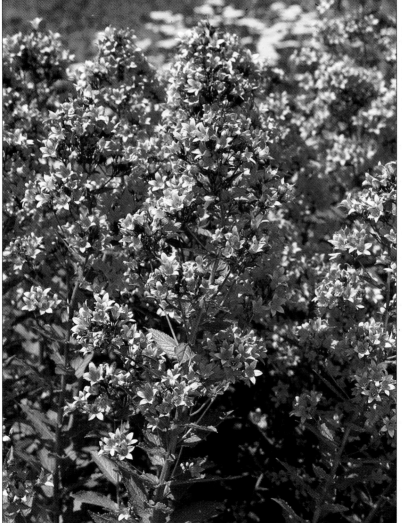

| Asteraceae/Compositae | GLOBE THISTLE |
|---|---|

## *ECHINOPS BANNATICUS*

**Habit** Clump-forming, upright. **Flowers** Tiny, in tight, globular heads, borne on branching stems in late summer. Pale to mid-blue. **Leaves** Narrow, deeply cut, cobwebbed with fine white hair. Green above, white-downy beneath.
• NATIVE HABITAT Scrub, grasslands, S.E. Europe.
• CULTIVATION Tolerates poor, dry soils. Grow in an open position in well-drained, not-too-fertile soil.
• PROPAGATION By division or seed in autumn, or by root cuttings in winter.
• OTHER NAMES *E. ritro.*

☀ ◐
❀ ❀ ❀

HEIGHT
2m (6ft)

SPREAD
1m (3ft)

| Gunneraceae | GIANT RHUBARB |
|---|---|

## *GUNNERA MANICATA*                     ▽

**Habit** Slow-growing, massive, clump-forming, rhizomatous. **Flowers** Tiny, in conical spikes, in early summer. Light green. **Leaves** Rounded, lobed, often heart-shaped at base, 1.5m (5ft) across, prickly at the margin, on prickly leaf stalks. Dull green.
• NATIVE HABITAT By streamsides, and among wet, mountain rocks, S. Brazil.
• CULTIVATION Grow in moist, fertile soil and provide shelter from wind. Mulch crowns with dead leaves in winter.
• PROPAGATION By seed in autumn or spring.

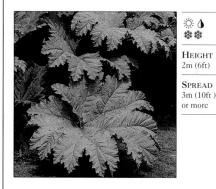

☀ ◐
❀ ❀

HEIGHT
2m (6ft)

SPREAD
3m (10ft )
or more

| Leguminosae/ Papilionaceae | |
|---|---|

## *GALEGA* × *HARTLANDII* 'Lady Wilson'

**Habit** Vigorous, upright. **Flowers** Small, pea-like, borne in branched spikes above the foliage in summer. Lilac-blue and pinkish-white. **Leaves** Divided, with 4–8 pairs of oval leaflets. Mid-green.
• NATIVE HABITAT Garden origin.
• CULTIVATION Grow in an open position, in any well-drained soil. Needs staking.
• PROPAGATION By division in winter.

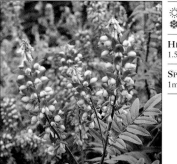

☀ ◐
❀ ❀ ❀

HEIGHT
1.5m (5ft)

SPREAD
1m (3ft)

| Apiaceae/Umbelliferae | ANGELICA |
|---|---|

## *ANGELICA ARCHANGELICA*

**Habit** Upright, perennial. **Flowers** Small, in broad, rounded umbels, in late summer. Greenish-white to cream. **Leaves** Aromatic, deeply divided, coarsely toothed. Bright green.
• NATIVE HABITAT Damp habitats throughout N. and E. Europe, to C. Asia.
• CULTIVATION Grow in any well-drained soil in sun or shade. Remove seed heads, otherwise plants may die, although they often self-seed. Stems may be crystallized for culinary use.
• PROPAGATION By seed when ripe

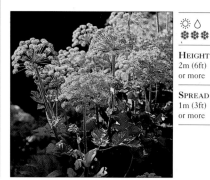

☀ ◐
❀ ❀ ❀

HEIGHT
2m (6ft)
or more

SPREAD
1m (3ft)
or more

| Scrophulariaceae | |
|---|---|

## *VERBASCUM OLYMPICUM*

**Habit** Rosette-forming biennial or short-lived perennial. **Flowers** Small, on tall, branching, white-felted spires from mid-summer onwards. Bright golden-yellow. **Leaves** Lance-shaped, covered in white, woolly felt, forming a dense basal clump.
• NATIVE HABITAT  Dry, rocky hillsides, Greece and Turkey.
• CULTIVATION  Tolerant of dry and limy soils. Grow in an open, sunny site in any well-drained soil.
• PROPAGATION  By seed in spring or late summer, or by root cuttings in winter. Self-seeds easily.

☼ ◊
❀ ❀ ❀

**Height**
2m (6ft)

**Spread**
1m (3ft)

| Apiaceae/Umbelliferae | GIANT FENNEL |
|---|---|

## *FERULA COMMUNIS*

**Habit** Robust, upright. **Flowers** Small, in rounded umbels, on long, stout, branched stems, from late spring to summer. Yellow. **Leaves** Large, finely cut into very slender, linear segments. Rich green.
• NATIVE HABITAT  Rough, rocky ground around the Mediterranean.
• CULTIVATION  Grow in any well-drained soil. Plants may die after flowering. Not to be confused with culinary fennel, *Foeniculum vulgaris*.
• PROPAGATION  By seed when ripe.

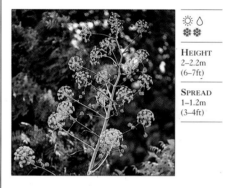

☼ ◊
❀ ❀

**Height**
2–2.2m
(6–7ft)

**Spread**
1–1.2m
(3–4ft)

| Dipsacaceae | GIANT SCABIOUS, YELLOW SCABIOUS |
|---|---|

## *CEPHALARIA GIGANTEA*

**Habit** Robust, clump-forming. **Flowers** Large, pincushion-like, on upright, wiry stems, in mid-summer. Pale primrose-yellow. **Leaves** Divided into broadly lance-shaped segments. Dark green.
• NATIVE HABITAT  Damp areas, Caucasus to Siberia.
• CULTIVATION  Grow in fertile, moist but well-drained soil, in full sun. Good for large borders or for naturalizing in a wild garden.
• PROPAGATION  By division in spring, or seed in autumn.
• OTHER NAMES  *C. tatarica*.

☼ ◊
❀ ❀ ❀

**Height**
2m (6ft)
or more

**Spread**
1.2m (4ft)

Asteraceae/Compositae

## RUDBECKIA 'Goldquelle' ♀

**Habit** Compact, upright, branching. **Flowers** Large, fully double, daisy-like, with many bright yellow petals around a green centre, in late summer and autumn. **Leaves** Deeply divided, with 3–7 pointed, toothed segments. Green.
• NATIVE HABITAT Garden origin.
• CULTIVATION Tolerates light shade. Grow in any moderately fertile, moisture-retentive but well-drained soil. Flowers are good for cutting.
• PROPAGATION By division in spring.
• OTHER NAMES *R. laciniata* 'Goldquelle'.

☼ ◐
❀ ❀ ❀

**HEIGHT**
1.2–1.5m
(4–5ft)

**SPREAD**
1m (3ft)

Asteraceae/Compositae

## LIGULARIA STENOCEPHALA

**Habit** Open, clump-forming. **Flowers** Small, daisy-like, in tall spikes, on long, dark purple stems, from mid- to late summer. Orange-yellow. **Leaves** Rounded with irregular jagged edges. Dark green.
• NATIVE HABITAT Wet mountains in Japan.
• CULTIVATION Grow in deep, fertile, humus-rich soil. Provide wind shelter and mulch annually with organic matter.
• PROPAGATION By division in spring or by seed in spring or autumn.

☼ ◐
❀ ❀ ❀

**HEIGHT**
1.2m (4ft)
or more

**SPREAD**
60cm (2ft)

Asteraceae/Compositae

## LIGULARIA PRZEWALSKII

**Habit** Loosely clump-forming. **Flowers** Small, daisy-like, on long, purple-stemmed spikes, from mid- to late summer. Yellow. **Leaves** Palmately lobed, with deep, jaggedly cut segments. Dark green.
• NATIVE HABITAT Damp mountains, N. China.
• CULTIVATION Tolerates dappled shade. Grow in deep, humus-rich soil in a sheltered site. Suited to waterside plantings. Leaves prone to slug damage.
• PROPAGATION By division in spring, or by seed in spring or autumn.
• OTHER NAMES *Senecio przewalskii*.

☼ ◐
❀ ❀ ❀

**HEIGHT**
1.2–2m
(4–6ft)

**SPREAD**
1m (3ft)

| Asphodelaceae/<br>Liliaceae | |
|---|---|

# *KNIPHOFIA* 'Wrexham Buttercup'

*Habit* Upright, clump-forming. *Flowers* Small, narrowly tubular, downward facing, borne in terminal spikes, on sturdy stems in late summer and autumn. Clear lemon-yellow. *Leaves* Grass-like, narrowly linear, arching to form basal clumps. Mid-green.

• NATIVE HABITAT Garden origin.
• CULTIVATION Grow in full sun, in moisture-retentive but well-drained soil. Needs ample moisture when in growth. Mulch crowns in cold winter areas. This plant is invaluable for its long flowering period, which is aided by the immediate removal of the dead flower stems. There are many bi-coloured cultivars of *Kniphofia* (red-hot poker), which are very garden-worthy, but considerably fewer single-coloured of which this is an excellent example.

• PROPAGATION By division in spring.

☼ ◊
❊ ❊

HEIGHT
1–1.4m
(3–4½ ft)

SPREAD
60–75cm
(2–2½ft)

| Asteraceae/Compositae | |
|---|---|

## *INULA MAGNIFICA*

**Habit** Vigorous, clump-forming, upright.
**Flowers** Large, daisy-like, with very slender petals, borne in clusters on long, leafy stems in late summer. Rich yellow. **Leaves** Lance-shaped, toothed, smooth above, hairy beneath. Dark green.
• NATIVE HABITAT  In scrub in the E. Caucasus.
• CULTIVATION  Tolerates part-shade. Prefers deep, fertile, moisture-retentive soils.
• PROPAGATION  By seed or division in spring or autumn.

☼ ◊
❀ ❀ ❀

HEIGHT
1.8m (6ft)

SPREAD
1m (3ft)

| Scrophulariaceae | |
|---|---|

## *VERBASCUM* 'Cotswold Queen'

**Habit** Upright, rosette-forming. **Flowers** Small, 5-lobed, in tall, branching racemes, throughout summer. Apricot-buff with a darker eye. **Leaves** Semi-evergreen, oval, mostly in basal rosettes, but with smaller, narrower stem leaves. Mid-green.
• NATIVE HABITAT  Garden origin.
• CULTIVATION  Grow in fertile, well-drained soil, in an open, sunny site. Is short-lived, so propagate regularly. A beautiful, long-flowering specimen for herbaceous borders and gravel plantings.
• PROPAGATION  By root cuttings in winter.

☼ ◊
❀ ❀ ❀

HEIGHT
1–1.2m
(3–4ft)
or more

SPREAD
30–60cm
(1–2ft)

| Asphodelaceae/ Liliaceae | |
|---|---|

## *EREMURUS ISABELLINUS*
## Shelford Hybrids

**Habit** Upright, clump-forming, with fleshy roots.
**Flowers** Small, shallowly cup-shaped, in tall, sturdy spires, in profusion in mid-summer. Yellow, orange, pink, buff, or creamy-white. **Leaves** Strap-shaped, in basal rosettes. Grey-green.
• NATIVE HABITAT  Garden origin.
• CULTIVATION  Requires a sheltered site. Protect crowns from frost with bracken litter. Needs staking
• PROPAGATION  By division in spring or early autumn, or by seed in autumn.

☼ ◊
❀ ❀

HEIGHT
1.5m (5ft)

SPREAD
60cm (2ft)

| Asteraceae/Compositae | |
|---|---|

## *HELIOPSIS HELIANTHOIDES* var. *SCABRA* 'Light of Loddon'

*Habit* Upright, clump-forming. *Flowers* Double, marguerite-like, in profusion, on strong stems, from late summer to early autumn. Rich golden-yellow. *Leaves* Coarse, lance-shaped, serrated. Dark green.
• NATIVE HABITAT Garden origin.
• CULTIVATION Prefers fertile, moist soil, but will tolerate poorer soils. Flowers are good for cutting. Very hardy, long-lived and easily grown. Lift and divide clumps periodically to maintain vigour.
• PROPAGATION By division in autumn or spring.

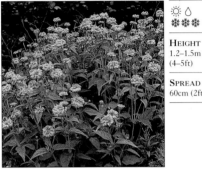

☀ ◊
❀ ❀ ❀

HEIGHT
1.2–1.5m
(4–5ft)

SPREAD
60cm (2ft)

| Asteraceae/Compositae | |
|---|---|

## *LIGULARIA* 'Gregynog Gold'  ♀

*Habit* Clump-forming. *Flowers* Small, daisy-like, in tall, pyramidal spires from mid- to late summer. Rich orange-yellow. *Leaves* Large, heart-shaped, saw-toothed. Dark green.
• NATIVE HABITAT Garden origin.
• CULTIVATION Grow in a wind-sheltered site, in moist, well-drained soil. Tolerates full sun where soils remain moist. Excellent for a damp border, or waterside plantings with the roots above water level.
• PROPAGATION By division in spring.
• OTHER NAMES *Senecio* 'Gregynog Gold'.

☀ ◊
❀ ❀ ❀

HEIGHT
2m (6ft)

SPREAD
60cm (2ft)

| Zingiberaceae | |
|---|---|

## *HEDYCHIUM DENSIFLORUM*

*Habit* Clump-forming, stoutly rhizomatous. *Flowers* Short-lived, small, fragrant, in dense, upright spikes, in late summer. Orange or yellow. *Leaves* Oblong to broadly lance-shaped, conspicuously ribbed, glossy, on reed-like stems. Dark green.
• NATIVE HABITAT Damp forest margins, Himalayas.
• CULTIVATION Grow in rich, moisture-retentive soil in a warm, sheltered border or cool conservatory.
• PROPAGATION By division when growth resumes in spring.

☀ ◊
❀ ❀

HEIGHT
1.2–2m
(4–6ft)

SPREAD
60cm (2ft)

| Heliconiaceae | PARROT'S FLOWER, PARROT'S PLANTAIN |
|---|---|

## *HELICONIA PSITTACORUM*

*Habit* Tufted, slender-stemmed. *Flowers* Cylindrical, in upright clusters (on mature plants only), in summer. Orange, green-tipped, enclosed in large, waxy, orange-red bracts. *Leaves* Evergreen, lance-shaped, on long, sometimes scarlet-tinted stalks.
• NATIVE HABITAT Tropical forests of E. Brazil.
• CULTIVATION Grow as a house or conservatory plant in cool climates. Water freely when in growth, otherwise water very sparingly.
• PROPAGATION By seed or division in spring.

☀ ◊

Min. 18°C
(64°F)

HEIGHT
To 2m (6ft)

SPREAD
1m (3ft)

# DELPHINIUMS

Delphiniums are a genus of annuals and perennials grown for their long spikes of cup-shaped, single to fully double flowers, in a range of colours from creamy-whites through lilac-pinks to deep indigo-blue, often with a contrasting "eye" or "bee" formed by the inner sepals. They are well suited to herbaceous borders, and are also grown in beds for cutting.

The delphiniums most usually seen in gardens are hybrids of *D. elatum*, and are clump-forming, fleshy-crowned perennials that flower from early to mid-summer. Their leaves are lobed, divided and range from mid- to bright green. Hybrids of *D. x belladonna*, are also clump-forming perennials, with more slender, wiry stems bearing branched spikes of spurred flowers.

Delphiniums should be grown in fertile, moist but well-drained soil in full sun with shelter from strong winds. During growth, especially in spring and early summer, they require regular watering and a weekly feed with a balanced liquid fertilizer. To produce good quality blooms, thin out the young shoots when they reach 7cm (3in) tall, leaving 2–3 shoots on young plants, 5–7 on well-established perennials. All but the dwarf cultivars need staking: the lower-growing cultivars with twiggy sticks; the taller ones with canes, or "grow-through" supports. To avoid damage, insert supports as plants reach 30cm (12in) high, usually by mid-spring. Well-fed and watered plants will produce a second, lesser crop of flowers in late summer. Dead-head flowered spikes, cutting back to the smaller, branching sideshoots. Cut back all growth in autumn.

Both *D. elatum* and *D. x belladonna* hybrids can be propagated by taking heeled basal cuttings, 7–10cm (3–4in) long, in early spring. The *D. x belladonna* hybrids can also be increased by division.

## D. 'Butterball'

**Flowers** Large, semi-double, borne in spikes to 50cm (20in) long. White, overlaid with very pale greenish-yellow, with creamy-yellow eyes.
• HEIGHT 1.5–1.7m (5–5½ft).
• SPREAD 75cm (2½ft).

**D. 'Butterball'**
*D. elatum* hybrid

☼ ◊ ❀ ❀ ❀

## D. 'Sandpiper'

**Flowers** Large, semi-double, borne in spikes to 75cm (30in) long. White with dark creamy-brown eyes.
• HEIGHT 1–1.35m (3–4½ft).
• SPREAD 75cm (2½ft).

**D. 'Sandpiper'**
*D. elatum* hybrid

☼ ◊ ❀ ❀ ❀  ♆

## *D.* 'Olive Poppleton'

*Flowers* Large, semi-double, borne in spikes to 1m (3ft) long. White with fawn eyes.
• HEIGHT 2–2.5m (6–8ft).
• SPREAD 75cm–1m (2½–3ft).

**D. 'Olive Poppleton'**
*D. elatum* hybrid

☼ ◊ ❋❋❋

## *D.* 'Emily Hawkins'

*Flowers* Large, semi-double, borne in spikes to 80cm (32in) long. Pale blue, flushed lilac with fawn eyes.
• HEIGHT 2–2.2m (6–7ft).
• SPREAD 75cm–1m (2½–3ft).

**D. 'Emily Hawkins'**
*D. elatum* hybrid

☼ ◊ ❋❋❋        ♙

## *D.* 'Langdon's Royal Flush'

*Flowers* Large, semi-double, borne in spikes to 85cm (34in) long. Pinkish-purple, with cream eyes. The petals of the upper flowers are darker than the lower, providing elegant gradation of colour.
• HEIGHT 2m (6ft).
• SPREAD 75cm–1m (2½–3ft).

**D. 'Langdon's Royal Flush'**
*D. elatum* hybrid

☼ ◊ ❋❋❋

## *D.* 'Fanfare'

*Flowers* Large, semi-double, borne in spikes to 60–75cm (2–2½ft) long. Pale blue to silvery-mauve, with white and violet eyes.
• HEIGHT 2–2.2m (6–7ft).
• SPREAD 75cm–1m (2½–3ft).

**D. 'Fanfare'**
*D. elatum* hybrid

☼ ◊ ❋❋❋        ♙

### D. 'Strawberry Fair'

*Flowers* Large, semi-double, borne in spikes to 78cm (31in) long. Mulberry-pink with white eyes.
• HEIGHT 1.7–2m (5½–6ft).
• SPREAD 75cm–1m (2½–3ft).

**D. 'Strawberry Fair'**
*D. elatum* hybrid

☼ ◊ ❀ ❀ ❀

### D. 'Gillian Dallas'

*Flowers* Large, semi-double, produced in spikes to 80cm (32in) long. Pale lilac, growing paler towards the petal margins, with white eyes.
• HEIGHT 2m (6ft).
• SPREAD 75–1m (2½–3ft).

**D. 'Gillian Dallas'**
*D. elatum* hybrid

☼ ◊ ❀ ❀ ❀ ♈

### D. 'Mighty Atom'

*Flowers* Large, semi-double, produced in spikes to 75cm (30in) long. Mid-violet with violet marked, yellowish-brown eyes.
• HEIGHT 1.5–2m (5–6ft).
• SPREAD 75cm (2½ft).

**D. 'Mighty Atom'**
*D. elatum* hybrid

☼ ◊ ❀ ❀ ❀ ♈

### D. 'Spindrift'

*Flowers* Large, semi-double, in spikes to 1m (3ft) long. Pink-purple, overlaid with pale blue, and with creamy-white eyes; becoming more intensely blue at the centre. On acid soils, the petal colour becomes green-tinted.
• HEIGHT 1.7–2m (5½–6ft).
• SPREAD 75cm–1m (2½–3ft).

**D. 'Spindrift'**
*D. elatum* hybrid

☼ ◊ ❀ ❀ ❀ ♈

### D. 'Bruce'

*Flowers* Large, semi-double, produced in spikes to 1.2m (4ft) long. Deep violet-purple, flushed silver at the centre, with grey-brown eyes.
• HEIGHT 1.7–2.2m (5½–7ft).
• SPREAD 75cm–1m (2½–3ft).

**D. 'Bruce'**
*D. elatum* hybrid

☼ ◊ ❀ ❀ ❀ ♈

### D. 'Blue Dawn'

*Flowers* Large, semi-double, borne in spikes to 1.2m (4ft) long. Pale blue, flushed pink-purple, with dark brown eyes.
• HEIGHT 2–2.2m (6–7ft).
• SPREAD 75cm–1m (2½–3ft).

**D. 'Blue Dawn'**
*D. elatum* hybrid

☼ ◊ ❀ ❀ ❀ ♈

*D.* × *BELLADONNA*
**'Blue Bees'**
*Habit* Upright, branching.
*Flowers* Single,
occasionally semi-
double, to 2cm (¾in)
or more across, borne in
loose, delicate spikes,
to 30cm (12in) long.
Sky-blue.
*Leaves* Palmately divided.
Mid- to bright green.
• HEIGHT 1.1–1.5m
(3½–5ft).
• SPREAD 60cm (2ft).

*D.* × *belladonna*
**'Blue Bees'**

☼ ◊ ❁❁❁

*D.* **'Loch Leven'**
*Flowers* Large, semi-
double, borne in spikes
to 1m (3ft) long. Clear
blue with white eyes.
• HEIGHT 1.7m (5½ft).
• SPREAD 75cm (2½ft).

*D.* **'Loch Leven'**
*D. elatum* hybrid

☼ ◊ ❁❁❁ ♛

*D.* **'Lord Butler'**
*Flowers* Large, semi-
double, produced in
spikes to 75cm (30in)
long. Pale blue flushed
pale lilac, with blue-
marked, white eyes.
• HEIGHT 1.5–1.7m
(5–5½ft).
• SPREAD 75cm (2½ft).

*D.* **'Lord Butler'**
*D. elatum* hybrid

☼ ◊ ❁❁❁ ♛

*D.* **'Blue Nile'**
*Flowers* Large, semi-
double, borne in spikes
to 68cm (27in) long. Rich
deep blue, with blue-
streaked, white eyes.
• HEIGHT 1.5–1.7m
(5–5½ft).
• SPREAD 75cm (2½ft).

*D.* **'Blue Nile'**
*D. elatum* hybrid

☼ ◊ ❁❁❁ ♛

*D. GRANDIFLORUM*
**'Blue Butterfly'**
*Habit* Upright,
short-lived.
*Flowers* Single,
to 3.5cm (1½in) across,
in loose, branching
spikes to 15cm (6in) long.
Deep blue.
*Leaves* Palmately
divided. Bright green.
• OTHER NAMES *D.
chinense* 'Blue Butterfly'.
• HEIGHT 45cm (18in).
• SPREAD 30cm (12in).

*D. grandiflorum*
**'Blue Butterfly'**

☼ ◊ ❁❁❁

*D.* **'Chelsea Star'**
*Flowers* Large, semi-
double, borne in spikes
to 1.1m (3½ft) long. Rich
deep violet with white
eyes.
• HEIGHT 2m (6ft).
• SPREAD 75cm–1m
(2½–3ft).

*D.* **'Chelsea Star'**
*D. elatum* hybrid

☼ ◊ ❁❁❁

*D.* **'Sungleam'**
*Flowers* Large, semi-
double, 40–75cm
(16–30in) long, borne in
spikes. White, overlaid
with pale yellow, with
yellow eyes.
• HEIGHT 1.7–2m
(5½–6ft).
• SPREAD 75cm–1m
(2½–3ft).

*D.* **'Sungleam'**
*D. elatum* hybrid

☼ ◊ ❁❁❁ ♛

| Ranunculaceae | |
| --- | --- |

## CIMICIFUGA SIMPLEX

*Habit* Upright, rhizomatous. *Flowers* Tiny, star-shaped, fragrant, borne in slender, dark-stemmed, arching spikes, in autumn. White. *Leaves* Divided into narrowly oval, toothed and irregularly lobed, leaflets. Fresh green.
• NATIVE HABITAT Alpine and sub-alpine meadows, Mongolia, Kamchatka, Japan.
• CULTIVATION Grow in moist, humus-rich soil, in shade or semi-shade. Needs staking. Excellent for shady borders and woodland gardens.
• PROPAGATION By fresh seed, or division in spring.

☼ ◐
❄ ❄ ❄

HEIGHT
1.2–1.5m
(4–5ft)

SPREAD
60cm (2ft)

| Ranunculaceae | |
| --- | --- |

## ANEMONE × HYBRIDA
### 'Honorine Jobert'

*Habit* Vigorous, branching, spreading. *Flowers* Single, slightly cupped, with 6–9 pure white petals surrounding a boss of golden stamens, borne on wiry stems, from late summer to early autumn. *Leaves* Deeply divided. Dark green.
• NATIVE HABITAT Garden origin.
• CULTIVATION Grow in moderately fertile, well-drained soil, in sun or part-shade. An invaluable, long-flowering specimen for a late summer border.
• PROPAGATION By division in spring or autumn.

☼ ◐
❄ ❄ ❄

HEIGHT
1.5m (5ft)

SPREAD
60cm (2ft)

| Asteraceae/Compositae | |
| --- | --- |

## LEUCANTHEMELLA SEROTINA

*Habit* Erect, bushy. *Flowers* Large, single, daisy-like, borne in sprays in late autumn. White with greenish centres. *Leaves* Lance-shaped, lobed, toothed. Dark green.
• NATIVE HABITAT Damp habitats in S. E. Europe.
• CULTIVATION Grow in moist but well-drained fertile soil in full sun. The flowers are good for cutting. A statuesque perennial for a large border.
• PROPAGATION By seed or division in spring or autumn.
• OTHER NAMES *Chrysanthemum uliginosum*.

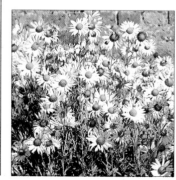

☼ ◑
❄ ❄ ❄

HEIGHT
2.2m (7ft)

SPREAD
60cm (2ft)

| Asteraceae/Compositae | JOE PYE WEED |
|---|---|

## *EUPATORIUM PURPUREUM*

**Habit** Robust, clump-forming, upright. **Flowers**
Tiny, tubular, in dense, terminal heads, from late
summer to autumn. Pink-purple. **Leaves** Coarse,
finely toothed, lance-shaped to oval, borne in
whorls along purple-tinted stems. Mid-green.
• NATIVE HABITAT Damp woodland, E.
North America.
• CULTIVATION Grow in moist, fertile, humus-rich
soil, in sun or part-shade. Suitable for wild or
woodland gardens. Very attractive to butterflies.
Difficult to place in a border because of its height.

Therefore, careful selection of its companions is
required: *Rudbeckia laciniata* and *Macleaya cordata*
would be suitable neighbours before descending
to tall Michaelmas daisies (*Aster*), *Helenium* and
*Persicaria* (*Polygonum*) *amplexicaule*.
• PROPAGATION By seed in spring, or by division
in early spring or autumn.

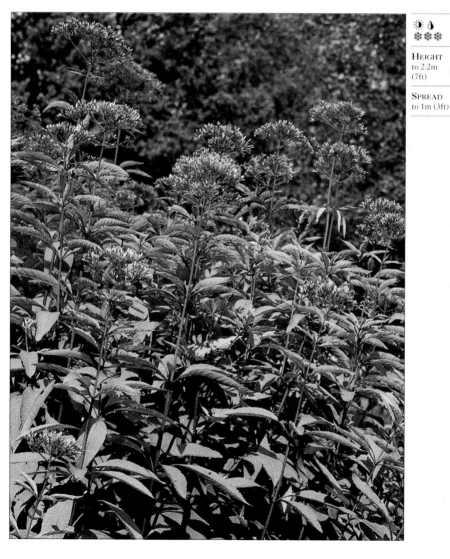

**HEIGHT**
to 2.2m
(7ft)

**SPREAD**
to 1m (3ft)

| Ranunculaceae | |
|---|---|

## *ANEMONE HUPEHENSIS* ♥
### 'September Charm'

***Habit*** Vigorous, branching, stoloniferous. ***Flowers***
Single, slightly cupped, in wiry-stemmed umbels,
from late summer to early autumn. Clear silvery-
pink, with a darker petal reverse. ***Leaves*** More or
less evergreen, deeply divided. Dark green.
• NATIVE HABITAT Garden origin.
• CULTIVATION Grow in well-drained soil, in sun or
part-shade. Excellent in a late summer border.
• PROPAGATION By division in spring or autumn, or
by root cuttings.

☀ ◊ pH
❄❄❄

HEIGHT
75cm (30in)

SPREAD
50cm (20in)

| Lamiaceae/Labiatae | |
|---|---|

## *SALVIA INVOLUCRATA* 'Bethellii'

***Habit*** Upright, woody-based, sub-shrubby.
***Flowers*** Large, 2-lipped, borne in dense, spike-
like heads, from late summer to autumn.
Cerise-crimson with pink bracts. ***Leaves*** Oval,
heart-shaped at the base. Mid-green.
• NATIVE HABITAT Garden origin.
• CULTIVATION Grow in a warm, sunny site, in any
moderately fertile, well-drained soil. Provide good
protection from cold wind.
• PROPAGATION By softwood cuttings in
mid-summer.

☀ ◊
❄

HEIGHT
1.2–1.5m
(4–5ft)

SPREAD
1m (3ft)

| Ranunculaceae | |
|---|---|

## *ANEMONE HUPEHENSIS* var. *JAPONICA*
### 'Bressingham Glow'

***Habit*** Vigorous, branching, clump-forming.
***Flowers*** Semi-double, slightly cupped, borne on
wiry stems, from late summer to early autumn.
Bright rose-purple. ***Leaves*** Deeply divided.
Dark green.
• NATIVE HABITAT Garden origin.
• CULTIVATION Grow in any moderately fertile,
well-drained soil, in sun or part-shade. A beautiful,
long-flowering perennial for a late summer border.
• PROPAGATION By division in spring or autumn.

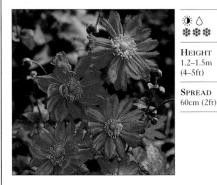

☀ ◊
❄❄❄

HEIGHT
1.2–1.5m
(4–5ft)

SPREAD
60cm (2ft)

| Phytolaccaceae | RED-INK PLANT, VIRGINIA POKEWEED |
|---|---|

## *PHYTOLACCA AMERICANA*

***Habit*** Stout, upright. ***Flowers*** Small, in dense,
upright spikes, on stout stems, in late spring or
summer. White or pink. ***Fruits*** Globose, shiny,
toxic. Black-purple. ***Leaves*** Large, oval to lance-
shaped. Bright green, purple in autumn.
• NATIVE HABITAT Grassland, E. North America.
• CULTIVATION Grow in moist but well-drained
fertile soil. The berries, although attractive, are
toxic. Not suitable for gardens where children play.
• PROPAGATION By seed in autumn or spring.
• OTHER NAMES *P. decandra.*

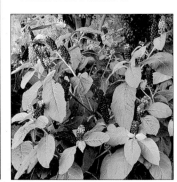

☀ ◉
❄❄❄

HEIGHT
1.2–1.5m
(4–5ft)

SPREAD
1.2–1.5m
(4–5ft)

| Asclepiadaceae | |
|---|---|

## GOMPHOCARPUS PHYSOCARPUS

**Habit** Upright, slender, sub-shrubby. **Flowers** 5-horned, borne in umbels during summer. Cream or greenish-white. **Fruits** Large, inflated, globose seed pods with soft bristles. **Leaves** Hairy, lance-shaped. Mid-green.
• NATIVE HABITAT South Africa.
• CULTIVATION Grow in full sun, in humus-rich, well-drained soil. Protect against cold winds in cool climates.
• PROPAGATION By division or seed in spring.
• OTHER NAMES *Asclepias physocarpa*.

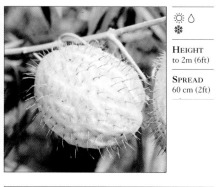

HEIGHT
to 2m (6ft)

SPREAD
60 cm (2ft)

| Zingiberaceae | KAHILI GINGER |
|---|---|

## HEDYCHIUM GARDNERIANUM

**Habit** Upright, stoutly rhizomatous. **Flowers** Short-lived, small, fragrant, borne in dense spikes from late summer to early autumn. Lemon-yellow, with conspicuous, bright red filaments. **Leaves** Lance-shaped, on reed-like stems. Greyish-green.
• NATIVE HABITAT Forests, N. India, Himalayas.
• CULTIVATION Grow in a warm, sunny site in fertile, moist, humus-rich soil. Give protection from cold wind. In cool climates overwinter indoors.
• PROPAGATION By division when growth resumes in spring.

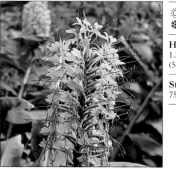

HEIGHT
1.5–2m
(5–6ft)

SPREAD
75cm (30in)

| Asphodelaceae/Liliaceae | |
|---|---|

## KNIPHOFIA 'Ice Queen'

**Habit** Upright, clump-forming. **Flowers** Small, narrowly tubular, borne on stout, upright stems in dense, terminal spikes, in early autumn. Creamy-white, opening from pale green buds. **Leaves** Grass-like, arching to form basal clumps. Mid-green.
• NATIVE HABITAT Garden origin.
• CULTIVATION Grow in full sun, in moisture-retentive but well-drained soil. Needs moisture when in growth. Mulch crowns in cold winter areas.
• PROPAGATION By division in spring.

HEIGHT
to 1.5m
(5ft)

SPREAD
60cm (2ft)

Asteraceae/Compositae

## *HELIANTHUS* × *MULTIFLORUS*

*Habit* Upright, spreading, rhizomatous. *Flowers*
Large, daisy-like, with ray florets in 2 ranks, from
late summer to early autumn. Yellow. *Leaves*
Coarse, lance-shaped to oval, thin-textured.
Mid-green.
• NATIVE HABITAT Garden origin.
• CULTIVATION Grow in any moderately fertile,
well-drained soil, in full sun. Needs staking.
Where conditions are favourable it may
spread rapidly.
• PROPAGATION By division in autumn or spring.

☼ ◊
❀ ❀ ❀

HEIGHT
to 1.5m
(5ft)

SPREAD
60cm (2ft)

Asteraceae/Compositae

## *HELIANTHUS* 'Capenoch Star'  ♧

*Habit* Upright, clump-forming. *Flowers*
Large, single, daisy-like, borne at the ends of
branching stems, from late summer to early
autumn. Lemon-yellow. *Leaves* Lance-shaped
to oval, toothed. Mid-green.
• NATIVE HABITAT Garden origin.
• CULTIVATION Grow in moderately fertile,
well-drained soil. Needs staking. Looks
good with blue-flowered plants in a late
summer border.
• PROPAGATION By division in autumn or spring.

☼ ◊
❀ ❀ ❀

HEIGHT
to 1.2m
(4ft)

SPREAD
60cm (2ft)

Asteraceae/Compositae

## *SOLIDAGO* 'Golden Wings'

*Habit* Vigorous, clump-forming. *Flowers* Tiny,
mimosa-like, borne in dense, clustered, branching
heads on upright stems, in late summer and
autumn. Bright golden-yellow. *Leaves* Toothed,
slightly hairy, lance-shaped. Mid-green.
• NATIVE HABITAT Garden origin.
• CULTIVATION Grow in any well-drained soil,
including poor soils, in sun. Good for cutting,
the bright flowers are much valued in a late
summer border.
• PROPAGATION By division in spring.

☼ ◊
❀ ❀ ❀

HEIGHT
1.5m (5ft)

SPREAD
1m (3ft)

Asteraceae/Compositae

## *HELENIUM* 'Sonnenwunder'

*Habit* Robust, dense, clump-forming.
*Flowers* Large, daisy-like, with reflexed, rich deep yellow ray florets and a rounded yellow disc, borne over long periods from late summer to autumn. *Leaves* Lance-shaped on stout stems. Dark green.

• NATIVE HABITAT Garden origin.
• CULTIVATION Easily grown in almost any soil except waterlogged soil, in full sun. A valuable long-flowering plant for a larger, late summer border. It is important to divide and replant regularly to maintain vigour. A trouble-free perennial for late in the season. This is one of the tallest in a genus that hails from North America. Popularly known as the sneezeweeds, heleniums hybridize freely and now provide cultivars for the entire border, ranging from the yellow-flowered 'The Bishop' at 60cm (2ft) and 'Moerheim Beauty', with reddish-mahogany-coloured flowers at 90–120cm (3–4ft). Excellent for cutting provided the lower leaves are removed.
• PROPAGATION By division in spring or autumn.

☼ ◊
❄ ❄ ❄

HEIGHT
to 1.5m
(5ft)

SPREAD
1m (3ft)

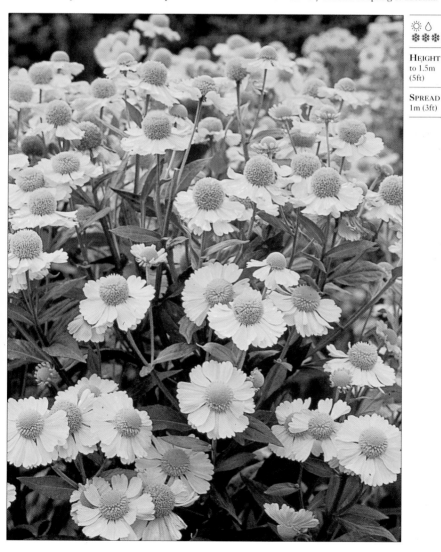

Asteraceae/Compositae

## HELIANTHUS 'Loddon Gold'  ♀

**Habit** Upright, spreading, rhizomatous.
**Flowers** Large, double, from late summer to early
autumn. Bright deep yellow. **Leaves** Coarse,
lance-shaped to oval, thin-textured. Mid-green.
• NATIVE HABITAT Garden origin.
• CULTIVATION Grow in any moderately fertile,
well-drained soil. Needs staking. May spread
quickly where conditions suit.
• PROPAGATION By division in autumn or spring.

Asteraceae/Compositae

## HELIANTHUS DECAPETALUS 'Morning Sun'

**Habit** Upright, clump-forming. **Flowers** Large,
semi-double, daisy-like, from late summer to early
autumn. Bright deep yellow with a yellow disc.
**Leaves** Coarse, lance-shaped, toothed. Mid-green.
• NATIVE HABITAT Garden origin.
• CULTIVATION Grow in any moderately fertile,
well-drained soil. Needs staking. A robust daisy
for the large, late summer border.
• PROPAGATION By division in autumn or spring.
• OTHER NAMES *H.* x *laetiflorus* 'Morning Sun'.

☼ ◌
❋ ❋ ❋
**HEIGHT** 1.5m (5ft)
**SPREAD** 60cm (2ft)

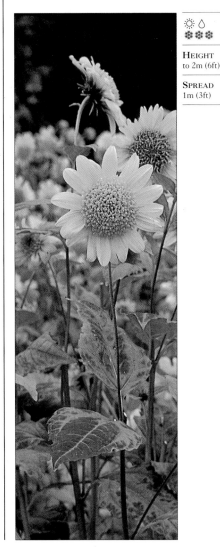

☼ ◌
❋ ❋ ❋
**HEIGHT** to 2m (6ft)
**SPREAD** 1m (3ft)

Asteraceae/Compositae

## HELIANTHUS 'Triomphe de Gand'

**Habit** Upright, clump-forming. **Flowers** Large,
semi-double, daisy-like, borne at the ends of
branching stems, from late summer to early
autumn. Rich golden-yellow. **Leaves** Lance-
shaped and toothed. Mid-green.
• NATIVE HABITAT Garden origin.
• CULTIVATION Grow in moderately fertile,
well-drained soil. Needs staking. Looks good
planted with blue-flowered plants in a late
summer border.
• PROPAGATION By division in autumn or spring.

☼ ◌
❋ ❋ ❋
**HEIGHT** 1.5m (5ft)
**SPREAD** 75cm (2½ft)

Asteraceae/Compositae

## *HELIANTHUS* 'Monarch' ♈

**Habit** Upright, spreading. **Flowers** Large, to 15cm (6in) across, semi-double, daisy-like, borne on sturdy stems from late summer to early autumn. Bright golden-yellow with a brown-black disc. **Leaves** Large, coarse, lance-shaped. Mid-green.
• NATIVE HABITAT Garden origin.
• CULTIVATION Grow in any moderately fertile, well-drained soil. Needs staking. May spread rapidly where conditions suit. A statuesque and robust perennial for the larger herbaceous border.
• PROPAGATION By division in autumn or spring.

☼ ◊
❄ ❄ ❄

HEIGHT
to 2.2m
(7ft)

SPREAD
1m (3ft)

Asteraceae/Compositae

## *RUDBECKIA* 'Herbstsonne'

**Habit** Robust, upright. **Flowers** Large, daisy-like, borne singly on strong, slender stems from late summer to autumn. Rich golden-yellow with a green, cone-shaped centre. **Leaves** Divided, shallowly lobed. Mid-green.
• NATIVE HABITAT Garden origin.
• CULTIVATION Grow in fertile, moist or well-drained soil, in full sun or light shade. Flowers particularly well during long, hot summers.
• PROPAGATION By division in spring or autumn.
• OTHER NAMES *R.* 'Autumn Sun'.

☼ ◊
❄ ❄ ❄

HEIGHT
1.5–2.3m
(5–7ft)

SPREAD
60–75cm
(2–2½ft)

Asteraceae/Compositae

## *HELIANTHUS DECAPETALUS* 'Soleil d'Or'

**Habit** Upright, spreading, rhizomatous. **Flowers** Large, double, from late summer to early autumn. The outer ray florets are larger than the inner ones. Bright deep yellow. **Leaves** Coarse, lance-shaped to oval, thin-textured. Mid-green.
• NATIVE HABITAT Garden origin.
• CULTIVATION Grow in any moderately fertile, well-drained soil. Needs staking. May spread quickly where conditions suit. A reliable old cultivar for the late summer border.
• PROPAGATION By division in autumn or spring.

☼ ◊
❄ ❄ ❄

HEIGHT
1.5m (5ft)
or more

SPREAD
1m (3ft)

Asteraceae/Compositae

## *HELENIUM* 'Riverton Gem'

**Habit** Upright, bushy, clump-forming. **Flowers** Large, daisy-like, with reflexed, ray florets and a rounded, brown disc, borne over long periods from late summer to autumn. Golden-yellow. **Leaves** Lance-shaped, on stout stems. Dark green.
• NATIVE HABITAT Garden origin.
• CULTIVATION Easily grown in almost any soil except waterlogged soil, in full sun. Divide and replant regularly to maintain vigour.
• PROPAGATION By division in spring or autumn.

☼ ◊
❄ ❄ ❄

HEIGHT
1.5m (5ft)

SPREAD
1m (3ft)

| Musaceae | FLOWERING BANANA |
|---|---|

## MUSA ORNATA     ♕

**Habit** Suckering, palm-like. **Flowers** Long, terminal spikes, with single rows of upright, yellow-orange flowers, each almost enclosed by a large, pink bract. **Fruits** Yellow-green, inedible bananas, about 6cm (2½in) long. **Leaves** Evergreen, paddle-shaped, waxy, to 2m (6ft) long. Bluish-green.
• NATIVE HABITAT Bangladesh, Burma.
• CULTIVATION Grow as a house or conservatory plant in cool climates.
• PROPAGATION By division year-round, by suckers after flowering, or by offsets in autumn.

☼ ◊

Min. 18°C
(64°F)

HEIGHT
to 3m
(10ft)

SPREAD
2.2m (7ft)

| Doryanthaceae/
Liliaceae | |
|---|---|

## DORYANTHES PALMERI

**Habit** Rosette-forming. **Flowers** Small, borne intermittently in dense panicles. Red-bracted, orange-red and white within. May produce bulbils in place of flowers. **Leaves** Evergreen, arching, sword-shaped, fleshy, to 2m (6ft) long. Rich green.
• NATIVE HABITAT Queensland, Australia.
• CULTIVATION Grow as a house or conservatory plant in cool climates. Water freely when in growth and keep just moist in winter.
• PROPAGATION By seed in spring, by mature bulbils, or by suckers after flowering.

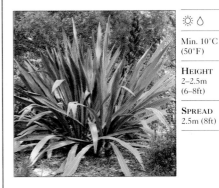

☼ ◊

Min. 10°C
(50°F)

HEIGHT
2–2.5m
(6–8ft)

SPREAD
2.5m (8ft)

| Strelitziaceae | |
|---|---|

## STRELITZIA NICOLAI

**Habit** Stout-trunked, palm-like. **Flowers** Short-stemmed, beak-like. White and pale blue, enclosed in a boat-shaped, dark purple bract. Produced intermittently. **Leaves** Evergreen, clumped, long-stalked, oval, to 1.5m (5ft) long. Blue-green.
• NATIVE HABITAT Natal, N.E. Cape, South Africa.
• CULTIVATION Grow as a house or conservatory plant in cool climates. Needs fertile, well-drained soil and good light, but shade from hot sun. Water freely when in growth but reduce water in winter.
• PROPAGATION By seed or suckers in spring.

◐ ◊

Min.
5–10°C
(41–50°F)

HEIGHT
to 8m (25ft)

SPREAD
5m (15ft)

| Marantaceae | |
|---|---|

## CALATHEA MAJESTICA 'Sanderiana'

**Habit** Clump-forming. **Flowers** Tubular, in short, dense spikes, produced occasionally. White or mauve, with yellow-brown bracts. **Leaves** Evergreen, broadly oval, leathery, glossy. Olive-green, striped pink and white, purplish beneath.
• NATIVE HABITAT Garden origin.
• CULTIVATION Grow as a house or conservatory plant in cool climates. Water with soft water. Maintain high humidity and constant temperature.
• PROPAGATION By division in spring.
• OTHER NAMES C. ornata 'Sanderiana'.

☀ ◊

Min. 15°C
(59°F)

HEIGHT
1.2–1.5m
(4–5ft)

SPREAD
1m (3ft)

| Lamiaceae/Labiatae | |
|---|---|

## PYCNOSTACHYS DAWEI

**Habit** Vigorous, bushy, upright. **Flowers** Tubular, 2-lipped, in short, dense, whorled spikes, from winter to spring. Brilliant blue. **Leaves** Narrowly lance-shaped, serrated, 12–30cm (5–12in) long. Mid-green, red-tinged beneath.
• NATIVE HABITAT Tropical C. Africa.
• CULTIVATION Grow as a house or conservatory plant in cool climates. Needs fertile, well-drained soil. Water freely when in full growth.
• PROPAGATION By stem cuttings in early summer.

☀ ◊

Min 15°C
(59°F)

HEIGHT
1.2–1.5m
(4–5ft)

SPREAD
30–90cm
(1–3ft)

| Agavaceae/Phormiaceae | |
|---|---|

## PHORMIUM TENAX    ♟
## Purpureum Group

**Habit** Upright, clump-forming. **Flowers** Tubular, dull in large panicles, to 5m (15ft) high, borne on blue-purple stems in summer. Dark red. **Leaves** Evergreen, stiff, sword-shaped, 2m (6ft) or more long, in basal clumps. Red-purple to deep copper.
• NATIVE HABITAT Garden origin.
• CULTIVATION Grow in deep, fertile, humus-rich soil, in a warm, sunny, sheltered site. Excellent for coastal gardens.
• PROPAGATION By division in spring.

☀ ◊
❄ ❄

HEIGHT
2–2.5m
(6–8ft)

SPREAD
1m (3ft)

| Musaceae | JAPANESE BANANA |
|---|---|

## MUSA BASJOO

**Habit** Suckering, palm-like. **Flowers** In long, terminal spikes, with drooping, pale yellow flowers and brown bracts, in summer. **Fruits** Yellow-green, banana-like, 6cm (2½in) long. **Leaves** Evergreen, arching, oblong to paddle-shaped, to 1m (3ft) long. Bright green.
• NATIVE HABITAT Ryuku Islands, Japan.
• CULTIVATION Grow in humus-rich soil out of wind or as a house, greenhouse or conservatory plant.
• PROPAGATION By division year-round, by suckers after flowering, or by offsets in autumn.

☀ ◊
❄

HEIGHT
3–5m
(10–15ft)

SPREAD
2–2.5m
(6–8ft)

| Musaceae | ABYSSINIAN BANANA, ETHIOPIAN BANANA |
|---|---|

## ENSETE VENTRICOSUM

**Habit** Palm-like, with a bulbous, trunk-like stem.
**Flowers** Long, terminal spikes, bearing red-green flowers with red bracts, are produced intermittently. **Fruits** Small, dry, banana-like, inedible. **Leaves** Evergreen, long, rather pointed, to 6m (20ft) long. Olive-green with a maroon midrib.

• NATIVE HABITAT Tropical Africa.
• CULTIVATION Grow in fertile, humus-rich soil. In cool climates this plant is only really suitable for a larger heated greenhouse where the temperature does not fall below 10°C (50°F) and the minimum height space is at least 8m (25ft). Can be planted either in a border or a large container. The latter will tend to restrict the growth and could be desirable in a confined space. Container-grown plants will need regular feeding.
• PROPAGATION By division year-round, or by seed in spring.
• OTHER NAMES *Musa arnoldiana, M. ensete.*

☼ ◊

Min. 10°C
(50°F)

**HEIGHT**
6m (20ft)
or more

**SPREAD**
3m (10ft)
or more

| Apiaceae/Umbelliferae | |
| --- | --- |

## *ANTHRISCUS SYLVESTRIS* 'Ravenswing'

*Habit* Clump-forming. *Flowers* Tiny, in small umbels, in late spring. Creamy-white, sometimes tinted pink. *Leaves* Finely divided fern-like. Green at first, black-purple when mature.
• NATIVE HABITAT Garden origin. Species (cow parsley) occurs in grassy habitats in Europe, N. Africa, to W. Asia.
• CULTIVATION Grow in moist but well-drained soil, in sun. Useful as foliage contrast in herbaceous borders, especially with silver-leaved plants.
• PROPAGATION By division in spring or autumn.

HEIGHT
1m (3ft)
or more

SPREAD
45cm (18in)

| Ranunculaceae | FAIR MAIDS OF FRANCE / KENT |
| --- | --- |

## *RANUNCULUS ACONITIFOLIUS* 'Flore Pleno'

*Habit* Clump-forming. *Flowers* Small, fully double, long-lasting, on sturdy branching stems, from late spring to summer. Pure white. *Leaves* Deeply divided, 3–5 lobed. Dark green.
• NATIVE HABITAT Origin uncertain. Species occurs in meadows and by streams, from W. to C. Europe.
• CULTIVATION Grow in moist, fertile, humus-rich soil in sun or part-shade. Suitable for borders, or stream- and watersides, above water level.
• PROPAGATION By division in spring or autumn.

HEIGHT
60–75cm
(24–30in)

SPREAD
50cm (20in)

| Ranunculaceae | |
| --- | --- |

## *RANUNCULUS ACONITIFOLIUS*

*Habit* Robust, clump-forming. *Flowers* Single, shallowly cupped, to 2.5cm (1in) across, in spring and early summer. White, sometimes pink-flushed beneath. *Leaves* Divided, 3–5 lobed. Dark green.
• NATIVE HABITAT Sub-alpine meadows, and by streams, from W. to C. Europe.
• CULTIVATION Grow in moist, fertile, humus-rich soil, in sun or part-shade. Suitable for a wildflower garden, border or streamside, above water level.
• PROPAGATION By seed in spring, or division in spring or autumn.

HEIGHT
1m (3ft)

SPREAD
1m (3ft)

| Convallariaceae/ Liliaceae | SOLOMON'S SEAL |
| --- | --- |

## *POLYGONATUM HIRTUM*

*Habit* Upright then arching, rhizomatous. *Flowers* Small, pendent, tubular, in clusters of 2–5, on arching stems, in late spring. White, tipped green. *Leaves* Alternate, lance-shaped to oval. Fresh green. Finely hairy stems, leaf stalks and leaves.
• NATIVE HABITAT Woodlands of E.C. and S.E. Europe, W. Russia, N.W. Turkey.
• CULTIVATION Grow in fertile, humus-rich, moisture-retentive but well-drained soil, in shade.
• PROPAGATION By seed or division in early spring.
• OTHER NAMES *P. latifolium.*

HEIGHT
1m (3ft)

SPREAD
30cm (1ft)

| Liliaceae/Liliaceae | FALSE SPIKENARD |
|---|---|

## SMILACINA RACEMOSA ♈

**Habit** Arching, clump-forming, rhizomatous.
**Flowers** Tiny, in dense, feathery sprays, from spring to mid-summer. White. **Fruits** Small, fleshy, red berries. **Leaves** Lance-shaped to oval, with pointed tips. Pale green.
• NATIVE HABITAT Damp woods, North America.
• CULTIVATION Grow in moist, fertile, humus-rich, neutral to acid soil. A beautiful specimen for shady borders and woodland gardens.
• PROPAGATION By division in spring or autumn, or by seed in autumn.

☼ ◐
❄ ❄ ❄

HEIGHT
90cm (36in)
or more

SPREAD
45cm (18in)

| Convallariaceae/ Liliaceae | |
|---|---|

## POLYGONATUM × HYBRIDUM ♈

**Habit** Arching, rhizomatous. **Flowers** Small, pendent, tubular, on arching stems in the leaf axils, in late spring. Greenish-white. **Leaves** Stem-clasping, oval. Fresh bright green.
• NATIVE HABITAT Long cultivated, origin uncertain.
• CULTIVATION Grow in any moderately fertile, moisture-retentive but well-drained soil. An elegant specimen for shady borders and woodland gardens. Leaves may be stripped by sawfly larvae.
• PROPAGATION By division in early spring.

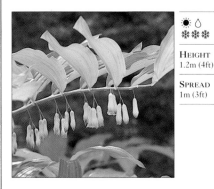

☼ ◐
❄ ❄ ❄

HEIGHT
1.2m (4ft)

SPREAD
1m (3ft)

| Saxifragaceae | UMBRELLA PLANT |
|---|---|

## DARMERA PELTATA ♈

**Habit** Spreading, rhizomatous. **Flowers** Small, in clusters, on sturdy, white-hairy stems, open before the leaves in spring. White or pale pink. **Leaves** Round, to 60cm (2ft) across, finely hairy. Mid-green.
• NATIVE HABITAT Mountain streambanks, in forests, N.W. California to S.W. Oregon.
• CULTIVATION Grow in sun or part-shade, in moist soil. Excellent as a marginal water plant.
• PROPAGATION By division in spring, or by seed in autumn or spring.
• OTHER NAMES *Peltiphyllum peltatum*.

☼ ◐
❄ ❄ ❄

HEIGHT
1–1.2m
(3–4ft)

SPREAD
60cm (2ft)

Asteraceae/Compositae

## *TANACETUM COCCINEUM* 'Brenda'

**Habit** Upright. **Flowers** Single, daisy-like, in late spring and summer. Bright magenta-pink, with yellow central discs. **Leaves** Faintly aromatic, finely divided. Grey-green.
• NATIVE HABITAT Garden origin.
• CULTIVATION Grow in an open, sunny site, in fertile, well-drained, preferably neutral to slightly acid soil. If cut back after the first flush of flowers, will usually produce a second flush of blooms later in the season. A long-established border plant, invaluable for cutting as the flowers last well in water. It does not do well in a poor, sandy soil, however, more frequent division and feeding will maintain vigour or encourage sturdier growth in a weaker plant.
• PROPAGATION By division in spring.
• OTHER NAMES *Pyrethrum* 'Brenda'.

☼ ◊
❀ ❀ ❀

**HEIGHT**
60cm (24in)

**SPREAD**
45cm (18in)
or more

---

Brassicaceae/Cruciferae

## *LUNARIA REDIVIVA*

**Habit** Upright, branching. **Flowers** Small, scented, 4-petalled, in upright, branching clusters, in spring. White, lilac or purple. **Fruits** Elliptical, silvery, translucent. **Leaves** Oval-lance-shaped, finely toothed. Mid-green, may be tinted maroon.
• NATIVE HABITAT Sub-alpine woodland and scrub, Europe to eastern Siberia.
• CULTIVATION Grow in fertile, moist, well-drained sun in semi-shade or sun. The seed heads dry well.
• PROPAGATION By seed in autumn or spring, or by division in spring.

☼ ◊
❀ ❀ ❀

**HEIGHT**
60–75cm
(24–30in)

**SPREAD**
30cm (12in)

---

Geraniaceae | MOURNING WIDOW

## *GERANIUM PHAEUM*

**Habit** Clump-forming, rhizomatous. **Flowers** Small, with 5 reflexed petals, borne in loose, clusters, from late spring to summer. Deep maroon-purple. **Leaves** Divided into 7–9 soft green lobes, sometimes spotted red-purple at base.
• NATIVE HABITAT Woods and sub-alpine meadows, S., C. and W. Europe.
• CULTIVATION Grow in any well-drained soil, in shade or semi-shade: Excellent for woodland and wild gardens, or for shady borders.
• PROPAGATION Seed or division in autumn or spring.

☼ ◊
❀ ❀ ❀

**HEIGHT**
up to 75cm
(30in)

**SPREAD**
45cm (18in)

# NON-BULBOUS IRISES

Grown for their distinctive and colourful flowers, irises form a large genus of perennials, some of which, like the plants featured on the following pages, are rhizomatous, and others bulbous. Each flower has 3 distinctive drooping "falls" which may have beards or crests, and 3 upright horizontal, occasionally drooping "standards". Irises can be grown in rock and woodland gardens, bog gardens, by water or in a herbaceous border.

Non-bulbous, rhizomatous irises, are divided into three groups: bearded, beardless and crested. Unless otherwise stated, all have rhizomatous rootstocks and sword-shaped leaves arranged in a basal fan.

**Bearded irises** flower from early spring to summer and are grouped by size into: Miniature dwarf, to 20cm (8in); Standard dwarf, 20–40cm (8–16in); Intermediate, 40–70cm (16–28in); and Standard tall, 70cm (28in) or more. They should be grown in well-drained, preferably slightly alkaline soil in full sun. Some tolerate poorer soils and light shade. Onocyclus and Regelia irises are both bearded irises but prefer drier summer conditions and may prove difficult to grow.

**Beardless irises** need similar conditions to bearded irises, but some prefer heavier, more moisture-retentive soils. The 16 group include the Pacific Coast, Spuria, Siberian and Japanese irises. They prefer moist waterside conditions, but may be grown in borders in moist soils, in an open, sunny site

**Crested irises**, including the Evansia irises, have ridges or crests instead of beards on the falls. Most thrive in similar conditions to the bearded irises, but a few prefer damp, humus-rich soils. A number in this group are half hardy to frost tender (min. 5°C/41°F).

Species can be propagated by division of rhizomes or offsets in late summer, or by seed in autumn; cultivars by division only.

---

*I. CONFUSA*
*Habit* Very robust, with aerial rhizomes.
*Flowers* To 5cm (2in) wide, borne in succession on branching stems, in mid-spring. White, yellow-crested falls are spotted yellow and purple.
*Leaves* Evergreen or semi-evergreen, broad, at the top of bamboo-like stems.
• TIPS Grow in well-drained soil. Best against a warm wall.
• HEIGHT 30cm–1m (1–3ft).
• SPREAD indefinite.

*I. confusa*
(Evansia)

☼ ◊ ✽✽

*I. 'Anniversary'*
*Habit* Robust, rhizomatous.
*Flowers* To 10cm (4in) across, borne 1–4 on branched stems from late spring to early summer. White, striped creamy-white at the throat of each fall.
• CULTIVATION Suitable for a bog garden or damp border.
• HEIGHT 60cm (2ft).
• SPREAD indefinite.

*I. 'Anniversary'*
(Beardless, Siberian)

☼ ◊ ✽✽✽

*I. 'Wisley White'*
*Habit* Robust, rhizomatous.
*Flowers* To 10cm (4in) across, borne 2–3 on branched stems in early summer. White standards and white falls stained yellow at the base.
• TIPS Suitable for a bog garden or damp border.
• HEIGHT 1m (3ft).
• SPREAD indefinite.

*I. 'Wisley White'*
(Beardless, Siberian)

☼ ◊ ✽✽✽

## *I.* 'Dreaming Yellow'

*Habit* Rhizomatous.
*Flowers* To 10cm (4in) across, borne 1–4 on branched stems from late spring to early summer. White standards, creamy-yellow falls, ageing to white.
• TIPS Suitable for a bog garden or damp border.
• HEIGHT 1m (3ft).
• SPREAD indefinite.

*I.* 'Dreaming Yellow'
(Beardless, Siberian)

☼ ◗ ❀❀❀

## *I.* 'Arnold Sunrise'

*Habit* Rhizomatous.
*Flowers* 10–12cm (4–5in) across, borne 2–3 on a branched stem in spring. White, tinted lilac with light orange on falls.
• TIPS Prefers moisture-retentive soil. Slow-spreading.
• HEIGHT 25cm (10in).
• SPREAD indefinite.

*I.* 'Arnold Sunrise'
(Beardless, Pacific Coast)

☼ ◗ ❀❀❀          ♆

## *I. KERNERIANA*

*Habit* Rhizomatous.
*Flowers* To 12cm (5in) wide, borne 2–4 from each pair of bracts on strong, branching stems. Soft lemon- or creamy-yellow. *Leaves* Narrow, grass-like. Fresh green.
• TIPS Tolerates semi-shade. Needs moist but well-drained soil.
• HEIGHT 16–25cm (6–10in).
• SPREAD indefinite.

*I. kerneriana*
(Beardless, Spuria)

☼ ◗ pH ❀❀❀

## *I. AFGHANICA*

*Habit* Rhizomatous.
*Flowers* To 9cm (3½in) across, borne singly on slender stems in spring. Creamy-yellow standards, white falls, heavily veined and blotched purple-brown at the base.
*Leaves* Curved, linear.
• TIPS Suitable for a rock garden or alpine house. Grow in fertile, sharply drained soil. Provide a period of dry dormancy after flowering.
• HEIGHT 15–30cm (6–12in).
• SPREAD to 30cm (12in).

*I. afghanica*
(Regelia)

☼ ◊ ❀❀❀

## *I. IBERICA*

*Habit* Rhizomatous.
*Flowers* To 12cm (5in) wide, singly in late spring. Standards white, pale blue or yellow, falls white or pale lilac, spoon-shaped, veined brown-purple.
*Leaves* Curved, linear. Grey-green.
• TIPS Dry rhizome after flowering. Drain well.
• HEIGHT 15–20cm (6–8in).
• SPREAD indefinite.

*I. iberica*
(Onocyclus)

☼ ◊ ❀❀❀

## *I.* 'Geisha Gown'

*Habit* Robust.
*Flowers* Double, 15–30cm (6–12in) across, borne 3–5 on branched stems in summer. White standards and falls with rose-purple veining; falls have a yellow blaze and purple styles.
• TIPS For a sunny, open bog or water garden in lime-free soil.
• HEIGHT 80cm (32in).
• SPREAD indefinite.

*I.* 'Geisha Gown'
(Beardless, Japanese)

☼ ◗ ❀❀

## I. MISSOURIENSIS
**Habit** Rhizomatous.
**Flowers** To 8cm (3in) wide, 2–3 per spathe on branched stems, in spring or early summer. Blue, pale lavender, lilac or white.
**Leaves** Smooth, grass-like. Pale green.
• TIPS Prefers sun, but tolerates semi-shade and shallow water. Resents root disturbance.
• HEIGHT to 75cm (30in).
• SPREAD indefinite.

*I. missouriensis*
(Beardless, Pacific Coast)

☼ ◊ pH ❋❋

## I. CRISTATA
**Habit** With branching rhizomes.
**Flowers** To 4cm (1½in) wide, almost stemless, 1–2 per stem, in early summer. Lilac, blue, lavender or white, with orange-crested falls.
**Leaves** Narrowly sword-shaped. Yellowish-green.
• TIPS Prefers moist, peaty, lime-free soil.
• HEIGHT 10cm (4in).
• SPREAD indefinite.

*I. cristata*
(Evansia)

☼ ◊ pH ❋❋❋

## I. PALLIDA
## 'Aurea Variegata'
**Habit** Rhizomatous.
**Flowers** Scented, 8–12cm (3–5in) across, on branched stems, in late spring and early summer. Pale lilac-blue, with yellow beards.
**Leaves** Sword-shaped. Green and yellow striped.
• TIPS Likes well-drained, fairly alkaline soil.
• HEIGHT 70cm–1m (28–36in).
• SPREAD indefinite.

*I. pallida* 'Aurea Variegata'
(Bearded)

☼ ◊ ❋❋❋

## I. 'Joette'
**Habit** Rhizomatous.
**Flowers** To 15cm (6in) across, borne on branched stems in late spring and early summer. Standards uniform lavender-blue; falls lavender-blue, with white veining at the base and a golden-yellow beard.
• TIPS Likes well-drained, slightly alkaline soil.
• HEIGHT 45cm (18in).
• SPREAD indefinite.

*I. 'Joette'*
(Bearded, Intermediate)

☼ ◊ ❋❋❋

## I. 'Paradise Bird'
**Habit** Rhizomatous.
**Flowers** To 15cm (6in) across, 8–10 borne on well-branched stems, in early summer. Pale magenta standards; falls darker magenta, with a dark golden beard.
• TIPS Grow in fertile, well-drained, slightly alkaline soil, in full sun.
• HEIGHT 85cm (34in).
• SPREAD indefinite.

*I. 'Paradise Bird'*
(Bearded, Standard tall)

☼ ◊ ❋❋❋

## I. 'Rippling Rose'
**Habit** Rhizomatous.
**Flowers** To 15cm (6in) across, 6–10 borne on well-branched stems in early summer. White standards and falls, with rose-purple markings and edges and a lemon-yellow beard.
• TIPS Grow in fertile, well-drained, slightly alkaline soil, in full sun.
• HEIGHT 1m (3ft).
• SPREAD indefinite.

*I. 'Rippling Rose'*
(Bearded, Standard tall)

☼ ◊ ❋❋❋

## I. TENAX
**Habit** Rhizomatous.
**Flowers** 8–12cm (3–5in) wide, 1–2 per spathe, in spring or early summer. Deep purple to lavender-blue, often marked yellow and white on the falls.
**Leaves** Smooth, grass-like. Dark green, stained pink at the base.
• TIPS Slightly acid soil.
• HEIGHT 15–30cm (6–12in).
• SPREAD indefinite.

*I. tenax*
(Beardless, Pacific Coast)

☼ ◊ pH ❋❋

## I. VERSICOLOR
**Habit** Robust.
**Flowers** 5–10cm (2–4in) wide, borne 3–5 per spathe on branched stems from early to mid-summer. Purple-blue, red-purple, lavender or slate-blue, falls usually with purple-veined, white centres.
**Leaves** Long, curved or upright. Green, stained purple at the base.
• HEIGHT 60cm (2ft).
• SPREAD indefinite.

*I. versicolor*
(Beardless)
Blue flag, Wild iris

☼ ◊ ❋❋❋

## *I.* 'Bold Print'

**Habit** Rhizomatous.
**Flowers** Up to 6 flowers, 13cm (5in) across, borne on branched stems in late spring/early summer. Standards white with a purple edge; falls white edged with purple "stitching" and a bronze-tipped, yellow beard.
• TIPS Grow in fertile, well-drained, preferably slightly alkaline soil, in full sun.
• HEIGHT 55cm (22in).
• SPREAD indefinite.

*I.* 'Bold Print'
(Bearded, Intermediate)

☼ ◊ ❈ ❈ ❈

## *I. TECTORUM*

**Habit** Rhizomatous.
**Flowers** 1–8cm (½–3in) across, 2–3 per spathe on sparsely branched stems in early summer. Dark-veined, bright lilac with white-crested falls.
**Leaves** Ribbed, broadly lance-shaped, in fans.
• TIPS Best in moist soil, by a warm, sheltered wall.
• HEIGHT 25–35cm (10–14in).
• SPREAD indefinite.

*I. tectorum*
(Evansia)

☼ ◖ ❈ ❈

## *I. UNGUICULARIS* 'Mary Barnard'

**Habit** Rhizomatous.
**Flowers** 5–8cm (2–3in) wide, long-tubed, almost stemless, scented, borne from late autumn to early spring. Deep violet-blue, with yellow-centred falls.
**Leaves** Evergreen, tough, narrow.
• TIPS Best in well-drained soil by a wall.
• HEIGHT to 20cm (8in).
• SPREAD indefinite.

*I. unguicularis* 'Mary Barnard'
(Beardless)

☼ ◊ ❈ ❈ ❈

## *I.* 'Krasnia'

**Habit** Rhizomatous.
**Flowers** 13–18cm (5–7in) across, 8–12 borne on well-branched stems in early summer. Standards purple; falls white, edged purple, with a dark golden-brown beard.
• TIPS Grow in fertile, well-drained, slightly alkaline soil, in full sun.
• HEIGHT 1m (3ft).
• SPREAD indefinite.

*I.* 'Krasnia'
(Bearded, Standard tall)

☼ ◊ ❈ ❈ ❈

## *I.* 'Fulvala'

**Habit** Rhizomatous.
**Flowers** 5–12cm (2–5in) across, in pairs on zigzag stems in summer. Velvety, deep red-purple standards; falls deep red-purple with a yellow blaze.
• TIPS Suited to a bog garden or damp border.
• OTHER NAMES *I.* × *fulvala*.
• HEIGHT 45cm (18in).
• SPREAD indefinite.

*I.* 'Fulvala'
(Beardless)

☼ ◖ ❈ ❈

## I. CHRYSOGRAPHES
**Habit** Rhizomatous.
**Flowers** 5–10cm (2–4in)
across, borne 1–4 on
branched stems in late
spring to early summer. ,
Deep red-purple to black-
purple standard and falls;
falls are gold-etched.
**Leaves** Linear, to 45cm
(18in) long.
• TIPS Good in a lime-
free bog garden.
• HEIGHT 40cm (16in).
• SPREAD indefinite.

*I. chrysographes*
(Beardless, Siberian)

☼ ◊ pH ❉❉❉

## I. 'Matinata'
**Habit** Rhizomatous.
**Flowers** 15cm (6in)
across, 6–9 (occasionally
12) borne on well-
branched stems in early
summer. Uniformly dark
purple-blue standards
and falls, with a dark
blue-purple beard.
• TIPS Grow in fertile,
well-drained, slightly
alkaline soil, in full sun.
• HEIGHT 1m (3ft).
• SPREAD indefinite.

*I. 'Matinata'*
(Bearded, Standard tall)

☼ ◊ ❉❉❉

## I. 'Mary Frances'
**Habit** Rhizomatous.
**Flowers** 15cm (6in)
across, 6–9 (occasionally
12) borne on well-
branched stems in early
summer. Uniformly pink.
lavender standards and
falls, delicately frilled,
with a white beard.
• TIPS Grow in fertile,
well-drained, slightly
alkaline soil, in full sun.
• HEIGHT 1m (3ft).
• SPREAD indefinite.

*I. 'Mary Frances'*
(Bearded, Standard tall)

☼ ◊ ❉❉❉

## I. DOUGLASIANA
**Habit** Rhizomatous.
**Flowers** To 12cm (5in)
wide, 1–3 on branched
stems in spring to
summer. Lavender to
purple or white, with
central yellowish zone
on falls.
**Leaves** Evergreen,
leathery. Dark green,
red-purple at the base.
• HEIGHT 25–70cm
(10–28in).
• SPREAD indefinite.

*I. douglasiana*
(Beardless, Pacific Coast)

☼ ◊ ❉❉

## I. LACUSTRIS
**Habit** Rhizomatous.
**Flowers** To 4cm (1½in)
wide, almost stemless,
long-tubed, borne 1–2
per stem in early
summer. Sky-blue, with
a brown-flecked, yellow
crest on the falls.
**Leaves** Linear, upright.
Bright green.
• TIPS Needs reliably
moist, lime-free soil.
• HEIGHT 10cm (4in).
• SPREAD indefinite.

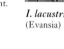

*I. lacustris*
(Evansia)

☼ ◊ pH ❉❉❉

## I. HOOGIANA
**Habit** Stout, rhizomatous.
**Flowers** To 10cm (4in)
wide, scented, 2–3 per
stem in early summer.
Lilac-blue, delicate
veined, golden-bearded.
**Leaves** Linear, slightly
arched. Mid-green, often
purple-tinted.
• TIPS Suited to a well-
drained rock garden.
• HEIGHT 45–80cm
(18–32in).
• SPREAD indefinite.

*I. hoogiana*
(Regelia)

☼ ◊ ❉❉❉

## I. 'Mountain Lake'
**Habit** Robust,
rhizomatous.
**Flowers** To 10cm (4in)
across, borne 1–4 on
branched stems from
late spring to early
summer. Mid-blue
standards; falls mid-blue
with darker veining
• TIPS Suitable for a
bog garden or damp
border.
• HEIGHT 1m (3ft).
• SPREAD indefinite.

*I. 'Mountain Lake'*
(Beardless, Siberian)

☼ ◊ ❉❉❉

## I. LAEVIGATA
**Habit** Rhizomatous.
**Flowers** To 12cm (5in)
wide, borne 2 to 4 per
sparsely branched stem,
from early to mid-summer.
Blue, blue-purple or white.
**Leaves** Smooth, grass-
like. Pale green.
• TIPS Grow in lime-free
soil. Tolerates semi-
shade and shallow water.
• HEIGHT 60cm–1m
(2–3ft).
• SPREAD indefinite.

*I. laevigata*
(Beardless, Japanese)

☼ ◊ pH ❉❉❉

## *I. SETOSA*
**Habit** Rhizomatous.
**Flowers** 5–8cm (2–3in) across, 2–13 per spathe, on branched stems, in summer. Small, bristle-like purple-blue standards; falls with paler markings.
**Leaves** Sword-shaped. Grey-green.
• TIPS Grow in moist soil. Suits a damp border.
• HEIGHT 10cm–1m (4in–3ft).
• SPREAD indefinite.

*I. setosa*
(Beardless)
Bristle-pointed iris

☼ ◐ ❀ ❀ ❀

## *I. VARIEGATA*
**Habit** Rhizomatous.
**Flowers** 5–8cm (2–3in) wide, 3–6 per spathe on branched stems, in early summer. Bright yellow standards; falls white or pale yellow, veined red-brown, appearing striped.
**Leaves** Ribbed, sickle-shaped. Bright green.
• TIPS For a bog garden.
• HEIGHT 30–50cm (12–20in).
• SPREAD indefinite.

*I. variegata*
(Bearded)
Variegated iris

☼ ◐ ❀ ❀ ❀

## *I.* 'Early Light'
**Habit** Rhizomatous.
**Flowers** To 18cm (7in) across, 8–10 borne on branched stems in early summer. Cream standards, flushed lemon-yellow; falls slightly darker with a yellow beard.
• TIPS Grow in fertile, well-drained, slightly alkaline soil, in full sun.
• HEIGHT 1m (3ft).
• SPREAD indefinite.

*I.* 'Early Light'
(Bearded, Standard tall)

☼ ◐ ❀ ❀ ❀          ♈

## *I. FORRESTII*
**Habit** Rhizomatous.
**Flowers** To 6cm (2½in) wide, fragrant, 1–2, in late spring to early summer. Yellow, with black-veined falls, and sometimes brown-flushed standards.
**Leaves** Linear, glossy. Mid-green.
• TIPS Needs reliably moist, lime-free soil.
• HEIGHT 15–40cm (6–16in).
• SPREAD indefinite.

*I. forrestii*
(Beardless, Siberian)

☼ ◐ pH ❀ ❀ ❀

## *I. PSEUDACORUS*
**Habit** Robust, rhizomatous.
**Flowers** 5–12cm (2–5in) across, borne 4–12 on strong branched stems, from early to mid-summer. Golden-yellow, usually with brown-violet veining and a darker yellow patch on the lower falls.
**Leaves** Sword-shaped. Grey-green.
• TIPS Grow in reliably moist soil in partial shade.
• HEIGHT to 2m (6ft).
• SPREAD indefinite.

*I. pseudacorus*
(Beardless)
Yellow flag

☼ ◐ ❀ ❀ ❀

## I. INNOMINATA

**Habit** Rhizomatous.
**Flowers** To 7.5cm (3in) wide, 1–2 per stem in late spring to early summer. Cream to orange, or lilac-pink to blue or purple; falls often maroon veined.
**Leaves** Evergreen, narrow. Purplish at base.
• TIPS Grow in the shelter of a warm, sunny wall.
• HEIGHT 16–25cm (6–10in).
• SPREAD indefinite.

*I. innominata*
(Beardless, Pacific Coast)

☼ ◊ pH ❋ ❋

## I. 'Sun Miracle'

**Habit** Rhizomatous.
**Flowers** 15–18cm (6–7in) across, 7–10 borne on well-branched stems in early summer. Pure yellow standards and falls, with a dark golden beard.
• TIPS Grow in fertile, well-drained, slightly alkaline soil, in full sun.
• HEIGHT 1m (3ft)
• SPREAD indefinite

*I. 'Sun Miracle'*
(Bearded, Standard tall)

☼ ◊ ❋ ❋ ❋

## I. 'Eyebright'

**Habit** Rhizomatous.
**Flowers** To 10cm (4in) across, 2–4 borne on usually unbranched stems in late spring. Standards bright yellow; falls bright yellow, marked dark brown, with a yellow beard.
• TIPS Grow in fertile, well-drained, slightly alkaline soil, in full sun.
• HEIGHT 30cm (12in).
• SPREAD indefinite.

*I. 'Eyebright'*
(Bearded, Standard dwarf)

☼ ◊ ❋ ❋ ❋

## I. 'Shepherd's Delight'

**Habit** Rhizomatous.
**Flowers** 15–18cm (6–7in) across, 6–10 on well-branched stems in early summer. Standards and falls clear pink with a yellowish cast, and a dark orange beard.
• TIPS Grow in fertile, well-drained, slightly alkaline soil, in full sun.
• HEIGHT 1m (3ft)
• SPREAD indefinite.

*I. 'Shepherd's Delight'*
(Bearded, Standard tall)

☼ ◊ ❋ ❋ ❋

## I. 'Peach Frost'

**Habit** Rhizomatous.
**Flowers** To 15cm (6in) across, 6–10 borne on well-branched stems in early summer. Peach-pink standards; falls white with peach-pink borders and a tangerine beard.
• TIPS Grow in fertile, well-drained, slightly alkaline soil, in full sun.
• HEIGHT 1m (3ft).
• SPREAD indefinite.

*I. 'Peach Frost'*
(Bearded, Standard tall)

☼ ◊ ❋ ❋ ❋

## I. FULVA

**Habit** Rhizomatous.
**Flowers** To 7cm (3in) wide, 1–2 in the leaf axils of sparsely branched stems in late spring to early summer. Coppery-orange or orange-red.
**Leaves** Linear, glossy. Mid-green.
• TIPS Prefers reliably moist soil.
• HEIGHT 45–80cm (18–32in).
• SPREAD indefinite.

*I. fulva*
(Beardless)

☼ ◊ ❋ ❋

## I. 'Blue-Eyed Brunette'

**Habit** Rhizomatous.
**Flowers** To 15cm (6in) across, 7–10 borne on well-branched stems, in early summer. Cigar-brown with a blue blaze and golden-bearded falls.
• TIPS Grow in fertile, well-drained, slightly alkaline soil, in full sun.
• HEIGHT 1m (3ft).
• SPREAD indefinite.

*I. 'Blue-Eyed Brunette'*
(Bearded, Standard tall)

☼ ◊ ❋ ❋ ❋      ▽

## I. 'Flamenco'

**Habit** Rhizomatous.
**Flowers** To 15cm (6in) across, 6–9 borne on well-branched stems in early summer. Standards gold infused red; falls white to yellow edged red, with a dark golden-brown beard.
• TIPS Grow in fertile, well-drained, slightly alkaline soil, in full sun.
• HEIGHT 1m (3ft)
• SPREAD indefinite

*I. 'Flamenco'*
(Bearded, Standard tall)

☼ ◊ ❋ ❋ ❋

# PEONIES

Herbaceous peonies (*Paeonia* species and cultivars) are valued for their showy flowers, bold foliage and, in some species, for their ornamental seed pods. The flowers vary from single to double or anemone form (with broad, outer petals and a mass of petaloids in the centre) and are often heavily scented.

Peony foliage is also striking, often tinged bronze when young and assuming rich, reddish tints in autumn. Unless otherwise stated, the leaves are large, alternate and divided into oval to lance-shaped linear leaflets.

Besides the wide variety of herbaceous border hybrids and species shown on these pages, there are also a number of tree peonies (cultivars of *P. suffruticosa*), which are open shrubs often over 2m (6ft).

Though they will tolerate a light shady position, peonies are best grown in sun in fertile, humus-rich, moist but well-drained soil. Before planting, prepare the ground by incorporating well-rotted manure or garden compost. Early in the season, provide tall border peonies with grow-through support.

Peonies are long-lived plants that should, if possible, be left undisturbed as they resent transplanting. If it is necessary to split the clumps, lift and divide them in autumn or early spring (p. 323). Species can be increased by seed sown as soon as it is ripe, although it can take as long as three years to germinate.

If shoots wilt, wither, and turn brown, this may be a sign that the plant is affected by peony wilt. This fungus may lie dormant in the soil until conditions are favourable, often in prolonged wet weather, when it starts to form a grey mould on the stems. The best method of control is to cut out the affected shoots to below ground level, and dust with a proprietary fungicide.

---

**P. EMODI**
*Habit* Clump-forming.
*Flowers* Large, fragrant, single, borne singly on tall stems in late spring and early summer. Pure white, with a central boss of golden stamens.
*Leaves* Divided into glossy leaflets. Mid-green.
• HEIGHT to 1.2m (4ft).
• SPREAD to 1m (3ft).

*P. emodi*

☼ ◊ ❋❋❋

---

**P. LACTIFLORA**
**'White Wings'**
*Habit* Clump-forming.
*Flowers* Large, well-scented, single to loosely semi-double, in early to mid-summer. Broad white petals, slightly ruffled at the tips, sometimes tinged pale sulphur-yellow, with golden stamens.
*Leaves* Dark green, provide autumn colour.
• HEIGHT 85cm (34in).
• SPREAD 85cm (34in).

*P. lactiflora*
**'White Wings'**

☼ ◊ ❋❋❋

---

**P. LACTIFLORA**
**'Whitleyi Major'**
*Habit* Clump-forming, floriferous.
*Flowers* Large, well-scented, single, in early to mid-summer. Broad, satiny, ivory-white petals, surrounding a boss of clear golden-yellow stamens.
*Leaves* Very dark green, flushed rich red-brown.
• HEIGHT 85cm (34in).
• SPREAD 85cm (34in).

*P. lactiflora*
**'Whitleyi Major'**

☼ ◊ ❋❋❋      ♔

---

**P. LACTIFLORA**
**'Baroness Schröder'**
*Habit* Vigorous, clump-forming, floriferous.
*Flowers* Large, fragrant, globe-shaped, double, in early to mid-summer. Flesh-pink at first, fading to white, with broad flat outer petals, and incurved, ruffled, tightly packed inner ones. Excellent for cutting.
• HEIGHT 1m (3ft).
• SPREAD 1m (3ft).

*P. lactiflora*
**'Baroness Schröder'**

☼ ◊ ❋❋❋

**P. *LACTIFLORA***
**'Krinkled White'**
**Habit** Robust,
clump-forming.
**Flowers** Large, single,
bowl-shaped, with large
petals having slightly
ruffled margins, and
surrounding a neat boss
of golden stamens, in
early to mid-summer.
Milky-white, sometimes
flushed very pale pink.
• HEIGHT 80cm (32in).
• SPREAD 80cm (32in).

*P. lactiflora*
**'Krinkled White'**

☼ ◊ ✳✳✳

---

**P. *OFFICINALIS***
**'Alba Plena'**
**Habit** Clump-forming.
**Flowers** Large, double,
with many slightly
ruffled petals, in early
to mid-summer. White,
often flushed pale pink.
• HEIGHT to 75cm
(30in).
• SPREAD to 75cm
(30in).

*P. officinalis*
**'Alba Plena'**

☼ ◊ ✳✳✳

**P. *LACTIFLORA***
**'Alice Harding'**
**Habit** Clump-forming.
**Flowers** Very large,
fragrant, in early to mid-
summer. Double, creamy
white.
• HEIGHT to 1m (3ft).
• SPREAD 1m (3ft).

*P. lactiflora*
**'Alice Harding'**

☼ ◊ ✳✳✳

---

**P. *LACTIFLORA***
**'Duchesse de
Nemours'**
**Habit** Vigorous, clump-
forming, free-flowering.
**Flowers** Fragrant, double,
in early to mid-summer.
Large outer petals green-
tinted fading to white;
narrow, creamy-white
inner petals yellow at base.
• OTHER NAMES *P.* 'Mrs
Gwyn Lewis'.
• HEIGHT to 70cm (28in).
• SPREAD 70cm (28in).

*P. lactiflora* **'Duchesse
de Nemours'**

☼ ◊ ✳✳✳          ♈

**P. *LACTIFLORA***
**'Cornelia Shaylor'**
**Habit** Erect, clump-
forming, floriferous.
**Flowers** Fragrant,
double, with ruffled
petals neatly and densely
arranged, from early to
mid-summer. Flushed
rose-pink on opening,
fading gradually to blush-
white.
• HEIGHT to 85cm
(34in).
• SPREAD 85cm (34in).

*P. lactiflora*
**'Cornelia Shaylor'**

☼ ◊ ✳✳✳

**P. *LACTIFLORA***
**'Shirley Temple'**
*Habit* Clump-
forming, floriferous.
*Flowers* Large, fragrant,
fully double, in late
spring to early summer.
Outer whorls of broad,
soft rose-pink petals,
fading to soft buff-white,
with slightly smaller,
loosely arranged inner
petals.
• HEIGHT 85cm (34in).
• SPREAD 85cm (34in).

*P. lactiflora*
**'Shirley Temple'**

☼ ◊ ❀❀❀

**P. *LACTIFLORA***
**'Kelway's Supreme'**
*Habit* Clump-forming,
freely branching,
floriferous.
*Flowers* Large, strongly
fragrant, double, borne
over long periods from
early to mid-summer.
Broad, incurving, soft
blush-pink petals, fading
to creamy-white, cupping
a boss of golden stamens.
• HEIGHT 1m (3ft).
• SPREAD 1m (3ft).

*P. lactiflora*
**'Kelway's Supreme'**

☼ ◊ ❀❀❀

**P. *LACTIFLORA***
**'Mother of Pearl'**
*Habit* Clump-forming.
*Flowers* Elegant,
single. with broad
petals, in late spring to
early summer. Dog-
rose-pink petals, paler
at the margins, cupping
a boss of golden
stamens.
*Leaves* Bright grey-
green.
• HEIGHT 75cm (30in).
• SPREAD 60cm (24in).

*P. lactiflora*
**'Mother of Pearl'**

☼ ◊ ❀❀❀

**P. *LACTIFLORA***
**'Avant Garde'**
*Habit* Clump-forming.
*Flowers* Medium to large,
fragrant, single, in mid-
spring. Pale rose-pink
petals with darker veins,
and a boss of golden
anthers with red filaments.
Stiff-stemmed flowers are
excellent for cutting.
*Leaves* Has particularly
luxuriant foliage.
• HEIGHT to 1m (3ft).
• SPREAD to 1m (3ft).

*P. lactiflora*
**'Avant Garde'**

☼ ◊ ❀❀❀

**P. *LACTIFLORA***
**'Sarah Bernhardt'**
*Habit* Vigorous, upright,
clump-forming,
floriferous.
*Flowers* Very large,
fragrant, fully double,
with large, slightly ruffled
petals, in early to mid-
summer. Clear rose-pink,
fading to soft silvery-pink
at the margins.
• HEIGHT to 1m (3ft).
• SPREAD to 1m (3ft).

*P. lactiflora* 'Sarah
Bernhardt'

☼ ◊ ❀❀❀    ♛

**P. *CAMBESSEDESII***
*Habit* Clump-forming.
*Flowers* Single, in mid-
spring. Deep rose-pink.
*Leaves* Very dark green,
with veins, stalks and
undersides flushed
purple-red.
• TIPS Needs a warm,
sheltered site, with
protection from late
spring frost and
excessive summer rain.
Can be grown in a
greenhouse.
• HEIGHT 45cm (18in).
• SPREAD 45cm (18in).

*P. cambessedesii*
Majorcan peony

☼ ◊ ❀❀

---

**P. *LACTIFLORA***
**'Ballerina'**
*Habit* Clump-forming.
*Flowers* Fragrant,
double, in spring to early
summer. Inner petals are
narrower and more
densely arranged often
with ruffled edges. Soft
blush-pink, lilac-tinted
at first, fading to white.
*Leaves* Provide good
autumn colour.
• HEIGHT 1m (3ft).
• SPREAD 1m (3ft).

*P. lactiflora* 'Ballerina'

☼ ◊ ❀❀❀

---

**P. *MASCULA***
*Habit* Clump-forming.
*Flowers* Single. Carmine-
or purple-red, or white,
around golden stamens
with purple filaments.
*Fruits* Downy, boat-
shaped capsules split to
reveal purple-black seeds.
*Leaves* Shiny, leaflets on
red stems. Dark green.
• OTHER NAMES
*P. corallina.*
• HEIGHT to 1m (3ft).
• SPREAD to 1m (3ft).

*P. mascula*

☼ ◊ ❀❀❀

---

**P. *LACTIFLORA***
**'Bowl of Beauty'**
*Habit* Clump-forming.
*Flowers* Very large,
anemone-form, in early
to mid-summer. Broad,
outer petals of pale
carmine-pink, and
numerous narrow, inner
petal-like stamens,
densely arranged, ivory-
white.
• HEIGHT 1m (3ft).
• SPREAD 1m (3ft).

*P. lactiflora*
'Bowl of Beauty'

☼ ◊ ❀❀❀ ♈

---

**P. *VEITCHII***
*Habit* Clump-
forming, spreading.
*Flowers* Small, single,
nodding, borne 2 or
more per stem in early
summer. Purple-pink.
*Leaves* Divided into
shiny narrowly oblong
to elliptic segments.
Bright green.
• HEIGHT to 75cm
(30in).
• SPREAD 75cm (30in)
or more.

*P. veitchii*

☼ ◊ ❀❀❀

**P. LACTIFLORA**
**'Globe of Light'**
*Habit* Clump-forming.
*Flowers* Large, fragrant,
anemone-form, in early
to mid-summer. Pure
pink outer petals with
narrow, inner, petal-like
stamens, of a clear
golden-yellow.
• HEIGHT 1m (3ft).
• SPREAD 1m (3ft).

*P. lactiflora*
'Globe of Light'

☼ ◊ ❀❀❀

**P. LACTIFLORA**
**'Kelway's Gorgeous'**
*Habit* Clump-
forming, floriferous.
*Flowers* Single, in early
summer. Intense
carmine, slightly flushed
salmon-pink, with a
central boss of golden
stamens.
• HEIGHT 85cm (34in).
• SPREAD 85cm (34in).

*P. lactiflora*
'Kelway's Gorgeous'

☼ ◊ ❀❀❀

**P. LACTIFLORA**
**'Silver Flare'**
*Habit* Clump-forming.
*Flowers* Large, single to
loosely semi-double, on
dark red-tinted stems in
spring to early summer.
Golden stamens
surrounded by carmine-
pink petals fading to a
silvery margin.
*Leaves* Provide good
autumn colour.
• HEIGHT to 1m (3ft).
• SPREAD to 1m (3ft).

*P. lactiflora*
'Silver Flare'

☼ ◊ ❀❀❀

**P. LACTIFLORA**
**'Magic Orb'**
*Habit* Clump-forming.
*Flowers* Large, fragrant,
double, with several
whorls of broad ruffles,
in early to mid-summer.
Intense cherry-pink outer
petals and pale blush-
white inner petals,
shaded carmine, surround
a central cluster of narrow
creamy-white petals.
• HEIGHT 1m (3ft).
• SPREAD 1m (3ft).

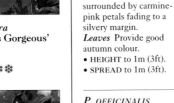

*P. lactiflora*
'Magic Orb'

☼ ◊ ❀❀❀

**P. OFFICINALIS**
**'China Rose'**
*Habit* Clump-forming.
*Flowers* Large, single,
in early to mid-summer.
Incurved, dark salmon-
rose petals cupping a
boss of golden-orange
anthers.
• HEIGHT to 45cm
(18in).
• SPREAD to 45cm
(18in).

*P. officinalis*
'China Rose'

☼ ◊ ❀❀❀

**P. LACTIFLORA**
## 'Auguste Dessert'
**Habit** Clump-forming.
**Flowers** Fragrant, semi-double, in early to mid-summer. Carmine-pink, tinted salmon-pink, with ruffled silvery-white petal margins, and a central boss of yellow stamens.
**Leaves** Colour richly in autumn.
• HEIGHT 75cm (30in).
• SPREAD 75cm (30in).

*P. lactiflora*
**'Auguste Dessert'**

☼ ◊ ❀❀❀

**P. LACTIFLORA**
## 'Instituteur Doriat'
**Habit** Clump-forming.
**Flowers** Large, anemone-form, in early summer. Outer petals, carmine-red, inner petal-like stamens paler pinkish-carmine, broader and densely arranged, with ruffled, silvery-white margins.
**Leaves** Provide good autumn colour.
• HEIGHT 1m (3ft).
• SPREAD 1m (3ft).

*P.* **'Instituteur Doriat'**

☼ ◊ ❀❀❀

**P. LACTIFLORA**
## 'Defender'
**Habit** Vigorous, clump-forming.
**Flowers** Strong-stemmed, large, single, in late spring to early summer. Satiny crimson petals, with a central boss of golden stamens.
• HEIGHT 1m (3ft).
• SPREAD 1m (3ft).

*P. lactiflora* **'Defender'**

☼ ◊ ❀❀❀    ♛

**P. 'Smouthii'**
**Habit** Vigorous, clump-forming, floriferous.
**Flowers** Large, fragrant, single. Glistening dark crimson, with conspicuous golden-yellow stamens.
**Leaves** Finely cut. Greyish green, but variable in colour.
• OTHER NAMES
*P.* x *smouthii.*
• HEIGHT to 45cm (18in).
• SPREAD to 45cm (18in).

*P.* **'Smouthii'**

☼ ◊ ❀❀❀

**P. PEREGRINA**
## 'Sunshine'
**Habit** Clump-forming.
**Flowers** Large, single, in late spring to early summer. Vermilion, tinged salmon-rose.
**Leaves** Glossy. Bright green.
• OTHER NAMES
*P. peregrina* 'Otto Freubel'.
• HEIGHT to 75cm (30in).
• SPREAD to 75cm (30in).

*P. peregrina*
**'Sunshine'**

☼ ◊ ❀❀❀

**P. LACTIFLORA 'Knighthood'**
*Habit* Clump-forming.
*Flowers* Large, very double, with many both broad and rather narrow, densely arranged, ruffled petals in early to mid-summer. Intense, deep, rich burgundy-red.
• HEIGHT 75cm (30in).
• SPREAD 75cm (30in).

*P. lactiflora* 'Knighthood'

☼ ◊ ❀❀❀

**P. OFFICINALIS 'Rubra Plena'**
*Habit* Clump-forming, long-lived.
*Flowers* Large, double, with many slightly ruffled petals, in early to mid-summer. Vivid pink-crimson.
*Leaves* Distinctively divided into rounded, broadly oval leaflets.
• HEIGHT to 75cm (30in).
• SPREAD to 75cm (30in).

*P. officinalis* 'Rubra Plena'

☼ ◊ ❀❀❀ ♛

**P. TENUIFOLIA**
*Habit* Clump-forming.
*Flowers* Small, bowl-shaped, single. Dark crimson with a central boss of conspicuous golden yellow stamens.
*Leaves* Elegant and very finely cut into filament-like segments. Bright green.
• HEIGHT to 45cm (18in).
• SPREAD to 45cm (18in).

*P. tenuifolia*

☼ ◊ ❀❀❀

**P. WITTMANNIANA**
*Habit* Robust, clump-forming, spreading.
*Flowers* Large, single, bowl-shaped, in late spring, and sometimes in mid-summer. Pale primrose-yellow, with a large central boss of yellow anthers on purple-red filaments.
*Leaves* Divided into oval segments. Dark green, paler beneath.
• HEIGHT to 1m (3ft).
• SPREAD to 1m (3ft).

*P. wittmanniana*

☼ ◊ ❀❀❀

**P. LACTIFLORA 'Chocolate Soldier'**
*Habit* Clump-forming.
*Flowers* Semi-double, in late spring to early summer. Purple-red, with yellow-mottled centres.
*Leaves* Mid- to dark green, usually tinged bronze-red when young.
• HEIGHT 1m (3ft).
• SPREAD 1m (3ft).

*P. lactiflora* 'Chocolate Soldier'

☼ ◊ ❀❀❀

**P. LACTIFLORA 'Laura Dessert'**
*Habit* Clump-forming.
*Flowers* Large, fragrant, double, in late spring to early summer. Creamy-blush-white outer petals, and densely arranged, incurved, inner petals flushed creamy lemon-yellow, often with cut and slightly ruffled margins.
• HEIGHT 75cm (30in).
• SPREAD 75cm (30in).

*P. lactiflora* 'Laura Dessert'

☼ ◊ ❀❀❀ ♛

**P. LACTIFLORA 'Sir Edward Elgar'**
*Habit* Clump-forming.
*Flowers* Large, single, in early to mid-summer. Solid, rich crimson petals tinted chocolate-brown arranged loosely around rather lax, lemon-yellow stamens.
*Leaves* Provide good autumn colour.
• HEIGHT 75cm (30in).
• SPREAD 75cm (30in).

*P. lactiflora* 'Sir Edward Elgar'

☼ ◊ ❀❀❀

**P. MLOKOSEWITSCHII**
*Habit* Clump-forming.
*Flowers* Large, single, bowl-shaped, in late spring. Pale lemon- to creamy-yellow, with a boss of golden stamens.
*Leaves* Divided into rounded leaflets. Bluish-green sometimes with red-purple edges, strongly suffused red-purple on emergence.
• HEIGHT to 75cm (30in).
• SPREAD to 75cm (30in).

*P. mlokosewitschii*

☼ ◊ ❀❀❀ ♛

| Boraginaceae | |
|---|---|

## SYMPHYTUM × UPLANDICUM 'Variegatum' ♀

*Habit* Clump-forming. *Flowers* Small, tubular, from late spring to early summer. Pale lilac-blue. *Leaves* Large, hairy, lance-shaped. Grey-green with broad cream margins.
• NATIVE HABITAT  The green-leaved hybrid occurs in the Caucasus, but is naturalized in N. Europe.
• CULTIVATION  Grow in any moist soil, in sun or shade. It produces its best foliage if the flowering stems are removed before they bloom.
• PROPAGATION  By division in autumn or spring.

☼ ◊
❁ ❁ ❁

HEIGHT
1m (3ft)

SPREAD
60cm (2ft)

| Boraginaceae | |
|---|---|

## SYMPHYTUM CAUCASICUM

*Habit* Robust, clump-forming, rhizomatous. *Flowers* Pendent, tubular, in short, paired cymes, from spring to early summer. Azure-blue. *Leaves* Coarse, hairy, oval pointed. Mid-green.
• NATIVE HABITAT  Scrub and streambanks, Caucasus
• CULTIVATION  Grow in moist soil in sun or shade. Is invasive, but is well suited to a wild garden, blooming over long periods. Will produce a second flush of bloom if cut back after first flowering.
• PROPAGATION  By division in spring or seed in autumn.

☼ ◊
❁ ❁ ❁

HEIGHT
60–90cm
(2–3ft)

SPREAD
60–90cm
(2–3ft)
or more

| Apiaceae/Umbelliferae | GOLDEN SPANIARD |
|---|---|

## ACIPHYLLA AUREA

*Habit* Rosette-forming. *Flowers* Small, in large, terminal, candelabra-like spikes, about 80cm (32in) tall, from late spring to early summer. Golden-cream. *Leaves* Evergreen, rigid, bayonet-like, to 70cm (28in) long. Usually golden-green.
• NATIVE HABITAT  Sub-alpine and mountain grassland, South Island, New Zealand.
• CULTIVATION  Grow in full sun, in humus-rich, well-drained soil. An excellent architectural shape; especially useful for planting in gravel.
• PROPAGATION  By seed sown fresh or in spring.

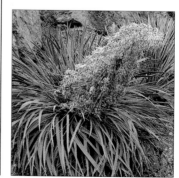

☼ ◊
❁ ❁

HEIGHT
60–75cm
(24–30in)

SPREAD
60–75cm
(24–30in)

| Asteraceae/Compositae | LEOPARD'S BANE |
|---|---|

## DORONICUM PARDALIANCHES

*Habit* Clump-forming, tuberous, spreading.
*Flowers* Small, daisy-like, borne on slender,
branching stems in late spring. Rich clear yellow.
*Leaves* Heart-shaped, softly hairy. Bright green.
• NATIVE HABITAT Woodlands of W. Europe.
• CULTIVATION Grow in any moist, well-drained
soil in shade or semi-shade. Is good for naturalizing
in wild and woodland gardens.
• PROPAGATION By division in autumn or seed in
autumn or spring.
• OTHER NAMES *D. cordatum.*

☀ ◊
❀❀❀

HEIGHT
75cm (30in)

SPREAD
60cm (24in)

| Asphodelaceae/ Liliaceae | KING'S SPEAR, YELLOW ASPHODEL |
|---|---|

## ASPHODELINE LUTEA

*Habit* Clump-forming. *Flowers* Small, scented,
star-shaped, in dense spikes, on leafy stems, in late
spring or summer. Yellow. *Leaves* Narrow, linear,
to 30cm (1ft) long. Silvery-green to grey-green.
• NATIVE HABITAT Rocky slopes, Mediterranean.
• CULTIVATION Grow in a sheltered site, in well-
drained soil. In cool climates protect in winter.
• PROPAGATION By seed in autumn or spring or by
careful division in early spring. The fleshy roots are
easily damaged.
• OTHER NAMES *Asphodelus lutea.*

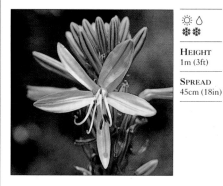

☀ ◊
❀❀

HEIGHT
1m (3ft)

SPREAD
45cm (18in)

| Papaveraceae | |
|---|---|

## CHELIDONIUM MAJUS 'Flore Pleno'

*Habit* Upright, with a fleshy rootstock. *Flowers*
Small, cupped, double, about 2.5cm (1in) across,
borne on slender, branching stems in late spring
and early summer. Bright yellow. *Leaves*
Deeply cut, with rounded lobes. Bright green.
• NATIVE HABITAT The species occurs in
woodland, from Europe to W. Asia.
• CULTIVATION Grow in sun or dappled shade, in
any well-drained soil. Suitable for naturalizing in
wild and woodland gardens. Seeds freely. Invasive.
• PROPAGATION By seed or division in autumn.

☀ ◊
❀❀❀

HEIGHT
60–90cm
(2–3ft)

SPREAD
30cm (1ft)

| Ranunculaceae | |
|---|---|

## TROLLIUS × CULTORUM 'Orange Princess'   ♛

*Habit* Robust, clump-forming. *Flowers* Rounded,
almost globular, borne on sturdy, slender stems,
above the leaves in spring. Golden-orange. *Leaves*
Deeply divided into jagged-toothed, leaflets,
mostly in dense, basal clumps. Mid-green.
• NATIVE HABITAT Garden origin.
• CULTIVATION Grow in moist, fertile, humus-rich
soil. Larger than most of the genus and good for
pool- and streamsides and damp borders.
• PROPAGATION By division in early autumn.

☀ ◊
❀❀❀

HEIGHT
75cm (30in)

SPREAD
45cm (18in)

Caryophyllaceae

## *GYPSOPHILA PANICULATA* 'Bristol Fairy' ♀

*Habit* Mound-forming, with a deep, stout rootstock. *Flowers* Tiny, double, in airy panicles, on wiry, very slender, branching stems, in summer. White. *Leaves* Slightly fleshy, narrowly lance-shaped. Blue-green.
• NATIVE HABITAT Garden origin.
• CULTIVATION Tolerates light, sandy soils but grows best in deep, moderately fertile, well-drained soil. Resents disturbance. The flowers dry well for winter arrangements. This plant looks charming when allowed to cascade over a low wall.

It is excellent for giving a feeling of space and balance in a border, where contrasting colours need a separating foil. The white flowers also emphasize other colours, and so it is important not to exclude them from a mixed border.
• PROPAGATION By grafting in winter.

☼ ◊
❀ ❀ ❀

**HEIGHT**
60–75cm
(24–30in)

**SPREAD**
1m (3ft)

| Asteraceae/Compositae | |
|---|---|

## *ACHILLEA PTARMICA* 'The Pearl'

*Habit* Upright, creeping, rhizomatous. *Flowers* Small, pompon-like, in large, branched heads, in summer. Pure white. *Leaves* Narrowly lance-shaped, more or less serrated. Glossy, dark green.
• NATIVE HABITAT Garden origin.
• CULTIVATION Grow in fertile, moist but well-drained soil. May spread rapidly. The flowers are good for air drying, for garlands and for winter arrangements.
• PROPAGATION By division in spring or autumn.
• OTHER NAMES *A. ptarmica* 'Boule de Neige'.

☀ ◊
❊ ❊ ❊

HEIGHT
to 75cm
(30in)

SPREAD
75cm (30in)

| Solanaceae | FLOWERING TOBACCO, JASMINE TOBACCO |
|---|---|

## *NICOTIANA ALATA*

*Habit* Rosette-forming, with a thick rootstock. *Flowers* Night-scented, tubular, borne in branched clusters, on sticky stems over long periods in summer. Creamy-white, flushed pale brownish-violet on the outside. *Leaves* Soft, spoon-shaped to oval. Mid-green.
• NATIVE HABITAT N.E. Argentina to S. Brazil.
• CULTIVATION Grow in fertile, well-drained soil, in sun or light shade. Best grown as an annual.
• PROPAGATION By seed in spring.
• OTHER NAMES *N. affinis*.

☀ ◊
❊

HEIGHT
75cm (30in)

SPREAD
30cm (12in)

| Asteraceae/Compositae | |
|---|---|

## *ACHILLEA AGERATUM* 'W. B. Childs'

*Habit* Upright, spreading. *Flowers* Small, in loose, branched heads, borne on lax stems in summer. Pure white, with creamy-white centres. *Leaves* Narrow, finely toothed and divided. Dark green.
• NATIVE HABITAT Garden origin.
• CULTIVATION Grow in fertile, moist but well-drained soil. May spread rapidly in good conditions. The flowers are good for air drying, for garlands and winter arrangements.
• PROPAGATION By division in spring or autumn.

☀ ◊
❊ ❊ ❊

HEIGHT
60–70cm
(24–28in)

SPREAD
60cm (24in)

| Iridaceae | NEW ZEALAND SATIN FLOWER |
|---|---|

## *LIBERTIA GRANDIFLORA*

*Habit* Loosely clump-forming, rhizomatous. *Flowers* Small, iris-like, to 2cm (¾in) across, in branched, spike-like clusters, in early summer. White. *Leaves* Rigid, linear, to 60cm (24in) long. Dark green, often turning brown at the tip.
• NATIVE HABITAT By streamsides and in forests, in New Zealand.
• CULTIVATION Grow in a warm, sheltered site, in sun or part-day shade, in well-drained soil.
• PROPAGATION By division in spring, or by seed in autumn or spring.

☀ ◊
❊ ❊

HEIGHT
75cm (30in)

SPREAD
60cm (24in)

| Brassicaceae/Cruciferae | DAME'S VIOLET, SWEET ROCKET |
|---|---|

### HESPERIS MATRONALIS

**Habit** Upright. **Flowers** Small, 4-petalled, in loose, spike-like racemes, in summer. White, lilac or violet. Strongly scented in the evening. **Leaves** Lance-shaped to oval, smooth. Mid-green.
• NATIVE HABITAT Mountain woods, scrub and streamsides, from S. Europe to Siberia.
• CULTIVATION Grow in moderately fertile, moist but well-drained soil, in sun or dappled shade. Is often short-lived, so propagate regularly.
• PROPAGATION By basal cuttings in spring, or by seed in autumn or spring.

☼ ◊
❀ ❀ ❀

HEIGHT
75cm (30in)
or more

SPREAD
60cm (24in)

| Geraniaceae | |
|---|---|

### GERANIUM PHAEUM 'Album'

**Habit** Clump-forming, rhizomatous. **Flowers** Larger than the dark-flowered species, with 5 reflexed petals, borne in loose, branched, one-sided clusters, from late spring to summer. White. **Leaves** Divided into 7–9 soft green lobes.
• NATIVE HABITAT Species occurs in woods and sub-alpine meadows, S., C. and W. Europe.
• CULTIVATION Grow in any well-drained soil, in shade or semi-shade. Excellent for woodland and wild gardens, or for shady borders.
• PROPAGATION By division in autumn or spring.

☼ ◊
❀ ❀ ❀

HEIGHT
75cm (30in)

SPREAD
45cm (18in)

| Papaveraceae | |
|---|---|

### DICENTRA SPECTABILIS 'Alba'                                    ♀

**Habit** Clump-forming. **Flowers** Pendent, heart-shaped, on fleshy, arching stems, in late spring and early summer. Pure white. **Leaves** Fern-like, deeply cut. Light green.
• NATIVE HABITAT Woods and shady valleys, from Siberia to Japan.
• CULTIVATION Grow in humus-rich, moist but well-drained soil, in semi-shade. Suitable for a shady border or woodland garden. It has proved hardier than originally thought, although, when planting, it is important to bear in mind that a severe late frost occasionally damages the fresh new growth. It is sometimes difficult to differentiate between this and the pink-flowered species when out of flower, so to avoid disappointment, it is best purchased during the flowering period.
• PROPAGATION By division when dormant in late winter.

☼ ◊
❀ ❀

HEIGHT
60–75cm
(24–30in)

SPREAD
60cm (24in)

| Asphodelaceae/ Liliaceae | WHITE ASPHODEL |
|---|---|

## *ASPHODELUS ALBUS*

**Habit** Upright, clump-forming, with fleshy roots.
**Flowers** Small, star-shaped, in stout-stemmed, terminal racemes, in late spring and early summer. White. **Leaves** Flattened, linear, to 60cm (2ft) long, in basal clumps. Mid-green.
• NATIVE HABITAT Woods, heaths and rocky places, C. and S. Europe.
• CULTIVATION Grow in a warm, sunny site, in light, well-drained soil.
• PROPAGATION By division in spring, or by seed in autumn.

☼ ◊
❉ ❉

HEIGHT
1m (3ft)

SPREAD
45cm (18in)

| Asteraceae/Compositae | PEARL EVERLASTING |
|---|---|

## *ANAPHALIS MARGARITACEA*

**Habit** Bushy, clump-forming. **Flowers** Tiny, with papery petals, in clustered heads, on upright stems, in late summer. White. **Leaves** Narrowly lance-shaped, white-margined. Silver- or grey-green.
• NATIVE HABITAT On dry, stony soils, in North America, N. and C. Europe and N.E. Asia.
• CULTIVATION Grow in any moderately fertile, well-drained, not-too-dry soil. Flowers dry well.
• PROPAGATION By seed in autumn, or by division in late winter or early spring.
• OTHER NAMES *A. yedoensis.*

☼ ◊
❉ ❉ ❉

HEIGHT
60–75cm
(24–30in)

SPREAD
60cm (24in)

| Lamiaceae/Labiatae | |
|---|---|

## *SALVIA ARGENTEA*  ♆

**Habit** Rosette-forming. **Flowers** Hooded, 2-lipped, sage-like, in branching, candelabra-like clusters, on strong, upright stems, in summer. White. **Leaves** Oval, wrinkled, woolly, in a large basal clump. Silver-green.
• NATIVE HABITAT Dry hills in the Mediterranean.
• CULTIVATION Grow in a warm, sunny, sheltered site, in very well-drained soil. Grown for its soft, felty-grey foliage, it is suited to a Mediterranean border, also dry walls and the alpine house.
• PROPAGATION By seed or division in spring.

☼ ◊
❉ ❉

HEIGHT
60cm–1m
(2–3ft)

SPREAD
45cm (18in)

| Rutaceae | BURNING BUSH |
|---|---|

## *DICTAMNUS ALBUS*  ♆

**Habit** Upright, woody-based. **Flowers** Fragrant, star-shaped, in erect racemes, in early summer. White, with conspicuous stamens. **Leaves** Aromatic, divided into lance-shaped, light green leaflets.
• NATIVE HABITAT Dry, rocky sites and open woods, in S.W. Europe, S. and C. Asia, China and Korea.
• CULTIVATION Grow in a warm, sunny, sheltered site, in fertile, well-drained soil. Resents disturbance. On warm, still evenings, the ripening seedpods give off oils that can be ignited, hence the common name.
• PROPAGATION By seed sown fresh in late summer.

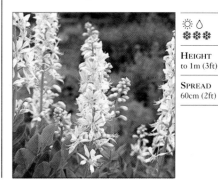

☼ ◊
❉ ❉ ❉

HEIGHT
to 1m (3ft)

SPREAD
60cm (2ft)

| Ranunculaceae | |
| --- | --- |

## *THALICTRUM AQUILEGIIFOLIUM*
## 'White Cloud'

*Habit* Dense, clump-forming, slow-growing.
*Flowers* Tiny, in dense, fluffy, terminal sprays,
in early summer. White. *Leaves* Smooth, finely
divided. Pale greyish-green.
• NATIVE HABITAT Garden origin.
• CULTIVATION Grow in moist but well-drained,
fertile soil, in sun or light, dappled shade. Suited
to border plantings; especially good in white or
silver borders.
• PROPAGATION By division in spring.

☼ ◊
❄ ❄ ❄

HEIGHT
1–1.2m
(3–4ft)

SPREAD
30cm (1ft)

| Asteraceae/Compositae | |
| --- | --- |

## *LEUCANTHEMUM* X *SUPERBUM* 'Elizabeth'

*Habit* Robust, clump-forming. *Flowers* Large,
solitary, semi-double, borne on sturdy stems, from
mid- to late summer. White, with a yellow central
disc. *Leaves* Coarse, spoon-shaped, lobed and
toothed. Dark green.
• NATIVE HABITAT Garden origin.
• CULTIVATION Grow in any moderately fertile,
well-drained soil in full sun. Suitable for cutting.
• PROPAGATION By division in spring or autumn.
• OTHER NAMES *Chrysanthemum* x *superbum*
'Elizabeth'.

☼ ◊
❄ ❄ ❄

HEIGHT
1m (3ft)

SPREAD
60cm (2ft)

| Asteraceae/Compositae | MARGUERITE PARIS DAISY |
| --- | --- |

## *ARGYRANTHEMUM FRUTESCENS*

*Habit* Bushy, woody-based. *Flowers* Large,
single, daisy-like, produced on strong, slender
stems throughout summer. Pure white, pink
or yellow. *Leaves* Finely divided, fern-like.
Blue-green.
• NATIVE HABITAT Canary Islands.
• CULTIVATION Grow in a warm, sunny site,
in moderately fertile, well-drained soil.
• PROPAGATION By stem cuttings in autumn,
or by seed in spring.
• OTHER NAMES *Chrysanthemum frutescens*.

☼ ◊
❄

HEIGHT
1m (3ft)

SPREAD
1m (3ft)

Asteraceae/Compositae

## *ERIGERON* 'White Quakeress'

*Habit* Clump-forming. *Flowers* Daisy-like, with slender, white ray florets around a greenish-yellow disc, borne in profusion over long periods in summer. *Leaves* Lance-shaped to spoon-shaped. Greyish-green.
• NATIVE HABITAT  Garden origin.
• CULTIVATION  Grow in moderately fertile, well-drained soil in full sun. A charming sport of the pale lilac-pink flowered 'Quakeress', it is noted for its long flowering period. Suitable for the front or middle of a mixed or herbaceous border. Cut back

any remnants of the previous year's growth in early spring to maintain a neat and compact habit. The flowers are good for cutting. The genus includes many garden-worthy plants, offering a range of heights, colours and flowering seasons.
• PROPAGATION  By division in spring or early autumn, or by basal cuttings in early summer.

☀ ◊
❀ ❀ ❀

**HEIGHT**
to 80cm
(32in)

**SPREAD**
60cm (24in)

Saxifragaceae

## RODGERSIA AESCULIFOLIA

**Habit** Vigorous, clump-forming, rhizomatous.
**Flowers** Fragrant, tiny, in branching, flat-topped
clusters, on strong, slender, rusty-hairy stems.
Pinkish-white. **Leaves** Divided into 7 toothed,
crinkled, veined. Bronze-green leaflets.
• NATIVE HABITAT Damp woods and streambanks,
in the mountains of W. China.
• CULTIVATION Grow in moist but well-drained,
fertile, humus-rich soil, in sun or semi-shade. This
is a statuesque perennial for damp woodland
gardens or pondsides, associating well with similar
damp-loving plants. Its horse-chestnut-like leaves
have excellent qualities that make it one of the
aristocrats of the garden. Best planted alone to give
full reign to its architectural features.
• PROPAGATION By division in spring, or seed
in autumn.

**HEIGHT**
1m (3ft)

**SPREAD**
1m (3ft)

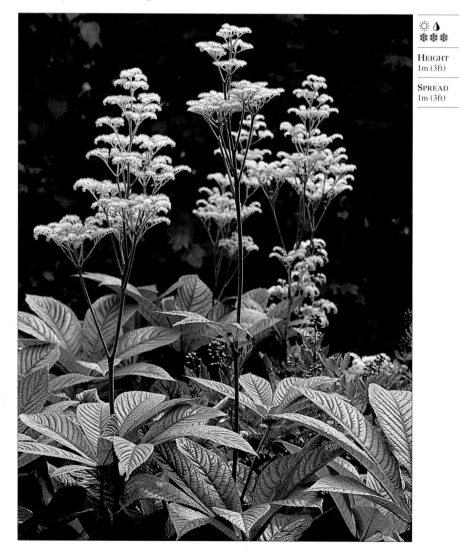

| Apiaceae/Umbelliferae | SWEET CICELY, GARDEN MYRRH |
|---|---|

## MYRRHIS ODORATA

**Habit** Vigorous, with a deep, woody rootstock.
**Flowers** Tiny, in dense, rounded umbels, in early summer. White. **Leaves** Aromatic, softly hairy, finely divided and fern-like. Fresh bright green.
• NATIVE HABITAT Damp woods, hedges and streambanks in Europe, but widely naturalized.
• CULTIVATION Grow in moist but well-drained, fertile soil, in sun or dappled shade. Grow in a herb garden, or in a border, to make an attractive, fresh green foil for more brightly coloured perennials.
• PROPAGATION By seed in autumn or spring.

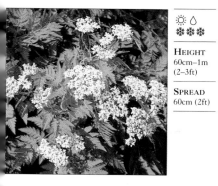

HEIGHT
60cm–1m
(2–3ft)

SPREAD
60cm (2ft)

| Saxifragaceae | |
|---|---|

## RODGERSIA PODOPHYLLA

**Habit** Clump-forming, rhizomatous. **Flowers** Tiny, borne in branching clusters above the foliage, in summer. Creamy-white. **Leaves** Large, divided into 5 shallowly lobed leaflets. Bronze when young; mid-green then coppery in autumn.
• NATIVE HABITAT Damp, mountain woodlands, Japan and Korea.
• CULTIVATION Grow in moist soil, in sun or semi-shade, with shelter from dry winds.
• PROPAGATION By division in spring, or by seed in autumn.

HEIGHT
to 1.2m
(4ft)

SPREAD
1m (3ft)

| Saxifragaceae | |
|---|---|

## RODGERSIA SAMBUCIFOLIA

**Habit** Clump-forming, rhizomatous. **Flowers** Tiny, in branching, feathery clusters, well above the foliage, in summer. Creamy-white or pale pink. **Leaves** Irregularly divided into 8–11 leaflets. Emerald-green, sometimes bronze-flushed.
• NATIVE HABITAT Rocky forest areas in W. China.
• CULTIVATION Grow in moist, fertile, humus-rich soil, in sun or semi-shade, with shelter from dry winds.
• PROPAGATION By division in spring, or by seed in autumn.

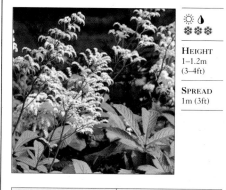

HEIGHT
1–1.2m
(3–4ft)

SPREAD
1m (3ft)

| Rosaceae | |
|---|---|

## ARUNCUS DIOICUS 'Kneiffii'

**Habit** Clump-forming. **Flowers** Tiny, star-shaped, in dense plumes, on slender, wiry stems, from mid- to late summer. Creamy-white. **Leaves** Feathery, deeply cut into very slender segments. Rich green.
• NATIVE HABITAT Garden origin.
• CULTIVATION Grow in moist but well-drained soil, in sun or semi-shade. Plant in a border or by a pond or stream, above water level.
• PROPAGATION By division in spring or autumn.
• OTHER NAMES *A. plumosus* 'Kneiffii', *A. sylvester* 'Kneiffii'.

HEIGHT
1m (3ft)

SPREAD
50cm (20in)

| Papaveraceae | |
|---|---|

## PAPAVER ORIENTALE 'Perry's White'

**Habit** Clump-forming. **Flowers** Large, deeply cupped, with satiny, white petals, each with a dark maroon-purple blotch at the base, borne on strong stems in early summer. **Leaves** Divided into hairy, toothed, lance-shaped segments, dying back after flowering. Dark grey-green.
• NATIVE HABITAT Garden origin.
• CULTIVATION Grow in moist, well-drained, fertile soil, in sun. Tends to sprawl and may need support.
• PROPAGATION By root cuttings in winter, or by division in autumn.

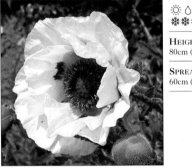

☼ ◊
❀ ❀ ❀

HEIGHT
80cm (32in)

SPREAD
60cm (24in)

| Scrophulariaceae | RUSTY FOXGLOVE |
|---|---|

## DIGITALIS FERRUGINEA

**Habit** Basal rosette-forming. **Flowers** Funnel-shaped, borne in dense, slender spires in mid-summer. Pale golden-brown and white.
**Leaves** Narrowly oval, in basal rosettes, with linear stem leaves. Olive to mid-green.
• NATIVE HABITAT Woodland, scrub and rocky sites in Turkey.
• CULTIVATION Tolerates dry soils. Grow in any moderately fertile, well-drained soil, in sun or semi-shade. Short-lived and best treated as a biennial.
• PROPAGATION By seed in autumn.

☼ ◊
❀ ❀ ❀

HEIGHT
1–1.2m
(3–4ft)

SPREAD
30cm (1ft)

| Asteraceae/Compositae | |
|---|---|

## ACHILLEA 'Wesersandstein'

**Habit** Mound-forming, vigorous. **Flowers** Small, in broad, branched heads, throughout summer. Bright salmon-pink, fading to a creamy, sand-yellow. **Leaves** Narrowly lance-shaped, feathery, finely divided, finely hairy. Green.
• NATIVE HABITAT Garden origin.
• CULTIVATION Grow in fertile, well-drained soil, in full sun. Divide and replant every third year to maintain vigour. Flower heads dry well.
• PROPAGATION By division in early spring or autumn.

☼ ◊
❀ ❀ ❀

HEIGHT
45–60cm
(18–24in)

SPREAD
60cm (24in)

| Primulaceae | GOOSENECK LOOSESTRIFE |
|---|---|

## LYSIMACHIA CLETHROIDES　　♈

**Habit** Vigorous, clump-forming, rhizomatous. **Flowers** Tiny, star-shaped, in dense, slender, spikes that are nodding when in bud, becoming erect when in full bloom. White.
**Leaves** Lance-shaped. Mid-green, yellow-green when young.
• NATIVE HABITAT Grassy hills in Japan.
• CULTIVATION Grow in moist but well-drained soil, in sun or semi-shade.
• PROPAGATION By division in spring, or by seed in autumn.

☼ ◊
❀ ❀ ❀

HEIGHT
1m (3ft)

SPREAD
60cm–1m
(2–3ft)

| Campanulaceae | |
|---|---|

## *Campanula lactiflora* 'Loddon Anna'

*Habit* Upright, branching, slender-stemmed, with a stout rootstock. *Flowers* Large, nodding, broadly bell-shaped, borne in broad, dense, leafy panicles, from mid- to late summer. Soft, dusty lilac-pink. *Leaves* Narrowly oval, borne in basal rosettes and scattered up the stems. Mid-green.
• NATIVE HABITAT Garden origin. The species occurs in forests and alpine and sub-alpine meadows in the Caucasus mountains.
• CULTIVATION Prefers fertile, moist but well-drained soil, in full sun, but tolerates partial shade. Needs staking especially on windy sites. Excellent for a mixed or herbaceous border.
This and other cultivars of the species associate particularly well with old-fashioned roses, since they bear their first flush of flowers at about the same time.
• PROPAGATION By division in spring or autumn.

HEIGHT
to 1.2m
(4ft)

SPREAD
60cm (2ft)

# PHLOX

Border phlox (cultivars of *Phlox maculata* and *P. paniculata*) produce often delicately fragrant, dome-shaped or conical heads of flowers in late summer in shades of mainly white, pink and purple. Unless otherwise indicated, the leaves are oval and mid-green.

Phlox thrive in moist but well-drained soil in full sun, or, on drier soils, in light shade. Taller cultivars may need staking. To produce larger flowers, cut back the weakest shoots in spring when the plant is about a third of its eventual height.

Border phlox are particularly prone to infestations of eelworm and any affected plants should be burnt. Propagate by taking root cuttings from healthy stock. Do not replant infested soil for at least two years.

**P. PANICULATA**
**'Fujiyama'**
*Habit* Upright, clump-forming.
*Flowers* Tubular, 5-lobed, borne in dense, long, conical heads, on very sturdy stems in late summer. Pure white.
• HEIGHT to 1m (3ft).
• SPREAD 45cm (18in).

*P. paniculata*
**'Fujiyama'**

☼ ◊ ❋❋❋        ♈

**P. PANICULATA**
**'Mia Ruys'**
*Habit* Upright, clump-forming.
*Flowers* Large, tubular, 5-lobed, borne in dense, rounded-conical heads, in late summer. Pure-white.
• HEIGHT 45cm (18in).
• SPREA 45cm (18in).

*P. paniculata*
**'Mia Ruys'**

☼ ◊ ❋❋❋

**P. MACULATA**
**'Omega'**
*Habit* Upright, clump-forming.
*Flowers* Tubular, 5-lobed, borne in long, cylindrical heads, in summer. White with a lilac eye.
• HEIGHT to 1m (3ft).
• SPREAD 45cm (18in).

*P. maculata* 'Omega'

☼ ◊ ❋❋❋        ♈

**P. PANICULATA**
**'White Admiral'**
*Habit* Upright, open, clump-forming.
*Flowers* Tubular, 5-lobed, borne in dense, conical heads, in late summer. Pure white.
• HEIGHT 1m (3ft).
• SPREAD 45cm (18in).

*P. paniculata*
**'White Admiral'**

☼ ◊ ❋❋❋        ♈

**P. PANICULATA**
**'Mother of Pearl'**
*Habit* Upright, clump-forming.
*Flowers* Tubular, 5-lobed, borne in dense, rounded-conical heads, in late summer. White, suffused palest pink.
• HEIGHT 1.2m (4ft).
• SPREAD 45cm (18in).

*P. paniculata*
**'Mother of Pearl'**

☼ ◊ ❋❋❋        ♈

**P. PANICULATA**
**'Graf Zeppelin'**
*Habit* Upright,
clump-forming.
*Flowers* Tubular,
5-lobed, borne in dense,
rounded-conical heads,
in late summer. White
with red eyes.
• HEIGHT to 1m (3ft).
• SPREAD 45cm (18in).

*P. paniculata*
**'Graf Zeppelin'**

☼ ◊ ❋❋❋

**P. MACULATA 'Alpha'**
*Habit* Upright,
clump-forming.
*Flowers* Tubular,
5-lobed, borne in long,
cylindrical heads in
summer. Rose-pink.
• HEIGHT to 1m (3ft).
• SPREAD 45cm (18in).

*P. maculata* 'Alpha'

☼ ◊ ❋❋❋   ♛

**P. PANICULATA**
**'Eva Cullum'**
*Habit* Upright,
clump-forming.
*Flowers* Tubular,
5-lobed, borne in open,
rounded-conical heads in
late summer. Clear pink
with magenta eyes.
• HEIGHT to 1m (3ft).
• SPREAD 45cm (18in).

*P. paniculata*
**'Eva Cullum'**

☼ ◊ ❋❋❋

**P. PANICULATA**
**'Sandringham'**
*Habit* Upright, open,
clump-forming.
*Flowers* Tubular,
5-lobed, with widely
spaced petals, borne in
dense, rounded-conical
heads, in late summer.
Pink, with a darker
pink eye.
• HEIGHT 1m (3ft).
• SPREAD 45cm (18in).

*P. paniculata*
**'Sandringham'**

☼ ◊ ❋❋❋

**P. PANICULATA**
**'Balmoral'**
*Habit* Upright,
clump-forming.
*Flowers* Large, tubular,
5-lobed, borne in
rounded-conical heads
in late summer. Rosy-
mauve.
• HEIGHT to 1m (3ft).
• SPREAD 45cm (18in).

*P. paniculata*
**'Balmoral'**

☼ ◊ ❋❋❋

**P. PANICULATA**
**'Windsor'**
*Habit* Upright,
open, clump-forming.
*Flowers* Tubular,
5-lobed, borne in dense,
conical heads, in late
summer. Carmine-rose
with red eyes.
• HEIGHT 1m (3ft).
• SPREAD 45cm (18in).

*P. paniculata* 'Windsor'

☼ ◊ ❋❋❋   ♛

*P. PANICULATA*
**'Prince of Orange'**
*Habit* Upright,
clump-forming.
*Flowers* Tubular,
5-lobed, borne in dense,
broad, rounded-conical
heads, in late summer.
Orange-red.
• HEIGHT 1m (3ft).
• SPREAD 45cm (18in).

*P. paniculata*
**'Prince of Orange'**

☼ ◊ ❋❋❋　　　♈

*P. PANICULATA*
**'Brigadier'**
*Habit* Upright,
clump-forming.
*Flowers* Tubular,
5-lobed, borne in
rounded-conical heads
in late summer. Deep
orange-red.
• HEIGHT to 1m (3ft).
• SPREAD 45cm (18in).

*P. paniculata*
**'Brigadier'**

☼ ◊ ❋❋❋　　　♈

*P. PANICULATA*
**'Harlequin'**
*Habit* Upright,
clump-forming.
*Flowers* Tubular,
5-lobed, borne in dense,
rounded-conical heads,
in late summer. Red-
purple.
*Leaves* Variegated
ivory-white.
• HEIGHT to 1m (3ft).
• SPREAD 45cm (18in).

*P. paniculata*
**'Harlequin'**

☼ ◊ ❋❋❋

*P. PANICULATA*
**'Aida'**
*Habit* Upright,
clump-forming.
*Flowers* Tubular,
5-lobed, borne in conical
heads in late summer.
Purple-red with a
purple eye.
• HEIGHT to 1m (3ft).
• SPREAD 45cm (18in).

*P. paniculata* **'Aida'**

☼ ◊ ❋❋❋

*P. PANICULATA*
**'Eventide'**
*Habit* Upright,
clump-forming.
*Flowers* Tubular,
5-lobed, borne in dense,
rounded-conical heads
in late summer.
Lavender-blue.
• HEIGHT to 1m (3ft).
• SPREAD 45cm (18in).

*P. PANICULATA*
**'Le Mahdi'**
*Habit* Upright,
clump-forming.
*Flowers* Tubular,
5-lobed, borne in dense,
rounded-conical heads,
in late summer. Deep
blue-purple, sometimes
white-eyed.
• HEIGHT to 1m (3ft).
• SPREAD 45cm (18in).

*P. paniculata*
'Eventide'

☼ ◊ ❀❀❀ ♉

*P. paniculata*
'Le Mahdi'

☼ ◊ ❀❀❀ ♉

*P. PANICULATA*
**'Norah Leigh'**
*Habit* Upright,
clump-forming.
*Flowers* Tubular,
5-lobed, borne in dense,
rounded-conical heads, in
late summer. Pale lilac.
*Leaves* Variegated
ivory-white.
• HEIGHT 1m (3ft).
• SPREAD 45cm (18in).

*P. PANICULATA*
**'Hampton Court'**
*Habit* Upright,
clump-forming.
*Flowers* Tubular,
5-lobed, borne in dense,
rounded-conical heads,
in late summer.
Mauve-blue.
*Leaves* Very dark green.
• HEIGHT to 1m (3ft).
• SPREAD 45cm (18in).

*P. paniculata*
'Norah Leigh'

☼ ◊ ❀❀❀

*P. paniculata*
'Hampton Court'

☼ ◊ ❀❀❀

| Morinaceae | WHORLFLOWER |
|---|---|

## MORINA LONGIFOLIA

**Habit** Rosette-forming. **Flowers** Tubular, hooded, waxy, borne in whorls on sturdy stems in mid-summer. White, pink after fertilization. **Leaves** Aromatic, spiny and thistle-like, mostly in a basal rosette. Bright green.
• NATIVE HABITAT  Damp, steep slopes, Himalayas.
• CULTIVATION  Grow in moist, open, well drained soil in sun. Shelter from cold, dry winds in spring. Suitable for borders, or as a specimen.
• PROPAGATION  By fresh seed in late summer, or by division after flowering.

☼ ◊
❄ ❄

HEIGHT
60–75cm
(24–30in)

SPREAD
30cm (1ft)

| Rosaceae | BOWMANS ROOT<br>INDIAN PHYSIC |
|---|---|

## GILLENIA TRIFOLIATA ♈

**Habit** Upright, clump-forming. **Flowers** Delicate, with 5 slender white petals, on wiry, branching, red stems, in summer. **Leaves** Divided into oval-oblong, olive-green leaflets, turning red in autumn.
• NATIVE HABITAT  Rocky areas in open woodland, N.E. North America.
• CULTIVATION  Grow in sun or semi-shade, in any well-drained soil. Can be difficult to establish, but worth the effort. A beautiful and very graceful border plant.
• PROPAGATION  By seed in autumn or spring.

☼ ◊
❄ ❄ ❄

HEIGHT
1–1.2m
(3–4ft)

SPREAD
60cm (2ft)

| Scrophulariaceae | |
|---|---|

## VERONICASTRUM VIRGINICUM ALBUM

**Habit** Upright. **Flowers** Small, tubular, borne in slender spires, in late summer. White, with prominent, pale pink stamens. **Leaves** Narrow, lance-shaped, in whorls. Dark green.
• NATIVE HABITAT  Woods and scrub, E. North America.
• CULTIVATION  Grow in moist, well drained soil.
• PROPAGATION  By division in spring or autumn, by seed in autumn, or by softwood or semi-ripe cuttings in summer.
• OTHER NAMES  *Veronica virginica* f. *alba*.

☼ ◊
❄ ❄ ❄

HEIGHT
1.2m (4ft)

SPREAD
45cm (18in)

| Valerianaceae | CAT'S VALERIAN, COMMON VALERIAN |
|---|---|

## VALERIANA OFFICINALIS

**Habit** Fleshy, clump-forming. **Flowers** Tiny, in branched, rounded clusters, in summer. White to pink. **Leaves** Divided into toothed or entire, narrow leaflets. Mid-green.
• NATIVE HABITAT Dry or damp meadows and ditches, from Europe to W. Asia.
• CULTIVATION Grow in sun, in moist but well-drained soil. Also tolerates dry soils. Good for wild gardens, herbaceous borders and sometimes grown in medicinal herb gardens.
• PROPAGATION By seed in spring.

☼ ◊
❀ ❀ ❀

**HEIGHT**
1–1.2m
(3–4ft)

**SPREAD**
1m (3ft)

| Scrophulariaceae | |
|---|---|

## LINARIA PURPUREA 'Canon Went'

**Habit** Upright, clump-forming. **Flowers** Small, snapdragon-like, borne in slender spikes, from mid- to late summer. Dusky-pink with orange-tinged throats. **Leaves** Linear, smooth, in basal clumps and along the stems. Grey-green.
• NATIVE HABITAT Garden origin.
• CULTIVATION Grow in any well-drained soil, in sun or light shade. Self-seeds freely. Suitable for herbaceous borders and gravel plantings. Makes excellent contrasts in a grey or silver border.
• PROPAGATION By seed in autumn or spring.

☼ ◊
❀ ❀ ❀

**HEIGHT**
60cm–1m
(2–3ft)

**SPREAD**
60cm (2ft)

| Asteraceae/Compositae | |
|---|---|

## ACHILLEA 'Forncett Candy'

**Habit** Upright. **Flowers** Tiny, uniform in large, flat heads, borne on rigid, leafy stems during summer. Chalky-pink, fading with age. **Leaves** Feathery, finely divided. Matt green.
• NATIVE HABITAT Garden origin.
• CULTIVATION Grow in fertile, well-drained soil, in full sun. Divide and replant every third year to maintain vigour. Valued for its clear flower colour. The flower heads dry well for winter arrangements.
• PROPAGATION By division in early spring or autumn.

☼ ◊
❀ ❀ ❀

**HEIGHT**
to 85cm
(34in)

**SPREAD**
60cm (24in)
or more

| Geraniaceae | |
|---|---|

## GERANIUM × OXONIANUM 'Winscombe'

**Habit** Dense, mound-forming. **Flowers** Small, cup-shaped, borne in profusion throughout summer. Pale pink, darkening with age. **Leaves** Semi-evergreen, with 5 deeply cut, toothed, mid-green lobes, sometimes blotched brown at the base.
• NATIVE HABITAT Garden origin.
• CULTIVATION Grow in any but waterlogged soil, in sun or light shade. Valued as weed-smothering ground cover and for its long flowering season.
• PROPAGATION By division in autumn or spring.

☼ ◊
❀ ❀ ❀

**HEIGHT**
60–75cm
(24–30in)

**SPREAD**
45cm (18in)

| Malvaceae | MUSK MALLOW |
|---|---|

## MALVA MOSCHATA

**Habit** Bushy, branching. **Flowers** Saucer-shaped, in spikes, produced in succession from early to late summer. Clear rose-pink. **Leaves** Slightly aromatic, deeply divided into 7 narrow, mid-green lobes.
• NATIVE HABITAT Grasslands of Europe to N.W Africa and Turkey.
• CULTIVATION Grow in fertile, well-drained soil, in sun. Ideal for borders and wildflower gardens.
• PROPAGATION By seed in autumn or basal cuttings in summer.

☼ ◊
❋ ❋ ❋

**HEIGHT**
60cm–1m
(2–3ft)

**SPREAD**
60cm (2ft)

| Malvaceae | CHECKERBLOOM |
|---|---|

## SIDALCEA MALVIFLORA

**Habit** Clump-forming. **Flowers** Bowl-shaped, borne in erect, terminal racemes in summer. Pink or lilac-pink, with pale-veined, silky petals. **Leaves** Divided into 7–9 rounded lobes, mostly basal. Bright green.
• NATIVE HABITAT Grassy slopes and damp hollows in Baja California, California and Oregon.
• CULTIVATION Grow in moist, well-drained soil, in sun or light shade. Flowers are good for cutting. Ideal for the front of a border; seldom needs staking.
• PROPAGATION By seed or division in spring.

☼ ◊
❋ ❋ ❋

**HEIGHT**
60–80cm
(24–32in)

**SPREAD**
80cm (32in)

| Polygonaceae | |
|---|---|

## PERSICARIA BISTORTA 'Superba'    ♈

**Habit** Clump-forming, rhizomatous. **Flowers** Tiny, in dense, cylindrical spikes, on slender stems, in summer. Soft, clear pink. **Leaves** Oval, with triangular stem leaves. Mid-green.
• NATIVE HABITAT Garden origin.
• CULTIVATION Grow in moist, fertile soil. Tolerate drier soils, but flowers less freely. Vigorous and long-flowering specimen for a moist border, but may swamp more delicate plants, so site carefully.
• PROPAGATION By division in spring or autumn.
• OTHER NAMES *Polygonum bistorta superbum.*

☼ ◊
❋ ❋ ❋

**HEIGHT**
60–75cm
(24–30in)

**SPREAD**
60cm (2ft)
or more

| Rutaceae | |
|---|---|

## *DICTAMNUS ALBUS* var. *PURPUREUS* ♥

*Habit* Upright, woody-based. *Flowers* Fragrant, star-shaped, borne in erect racemes in early summer. Pale to deep purplish-pink, with conspicuous stamens. *Leaves* Highly aromatic, divided into lance-shaped, leaflets. Light green.
• NATIVE HABITAT Dry rocks and open woods, from S.W. Europe, S. and C. Asia, China and Korea.
• CULTIVATION Grow in a warm, sunny, sheltered site, in fertile, well-drained soil. Dislikes disturbance.
• PROPAGATION By seed sown fresh in late summer.

☼ ◊
❀ ❀ ❀

HEIGHT
1m (3ft)

SPREAD
60cm (2ft)

| Saxifragaceae | BRIDAL WREATH |
|---|---|

## *FRANCOA SONCHIFOLIA*

*Habit* Clump- or mat-forming. *Flowers* Small, cup-shaped, borne in short, dense racemes on slender, upright stems in summer and early autumn. Pink, marked red. *Leaves* Evergreen, rounded, deeply lobed, with winged leaf stalks, in dense, basal clumps. Dark green, softly hairy.
• NATIVE HABITAT Rocky, cliffside crevices, Chile.
• CULTIVATION Grow in light, well-drained soil in sun or light shade, in a warm, sheltered site. Good for the front of a border.
• PROPAGATION By seed or division in spring.

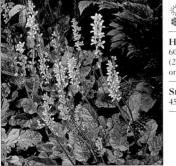

☼ ◊
❀ ❀

HEIGHT
60–75cm
(24–30in)
or more

SPREAD
45cm (18in)

| Lamiaceae/Labiatae | BERGAMOT, BEE BALM OSWEGO TEA |
|---|---|

## *MONARDA* 'Croftway Pink' ♥

*Habit* Clump-forming. *Flowers* Small, hooded, in dense, terminal heads, throughout summer. Soft rose-pink. *Leaves* Aromatic, toothed, oval, triangular or lance-shaped. Mid-green.
• NATIVE HABITAT Garden origin.
• CULTIVATION Grow in any moist, fertile soil, in sun or light shade. Suitable for herbaceous borders and herb gardens. The flowers attract bees and other insects. Prone to mildew in dry conditions.
• PROPAGATION By division in spring.
• OTHER NAMES *M. didyma* 'Croftway Pink'.

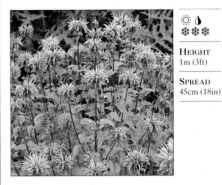

☼ ◊
❀ ❀ ❀

HEIGHT
1m (3ft)

SPREAD
45cm (18in)

| Geraniaceae | |
|---|---|

## *GERANIUM* × *OXONIANUM* 'Southcombe Star'

*Habit* Dense, mound-forming. *Flowers* Small, star-shaped, in profusion through summer. Pink with darker veins. Sometimes produces double flowers with petal-like stamens. *Leaves* Semi-evergreen, with 5 deeply cut, toothed lobes. Mid-green, sometimes blotched brown at the base.
• NATIVE HABITAT Garden origin.
• CULTIVATION Grow in any but waterlogged soil, in sun or light shade. Is good for ground cover.
• PROPAGATION By division in autumn or spring.

☼ ◊
❀ ❀ ❀

HEIGHT
60–75cm
(24–30in)

SPREAD
45cm (18in)

Malvaceae

## *SIDALCEA* 'Jimmy Whittet'

*Habit* Clump-forming. *Flowers* Bowl-shaped, borne in erect, terminal racemes in summer. Purplish-pink, with silky petals. *Leaves* Divided into 7–9 rounded lobes, mostly in basal clumps. Bright green.
• NATIVE HABITAT Garden origin.
• CULTIVATION Grow in moist but well-drained soil, in sun or light shade. Provide unobtrusive support. Flowers are good for cutting. A useful perennial for the middle of a border. Its graceful and handsome spikes carry long-lasting flowers.

For a second show of flowers cut back after the first flush – this will prolong the season to the autumn. A winter mulch of bracken litter, for example, will help protect during long periods of low temperatures.
• PROPAGATION By division in spring.
• OTHER NAMES *S.* 'Jimmy Whitelet'.

☼ ◊
❋ ❋ ❋

HEIGHT
1–1.2m
(3–4ft)

SPREAD
1m (3ft)

| Asteraceae/Compositae | |
|---|---|

## *ARGYRANTHEMUM* 'Mary Wootton'

**Habit** Bushy, woody-based. **Flowers** Large, daisy-like, produced on strong, slender stems throughout summer. Pink. **Leaves** Finely divided, fern-like. Pale green.
• NATIVE HABITAT Garden origin.
• CULTIVATION Grow in moderately fertile, well-drained soil. Needs a warm, sunny site with protection from cold winds.
• PROPAGATION By stem cuttings in autumn.
• OTHER NAMES *A. frutescens* 'Mary Wootton', *Chrysanthemum frutescens* 'Mary Wootton'.

HEIGHT
1m (3ft)

SPREAD
1m (3ft)

| Asteraceae/Compositae | KNAPWEED |
|---|---|

## *CENTAUREA PULCHERRIMA*

**Habit** Upright. **Flowers** Cornflower-like, borne singly on slender stems in summer. Rose-pink, with paler centres. **Leaves** Narrowly lance-shaped, deeply cut, mostly in basal clumps. Silvery-green.
• NATIVE HABITAT Meadows, Caucasus mountains.
• CULTIVATION Grow in open, freely draining and moderately fertile soils in full sun. Thrives on limy soils. Good for herbaceous borders and wildflower gardens.
• PROPAGATION By seed or division in autumn or spring.

HEIGHT
75cm (30in)

SPREAD
60cm (24in)

| Saxifragaceae | |
|---|---|

## *ASTILBE* 'Venus'

**Habit** Clump-forming. **Flowers** Tiny, in dense, feathery plumes, in summer. Pale pink. **Leaves** Divided into toothed, oval leaflets. Fresh green.
• NATIVE HABITAT Garden origin.
• CULTIVATION Grow in moist, fertile, humus-rich soil, in sun or semi-shade. Mulch in spring. Good for damp borders, bog gardens, or waterside plantings. Flower heads turn brown and dry.and will persist into winter unless removed.
• PROPAGATION By division in spring or autumn.
• OTHER NAMES *A.* x *arendsii* 'Venus'.

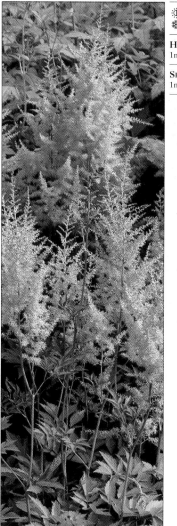

HEIGHT
1m (3ft)

SPREAD
1m (3ft)

| Saxifragaceae | |
|---|---|

## ASTILBE 'Straussenfeder'  ☑

**Habit** Clump-forming. **Flowers** Tiny, in arching, tapering plumes, in summer. Coral-pink. **Leaves** Divided into toothed, oval leaflets. Dark green.
• NATIVE HABITAT Garden origin.
• CULTIVATION Grow in moist, fertile, humus-rich soil, in sun or semi-shade. Apply an annual spring mulch of organic matter. Good for damp borders, bog gardens or waterside plantings. Flower heads turn brown and dry and persist into winter.
• PROPAGATION By division in spring or autumn.
• OTHER NAMES *A.* 'Ostrich Plume'.

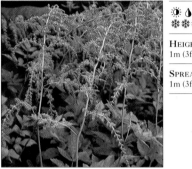

☀ ◐
❄ ❄ ❄

HEIGHT
1m (3ft)

SPREAD
1m (3ft)

| Apiaceae/Umbelliferae | |
|---|---|

## CHAEROPHYLLUM HIRSUTUM 'Roseum'

**Habit** Robust, clump-forming. **Flowers** Tiny, borne in small umbels on stout, upright stems in mid-summer. Pink, with fringed petals. **Leaves** Large, soft, fern-like, divided into overlapping, purple-flushed segments, borne on purplish-green stems.
• NATIVE HABITAT Species occurs in mountain scrub and grassland in Europe.
• CULTIVATION Grow in moist, fertile soil in sun or part-shade. Suitable for borders and wild gardens.
• PROPAGATION By division in early spring.

☀ ◐
❄ ❄ ❄

HEIGHT
to 1.2m
(4ft)

SPREAD
60cm (2ft)

| Scrophulariaceae | |
|---|---|

## DIGITALIS × MERTONENSIS  ☑

**Habit** Clump-forming. **Flowers** Tubular, to 6cm (2½in) long, borne in open, upright spikes from late spring to early summer. Buff-tinted, strawberry pink. **Leaves** Evergreen, lance-shaped, strongly veined, in basal rosettes. Dark green.
• NATIVE HABITAT Garden origin.
• CULTIVATION Tolerates dry soil and sun, but best in moist, well-drained soil in dappled shade. Ideal for a herbaceous border or woodland garden.
• PROPAGATION By seed in spring or division after flowering.

☀ ◐
❄ ❄ ❄

HEIGHT
75–90cm
(30–36in)

SPREAD
30cm (12in)

Leguminosae/
Papilionaceae

## *LUPINUS* 'The Chatelaine'

*Habit* Clump-forming. *Flowers* Small, pea-like, in dense, terminal spires, in early summer. Pink and white. *Leaves* Palmate, deeply divided into oval-lance-shaped leaflets. Dark bluish-green.
• NATIVE HABITAT Garden origin.
• CULTIVATION Grows best in well-drained, sandy, preferably slightly acid soils. Young foliage is very susceptible to slugs. Dead-head to help maintain vigour.
• PROPAGATION By cuttings of non-flowering sideshoots in spring or early summer.

☼ ◊
❀ ❀ ❀

HEIGHT
1.2m (4ft)

SPREAD
45cm (18in)

Asteraceae/Compositae

## *ACHILLEA MILLEFOLIUM* 'Cerise Queen'

*Habit* Upright, vigorous. *Flowers* Tiny, in large, flat heads, borne on rigid, leafy stems over long periods in summer. Vivid crimson-pink. *Leaves* Feathery, finely divided into lance-shaped segments. Grey-green, finely hairy.
• NATIVE HABITAT Garden origin.
• CULTIVATION Grow in fertile, well-drained soil, in full sun. Excellent for a silver border. Divide and replant every third year to maintain vigour. The flower heads dry well for winter decoration.
• PROPAGATION By division in spring or autumn.

☼ ◊
❀ ❀ ❀

HEIGHT
1–1.2m
(3–4ft)

SPREAD
60cm (24in)
or more

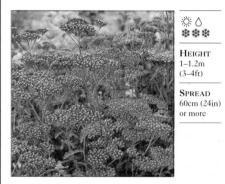

Asteraceae/Compositae

## *ECHINACEA PURPUREA* 'Robert Bloom'

*Habit* Upright, vigorous. *Flowers* Large, solitary, single, daisy-like, borne on stout stems, in summer. Intense cerise-crimson petals surrounding a domed, brown centre. *Leaves* Lance-shaped. Dark green.
• NATIVE HABITAT Garden origin.
• CULTIVATION Grow in moist, fertile, humus-rich soils, in sun. Contrasts well with softer pink flowers in a herbaceous border. Flowers are good for cutting.
• PROPAGATION By division or root cuttings in spring.

☼ ◐
❀ ❀ ❀

HEIGHT
1.2m (4ft)

SPREAD
50cm (20in)

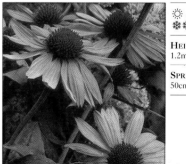

| Lamiaceae/Labiatae | |
|---|---|

## PHYSOSTEGIA VIRGINIANA subsp. SPECIOSA 'Variegata'

*Habit* Upright, rhizomatous. *Flowers* Tubular, hooded, in erect spikes, in late summer. Purplish-pink. *Leaves* Toothed, elliptic or lance-shaped. Mid-green, edged with white.
• NATIVE HABITAT Garden origin.
• CULTIVATION Grow in moist, humus-rich, fertile soil, in sun. The flowers have hinged stalks, which remain fixed when moved. Suitable for herbaceous borders. The flowers are good for cutting.
• PROPAGATION By division in spring.

| Gesneriaceae | |
|---|---|

## KOHLERIA WARSCEWICZII

*Habit* Upright, bushy, rhizomatous. *Flowers* Tubular, borne in long-stalked clusters in summer and autumn. Pink and white, very hairy, with purple-spotted, green lobes. *Leaves* Scalloped. Densely hairy, dark green.
• NATIVE HABITAT Colombia.
• CULTIVATION Grow as a house or conservatory plant in cool climates. Plant in moist but well-drained soil, in sun or semi-shade.
• PROPAGATION By division or seed in spring.
• OTHER NAMES *K. digitaliflora.*

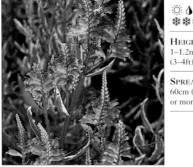

☼ ◊
❄ ❄ ❄

HEIGHT
1–1.2m
(3–4ft)

SPREAD
60cm (2ft)
or more

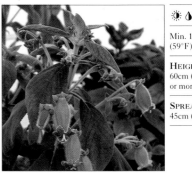

☼ ◊

Min. 15°C
(59°F)

HEIGHT
60cm (24in)
or more

SPREAD
45cm (18in)

| Scrophulariaceae | |
|---|---|

## REHMANNIA ELATA

*Habit* Much-branched, rather straggly. *Flowers* Foxglove-like, borne on slender stalks, in the leaf axils from early to mid-summer. Bright rose-purple, with yellow throats. *Leaves* Hairy, soft, oval, lobed and sometimes toothed. Bright green.
• NATIVE HABITAT Stony ground, China.
• CULTIVATION Grow in light, sharply drained soil, in a warm, sunny sheltered site. Dislikes winter wet and can be grown in a cold greenhouse.
• PROPAGATION By seed in autumn or spring, or by root cuttings in winter.

| Papaveraceae | BLEEDING HEART |
|---|---|

## DICENTRA SPECTABILIS ♥

*Habit* Hummock-forming. *Flowers* Pendent, heart-shaped, on fleshy, arching stems, in late spring and early summer. Red-pink. *Leaves* Fern-like, deeply cut. Mid-green.
• NATIVE HABITAT Woods and shady valleys, from Siberia to Japan.
• CULTIVATION Grow in humus-rich, moist but well-drained soil, in semi-shade. A beautiful plant for a shady border or woodland garden.
• PROPAGATION By division when dormant in late winter, or seed in autumn.

☼ ◊

Min. 1°C
(34°F)

HEIGHT
1m (3ft)

SPREAD
45cm (18in)

☼ ◊
❄ ❄

HEIGHT
60cm (2ft)

SPREAD
60–75cm
(24–30in)

| Lythraceae | |
|---|---|

## *LYTHRUM VIRGATUM* 'The Rocket'

*Habit* Erect, clump-forming. *Flowers* Small, 4-petalled, borne on slender, upright spikes, over long periods in summer. Vivid rose-pink. *Leaves* Narrowly lance-shaped, all along the stems. Mid-green.
• NATIVE HABITAT Garden origin.
• CULTIVATION Grow in moist, fertile soil, in sun or light shade. Suitable for bog gardens, waterside plantings and herbaceous borders where soil remains reliably moist.
• PROPAGATION By division in spring or autumn.

☼ ◐
❊ ❊ ❊

HEIGHT
1m (3ft)

SPREAD
45cm (18in)

| Malvaceae | |
|---|---|

## *SIDALCEA* 'Elsie Heugh'

*Habit* Clump-forming. *Flowers* Bowl-shaped, , borne in erect, terminal racemes in summer. Pale pink, with silky, fringed petals. *Leaves* Divided into 7–9 rounded lobes, mostly in basal clumps. Bright green.
• NATIVE HABITAT Garden origin.
• CULTIVATION Grow in any moist but well-drained soil, in sun or light shade. Provide unobtrusive support. Flowers are good for cutting.
• PROPAGATION By division in spring.

☼ �○
❊ ❊ ❊

HEIGHT
1–1.2m
(3–4ft)

SPREAD
1m (3ft)

| Lythraceae | |
|---|---|

## *LYTHRUM SALICARIA* 'Feuerkerze' ♀

*Habit* Upright, clump-forming. *Flowers* Small, 4-petalled, borne in dense, upright spikes from mid- to late summer. Rose-pink. *Leaves* Oval to narrowly lance-shaped, opposite or in whorls, all along the stem. Mid-green.
• NATIVE HABITAT Garden origin.
• CULTIVATION Grow in moist, fertile soil, in sun or light shade. Suitable for waterside plantings, bog gardens and permanently damp herbaceous borders.
• PROPAGATION By division in spring or autumn.
• OTHER NAMES *L. salicaria* 'Firecandle'.

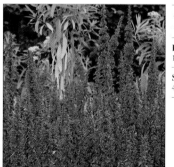

☼ ◐
❊ ❊ ❊

HEIGHT
1m (3ft)

SPREAD
45cm (18in)

| Geraniaceae | |
|---|---|

## GERANIUM PSILOSTEMON

**Habit** Clump-forming. **Flowers** Single, cup-shaped, borne in profusion in mid-summer. Bright magenta-pink, with black centres. **Leaves** Divided into 7, deeply cut and lobed. Mid-green, turning red in autumn.
• NATIVE HABITAT  Scrub, open forest and meadows, N.E. Turkey.
• CULTIVATION  Grow in fertile, well-drained soil, in full sun. Suitable for wild gardens. A vigorous herbaceous perennial with distinctly coloured flowers that need to be carefully placed in a border. While it undoubtedly forms an attractive specimen plant in its own right, it also blends well in mixed company. The early growth has attractive leaf buds tinged with red.
• PROPAGATION  By seed or division in autumn or spring.
• OTHER NAMES  *G. armenum.*

HEIGHT
To 1.2m
(4ft)

SPREAD
1.2m (4ft)

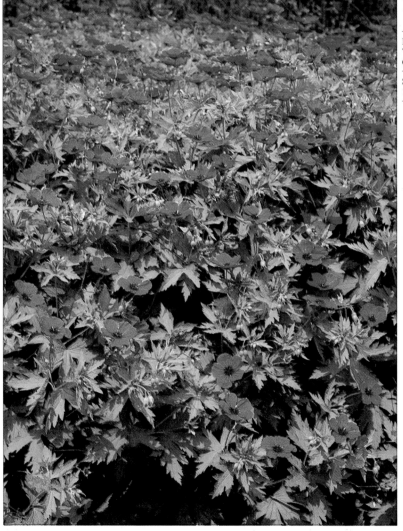

| Geraniaceae | |
|---|---|

## GERANIUM X OXONIANUM

**Habit** Dense, mound-forming. **Flowers** Small, funnel-shaped, in abundance through summer. Pink with darker veins, darkening with age. **Leaves** Semi-evergreen, with 5 deeply cut, toothed lobes. Mid-green sometimes blotched brown at the base.
• NATIVE HABITAT Garden origin.
• CULTIVATION Tolerant of dry soils. Grow in any but waterlogged soil, in sun or light shade. Good as ground cover, in herbaceous borders and cottage gardens.
• PROPAGATION By division in autumn or spring.

☼ ◊
❄ ❄ ❄

HEIGHT
60–75cm
(24–30in)

SPREAD
45cm (18in)

| Leguminosae/ Papilionaceae | |
|---|---|

## LUPINUS 'Inverewe Red'

**Habit** Upright, clump-forming. **Flowers** Small, pea-like, in dense, erect racemes, in early summer. Rich red. **Leaves** Palmate, deeply divided into lance-shaped leaflets. Dark green.
• NATIVE HABITAT Garden origin.
• CULTIVATION Grows best in well-drained, sandy, preferably slightly acid soils. Young foliage is very susceptible to slugs. Dead-head to help maintain vigour. May be short-lived.
• PROPAGATION By cuttings of non-flowering sideshoots in spring or early summer.

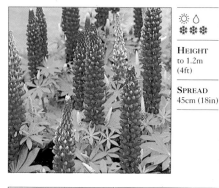

☼ ◊
❄ ❄ ❄

HEIGHT
to 1.2m
(4ft)

SPREAD
45cm (18in)

| Nyctaginaceae | FOUR O'CLOCK PLANT MARVEL OF PERU |
|---|---|

## MIRABILIS JALAPA

**Habit** Bushy, tuberous-rooted. **Flowers** Fragrant, trumpet-shaped, opening late on summer afternoons. Crimson, pink, white or yellow. **Leaves** Oval, heart-shaped at the base. Mid-green.
• NATIVE HABITAT Peru.
• CULTIVATION Grow in fertile, well-drained soil, in a sunny, sheltered site. Lift tubers and store over winter in frost-free conditions.
• PROPAGATION By seed or division of tubers in early spring.

☼ ◊
❄

HEIGHT
60cm–1.2m
(2–4ft)

SPREAD
60–75cm
(2–2½ft)

| Rosaceae | MEADOWSWEET |
|---|---|

## FILIPENDULA PURPUREA     ♈

**Habit** Upright, rhizomatous. **Flowers** Tiny, rich in dense, branched, terminal heads, on slender, purple-tinged stems, in summer. Red-purple. **Leaves** Deeply divided into 5–7 finely hairy, serrated lobes. Dark green.
• NATIVE HABITAT Damp habitats in Japan.
• CULTIVATION Grow in moist, humus-rich soil, in semi-shade, or in sun where soils remain reliably moist. Good for waterside plantings.
• PROPAGATION By seed in autumn, or by division in autumn or winter.

☼ ◊
❄ ❄ ❄

HEIGHT
1.2m (4ft)

SPREAD
60cm (2ft)
or more

# PELARGONIUMS

Pelargoniums make up a genus of mostly evergreen perennials and sub-shrubs, many of which are treated as annuals. Cultivated primarily for their exuberantly coloured flowers, and valued for their long flowering period, pelargoniums are grown as house-plants, as summer bedding, and as container plants, in patio pots, window boxes, and hanging baskets. A number are also grown for their beautifully scented foliage.

Pelargoniums are divided according to type into the following five groups:

**Zonal** – often sold as bedding geraniums, they have rounded leaves marked with a central darker zone, bearing fully double, semi-double or single (5-petalled) flowers.

**Ivy-leaved** – trailing plants with ivy-shaped, slightly fleshy leaves, and flowers similar to those of zonal pelargoniums.

**Scented-leaved** and **species** – plants with small, often irregularly star-shaped flowers and scented leaves.

**Regal** – shrubby perennials with deeply serrated leaves and brilliantly coloured, broadly trumpet-shaped flowers that are prone to rain damage when grown outdoors

**Unique** –tall sub-shrubs, with brightly coloured flowers, similar to those of the regal types, throughout the season. The variably shaped leaves may be scented.

Grow bedding plants in well-drained soil or compost in full sun, setting out when danger of frost has passed. Dead-head regularly. To overwinter, cut back plants to 12cm (5in) in late autumn/winter and move into the greenhouse. If grown in the house or conservatory, provide good ventilation and full light with shade from the hottest summer sun. Feed regularly when in growth. Repot and cut back hard in early spring.

Propagate by softwood cuttings between spring and autumn. Sow seed under glass in late winter at 16–18°C (61–64°F).

---

*P. ODORATISSIMUM*
*Habit* Low-growing.
*Flowers* Tiny, borne in trailing, branched clusters of 5–10, in late spring and summer. White, with red veins on the upper petals.
*Leaves* Evergreen, rounded, heart-shaped at the base, scalloped, apple-scented. Light green.
• HEIGHT 30–45cm (12–18in).
• SPREAD 30–45cm (12–18in).

*P. odoratissimum*
(Scented-leaved)
Apple pelargonium
☼ ◊
Min. 1°C (34°F)

*P. 'Fraicher Beauty'*
*Habit* Compact, upright.
*Flowers* Double, from early summer to autumn. White petals finely edged with red-pink, becoming deeper in warm, dry conditions.
*Leaves* Rounded. Mid-green with a darker zone.
• TIPS Excellent pot plant.
• HEIGHT 30cm (12in).
• SPREAD 23cm (9in).

*P. 'Fraicher Beauty'*
(Zonal)
☼ ◊
Min. 1°C (34°F)

---

*P. 'Mauritania'*
*Habit* Compact.
*Flowers* Single, borne in rounded clusters from summer to autumn. White, flushed pale salmon-pink at the base of the petals.
*Leaves* Rounded. Mid-green with a darker central zone.
• HEIGHT 30cm (12in).
• SPREAD 23cm (9in).

*P. 'Mauritania'*
(Zonal)
☼ ◊
Min. 1°C (34°F)

*P. 'Brookside Primrose'*
*Habit* Compact, bushy.
*Flowers* Double, borne from summer to autumn. Pale pink.
*Leaves* With a central, butterfly-shaped mark.
• TIPS Good for window boxes, pots and bedding.
• HEIGHT 10–12cm (4–5in).
• SPREAD 7–10cm (3–4in).

*P. 'Brookside Primrose*
(Dwarf zonal)
☼ ◊
Min. 1°C (34°F)

## P. 'Golden Lilac Mist'

*Habit* Bushy.
*Flowers* Double, in dense heads from summer to autumn. Lavender-pink.
*Leaves* Evergreen, rounded. Yellow-green, marked bronze.
• TIPS Good for window boxes.
• HEIGHT 25–30cm (10–12in).
• SPREAD 15–20cm (6–8in).

P. 'Golden Lilac Mist'
(Zonal)

☼ ◊
Min. 1°C (34°F)

## P. 'Fair Ellen'

*Habit* Shrubby, bushy.
*Flowers* Small, delicate, irregularly star-shaped, produced in flushes from early summer to autumn. Pale pink, intricately marked red.
*Leaves* Evergreen, crinkled, 3-lobed, scented. Dark green.
• TIPS Good for pots indoors.
• HEIGHT 38cm (15in).
• SPREAD 30cm (12in).

P. 'Fair Ellen'
(Scented-leaved)

☼ ◊
Min. 1°C (34°F)

## P. 'Mr Henry Cox'

*Habit* Upright.
*Flowers* Single, borne in small clusters from summer to autumn. Pale pink.
*Leaves* Evergreen, rounded. Zoned red, yellow, and purple-brown on a mid-green ground.
• TIPS Grown primarily for foliage.
• HEIGHT 30cm (12in).
• SPREAD 15cm (6in).

P. 'Mr Henry Cox'
(Zonal)

☼ ◊
Min. 1°C (34°F)  ♛

## P. 'The Boar'

*Habit* Trailing.
*Flowers* Single, long-stemmed, from summer to autumn. Salmon-pink.
*Leaves* Evergreen, with 5 notched lobes. Dark green with a central dark brown blotch.
• TIPS Excellent for hanging baskets.
• HEIGHT to 60cm (24in).
• SPREAD to 60cm (24in).

P. 'The Boar'
(Trailing)

☼ ◊
Min. 1°C (34°F)  ♛

## P. 'Bird Dancer'

*Habit* Dwarf, compact.
*Flowers* Narrow petalled, star-like, carried high, in ball-headed clusters from summer to autumn. Pale salmon-pink.
*Leaves* Palmate, lobed. Mid-green with wide, dark green central zone.
• TIPS Good as a house plant or in a window box.
• HEIGHT 10–12cm (4–5in).
• SPREAD 7–10cm (3–4in).

P. 'Bird Dancer'
(Zonal)

☼ ◊
Min. 1°C (34°F)  ♛

## P. 'Sweet Mimosa'

*Habit* Vigorous, upright, branching.
*Flowers* Trumpet-shaped, in small clusters, from summer to autumn. Pink.
*Leaves* Large, lobed. Mid-green.
• TIPS Good as a specimen plant in a container.
• HEIGHT 50cm (20in).
• SPREAD 30cm (12in).

P. 'Sweet Mimosa'
(Scented-leaved)

☼ ◊
Min. 1°C (34°F)

## P. 'Apple Blossom Rosebud'

*Habit* Compact, upright.
*Flowers* Fully double, resembling miniature rosebuds, from summer to autumn. Pale pinkish-white, with red-flushed petal margins, colouring more strongly in hot, sunny conditions.
*Leaves* Rounded. Mid-green with a dark centre.
• HEIGHT 30cm (12in).
• SPREAD 23cm (9in).

P. 'Apple Blossom Rosebud'
(Zonal)

☼ ◊
Min. 1°C (34°F)  ♛

## P. 'Timothy Clifford'

*Habit* Compact, miniature, short-jointed.
*Flowers* Large, fully double, in neat, rounded clusters from summer to autumn. Salmon-pink.
*Leaves* Very dark green.
• TIPS Good for a sunny windowsill.
• HEIGHT 15–20cm (6–8in).
• SPREAD 10cm (4in).

P. 'Timothy Clifford'
(Zonal)

☼ ◊
Min. 1°C (34°F)

## *P.* 'Autumn Festival'

*Habit* Bushy.
*Flowers* Large, broadly trumpet-shaped, with waved petals, from summer to autumn. Salmon-pink petals, and a white throat marked with darker salmon-pink veining.
*Leaves* Oval, deeply serrated. Mid-green.
• HEIGHT 30cm (12in).
• SPREAD 30cm (12in).

*P.* 'Autumn Festival'
(Regal)

☼ ◊
Min. 1°C (34°F)

## *P.* 'Leslie Judd'

*Habit* Vigorous, bushy.
*Flowers* Large, broadly trumpet-shaped, with wavy petals, from summer to autumn. Soft salmon-pink with a red blotch.
*Leaves* Oval, serrated. Mid-green.
• TIPS Pinch out growing tips before flowering to maintain a dense habit.
• HEIGHT 45–60cm (18–24in).
• SPREAD 30cm (12in).

*P.* 'Leslie Judd'
(Regal)

☼ ◊
Min. 1°C (34°F)

## *P.* Schöne Helena

*Habit* Vigorous, floriferous.
*Flowers* Large, semi-double, borne in dense, rounded clusters from summer to autumn. Salmon-pink.
*Leaves* Rounded. Mid-green with a darker central zone.
• HEIGHT 30–45cm (12–18in).
• SPREAD 23cm (9in).

*P.* Schöne Helena
(Zonal)

☼ ◊
Min. 1°C (34°F)

## *P.* 'Cherry Blossom'

*Habit* Vigorous, upright.
*Flowers* Semi-double, from summer to autumn. Mauve-pink with white centres.
*Leaves* Rounded. Mid-green with a darker central zone.
• TIPS An excellent pot plant for a windowsill.
• HEIGHT to 45cm (18in).
• SPREAD 45cm (18in).

*P.* 'Cherry Blossom'
(Zonal)

☼ ◊
Min. 1°C (34°F)

## *P. CUCULLATUM*

*Habit* Upright, sub-shrubby.
*Flowers* Small, with broad petals, borne in clusters of 5 in spring and summer. Bright purple-pink, with darker veining on the 2 upper petals.
*Leaves* Evergreen, rounded, to triangular, lobed, cupped. Green with red-tinted margins.
• TIPS Good for home or conservatory.
• HEIGHT to 2m (6ft).
• SPREAD 60cm (24in) or more.

*P. cucullatum*
(Species)

☼ ◊
Min. 1°C (34°F)

## P. 'Purple Emperor'
**Habit** Vigorous.
**Flowers** Large, broadly trumpet-shaped, profusely from summer, and well into autumn. Pink-mauve darker at the centre.
**Leaves** Oval, serrated. Mid-green.
• TIPS Excellent for pots in the conservatory or on a patio.
• HEIGHT 45cm (18in) or more.
• SPREAD 30cm (12in).

**P. 'Purple Emperor'**
(Regal)

☼ ◊
Min. 1°C (34°F)

## P. 'Alberta'
**Habit** Upright.
**Flowers** Small, single, borne in rounded, open clusters from summer to autumn. Crimson and white.
**Leaves** Rounded. Mid-green with a darker central zone.
• TIPS Good for bedding.
• HEIGHT 45cm (18in).
• SPREAD 30cm (12in).

**P. 'Alberta'**
(Zonal)

☼ ◊
Min. 1°C (34°F)

## P. 'Francis Parrett'
**Habit** Compact, miniature, short-jointed.
**Flowers** Fully double, from early summer to autumn. Purplish-mauve.
**Leaves** Evergreen, rounded, very small. Mid-green.
• TIPS An excellent pot plant for a sunny windowsill.
• HEIGHT 15–20cm (6–8in).
• SPREAD 10cm (4in).

**P. 'Francis Parrett'**
(Zonal)

☼ ◊
Min. 1°C (34°F)      ♏

## P. 'Clorinda'
**Habit** Vigorous, upright.
**Flowers** Large, single, in flushes from early summer to autumn. Rose-pink.
**Leaves** Evergreen, crinkled, 3-lobed, cedar-scented.
• TIPS Good in large pots on a patio or in a conservatory.
• HEIGHT 45–60cm (18–24in) or more.
• SPREAD 20–25cm (8–10in).

**P. 'Clorinda'**
(Scented-leaved)

☼ ◊
Min. 1°C (34°F)

## P. 'Lavender Grand Slam'
**Habit** Vigorous, bushy.
**Flowers** Large, broadly trumpet-shaped, with wavy petals, borne from summer to autumn. Silvery-mauve with a light maroon blotch.
**Leaves** Oval, serrated. Mid-green.
• HEIGHT 45–60cm (18–24in).
• SPREAD 30cm (12in).

**P. 'Lavender Grand Slam'**
(Regal)
☼ ◊
Min. 1°C (34°F)      ♏

## P. 'Manx Maid'
**Habit** Compact.
**Flowers** Relatively small, broadly trumpet-shaped, from summer to autumn. Pink, blotched and veined with burgundy.
**Leaves** Smaller than most other regals. Bright green.
• TIPS Good for a hanging basket.
• HEIGHT 30–38cm (12–15in).
• SPREAD 25cm (10in).

**P. 'Manx Maid'**
(Regal)

☼ ◊
Min. 1°C (34°F)

## P. 'Paton's Unique'
**Habit** Vigorous, sub-shrubby.
**Flowers** Single, in neat clusters, from summer to autumn. Red or pale pink with a white eye.
**Leaves** Evergreen, lobed, pungent, shiny. Mid-green.
• TIPS Good for pots in a conservatory.
• HEIGHT 38–45cm (15–18in).
• SPREAD 15–20cm (6–8in).

**P. 'Paton's Unique'**
(Unique)

☼ ◊
Min. 1°C (34°F)

## P. 'Amethyst'
**Habit** Trailing.
**Flowers** Fully double, from summer to autumn. Mauve-purple.
**Leaves** Evergreen, fleshy, ivy-shaped with pointed lobes. Fresh green.
• HEIGHT to 1.5m (5ft).
• SPREAD to 1.5m (5ft).

**P. 'Amethyst'**
(Ivy-leaved)

☼ ◊
Min. 1°C (34°F)

## P. 'Tip Top Duet'
**Habit** Bushy, dainty.
**Flowers** Broadly trumpet-shaped, from early summer to autumn. White, veined pink, with deep burgundy blotches on uppermost petals.
**Leaves** Small, oval, serrated. Mid-green.
• TIPS Good for a hanging basket or container.
• HEIGHT 30–38cm (12–15in).
• SPREAD 25cm (10in).

**P. 'Tip Top Duet'**
(Regal)

☼ ◊
Min. 1°C (34°F)

## P. 'Mini Cascade'
**Habit** Trailing, short-jointed.
**Flowers** Single, borne in large clusters in profusion from summer to autumn. Pinkish-red.
• TIPS Dead-heading is essential for continuous flowering. Excellent for hanging baskets.
• HEIGHT 30–45cm (12–18in).
• SPREAD 30–45cm (12–18in).

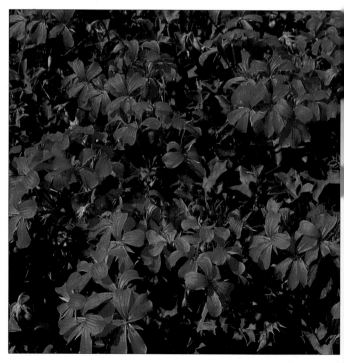

**P. 'Mini Cascade'**
(Ivy-leaved)

☼ ◊
Min. 1°C (34°F)

## P. 'Friesdorf'

*Habit* Compact, dwarf.
*Flowers* Single, delicate,
with narrow petals, borne
in open clusters from
summer to autumn.
Orange-scarlet.
*Leaves* Rounded.
Purple-green with a
darker central ring.
• TIPS Good for window
boxes, bedding and
border edging.
• HEIGHT 25cm (10in).
• SPREAD 15cm (6in).

**P. 'Friesdorf'**
(Zonal)

☼ ◊
Min. 1°C (34°F)

## P. 'Irene'

*Habit* Bushy. upright.
*Flowers* Large, semi-
double, borne in dense,
rounded clusters from
summer to autumn.
Light crimson.
*Leaves* Rounded. Mid-
green with a darker
central zone.
• HEIGHT 45cm (18in).
• SPREAD 23–30cm
(9–12in).

**P. 'Irene'**
(Zonal)

☼ ◊
Min. 1°C (34°F)    ⬡

## P. 'Rollisson's Unique'

*Habit* Vigorous, upright,
sub-shrubby.
*Flowers* Small, single,
open, in clusters, from
summer to autumn. Wine-
red with purple veins.
*Leaves* Evergreen, oval,
notched, pungent.
• TIPS Suitable for large
pots in a conservatory.
• HEIGHT 60cm (24in)
or more.
• SPREAD 60cm (24in).

**P. 'Rollisson's Unique'**
(Unique)

☼ ◊
Min. 1°C (34°F)

## P. 'Alice Crousse'

*Habit* Trailing.
*Flowers* Double, borne
in clusters. Cerise
rose-pink.
*Leaves* Green, ivy-
shaped.
• TIPS Suited to hanging
baskets or window boxes.
Take cuttings in autumn
or spring.
• HEIGHT 25–30cm
(10–12in)
• SPREAD 30–35cm
(12–14in)

**P. 'Alice Crousse'**
(Ivy-leaved)

☼ ◊
Min. 1°C (34°F)    ⬡

## P. 'Rouletta'

*Habit* Vigorous, trailing.
*Flowers* Semi-double,
from summer to autumn.
Red petal edges, fading to
white at the centre.
*Leaves* Rounded, lobed.
Mid-green.
• TIPS Excellent for
hanging baskets. Pinch
out growing tips regularly
to promote branching.
• HEIGHT 60cm–1m
(2–3ft).
• SPREAD to 1m (3ft).

**P. 'Rouletta'**
(Ivy-leaved)

☼ ◊
Min. 1°C (34°F)

## P. 'Caligula'

*Habit* Compact,
miniature.
*Flowers* Small, double,
from summer to autumn.
Crimson.
*Leaves* Tiny.
Dark green.
• TIPS An excellent pot
plant for a windowsill.
• HEIGHT 15–20cm
(6–8in).
• SPREAD 10cm (4in).

**P. 'Caligula'**
(Zonal)

☼ ◊
Min. 1°C (34°F)

## P. 'Paul Humphries'

*Habit* Bushy, compact.
*Flowers* Fully double,
in dense, rounded heads,
from summer to autumn.
Deep wine-red.
*Leaves* Rounded. Mid-
green with a darker
central zone.
• TIPS A good pot plant.
• HEIGHT 30cm (12in).
• SPREAD 23cm (9in).

**P. 'Paul Humphries'**
(Zonal)

☼ ◊
Min. 1°C (34°F)

## P. 'Dolly Varden'

*Habit* Compact.
*Flowers* Small, single,
borne in open clusters
from early summer to
autumn. Clear bright
scarlet.
*Leaves* Evergreen,
rounded. Zoned purple-
brown, creamy-white
and crimson.
• TIPS Grown primarily
for its foliage.
• HEIGHT 30cm (12in).
• SPREAD 23cm (9in).

**P. 'Dolly Varden'**
(Zonal)

☼ ◊
Min. 1°C (34°F)    ⬡

## P. 'Happy Thought'
**Habit** Vigorous, upright.
**Flowers** Small, single, in small clusters from summer to autumn. Red.
**Leaves** Rounded. Mid-green, with paler golden-green central zone.
• TIPS Foliage and flowers suits it to outdoor bedding, tubs and window boxes.
• OTHER NAMES
P. 'A Happy Thought'.
• HEIGHT 50cm (20in).
• SPREAD 30cm (12in).

**P. 'Happy Thought'**
(Zonal)
☼ ◊
Min. 1°C (34°F)    ♀

## P. 'Flower of Spring'
**Habit** Vigorous, upright.
**Flowers** Small, single, from early summer to autumn. Bright scarlet.
**Leaves** Evergreen, rounded. Grey-green, edged with white.
• HEIGHT 60cm (24in).
• SPREAD 30cm (12in).

**P. 'Flower of Spring'**
(Zonal)
Silver-leaved geranium
☼ ◊
Min. 1°C (34°F)    ♀

## P. 'Orange Ricard'
**Habit** Vigorous, robust.
**Flowers** Large, semi-double, borne in rounded clusters, in profusion, from summer to autumn. Orange.
**Leaves** Rounded. Mid-green with darker zone.
• HEIGHT 45–60cm (18–24in).
• SPREAD 30cm (12in).

**P. 'Orange Ricard'**
(Zonal)
☼ ◊
Min. 1°C (34°F)

## P. 'Mrs Pollock'
**Habit** Upright.
**Flowers** Small, single, borne in small clusters from summer to autumn. Orange-red.
**Leaves** Evergreen, rounded. Golden-yellow with a central grey-green, butterfly mark, shot throughout with bronze.
• TIPS Grown primarily for foliage.
• HEIGHT 30cm (12in).
• SPREAD 15cm (6in).

**P. 'Mrs Pollock'**
(Zonal)
☼ ◊
Min. 1°C (34°F)

## P. 'Voodoo'
**Habit** Vigorous, upright, sub-shrubby.
**Flowers** Small, single, open, borne in open clusters, from early summer to autumn. Pale burgundy, with a purple-black blaze on each petal.
**Leaves** Evergreen, lobed, aromatic.
• TIPS Suitable for a conservatory or greenhouse.
• HEIGHT 50–60cm (20–24in).
• SPREAD 20–25cm (8–10in).

**P. 'Voodoo'**
(Unique)
☼ ◊
Min. 1°C (34°F)

## P. 'Bredon'
**Habit** Upright, vigorous, bushy.
**Flowers** Large, broadly trumpet-shaped, borne from summer to autumn. Deep maroon.
**Leaves** Rounded, serrated. Mid-green.
• TIPS Makes a good feature plant in a container for the patio or conservatory.
• HEIGHT 45cm (18in).
• SPREAD 30cm (12in).

**P. 'Bredon'**
(Regal)
☼ ◊
Min. 1°C (34°F)    ♀

## P. CAPITATUM
**Habit** Erect to arching.
**Flowers** Small, with slender petals, from summer to autumn. Mauve, with darker veins on the upper 2 petals.
**Leaves** Evergreen, 3–5 lobed, velvety, with crinkled margins, rose-scented.
• HEIGHT 30–60cm (12–24in).
• SPREAD 30cm (12in).

**P. capitatum**
(Scented-leaved species)
Rose-scented geranium
☼ ◊
Min. 1°C (34°F)

## P. 'Lady Plymouth'
**Habit** Bushy, vigorous.
**Flowers** Small, with delicate petals, borne in clusters of 5, from early summer to autumn. White to pale pink.
**Leaves** Evergreen, triangular, deeply lobed, rose-scented. Greyish-green, margined with cream.
• TIPS Excellent in large pots in a warm conservatory.
• HEIGHT 45–60cm (18–24in).
• SPREAD 45cm (18in).

P. 'Lady Plymouth'
(Scented-leaved)
Min. 1°C (34°F)

## P. 'Prince of Orange'
**Habit** Compact.
**Flowers** Small, single, from early summer to autumn. Pale mauve with maroon veining.
**Leaves** Evergreen, small, rounded, rough, orange-scented. Light green.
• TIPS Good as a pot plant indoors.
• HEIGHT 25–30cm (10–12in).
• SPREAD 15–20cm (6–8in).

P. 'Prince of Orange'
(Scented-leaved)
Min. 1°C (34°F)

## P. 'L'Elégante'
**Habit** Trailing.
**Flowers** Small, single to semi-double, borne in open clusters from early summer to autumn. Pale mauve.
**Leaves** Evergreen, ivy-shaped. Creamy-white and green, tinted pink in warm, dry conditions.
• TIPS Good for hanging baskets.
• HEIGHT to 60cm (24in).
• SPREAD to 60cm (24in).

P. 'L'Elégante'
(Ivy-leaved)
Min. 1°C (34°F)

## P. 'Purple Unique'
**Habit** Vigorous, upright, sub-shrubby.
**Flowers** Single, open trumpet-shaped, in small clusters, early summer to autumn. Light purple.
**Leaves** Evergreen, large-lobed, strongly scented. Mid-green.
• TIPS Train against a sunny wall.
• HEIGHT 1m (3ft) or more.
• SPREAD 1m (3ft).

P. 'Purple Unique'
(Unique)
Min. 1°C (34°F)

## P. 'Old Spice'
**Habit** Compact, upright.
**Flowers** Small, single, from early summer. Pale purplish-pink.
**Leaves** Evergreen, small, rounded, shallowly lobed, softly hairy, with crisped margins; spice-scented. Grey-green and cream.
• TIPS Good for medium-sized pots indoors.
• HEIGHT to 1m (3ft).
• SPREAD 30–45cm (12–18in).

P. 'Old Spice'
(Scented-leaved)
Min. 1°C (34°F)

## P. 'Mabel Grey'
**Habit** Vigorous.
**Flowers** Small, with delicate petals, borne in clusters of 5–10, from early summer to autumn. Mauve.
**Leaves** Evergreen, diamond-shaped, with 5–7 pointed lobes, lemon-scented. Bright green.
• HEIGHT 45–60cm (18–24in).
• SPREAD 30–45cm (12–18in).

P. 'Mabel Grey'
(Scented-leaved)
Min. 1°C (34°F)

## P. CRISPUM 'Variegatum'
**Habit** Upright, bushy.
**Flowers** Small, in clusters from early summer to autumn. Pale lilac.
**Leaves** Evergreen, rough-textured, 3-lobed with crisped margins, lemon-scented. Edged golden-yellow, becoming creamy-white in winter.
• HEIGHT to 1m (3ft).
• SPREAD 30–45cm (12–18in).

P. crispum 'Variegatum'
(Scented-leaved)
Min. 1°C (34°F)

# PENSTEMONS

These elegant and reliable border perennials are increasingly valued by gardeners for their spires of foxglove-like flowers. There are many cultivars available in a wide range of colours including white, pastel and deep pink, warm cherry-red, clear blue and dusky purple.

Penstemons thrive well in humus-rich, well-drained soil in full sun. Where severe winters are expected, lift the plants after flowering and overwinter in a cold frame. Deadhead regularly to prolong flowering.

Penstemons are generally not long-lived plants and tend to become woody at the base after a few seasons. Replace regularly with new plants propagated from softwood cuttings of non-flowering shoots taken in mid- to late summer.

## P. 'White Bedder'
*Habit* Vigorous, erect, clump-forming, floriferous.
*Flowers* Widely tubular, 2-lipped, in long flower heads from mid-summer to autumn. Pure white with dark anthers, opening from pink-flushed buds.
*Leaves* Semi-evergreen, narrowly lance-shaped. Fresh green.
• OTHER NAMES
P. 'Burford White',
P. 'Royal White',
P. 'Snow Storm',
P. 'Snowflake',
,P. 'Bisham Seedling'.
• HEIGHT 70cm (28in).
• SPREAD 60cm (2ft).

*P.* 'White Bedder'

☀ ◊ ❋ ❋     ♀

## P. 'Mother of Pearl'
*Habit* Bushy, clump-forming.
*Flowers* Small, tubular, 2-lipped, in long, slender spires from mid-summer to autumn. Pearly-mauve, tinted pink and white; throat streaked with dark pink.
*Leaves* Semi-evergreen, linear. Light green.
• HEIGHT to 1m (3ft).
• SPREAD 60cm (2ft).

*P.* 'Mother of Pearl'

☀ ◊ ❋ ❋

## P. 'Beech Park'
*Habit* Bushy, clump-forming.
*Flowers* Small, tubular, 2-lipped, in long, slender heads from mid-summer to autumn. Bright pink, with a white throat.
*Leaves* Semi-evergreen, linear. Light green.
• OTHER NAMES
P. 'Barbara Barker'.
• HEIGHT 60cm (2ft).
• SPREAD 60cm (2ft).

*P.* 'Beech Park'

☀ ◊ ❋ ❋     ♀

## P. 'Apple Blossom'
*Habit* Bushy, clump-forming.
*Flowers* Small, tubular, 2-lipped, in long, slender heads from mid- to late summer or early autumn. Pale pink, with white throat.
*Leaves* Semi-evergreen, narrow. Fresh green.
• HEIGHT 60cm (2ft).
• SPREAD 60cm (2ft).

*P.* 'Apple Blossom'

☀ ◊ ❋ ❋     ♀

## P. 'Maurice Gibbs'
*Habit* Bushy, clump-forming.
*Flowers* Small, tubular. 2-lipped, in long, slender heads from mid-summer to autumn. Claret-red with white throats.
*Leaves* Semi-evergreen, narrowly lance-shaped. Light green.
• HEIGHT 90cm (3ft).
• SPREAD 60cm (2ft).

P. 'Maurice Gibbs'

☀ ◊ ❀ ❀

## P. 'Chester Scarlet'
*Habit* Robust, bushy, clump-forming.
*Flowers* Large, tubular, 2-lipped, in long, slender heads from mid-summer to autumn. Bright red.
*Leaves* Semi-evergreen, narrowly lance-shaped. Light green.
• OTHER NAMES P. 'Mrs Morse'.
• HEIGHT 90cm (3ft).
• SPREAD 90cm (3ft).

P. 'Chester Scarlet'

☀ ◊ ❀ ❀        ♔

## P. 'Evelyn'
*Habit* Erect, bushy, clump-forming, floriferous.
*Flowers* Small, tubular, 2-lipped, in long, slender heads from mid-summer to autumn. Pink.
*Leaves* Semi-evergreen, narrowly lance-shaped. Mid-green.
• OTHER NAMES P. 'Phyllis'.
• HEIGHT 45cm (18in).
• SPREAD 45cm (18in).

P. 'Evelyn'

☀ ◊ ❀ ❀        ♔

## P. BARBATUS
*Habit* Rosette-forming.
*Flowers* Small, tubular, 2-lipped, well-spaced in long, open heads from mid-summer to early autumn. Rose-red.
*Leaves* Semi-evergreen, oblong to oval, mostly basal, but with linear stem leaves. Mid-green.
• OTHER NAMES *Chelone barbata*.
• HEIGHT 1m (3ft).
• SPREAD 30cm (1ft).

P. barbatus

☀ ◊ ❀ ❀

## P. 'Pink Endurance'
*Habit* Dwarf, bushy, clump-forming.
*Flowers* Small, tubular. 2-lipped, in short heads in mid-summer. Rose-pink.
*Leaves* Semi-evergreen, linear. Mid-green.
• HEIGHT 30–38cm (12–15in).
• SPREAD 30–38cm (12–15in).

P. 'Pink Endurance'

☀ ◊ ❀ ❀

## P. 'Andenken an Friedrich Hahn'
*Habit* Vigorous, bushy, clump-forming.
*Flowers* Small, tubular, 2-lipped, in long, slender heads from mid-summer to autumn. Deep wine-red.
*Leaves* Semi-evergreen, narrowly lance-shaped. Fresh green.
• OTHER NAMES P. 'Garnet'.
• HEIGHT 60–75cm (2–2½ft).
• SPREAD 60cm (2ft).

P. 'Andenken an Friedrich Hahn'

## P. 'Pennington Gem'
*Habit* Vigorous, bushy, clump-forming.
*Flowers* Small, tubular. 2-lipped, in long, slender heads from mid-summer to autumn. Pink.
*Leaves* Semi-evergreen, linear. Fresh green.
• HEIGHT to 1m (3ft).
• SPREAD 60cm (2ft).

P. 'Pennington Gem'

☀ ◊ ❀ ❀        ♔

☀ ◊ ❀ ❀        ♔

## P. 'King George V'
*Habit* Bushy, clump-forming.
*Flowers* Small, funnel-shaped, in long, slender heads from mid-summer to autumn. Bright crimson with white throats.
*Leaves* Semi-evergreen, narrowly oval. Mid-green.
• HEIGHT 75cm (30in).
• SPREAD 45–60cm (18–24in).

P. 'King George V'

☼ ◊ ❀ ❀

## P. 'Prairie Fire'
*Habit* Vigorous, erect, clump-forming.
*Flowers* Small, tubular, 2-lipped, well-spaced in long, open, heads from mid-summer to autumn. Pinkish-red.
*Leaves* Semi-evergreen, narrowly lance-shaped, mostly in basal rosettes. Mid-green.
• HEIGHT 1.5m (5ft).
• SPREAD 60cm (2ft).

P. 'Prairie Fire'

☼ ◊ ❀ ❀

## P. 'Burgundy'
*Habit* Robust, bushy, clump-forming.
*Flowers* Small, tubular, 2-lipped, in long, slender heads from mid-summer to autumn. Purplish-red with dark red-streaked white throats.
*Leaves* Semi-evergreen, linear. Light green.
• OTHER NAMES
P. 'Burford Seedling'.
• HEIGHT 1.2m (4ft).
• SPREAD 60cm (2ft).

P. 'Burgundy'

☼ ◊ ❀ ❀

## P. 'Schoenholzeri'
*Habit* Vigorous, erect, clump-forming, floriferous.
*Flowers* Large, trumpet-shaped, in long racemes from mid-summer to autumn. Brilliant scarlet.
*Leaves* Semi-evergreen, lance-shaped to narrowly oval. Mid-green.
• HEIGHT 1m (3ft).
• SPREAD 30–45cm (12–18in).

P. 'Schoenholzeri'

☼ ◊ ❀ ❀ ∇

## P. 'Rubicundus'
*Habit* Erect, clump-forming.
*Flowers* Very large, tubular, 2-lipped, in long, open heads from mid-summer to autumn. Bright red with white throats.
*Leaves* Semi-evergreen, linear. Light green.
• HEIGHT 1.2m (4ft).
• SPREAD 60cm (2ft).

P. 'Rubicundus'

☼ ◊ ❀ ❀ ∇

## P. 'Countess of Dalkeith'
*Habit* Erect, bushy, clump-forming.
*Flowers* Large, tubular, 2-lipped, in long, slender heads from mid-summer to autumn. Deep purple with white throats.
*Leaves* Semi-evergreen, linear. Light green.
• HEIGHT 1m (3ft).
• SPREAD 60cm (2ft).

P. 'Countess of Dalkeith'

☼ ◊ ❀ ❀

## P. 'Sour Grapes'
*Habit* Vigorous, erect, clump-forming, floriferous.
*Flowers* Small, tubular, 2-lipped, in long heads from mid-summer to autumn. Deep purple-blue, suffused violet.
*Leaves* Semi-evergreen, narrowly lance-shaped. Light green.
• HEIGHT 90cm (3ft).
• SPREAD 60cm (2ft).

P. 'Sour Grapes'

☼ ◊ ❀ ❀

## P. 'Alice Hindley'
*Habit* Upright, clump-forming.
*Flowers* Small, tubular, 2-lipped, in long heads from mid- to late summer or early autumn. Pale blue-lilac, flushed lilac-pink.
*Leaves* Semi-evergreen, narrowly lance-shaped, dark green.
• HEIGHT 1.2m (4ft).
• SPREAD 60cm (2ft).

P. 'Alice Hindley'

☼ ◊ ❀ ❀ ∇

| Valerianaceae | RED VALERIAN |
| --- | --- |

## CENTRANTHUS RUBER

**Habit** Loosely clump-forming. **Flowers** Small, star-shaped, in branching heads, borne above the foliage from late spring to autumn. Deep red-pink. **Leaves** Fleshy, oval or lance-shaped. Blue-green.
• NATIVE HABITAT Rocks and coastal shingle, in Mediterranean Europe and N. Africa to Turkey.
• CULTIVATION Grow in full sun in well-drained soil. Thrives in exposed sites, in poor, especially alkaline soils and in seaside gardens. Excellent for naturalizing in dry walls or gravel.
• PROPAGATION By seed in autumn or spring.

☼ ◊
❋ ❋ ❋

HEIGHT
60cm–1m
(2–3ft)

SPREAD
45–60cm
(1½–2ft)
or more

| Ranunculaceae | |
| --- | --- |

## AQUILEGIA VULGARIS
### 'Nora Barlow'

**Habit** Clump-forming. **Flowers** Funnel-shaped, double, with short spurs and many narrow, red-pink, petals, tipped with pale-green, borne on slender stems in summer. **Leaves** Rounded, deeply divided into narrow lobes. Grey-green.
• NATIVE HABITAT Garden origin.
• CULTIVATION Grow in an open, sunny site, in well-drained soil. Long cultivated for its curious flowers, it is suited to borders and cottage gardens.
• PROPAGATION By division when dormant.

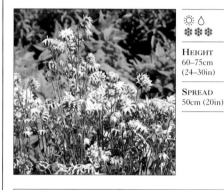

☼ ◊
❋ ❋ ❋

HEIGHT
60–75cm
(24–30in)

SPREAD
50cm (20in)

| Asteraceae/Compositae | |
| --- | --- |

## ACHILLEA 'Lachsschönheit'

**Habit** Upright. **Flowers** Tiny, in flat heads, on rigid, leafy stems, during summer. Pale salmon-red, fading to creamy-yellow. **Leaves** Feathery, finely divided into oblong to lance-shaped segments. Grey-green, finely hairy.
• NATIVE HABITAT Garden origin.
• CULTIVATION Grow in fertile, well-drained soil, in full sun. Excellent for a silver border. Divide and replant every third year to maintain vigour.
• PROPAGATION By division in spring or autumn.
• OTHER NAMES A. 'Salmon Beauty'.

☼ ◊
❋ ❋ ❋

HEIGHT
up to 1.2m
(4ft)

SPREAD
60cm (24in)

| Ranunculaceae | CANADIAN COLUMBINE |
| --- | --- |

## AQUILEGIA CANADENSIS

**Habit** Clump-forming. **Flowers** Bell-shaped, nodding, yellow, with long, straight, red spurs, borne on slender stems in early to mid-summer. **Leaves** Rounded, deeply divided into narrow lobes. Dark green.
• NATIVE HABITAT Rocky woods, North America.
• CULTIVATION Grow in well-drained, preferably sandy soil, in dappled shade or sun. Suitable for borders and cottage or woodland gardens.
• PROPAGATION By seed in autumn or spring, or by division when dormant.

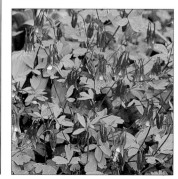

☼ ◊
❋ ❋ ❋

HEIGHT
60–75cm
(24–30in)

SPREAD
50cm (20in)

| Saxifragaceae | |
|---|---|

## *ASTILBE* 'Montgomery'

*Habit* Clump-forming. *Flowers* Tiny, in dense, feathery, branching spires, in summer. Deep salmon-red. *Leaves* Divided into toothed, oval, leaflets. Fresh green.
- NATIVE HABITAT Garden origin.
- CULTIVATION Grow in moist, fertile, humus-rich soil, in sun or semi-shade. Good for damp borders, bog gardens, or waterside plantings, associating well with *Hosta* and *Rodgersia*. Flower heads turn brown and dry, persisting into winter unless dead-headed.
- PROPAGATION By division in spring or autumn.

☀ ◐
❋ ❋ ❋

**HEIGHT**
1m (3ft)

**SPREAD**
1m (3ft)

| Polygonaceae | |
|---|---|

## *PERSICARIA AMPLEXICAULIS* ♆ 'Firetail'

*Habit* Clump-forming. *Flowers* Tiny, in slender spikes, in late summer and autumn. Bright crimson. *Leaves* Pointed, oval-lance-shaped, heart-shaped at the base. Mid-green.
- NATIVE HABITAT Garden origin.
- CULTIVATION Grow in sun or part-shade, in moist but well-drained soil. Suited to a herbaceous border, but may swamp less vigorous species.
- PROPAGATION By division in autumn or spring.
- OTHER NAMES *Polygonum amplexicaule* 'Firetail'.

☀ ◐
❋ ❋ ❋

**HEIGHT**
1–1.2m
(3–4ft)

**SPREAD**
1–1.2m
(3–4ft)

| Dipsacaceae | |
|---|---|

## *KNAUTIA MACEDONICA*

*Habit* Upright, clump-forming. *Flowers* Double, almost globular, borne on lax, branching stems, in mid-summer. Very deep crimson. *Leaves* Deeply divided stem leaves. Dark green. Basal leaves wither before flowering.
- NATIVE HABITAT Scrub, open woods, C. Europe.
- CULTIVATION Grow in a warm, sunny, sheltered site, in well-drained soil. May require staking.
- PROPAGATION By basal cuttings in spring, or by seed in autumn.
- OTHER NAMES *Scabiosa rumelica* of gardens.

☀ ◊
❋ ❋ ❋

**HEIGHT**
80cm (30in)

**SPREAD**
60cm (2ft)

| Campanulaceae | |
|---|---|

## LOBELIA 'Cherry Ripe'

*Habit* Clump-forming. *Flowers* 2-lipped, with 3 spreading lower lobes, borne in spikes, from mid- to late summer. Cerise-scarlet. *Leaves* Oval. Fresh green, often tinted red-bronze.
• NATIVE HABITAT Garden origin.
• CULTIVATION Grow in moist, fertile, humus-rich soil, in sun or part-shade. Suitable for waterside plantings. In cold areas, pot up over winter and protect from frost in a cold frame.
• PROPAGATION By division in spring.

HEIGHT
1m (3ft)

SPREAD
23cm (9in)

| Campanulaceae | |
|---|---|

## LOBELIA 'Queen Victoria'   ♥

*Habit* Clump-forming. *Flowers* 2-lipped, with 3 spreading lower lobes, in spikes, from late summer to mid-autumn. Almost luminous, vivid red. *Leaves* Oblong-oval, mostly basal. Deep red-purple.
• NATIVE HABITAT Garden origin.
• CULTIVATION Grow in moist, fertile, humus-rich soil, in sun or part-shade. Suitable for waterside plantings and damp borders. In cold areas, pot up over winter and protect from frost in a cold frame. Dislikes cold, wet conditions in winter.
• PROPAGATION By division in spring.

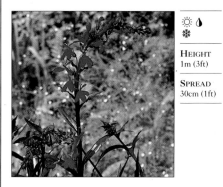

HEIGHT
1m (3ft)

SPREAD
30cm (1ft)

| Asteraceae/Compositae | CHOCOLATE COSMOS |
|---|---|

## COSMOS ATROSANGUINEUS

*Habit* Upright, tuberous-rooted. *Flowers* Single, with an elusive chocolate scent, borne on slender stems, from late summer till first frost. Velvety, maroon-crimson. *Leaves* Spoon-shaped, divided. Dark green, sometimes purple-flushed.
• NATIVE HABITAT Mexico.
• CULTIVATION Grow in a warm, sheltered site, in well-drained soil. In winter provide a dry mulch, or lift tubers and store in a cool, dry, frost-free place.
• PROPAGATION By basal cuttings in spring.
• OTHER NAMES *Bidens atrosanguinea*.

HEIGHT
60cm (24in)

SPREAD
45cm (18in)

| Acanthaceae | |
|---|---|

## RUELLIA GRAECIZANS

*Habit* Bushy, sub-shrubby. *Flowers* Small, tubular, borne in long-stalked clusters, intermittently throughout the year. Scarlet. *Leaves* Evergreen, pointed, narrowly oval. Glossy green.
• NATIVE HABITAT Forest edges, tropical South America.
• CULTIVATION Grow as a house or conservatory plant in cool climates. Plant in moist, well-drained soil, in partial shade; keep in a humid atmosphere.
• PROPAGATION By stem cuttings or seed in spring.
• OTHER NAMES *R. amoena*.

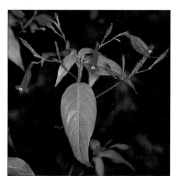

Min. 15°C
(59°F)

HEIGHT
60cm (2ft)
or more

SPREAD
60cm (2ft)
or more

| Leguminosae/ Papilionaceae | FRENCH HONEYSUCKLE |
|---|---|

## HEDYSARUM CORONARIUM

**Habit** Shrub-like, spreading. **Flowers** Small, pea-like, in spikes on sturdy stems, in early summer. Red-purple or carmine-red. **Leaves** Divided into 3–5 pairs of elliptic to rounded leaflets. Mid-green.
• NATIVE HABITAT Grasslands of the W. Mediterranean.
• CULTIVATION Grow in a warm, sheltered site, in well-drained soil. Tolerant of poor, stony soils. Cut back the previous season's growth in spring. Good for Mediterranean borders or gravel plantings.
• PROPAGATION By seed in autumn or spring.

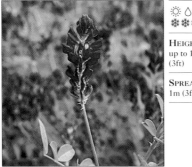

☀ ◊
❄ ❄ ❄

HEIGHT
up to 1m.
(3ft)

SPREAD
1m (3ft)

| Gesneriaceae | |
|---|---|

## COLUMNEA × BANKSII

**Habit** Trailing. **Flowers** Tubular, hooded, to 8cm (3in) long, produced in succession from spring to winter. Brilliant red. **Leaves** Evergreen, fleshy, oval, borne on long, pendent stems. Glossy green above, purplish-red beneath.
• NATIVE HABITAT Garden origin.
• CULTIVATION In cool climates, grow as a house or conservatory plant in moist, fertile soil or compost with bright, indirect light and moderate humidity. Reduce water in winter. Good for hanging baskets.
• PROPAGATION By tip cuttings after flowering.

☀ ◊

Min. 15°C
(59°F)

HEIGHT
90cm (3ft)

SPREAD
indefinite

| Lamiaceae/Labiatae | |
|---|---|

## MONARDA 'Cambridge Scarlet'    ♥

**Habit** Clump- or mound-forming. **Flowers** Small, hooded, in dense, terminal heads, through summer. Rich red. **Leaves** Aromatic, hairy, toothed, oval, triangular or lance-shaped. Mid-green.
• NATIVE HABITAT Garden origin.
• CULTIVATION Grow in moist, fertile soil, in sun or light shade. Suitable for herbaceous borders and herb gardens. The flowers attract bees and other insects. Susceptible to mildew in dry conditions.
• PROPAGATION By division in spring.
• OTHER NAMES M. didyma 'Cambridge Scarlet'.

☀ ◊
❄ ❄ ❄

HEIGHT
1m (3ft)

SPREAD
45cm (18in)

| Scrophulariaceae | CORAL PLANT, FIRECRACKER PLANT |
|---|---|

## RUSSELIA EQUISETIFORMIS    ♥

**Habit** Sub-shrubby, weeping. **Flowers** Tubular, scarlet, in pendent clusters, in summer and autumn. **Leaves** Evergreen, tiny, scale-like, dark green, on slender, green, rush-like stems.
• NATIVE HABITAT Arid areas of Mexico.
• CULTIVATION Grow as a house or conservatory plant in cool climates. Plant in light, well-drained, compost or humus-rich soil, in sun or part-shade. Good for hanging baskets.
• PROPAGATION Stem cuttings or division in spring.
• OTHER NAMES R. juncea.

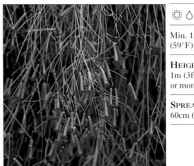

☀ ◊

Min. 15°C
(59°F)

HEIGHT
1m (3ft)
or more

SPREAD
60cm (2ft)

Papaveraceae

## PAPAVER ORIENTALE 'Allegro Viva'

**Habit** Clump-forming. **Flowers** Large, deeply cupped, borne on strong stems, in early summer. Satiny, bright scarlet petals, each with a black-purple blotch at the base. **Leaves** Divided into hairy, toothed, lance-shaped segments, dying back after flowering. Dark grey-green.
• NATIVE HABITAT Garden origin.
• CULTIVATION Grow in moist but well-drained, fertile soil, in sun. May need support. This cultivar is especially valued for the brilliance of its flowers. The leaves die back after flowering

and, as with other oriental poppies, this can leave a gap in the border. Compensate for this by filling in with later-flowering plants to conceal the space. A second flush of flowers can be encouraged by cutting back the old flower stems as soon as the petals have dropped. This particular cultivar makes a spectacular display in a completely red border or as a contrast to white-flowered plants.
• PROPAGATION By root cuttings in winter, or by division in autumn.

HEIGHT
60–75cm
(24–30in)

SPREAD
45cm (18in)

| Campanulaceae | |
|---|---|

## *LOBELIA* × *SPECIOSA* 'Bees' Flame'

*Habit* Clump-forming. *Flowers* 2-lipped, with 3 spreading lower lobes, borne in spikes, from late summer to mid-autumn. Brilliant scarlet. *Leaves* Oblong-oval, mostly basal. Deep bronze-red.
• NATIVE HABITAT Garden origin.
• CULTIVATION Grow in moist, fertile, humus-rich soil, in sun or part-shade. Suitable for waterside plantings and damp borders. In cold areas, pot up over winter and protect from frost in a cold frame. Dislikes cold, wet conditions in winter.
• PROPAGATION By division in spring.

☼ ◊
❄

HEIGHT
1m (3ft)

SPREAD
30cm (1ft)

| Haemodoraceae | RED-AND-GREEN KANGAROO PAW |
|---|---|

## *ANIGOZANTHOS MANGLESII*

*Habit* Vigorous, rhizomatous. *Flowers* Large, tubular, woolly, on slender stems, in spring and early summer. Red-and-green. *Leaves* Linear-lance-shaped, to 40cm (16in) long. Grey-green.
• NATIVE HABITAT W. Australia.
• CULTIVATION Grow in an open, sunny site, in well-drained, peaty or leafy soil. In cool areas, grow in a cool conservatory. Flowers cut and dry well. Ink spot disease may be a problem.
• PROPAGATION By division in spring, or by seed sown fresh in late summer.

☼ ◊ pH
❄

HEIGHT
1m (3ft)

SPREAD
45cm (18in)

| Asteraceae/Compositae | |
|---|---|

## *ACHILLEA* 'Fanal'

*Habit* Mound-forming. *Flowers* Tiny, in large, flat heads, on stiff, leafy stems in summer. Bright red, fading to yellowish-red. *Leaves* Feathery, divided into oblong to lance-shaped segments. Grey-green.
• NATIVE HABITAT Garden origin.
• CULTIVATION Grow in fertile, well-drained soil, in full sun. Divide and replant every third year to maintain vigour. Cut flowers dry well.
• PROPAGATION By division in early spring or autumn and cuttings in summer.
• OTHER NAMES *A.* 'The Beacon'.

☼ ◊
❄ ❄ ❄

HEIGHT
75cm (30in)

SPREAD
60cm (24in)

| Gesneriaceae | |
|---|---|

## *KOHLERIA ERIANTHA*

*Habit* Robust, bushy, with scaly rhizomes. *Flowers* Tubular, borne in nodding clusters, in summer. Bright orange-red, with yellow-spotted lobes. *Leaves* Oval to lance-shaped, borne on hairy stems. Dark green, fringed at the margin with red hairs.
• NATIVE HABITAT Colombia.
• CULTIVATION Grow as a house or conservatory plant in cool climates. Plant in moist but well-drained compost or soil, in sun or semi-shade.
• PROPAGATION By division or seed in spring.

☼ ◊

Min. 15°C
(59°F)

HEIGHT
1m (3ft)

SPREAD
1m (3ft)

| Leguminosae/ Papilionaceae | LIQUORICE |
|---|---|

## GLYCYRRHIZA GLABRA

**Habit** Upright, deep-rooted. **Flowers** Small, pea-like, in short spikes in the leaf axils, on erect stems in late summer. Pale purple-blue and white. **Leaves** Divided into oval, bluish-green leaflets.
• NATIVE HABITAT Dry scrub and damp ditches from the Mediterranean to S.W. Asia.
• CULTIVATION Grow in deep, fertile, moist but well-drained soil, in full sun. Cultivated commercially for its roots (liquorice).
• PROPAGATION By division in spring, or by seed in autumn or spring.

☼ ◊
❀ ❀ ❀

HEIGHT
1.2m (4ft)

SPREAD
1m (3ft)

| Campanulaceae | |
|---|---|

## LOBELIA × GERARDII 'Vedrariensis'

**Habit** Robust, clump-forming. **Flowers** 2-lipped, with 3 spreading lower lobes, borne in spikes, from late summer to mid-autumn. Rich purple. **Leaves** Oval to elliptic, in a basal rosette. Dark green.
• NATIVE HABITAT Garden origin.
• CULTIVATION Grow in moist, fertile, humus-rich soil, in sun or part-shade. Suitable for damp borders but dislikes cold, wet conditions in winter. Provide a deep, dry winter mulch of bracken litter or similar.
• PROPAGATION By division in spring.

☼ ◊
❀ ❀

HEIGHT
1m (3ft)

SPREAD
30cm (1ft)

| Acanthaceae | |
|---|---|

## ACANTHUS HUNGARICUS

**Habit** Densely clump-forming. **Flowers** Funnel-shaped, in spikes, 60–150cm (2–5ft) long, in summer. White or pink-flushed, enclosed in spiny, red-purple bracts. **Leaves** Lance-shaped in outline, deeply lobed. Glossy, dark green.
• NATIVE HABITAT Woods, scrub and rocky hills, in the Balkans, Romania and Greece.
• CULTIVATION Grow in well-drained soil, in full sun.
• PROPAGATION By seed or division in autumn or spring, or by root cuttings in winter.
• OTHER NAMES A. balcanicus, A. longifolius.

☼ ◊
❀ ❀ ❀

HEIGHT
60cm–1m
(2–3ft)

SPREAD
1m (3ft)

| Acanthaceae | |
|---|---|

## *ACANTHUS SPINOSUS*

**Habit** Densely clump-forming. **Flowers** Funnel-shaped, borne freely in spikes, to 1.5m (5ft) long, in summer. White, enclosed in spiny, soft mauve-purple bracts. **Leaves** Lance-shaped in outline, deeply dissected, with scattered spines. Glossy, dark green.

• NATIVE HABITAT Scrub and grassland, E. Mediterranean.

• CULTIVATION Grow in any well-drained soil in full sun. This stately perennial requires plenty of space for its undoubted architectural merits. The leaves are attractive in their own right when the plant is not in flower and are sufficiently spectacular to be allocated a corner where they can be seen to their best advantage. The flower spikes may also be air-dried for winter arrangements.

• PROPAGATION By seed or division in autumn or spring, or by root cuttings in winter.

HEIGHT
1.2m (4ft)

SPREAD
60cm (2ft)
or more

| Scrophulariaceae | THREE BIRDS TOADFLAX |
|---|---|

## LINARIA TRIORNITHOPHORA

**Habit** Upright, clump-forming. **Flowers** Small, snapdragon-like, borne in slender spikes, from mid-to late summer. Purple with yellow throats. **Leaves** Lance-shaped, smooth, borne in whorls of 3–4 along the stems. Grey-green.
• NATIVE HABITAT Scrub and hedgerows, Spain and Portugal.
• CULTIVATION Grow in any well-drained soil, in sun or light shade. May self-seed. Suitable for herbaceous borders and gravel plantings.
• PROPAGATION By seed in autumn or spring.

☼ ◊
❀ ❀

HEIGHT
60cm–1m
(2–3ft)

SPREAD
60cm (2ft)

| Lamiaceae/Labiatae | |
|---|---|

## ORIGANUM LAEVIGATUM ♈
### 'Herrenhausen'

**Habit** Mat-forming, suckering. **Flowers** Tiny, tubular, 2-lipped, in large diffuse, branching sprays, in summer. Lilac-pink. **Leaves** Aromatic, basal, oval to elliptic, slightly leathery. Green, flushed purple when young and in winter.
• NATIVE HABITAT Garden origin.
• CULTIVATION Grow in very well-drained soil in a sunny, sheltered site. Suitable for a border front, a Mediterranean-type border or planting in gravel.
• PROPAGATION By division in spring.

☼ ◊
❀ ❀

HEIGHT
45–70cm
(18–28in)
in flower

SPREAD
20cm (8in)
or more

| Brassicaceae/Cruciferae | |
|---|---|

## ERYSIMUM 'Bowles' Mauve' ♈

**Habit** Bushy, mound-forming. **Flowers** Small, 4-petalled, in dense, rounded, terminal clusters, in spring and summer. Rich mauve. **Leaves** Evergreen, narrowly lance-shaped. Grey-green.
• NATIVE HABITAT Garden origin.
• CULTIVATION Grow in any well-drained soil, including poor soils in full sun. Is often short-lived, so propagate regularly. Excellent for a border, valued for its long flowering period.
• PROPAGATION By softwood cuttings in summer.
• OTHER NAMES *Cheiranthus* 'Bowles' Mauve'.

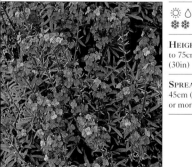

☼ ◊
❀ ❀

HEIGHT
to 75cm
(30in)

SPREAD
45cm (18in)
or more

| Lamiaceae/Labiatae | |
|---|---|

## MONARDA 'Beauty of Cobham' ♈

**Habit** Clump-forming. **Flowers** Small, hooded, in dense, terminal heads, throughout summer. Soft, pale lilac-pink, with dark brown-purple bracts beneath. **Leaves** Aromatic, toothed, oval, triangular or lance-shaped. Purple-tinted, green.
• NATIVE HABITAT Garden origin.
• CULTIVATION Grow in any moist, fertile soil, in sun or light shade. Suitable for herbaceous borders and herb gardens. The flowers attract bees and other insects. Susceptible to powdery mildew.
• PROPAGATION By division in spring.

☼ ◊
❀ ❀ ❀

HEIGHT
1m (3ft)

SPREAD
45cm (18in)

| Ranunculaceae | |
|---|---|

## THALICTRUM AQUILEGIIFOLIUM

**Habit** Dense, clump-forming, slow-growing.
**Flowers** Tiny, in dense, fluffy, terminal sprays,
in summer. Lilac-purple. **Leaves** Smooth, finely
divided, resembling those of maidenhair fern.
Grey-green.
• NATIVE HABITAT Meadows and shady rocks,
from Europe to temperate Asia.
• CULTIVATION Grow in moist, well-drained,
fertile soil, in sun or light, dappled shade.
Provides excellent contrast in a silver border.
• PROPAGATION By seed or division in spring.

☼ ◊
✿ ✿ ✿

HEIGHT
1–1.2m
(3–4ft)

SPREAD
45cm (18in)

| Geraniaceae | |
|---|---|

## GERANIUM SYLVATICUM 'Mayflower' ✿

**Habit** Clump-forming, deep-rooted.
**Flowers** Single, cup-shaped, borne on
branching stems, in profusion in early summer.
Violet-blue with a white centre. **Leaves** Mostly
basal, divided into 7–9 deeply cut and lobed
segments. Mid-green.
• NATIVE HABITAT Garden origin.
• CULTIVATION Grow in fertile, moist but
well-drained soil, in partial shade. Suitable for
borders and wild or woodland gardens.
• PROPAGATION By division in autumn or spring.

☼ ◊
✿ ✿ ✿

HEIGHT
1m (3ft)

SPREAD
60cm (2ft)

| Lamiaceae/Labiatae | WILD BERGAMOT |
|---|---|

## MONARDA FISTULOSA

**Habit** Clump-forming. **Flowers** Small, hooded,
downy, borne in loose, terminal heads, throughout
summer. Soft lilac-purple. **Leaves** Aromatic,
toothed, oval to lance-shaped. Grey-green.
• NATIVE HABITAT Woodland margins and dry
scrub, in Canada, USA and Mexico.
• CULTIVATION Grow in any moist, fertile soil, in
sun or light shade. Suitable for herbaceous borders,
herb and wildflower gardens. The flowers are
attractive to bees and other beneficial insects.
• PROPAGATION By seed or division in spring.

☼ ◊
✿ ✿ ✿

HEIGHT
1.2m (4ft)

SPREAD
45cm (18in)

| Campanulaceae | NETTLE-LEAVED BELLFLOWER |
|---|---|

## CAMPANULA TRACHELIUM

**Habit** Upright. **Flowers** Short-stalked, bell-
shaped, widely spaced on erect stems in mid- to late
summer. Mid-blue to purple-blue. **Leaves** Coarse,
serrated, oval, heart-shaped at base. Mid-green.
• NATIVE HABITAT Woodland margins, hedgerows,
on chalky soils, Europe to N. Africa and Siberia.
• CULTIVATION Tolerates dry shade. Grow in any
moderately fertile, well-drained soil, in sun or part-
shade. Suitable for borders, or for naturalizing in
wild and woodland gardens. May self-seed.
• PROPAGATION Seed or division in autumn or spring

☼ ◊
✿ ✿ ✿

HEIGHT
60cm–1m
(2–3ft)

SPREAD
30cm (1ft)

| Ranunculaceae | |
|---|---|

## CLEMATIS INTEGRIFOLIA

**Habit** Upright or sprawling, sub-shrubby. **Flowers** Single, star- to bell-shaped, nodding, borne singly at the stem tips, in mid-summer. Dark violet or blue, with creamy-white anthers. **Leaves** Entire, lance-shaped, slightly leathery. Mid-green.
• NATIVE HABITAT Grasslands from C. Europe, S.W. Russia, W. and C. Asia.
• CULTIVATION Grow in fertile, moist but well-drained, loamy soil, in sun. Cut old, flowered stems back to 2 basal buds in late winter.
• PROPAGATION Seed in autumn or division in spring.

☼ ◊
❀ ❀ ❀

HEIGHT
75m (30in)

SPREAD
75cm (30in)

| Campanulaceae | |
|---|---|

## CAMPANULA GLOMERATA 'Superba' ♔

**Habit** Vigorous, clump-forming, suckering. **Flowers** Large, bell-shaped, borne in dense, rounded, mainly terminal heads, in summer. Rich purplish-blue. **Leaves** Oval to lance-shaped, scallop-toothed, in basal rosettes and up the stem. Mid-green,
• NATIVE HABITAT Garden origin.
• CULTIVATION Grow in any fertile, well-drained soil, in sun or light shade. Divide and replant regularly to maintain vigour.
• PROPAGATION By division in spring or autumn.

☼ ◊
❀ ❀ ❀

HEIGHT
75cm (30in)

SPREAD
1m (3ft)
or more

| Scrophulariaceae | |
|---|---|

## VERONICA LONGIFOLIA 'Romiley Purple'

**Habit** Clump-forming. **Flowers** Small, funnel-shaped, borne in long, slender spikes, in profusion in summer. Rich purple. **Leaves** Whorled, lance-shaped or narrowly lance-shaped, toothed. Mid-green.
• NATIVE HABITAT Garden origin.
• CULTIVATION Grow in fertile, preferably loamy, well-drained soil, in sun. May need unobtrusive support. A beautiful border perennial; the flowers last quite well when cut.
• PROPAGATION By division in spring or autumn.

☼ ◊
❀ ❀ ❀

HEIGHT
1–1.2m
(3–4ft)

SPREAD
30–60cm
(1–2ft)

| Ranunculaceae | |
|---|---|

## ACONITUM 'Bressingham Spire' ♀

**Habit** Compact, erect, tuberous-rooted.
**Flowers** Large, hooded, helmet-shaped, borne in dense, upright, tapering spires, in summer. Deep violet-blue. **Leaves** Divided, deeply cut. Glossy, dark green.
• NATIVE HABITAT Garden origin.
• CULTIVATION Grow in moist but well-drained, fertile soil, in sun or part-shade. Divide every 2–3 years to maintain vigour. Excellent as part of a herbaceous border. The roots are toxic.
• PROPAGATION By division in autumn.

☀ ◊
❁ ❁ ❁

HEIGHT
to 1m (3ft)

SPREAD
30cm (12in)

| Asteraceae/Compositae | |
|---|---|

## ECHINOPS RITRO 'Veitch's Blue'

**Habit** Upright, clump-forming. **Flowers** Tiny, in tight, globular flower heads, borne on erect, silvery stems, in late summer. Purplish-blue. **Leaves** Sharply divided, firm, leathery, spiny. Green above and white-downy beneath.
• NATIVE HABITAT Garden origin.
• CULTIVATION Grow in well-drained, poor or only moderately fertile soil, in sun. Excellent for a silver border. The flowers dry well if cut before fully open
• PROPAGATION By division in autumn or root cuttings in winter.

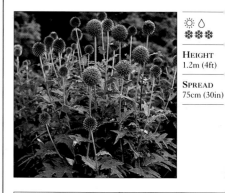

☀ ◊
❁ ❁ ❁

HEIGHT
1.2m (4ft)

SPREAD
75cm (30in)

| Commelinaceae | |
|---|---|

## DICHORISANDRA REGINAE

**Habit** Upright, clump-forming. **Flowers** Small, in dense spikes, from summer to autumn. Purple-blue. **Leaves** Evergreen, large, elliptic. Glossy green, banded and flecked with silver, purple-red beneath.
• NATIVE HABITAT Tropical areas in Peru.
• CULTIVATION In cool climates, grow as a house or conservatory plant in fertile, moist, well-drained soil or compost, in part-shade. Keep humid and water freely when in growth, otherwise moderately.
• PROPAGATION By division in spring, or by stem cuttings in summer.

☀ ◖

Min. 20°C
(68°F)

HEIGHT
60–75cm
(24–30in)

SPREAD
30cm (1ft)

| Campanulaceae | |
|---|---|

## CAMPANULA TRACHELIUM 'Bernice'

**Habit** Upright. **Flowers** Short-stalked, double, narrowly bell-shaped, borne on erect stems in mid- to late summer. Purple-violet. **Leaves** Coarse, serrated, oval, heart-shaped at the base. Mid-green.
• NATIVE HABITAT Garden origin.
• CULTIVATION Tolerates dry shade. Grow in any moderately fertile, well-drained soil, in sun or part-shade. Suitable for borders, or wild and woodland gardens.
• PROPAGATION By division in autumn or spring.

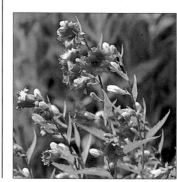

☀ ◊
❁ ❁ ❁

HEIGHT
75cm (30in)

SPREAD
30cm (1ft)

Lamiaceae/Labiatae

## *SALVIA* × *SYLVESTRIS* 'Mainacht'

*Habit* Neat, clump-forming. *Flowers* Small,
2-lipped, borne in dense, upright racemes, in
early to mid-summer. Rich, dark violet-blue with
red-purple bracts. *Leaves* Oblong-lance-shaped,
heart-shaped at the base, wrinkled. Mid-green.
• NATIVE HABITAT Garden origin.
• CULTIVATION Grow in fertile, well-drained soil
in sun. Valued for the fine deep violet-blue of its
flowers, this cultivar associates well with old-
fashioned roses, and *Paeonia officinalis* and
*Papaver orientale* cultivars. It also provides

strong contrast when planted with silver-leaved
plants. If cut back after the first flush of flowers,
it may produce a second, lesser flush later in the
season. Its sturdy habit will require little or no
staking in the second row of a herbaceous border.
It tolerates drought conditions, and the flowers
are excellent for cutting, lasting well in water.
The plant is pleasantly aromatic and attractive
to bees.
• PROPAGATION By division in spring or autumn.
• OTHER NAMES *S.* x *sylvestris* 'May Night'.

HEIGHT
1m (3ft)

SPREAD
45cm (18in)

| Ranunculaceae | |
|---|---|

## *ACONITUM* × *CAMMARUM* 'Bicolor' ♟

**Habit** Erect, tuberous-rooted. **Flowers** Large, hooded, helmet-shaped, borne in short, dense, spikes on upright, sparsely branched stems in summer. Violet-blue and white. **Leaves** Divided, deeply cut. Glossy dark green.
• NATIVE HABITAT Garden origin.
• CULTIVATION Grow in moist but well-drained, fertile soil, in sun or part-shade. The roots are poisonous.
• PROPAGATION By division in autumn. Divide every 2–3 years to maintain vigour.

☀ ◊
❀ ❀ ❀

HEIGHT
1.2m (4ft)

SPREAD
50cm (20in)

| Leguminosae/ Papilionaceae | |
|---|---|

## *GALEGA ORIENTALIS*

**Habit** Vigorous, upright. **Flowers** Small, pea-like, borne in slender, upright spikes above the foliage, in summer. Blue-tinged, violet. **Leaves** Divided, with 4–10 pairs of oval leaflets. Green, tinted with grey.
• NATIVE HABITAT Meadows, scrub, riversides, in the Caucasus.
• CULTIVATION Grow in an open position, in well-drained soil. Needs staking and may spread freely. Suitable for borders and wildflower meadows.
• PROPAGATION By division in winter.

☀ ◊
❀ ❀ ❀

HEIGHT
1.2m (4ft)

SPREAD
60cm (2ft)

| Leguminosae/ Papilionaceae | BLUE FALSE INDIGO |
|---|---|

## *BAPTISIA AUSTRALIS* ♟

**Habit** Upright, deep-rooted. **Flowers** Small, pea-like, in erect, open spikes in early or mid-summer. Indigo-blue. **Leaves** Divided into 3 oval leaflets. Bright blue-green, borne on grey-green stems.
• NATIVE HABITAT Usually on damp soils, by riverbanks, in eastern USA.
• CULTIVATION Grow in deep, fertile, moist but well-drained soil in full sun. Has a long season of interest, being beautiful in both foliage and flower.
• PROPAGATION By seed in autumn, or division in spring.

☀ ◊
❀ ❀ ❀

HEIGHT
75cm (30in) or more

SPREAD
60cm (2ft)

Plumbaginaceae

## LIMONIUM PLATYPHYLLUM

**Habit** Clump-forming. **Flowers** Tiny, borne in diffuse, airy panicles on wiry, branching stems, in late summer. Pale violet. **Leaves** Leathery, spoon-shaped to long-elliptic, in basal rosettes. Dark green.
• NATIVE HABITAT Dry grassland, from S.E. and C. Europe to S. Russia.
• CULTIVATION Grow in well-drained, preferably sandy soil, in full sun. Flowers are good for cutting and drying. Cut before fully open and hang upside down in a cool place with plenty of ventilation. An extremely useful foil in a herbaceous or mixed border where its "fluffy" flower heads contrast well with more solid neighbours. It also associates well with silver-leaved artemisias. This plant has a general lightening effect and its basal rosette of dark green leaves is distinctive even when it is out of flower.
• PROPAGATION By seed or division in spring or root cuttings in winter.
• OTHER NAMES *L. latifolium.*

☼ ◌
✲ ✲ ✲

HEIGHT
Up to 80cm
(32in)

SPREAD
45cm (18in)

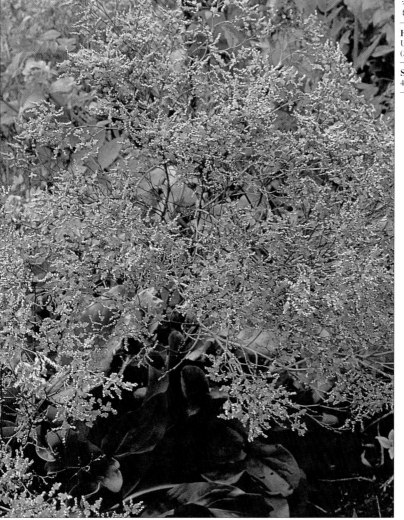

| Geraniaceae | |
|---|---|

### GERANIUM PRATENSE
## 'Mrs Kendall Clark' ♀

**Habit** Vigorous, clump-forming. **Flowers** Large, saucer-shaped, borne in clusters above the foliage, in summer. Light violet-blue. **Leaves** Deeply divided into 7 or 9 narrow, toothed and divided segments. Dark green.
• NATIVE HABITAT Garden origin.
• CULTIVATION Grow in well-drained, fertile soil, in light shade or full sun. Excellent in cottage gardens and borders where it associates well with old roses.
• PROPAGATION By division in autumn or spring.

☀ ◌
❋ ❋ ❋

HEIGHT
60cm (24in)
or more

SPREAD
60cm (24in)

| Apiaceae/Umbelliferae | |
|---|---|

### ERYNGIUM ALPINUM ♀

**Habit** Upright, rosette-forming. **Flowers** Tiny, in dense, conical heads amidst long, spiny, blue-purple bracts, borne on stout stems in late summer. Purple-blue. **Leaves** Deeply toothed, oval to triangular, in basal rosettes, heart-shaped at the base.
• NATIVE HABITAT Sub-alpine meadows, usually on limestone, in the mountains of Europe.
• CULTIVATION Grow in moderately fertile, freely draining soil, in full sun. Flowers dry well.
• PROPAGATION By seed in autumn, by division in spring, or by root cuttings in winter.

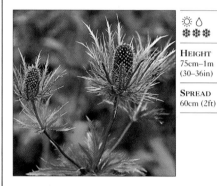

☀ ◌
❋ ❋ ❋

HEIGHT
75cm–1m
(30–36in)

SPREAD
60cm (2ft)

| Phormiaceae/Liliaceae | FLAX LILY |
|---|---|

### DIANELLA TASMANICA

**Habit** Upright, clump-forming, fibrous-rooted. **Flowers** Small, nodding, star-shaped, borne in loose, branching panicles, in summer. Bright blue. **Fruits** Deep blue berries in autumn. **Leaves** Evergreen, stiff, strap-shaped. Dark green.
• NATIVE HABITAT Cool, moist forests of Tasmania and S.E. Australia.
• CULTIVATION Grow in a sheltered site, in cool, moist but well-drained, neutral to acid, peaty soil in semi-shade, or in sun where soil stays reliably moist.
• PROPAGATION By division or seed in spring.

☀ ◌
❋ ❋

HEIGHT
1.2m (4ft)

SPREAD
50cm (20in)

| Apiaceae/Umbelliferae | |
|---|---|

### ERYNGIUM × TRIPARTITUM ♀

**Habit** Upright, rosette-forming. **Flowers** Tiny, in dense, rounded-conical heads, with a star of slender bracts beneath, borne on wiry, blue-tinted stems, in late summer and autumn. Metallic blue. **Leaves** Coarsely toothed, in basal rosettes. Grey-green.
• NATIVE HABITAT Dry, stony habitats, probably around the Mediterranean.
• CULTIVATION Grow in moderately fertile, freely draining soil, in full sun. Flowers dry well.
• PROPAGATION By division in spring, or by root cuttings in winter.

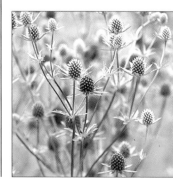

☀ ◌
❋ ❋ ❋

HEIGHT
1–1.2m
(3–4ft)

SPREAD
50cm (20in)

Apiaceae/Umbelliferae

## *ERYNGIUM* × *OLIVERIANUM*

**Habit** Upright. **Flowers** Tiny, in large, rounded, cylindrical heads, with spiny, narrow, silvery bracts, in late summer. Steel-blue to lavender-blue. **Leaves** Oval, 3-lobed or 5-parted, spiny-toothed, heart-shaped at the base and mostly basal. Mid-green.

• NATIVE HABITAT Garden origin.
• CULTIVATION Grow in moderately fertile, freely draining soil, in full sun. This is one of the most sturdy of the sea hollies for the middle of a mixed or herbaceous border, especially one with a silver- or grey-leaved theme. Site where the attractive basal leaves will not be obscured by neighbouring plants. The stiff, silvery ruffs contrast with the large metallic blue cones to give this plant considerable architectural status. Hang the cut flowers upside down to dry in a cool, airy place.
• PROPAGATION By division in spring, or by root cuttings in winter.

HEIGHT
60cm–1m
(2–3ft)
or more

SPREAD
45–60cm
(18–24in)

| Alliaceae/Liliaceae | |
| --- | --- |

## *AGAPANTHUS* 'Blue Giant'

*Habit* Clump-forming, fleshy-rooted. *Flowers* Small, tubular-bell-shaped, in large, rounded, heads, borne on sturdy, upright stems, in late summer. Rich purple-blue. *Leaves* Long, narrow, in basal clumps. Green.
• NATIVE HABITAT Garden origin.
• CULTIVATION Grow in moist but well-drained soil, in a warm, sunny site. Mulch the crowns with dry bracken litter or similar in winter.
• PROPAGATION By careful division of established clumps in spring.

☼ ◊
❋ ❋

HEIGHT
1m (3ft)

SPREAD
50cm (20in)

| Alliaceae/Liliaceae | |
| --- | --- |

## *AGAPANTHUS* 'Dorothy Palmer'

*Habit* Clump-forming, fleshy-rooted. *Flowers* Small, tubular-bell-shaped, in large, rounded, heads, borne on sturdy, upright stems, in late summer. Rich blue. *Leaves* Long, narrow, in basal clumps. Grey-green.
• NATIVE HABITAT Garden origin.
• CULTIVATION Grow in moist but well-drained soil, in a warm, sunny site. Mulch the crowns with dry bracken litter or similar in winter.
• PROPAGATION By careful division of established clumps in spring.

☼ ◊
❋ ❋

HEIGHT
1m (3ft)

SPREAD
50cm (20in)

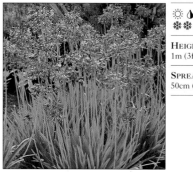

| Ranunculaceae | |
| --- | --- |

## *CLEMATIS HERACLEIFOLIA* ♥ var. *DAVIDIANA* 'Wyevale'

*Habit* Upright, woody-based. *Flowers* Scented, small, tubular, with reflexed petal tips, borne in clusters in summer. Pale sky-blue. *Leaves* Divided into irregularly serrated leaflets. Dark green.
• NATIVE HABITAT Garden origin.
• CULTIVATION Grow in fertile, moist, well-drained, loamy soil in sun or dappled shade. Cut flowered stems back to 2 basal buds in late winter. Mulch with well-rotted organic matter.
• PROPAGATION By division in spring.

☼ ◊
❋ ❋ ❋

HEIGHT
1m (3ft)

SPREAD
75cm (30in)

| Campanulaceae | |
| --- | --- |

## *CAMPANULA PERSICIFOLIA* 'Telham Beauty'

*Habit* Upright, rosette-forming. *Flowers* Large, nodding, bell-shaped, in slender, upright spikes in summer. Soft, clear blue. *Leaves* Lance-shaped to narrowly oval, mostly in basal rosettes, but with scattered, narrow stem leaves. Bright green.
• NATIVE HABITAT Garden origin.
• CULTIVATION Grow in fertile, moist, well-drained soil, in sun. Young leaves are prone to attack by slugs. The cut flowers last reasonably well in water.
• PROPAGATION By division in spring or autumn.

☼ ◊
❋ ❋ ❋

HEIGHT
1m (3ft)

SPREAD
30cm (1ft)

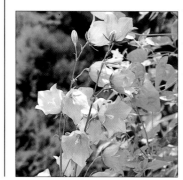

| Asteraceae/Compositae | CHICORY |
|---|---|

### *CICHORIUM INTYBUS* ♥

**Habit** Clump-forming. **Flowers** Daisy-like, open
in the mornings and closing at midday, borne at the
ends of willowy stems, in summer. Bright blue.
**Leaves** Pinnately lobed to deeply toothed, broadly
lance-shaped, mostly basal. Light green.
• NATIVE HABITAT Rough grassland and waste
ground, in Europe, W. Asia, N. Africa.
• CULTIVATION Grow in moderately fertile, well-
drained, preferably limy soil, in full sun. Good for
borders and wildflower gardens. May self-seed.
• PROPAGATION By seed in autumn or spring.

☀ ◐
❀ ❀ ❀

**HEIGHT**
1.2m (4ft)

**SPREAD**
45cm (18in)

| Papaveraceae | BLUE POPPY |
|---|---|

### *MECONOPSIS BETONICIFOLIA* ♥

**Habit** Erect, clump-forming. **Flowers** Large,
poppy-like, borne in pendent, few-flowered clusters,
on sturdy, leafy stems in early summer. Blue.
**Leaves** Erect, toothed and hairy, oblong, slightly
heart-shaped at the base, mostly basal. Mid-green.
• NATIVE HABITAT Damp, alpine meadows in China.
• CULTIVATION Grow in a cool, shaded, sheltered
site, in moist, leafy, acid soil. Tolerates dappled sun
in cool, damp climates. Will not thrive in warm, dry
climates. Suited to a peat bed or woodland garden.
• PROPAGATION By fresh seed in late summer.

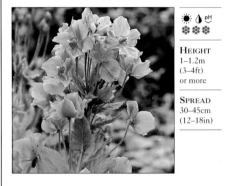

☀ ◐ pH
❀ ❀ ❀

**HEIGHT**
1–1.2m
(3–4ft)
or more

**SPREAD**
30–45cm
(12–18in)

| Papaveraceae |  |
|---|---|

### *MECONOPSIS GRANDIS* 'Branklyn'

**Habit** Erect, clump-forming. **Flowers** Large,
pendent, poppy-like, on sturdy stems in early
summer. Blue. **Leaves** Erect, oblong, slightly
toothed and hairy, mostly in basal clumps. Mid-
green.
• NATIVE HABITAT Garden origin.
• CULTIVATION Grow in a cool, shaded, sheltered
site, in moist, leafy, acid soil. Tolerates dappled sun
in cool, damp climates. Will not thrive in warm, dry
climates. Suited to a peat bed or woodland garden.
• PROPAGATION By division after flowering.

☀ ◐ pH
❀ ❀ ❀

**HEIGHT**
1–1.2m
(3–4ft)
or more

**SPREAD**
30–45cm
(12–18in)

| Lamiaceae/Labiatae |  |
|---|---|

### *SALVIA PATENS* 'Cambridge Blue' ♥

**Habit** Upright, branching, compact. **Flowers**
Hooded, tubular, 2-lipped, borne in whorls in
long, spike-like heads, in late summer. Pale blue.
**Leaves** Sticky-hairy, oval to diamond-shaped.
Mid-green.
• NATIVE HABITAT Garden origin.
• CULTIVATION Grow in well-drained soil, in full
sun. Excellent for borders, bedding and patio tubs.
Overwinter young plants in frost-free conditions.
• PROPAGATION By seed in spring or by softwood
cuttings in mid-summer.

☀ ◐
❀

**HEIGHT**
45–60cm
(18–24in)

**SPREAD**
45cm (18in)

Alliaceae/Liliaceae

## *AGAPANTHUS PRAECOX* subsp. *ORIENTALIS*

***Habit*** Clump-forming. ***Flowers*** Small, tubular-bell-shaped, borne in rounded heads, on sturdy stems, in late summer. Sky-blue. ***Leaves*** Almost evergreen, fleshy, broadly lance-shaped, in basal clumps. Dark green.

• NATIVE HABITAT South Africa.
• CULTIVATION Grow in moist but well-drained soil, in a warm, sunny site. The very striking late-summer flower heads make the entire genus *Agapanthus* extremely useful at a time when borders are beginning to slow down. They require generous provision of moisture. In frost-prone areas, plants can be grown in large pots or tubs and left over winter in a cool greenhouse or conservatory; during the warm summer months they can be moved outdoors again to decorate a courtyard or patio. The seed heads dry well for winter decoration.
• PROPAGATION By careful division of established clumps in spring, or by seed in autumn or spring.
• OTHER NAMES *A. orientalis.*

☼ ◐
❄

**HEIGHT**
1m (3ft)

**SPREAD**
50cm (20in)

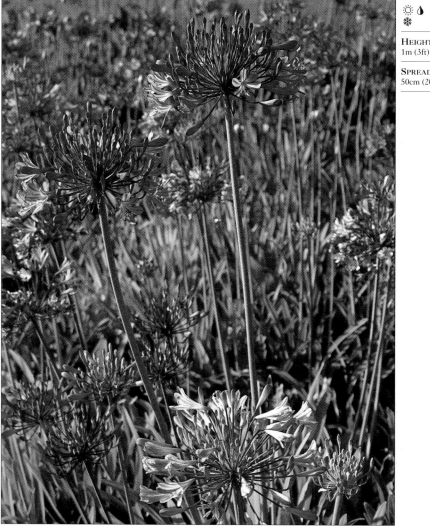

| Boraginaceae | HIMALAYAN HOUND'S TONGUE |
| --- | --- |

## CYNOGLOSSUM NERVOSUM

**Habit** Clump-forming. **Flowers** Small, forget-me-not-like, borne in terminal, branching cymes, in early summer. Bright blue. **Leaves** Oval to oblong basal leaves, with narrower stem leaves. Mid-green.
• NATIVE HABITAT Grassy areas in the Himalayas.
• CULTIVATION Grow in sun, in moist but well-drained, not too fertile soil. Plants become lax and leafy in fertile soils.
• PROPAGATION By division in spring, or by seed in autumn or spring.

HEIGHT
75cm (30in)

SPREAD
50cm (20in)

| Boraginaceae | |
| --- | --- |

## ANCHUSA AZUREA 'Loddon Royalist'

**Habit** Upright, clump-forming. **Flowers** Small, forget-me-not-like, borne in dense, branching spikes, on upright stems, in early summer. Intense deep blue. **Leaves** Hairy, coarse, lance-shaped, mostly basal. Mid-green.
• NATIVE HABITAT Garden origin.
• CULTIVATION Grow in deep, fertile, moist but well-drained soil, in sun. May need unobtrusive staking. Is often short-lived, so propagate regularly. Much-valued for its intense blue flowers.
• PROPAGATION By root cuttings in winter.

HEIGHT
1.2m (4ft)

SPREAD
60cm (2ft)

| Asteraceae/Compositae | |
| --- | --- |

## ARTEMISIA ALBA 'Canescens'

**Habit** Upright, bushy. **Flowers** Tiny, insignificant, in narrow spikes, in summer. Greyish-yellow. **Leaves** Semi-evergreen, finely divided into slender, delicate, curling segments. Ash-grey.
• NATIVE HABITAT Origin uncertain.
• CULTIVATION Grow in an open, sunny site, in well-drained soil. Cut back in spring for best foliage effects. Indispensable at the front of a silver border and cut stems are attractive in floral arrangements.
• PROPAGATION By division in spring or autumn.

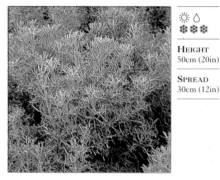

HEIGHT
50cm (20in)

SPREAD
30cm (12in)

| Asteraceae/Compositae | |
| --- | --- |

## ARTEMISIA LUDOVICIANA 'Silver Queen'

**Habit** Upright, bushy, stoloniferous. **Flowers** Tiny, in slender plumes, in summer. Greyish-yellow. **Leaves** Evergreen, entire and lance-shaped, sometimes jaggedly toothed, densely hairy. Silvery-white.
• NATIVE HABITAT Garden origin.
• CULTIVATION Grow in an open, sunny site, in well-drained soil. Cut back in spring for best foliage effects. Indispensable in a silver border.
• PROPAGATION By division in spring or autumn.

HEIGHT
75-90cm
(30–36in)

SPREAD
60cm (24in)

| Apiaceae/Umbelliferae | |
|---|---|

## *ASTRANTIA MAJOR* 'Sunningdale Variegated'  ♈

**Habit** Clump-forming. **Flowers** A dome of tiny greenish-pink florets, with a star-shaped collar of papery white, pink and green bracts beneath, borne throughout summer and autumn. **Leaves** Divided into 3–5 coarsely toothed lobes. Mid-green, heavily variegated with pale yellow and cream.
• NATIVE HABITAT Garden origin.
• CULTIVATION Grow in any fertile, well-drained soil in sun. Flowers are good for cutting and drying.
• PROPAGATION By division in spring.

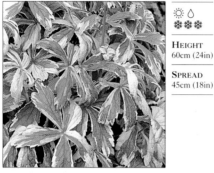

☼ ◊
❉ ❉ ❉

HEIGHT
60cm (24in)

SPREAD
45cm (18in)

| Polygonaceae | |
|---|---|

## *RHEUM ALEXANDRAE*

**Habit** Clump-forming. **Flowers** Small, borne in upright panicles, in early summer. Creamy-white, almost obscured by a large, yellow-green bract. **Leaves** Large, oval-oblong, heart-shaped at the base, in neat, basal rosettes. Glossy, dark green.
• NATIVE HABITAT Marshes, streamsides, W. China.
• CULTIVATION Grow in moist but well-drained, fertile soil, in full sun. An unusual, very ornamental perennial for the border, related to edible rhubarb.
• PROPAGATION By division in spring, or by seed in autumn.

☼ ◊
❉ ❉ ❉

HEIGHT
1m (3ft)

SPREAD
60cm (2ft)

| Lamiaceae/Labiatae | |
|---|---|

## *NEPETA GOVANIANA*

**Habit** Upright, much-branched. **Flowers** Small, long-tubed, 2-lipped, often paired, borne in open spikes over many weeks from mid- to late summer. Light yellow. **Leaves** Aromatic, pointed, oval to elliptic. Grey-green.
• NATIVE HABITAT Open woodland, Himalayas.
• CULTIVATION Grow in moist, well-drained, fertile soil, in a cool position, in sun or dappled shade. A graceful, elegant perennial for herbaceous borders.
• PROPAGATION By division in spring, stem tip cuttings in summer, or seed in autumn.

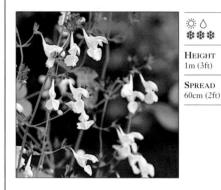

☼ ◊
❉ ❉ ❉

HEIGHT
1m (3ft)

SPREAD
60cm (2ft)

| Haemodoraceae | YELLOW KANGAROO PAW |
|---|---|

## *ANIGOZANTHOS FLAVIDUS*

**Habit** Vigorous, rhizomatous. **Flowers** Large, tubular, woolly, on sturdy stems, in spring to early summer. Yellow-green, sometimes red-flushed. **Leaves** Long, linear-lance-shaped. Mid-green.
• NATIVE HABITAT W. Australia.
• CULTIVATION Grow in an open, sunny site, in well-drained, peaty soil. In cold climates, grow in a cool conservatory. Flowers are excellent for cutting and drying. Ink-spot disease may be a problem.
• PROPAGATION By division in spring, or by seed sown fresh in late summer.

☼ ◊ pH
❉

HEIGHT
1.2m (4ft)

SPREAD
45cm (18in)

| Dipsacaceae | |
| --- | --- |

## SCABIOSA COLUMBARIA var. OCHROLEUCA

**Habit** Clump-forming. **Flowers** Borne on strong, wiry stems, in summer. Pale yellow petals around a domed centre. **Leaves** Lower leaves lance-shaped, toothed stem leaves pinnately divided. Grey-green.
• NATIVE HABITAT Garden origin.
• CULTIVATION Grow in moderately fertile, well-drained soil, in full sun. Excellent for cutting. Suited to herbaceous borders or cottage gardens.
• PROPAGATION By seed or division in spring or autumn.
• OTHER NAMES *S. ochroleuca.*

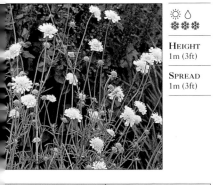

☼ ◊
❀ ❀ ❀

**HEIGHT**
1m (3ft)

**SPREAD**
1m (3ft)

| Scrophulariaceae | YELLOW FOXGLOVE |
| --- | --- |

## DIGITALIS GRANDIFLORA

**Habit** Clump-forming. **Flowers** Tubular, 2-lipped, in open, upright spikes from early to mid-summer. Pale yellow, veined brown. **Leaves** Evergreen, oval-oblong, veined and in basal rosettes. Mid-green, usually glossy.
• NATIVE HABITAT Woods and by streams, C. Europe.
• CULTIVATION Grows best in moist, well-drained soil in dappled shade but tolerates sun. Excellent for a herbaceous border or woodland garden.
• PROPAGATION By seed in spring.
• OTHER NAMES *D. ambigua.*

☀ ◊
❀ ❀ ❀

**HEIGHT**
75–90cm
(30–36in)

**SPREAD**
30cm (12in)

| Scrophulariaceae | |
| --- | --- |

## VERBASCUM CHAIXII 'Gainsborough' ♈

**Habit** Upright, rosette-forming. **Flowers** Small, 5-lobed, in tall, branching racemes, throughout summer. Pale sulphur-yellow. **Leaves** Semi-evergreen, oval, mostly in basal rosettes, but with smaller, narrower stem leaves. Grey-green.
• NATIVE HABITAT Garden origin.
• CULTIVATION Grow in fertile, well-drained soil, in an open, sunny site. Is short-lived, so propagate regularly. A beautiful, long-flowering specimen for herbaceous borders and gravel plantings.
• PROPAGATION By root cuttings in winter.

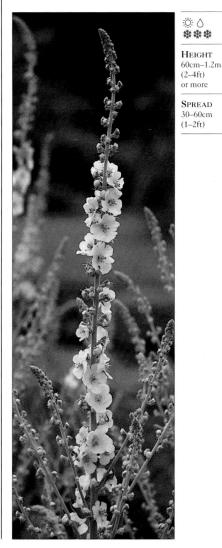

☼ ◊
❀ ❀ ❀

**HEIGHT**
60cm–1.2m
(2–4ft)
or more

**SPREAD**
30–60cm
(1–2ft)

| Ranunculaceae | |
|---|---|

### THALICTRUM LUCIDUM

**Habit** Dense, clump-forming. **Flowers** Tiny, in loose, fluffy, terminal sprays, in summer. Greenish-yellow. **Leaves** Finely divided into narrowly oblong leaflets, with linear stem leaves. Smooth, glossy green.
• NATIVE HABITAT Meadows, ditches and marshy habitats, from Europe to temperate Asia.
• CULTIVATION Grow in moist, but well-drained, fertile soil, in sun or light, dappled shade. Ideal for borders or for a damp site such as by water.
• PROPAGATION By seed or division in spring.

☀ ◊
❀ ❀ ❀

HEIGHT
1–1.2m
(3–4ft)

SPREAD
50cm (20in)

| Asteraceae/Compositae | |
|---|---|

### ARGYRANTHEMUM 🏆
### 'Jamaica Primrose'

**Habit** Bushy, woody-based. **Flowers** Large, daisy-like, on slender stems through summer. Soft yellow. **Leaves** Evergreen, fern-like. Pale green.
• NATIVE HABITAT Garden origin.
• CULTIVATION Grow in a warm, sunny site, in moderately fertile, well-drained soil.
• PROPAGATION By stem cuttings in early autumn; overwinter young plants under glass, in cool areas.
• OTHER NAMES *A. frutescens* 'Jamaica Primrose', *Chrysanthemum frutescens* 'Jamaica Primrose'.

☀ ◊
❄

HEIGHT
1m (3ft)

SPREAD
1m (3ft)

| Leguminosae/ Papilionaceae | |
|---|---|

### LUPINUS 'Chandelier'

**Habit** Clump-forming. **Flowers** Small, pea-like, in dense, terminal spires in early summer. Yellow. **Leaves** Palmate, deeply divided into oval to lance-shaped leaflets. Dark blue-green.
• NATIVE HABITAT Garden origin.
• CULTIVATION Grows best in well-drained, sandy, preferably slightly acid soils. Young foliage is very susceptible to slugs. Dead-head to help maintain vigour.
• PROPAGATION By cuttings of non-flowering sideshoots in spring or early summer.

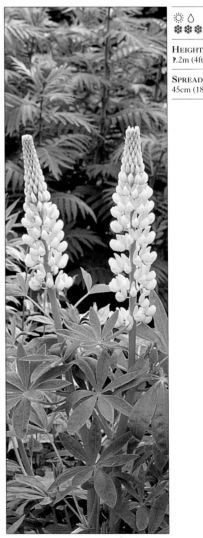

☀ ◊
❀ ❀ ❀

HEIGHT
1.2m (4ft)

SPREAD
45cm (18in

| Ranunculaceae | WOLF'S BANE |
|---|---|

## *ACONITUM LYCOCTONUM* subsp. *VULPARIA*

*Habit* Erect, fibrous-rooted. *Flowers* Narrow, hooded, in short spikes on upright, sparsely branched stems in summer. Pale buff-yellow.
*Leaves* Divided, deeply cut. Glossy, dark green.
• NATIVE HABITAT Meadows in Europe and E. Asia.
• CULTIVATION Grow in moist, but well-drained, fertile soil, in part-shade. Needs staking. Roots are toxic. Divide every 2–3 years to maintain vigour.
• PROPAGATION By seed or division in autumn.
• OTHER NAMES *A. vulparia.*

HEIGHT
1–1.2m
(3–4ft)

SPREAD
30–60cm
(1–2ft))

| Gentianaceae | GREAT YELLOW GENTIAN |
|---|---|

## *GENTIANA LUTEA*

*Habit* Upright. *Flowers* Small, short-tubed, star-shaped, borne in summer in the upper leaf axils in dense, whorled clusters with cupped, green bracts beneath. Yellow. *Leaves* Large, lance-shaped to elliptic; upper leaves clasp the stem. Bluish-green.
• NATIVE HABITAT Alpine meadows and woodland margins in the mountains of Europe.
• CULTIVATION Grow in deep, fertile, moist but well-drained soil, in sun. A stately perennial for herbaceous borders.
• PROPAGATION Division in spring; seed in autumn.

HEIGHT
1–1.2m
(3–4ft)

SPREAD
60cm (2ft)

| Asteraceae/Compositae |
|---|

## *ANTHEMIS TINCTORIA* 'E. C. Buxton'

*Habit* Clump-forming. *Flowers* Large, single, daisy-like, borne singly on slender, sturdy stems and produced in profusion during summer. Pale lemon-yellow. *Leaves* Fern-like, finely divided into narrow segments. Dark.green.
• NATIVE HABITAT Garden origin.
• CULTIVATION Grow in well-drained soil, in full sun. Cut flowers last well in water. Cut back hard immediately after flowering to maintain vigour.
• PROPAGATION By basal cuttings in spring or late summer.

HEIGHT
1m (3ft)

SPREAD
1m (3ft)

| Primulaceae | GARDEN LOOSESTRIFE |
|---|---|

## *LYSIMACHIA PUNCTATA*

*Habit* Upright, rhizomatous. *Flowers* Small, star-shaped, borne in whorls at the ends of upright stems, over long periods in summer. Bright yellow. *Leaves* Lance-shaped to elliptic, opposite or in whorls of 3–4. Mid-green.
• NATIVE HABITAT Ditches, marshes and riversides, from S.E. and C. Europe to Turkey.
• CULTIVATION Grow in moist, fertile soil in part-shade. *L. punctata* is a long-lived perennial that is valued for its strongly upright habit and long flowering season. It can be invasive, since it spreads widely by means of rhizomes. It is ideal for plantings in broad drifts to give strong colour in damp areas of the wild garden or in informal plantings by the sides of pools or streams. In a damp border, if necessary, control spread by digging out excess growth from the margins of the clumps.
• PROPAGATION By seed or division in spring or autumn.

☼ ◑
❀ ❀ ❀

**HEIGHT**
75cm–1m
(2½–3ft)

**SPREAD**
60cm (2ft)

| Euphorbiaceae | |
|---|---|

## *EUPHORBIA SIKKIMENSIS*

***Habit*** Clump-forming, rhizomatous. ***Flowers***
Small, surrounded by large, rounded, yellow bracts,
in terminal clusters, in early or mid-summer.
***Leaves*** Lance-shaped, smooth. Green, deep pink
at base and margins, with a white, pink-tinted
midrib, on reddish stems.
• NATIVE HABITAT Woodland clearings, Himalayas.
• CULTIVATION Grow in fertile, humus-rich, moist
or wet soil, in sun or light dappled shade.
• PROPAGATION By seed or division in spring or early
autumn, or by basal cuttings in spring or summer.

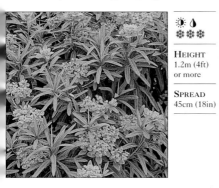

☀ ◐
❀ ❀ ❀

**HEIGHT**
1.2m (4ft)
or more

**SPREAD**
45cm (18in)

| Euphorbiaceae | |
|---|---|

## *EUPHORBIA PALUSTRIS* ♔

***Habit*** Upright, bushy, rhizomatous. ***Flowers***
Small, but surrounded by bright lime-yellow bracts,
borne in terminal clusters from spring to late
summer. ***Leaves*** Smooth, oblong to lance-shaped.
Yellowish-green, yellow and orange in autumn.
• NATIVE HABITAT Damp areas, Europe, Caucasus.
• CULTIVATION Grow in fertile, humus-rich, moist
or wet soil, in sun or dappled shade. Good for damp
borders, waterside plantings or woodland gardens.
• PROPAGATION By seed or division in spring or
early autumn; by basal cuttings in spring or summer.

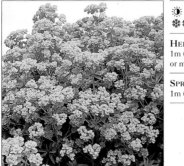

☀ ◐
❀ ❀ ❀

**HEIGHT**
1m (3ft)
or more

**SPREAD**
1m (3ft)

| Asteraceae/Compositae | |
|---|---|

## *SOLIDAGO* 'Goldenmosa' ♔

***Habit*** Vigorous, clump-forming. ***Flowers*** Tiny,
mimosa-like, borne in dense, clustered, branching
heads, on upright stems, in late summer and
autumn. Bright golden-yellow. ***Leaves*** Toothed,
hairy, lance-shaped. Yellowish-green.
• NATIVE HABITAT Garden origin.
• CULTIVATION Grow in any well-drained soil,
including poor soils, in sun. Good for cutting, the
bright flowers are much valued in a late
summer border.
• PROPAGATION By division in spring.

☀ ◊
❀ ❀ ❀

**HEIGHT**
1m (3ft)

**SPREAD**
60cm (2ft)

| Lamiaceae/Labiatae | |
|---|---|

## *PHLOMIS RUSSELIANA* ♈

*Habit* Mound-forming. *Flowers* Hooded, tubular, 2-lipped, borne in whorls, on stout stems in summer. Pale creamy-yellow. *Leaves* Evergreen, coarse, hairy, broadly oval, and heart-shaped at the base. Sage-green.
• NATIVE HABITAT Scrub and woodland in Turkey.
• CULTIVATION Grow in any moderately fertile, well-drained soil, in sun. Makes excellent, weed-smothering ground cover. The dried flower stems are persistent and attractive in winter. May self-seed.
• PROPAGATION Seed in autumn; division in spring.

☼ ◊
❄ ❄ ❄

HEIGHT
1m (3ft)

SPREAD
60cm (2ft)
or more

| Leguminosae/<br>Papilionaceae | |
|---|---|

## *THERMOPSIS MONTANA*

*Habit* Upright, rhizomatous, clump-forming. *Flowers* Small, pea-like, in erect, open, lupin-like spikes, during summer. Bright or pale yellow. *Leaves* Divided into 3 broadly oval to lance-shaped leaflets. Dark green.
• NATIVE HABITAT Rockies, North America.
• CULTIVATION Grow in light, well-drained, fertile soil, in sun or dappled shade. May spread rapidly.
• PROPAGATION By seed in autumn; division in spring.
• OTHER NAMES *T. rhombifolia.*

☼ ◊
❄ ❄ ❄

HEIGHT
60cm–1m
(2–3ft)

SPREAD
60cm (2ft)
or more

| Asteraceae/Compositae | |
|---|---|

## *INULA HOOKERI*

*Habit* Clump-forming. *Flowers* Slightly scented, daisy-like, with very slender, greenish-yellow ray florets and a golden-yellow disc, borne on strong, slender, leafy stems, in late summer. *Leaves* Coarse, hairy, elliptic to lance-shaped. Mid-green.
• NATIVE HABITAT Mountain scrub, Himalayas.
• CULTIVATION Grow in moist but well-drained soil, in sun or light shade. May spread rapidly. Suitable for borders and wild or woodland gardens.
• PROPAGATION By seed or division in spring or autumn.

☼ ◊
❄ ❄ ❄

HEIGHT
75cm (30in)

SPREAD
45cm (18in)

| Asteraceae/Compositae | |
|---|---|

## *CENTAUREA MACROCEPHALA*

*Habit* Robust, clump-forming. *Flowers* Large, thistle-like, on leafy stems, in summer. Bright yellow, enclosed in silvery-brown bracts. *Leaves* Stalkless, lance-shaped, slightly hairy. Mid-green.
• NATIVE HABITAT Sub-alpine meadows in the Caucasus and N.E. Turkey.
• CULTIVATION Grow in fertile, moist, well-drained soil in full sun. Excellent for a summer border or cottage garden.
• PROPAGATION By seed or division in spring or autumn.

☼ ◊
❄ ❄ ❄

HEIGHT
1m (3ft)

SPREAD
60cm (2ft)

Asteraceae/Compositae

## *RUDBECKIA FULGIDA* var. *SULLIVANTII* 'Goldsturm'

*Habit* Upright, clump-forming. *Flowers* Large, daisy-like, with narrow, rich golden-yellow ray florets and a conical black centre, borne singly on strong stems, in late summer and autumn.
*Leaves* Coarse, rough-textured, oval to lance-shaped. Mid-green.
• NATIVE HABITAT Garden origin.
• CULTIVATION Grow in any moist but well-drained soil, in sun or light shade. Valued for its strongly upright form and the prolific production of brilliantly coloured flowers that are borne well above the substantial clumps of foliage. It has a long flowering period and is an invaluable addition to the late summer border, especially when planted in bold drifts. The cut flowers last reasonably well in water.
• PROPAGATION By division in spring.
• OTHER NAMES *R. fulgida* 'Goldsturm'.

HEIGHT
75cm (30in)

SPREAD
30cm (12in)
or more

| Scrophulariaceae | DARK MULLEIN |
|---|---|

## VERBASCUM NIGRUM ♀

**Habit** Upright, clump-forming. **Flowers** Small, 5-lobed, in narrow spikes, from summer to autumn. Golden-yellow, purple-centred. **Leaves** Semi-evergreen, oblong. Grey-green, downy beneath.
• NATIVE HABITAT Grassland and rocky places, W. Europe to the Caucasus and Siberia.
• CULTIVATION Grow in fertile, well-drained soil, in an open, sunny site. Suitable for borders, gravel plantings and wildflower gardens.
• PROPAGATION By seed in spring or late summer, or by root cuttings in winter.

☼ ◊
❀ ❀ ❀

HEIGHT
60cm–1m
(2–3ft) or
more

SPREAD
60cm (2ft)

| Asteraceae/Compositae | |
|---|---|

## SOLIDAGO 'Laurin'

**Habit** Compact, clump-forming. **Flowers** Tiny, mimosa-like, borne in dense, clustered, branching spikes, at the ends of upright stems, in late summer and autumn. Bright golden-yellow. **Leaves** Toothed, lance-shaped. Mid-green, hairy.
• NATIVE HABITAT Garden origin.
• CULTIVATION Grow in any well-drained soil, including poor soils, in sun. A compact plant suitable for smaller herbaceous borders. Good for cutting, the bright flowers are valuable in late summer borders.
• PROPAGATION By division in spring.

☼ ◊
❀ ❀ ❀

HEIGHT
60–75cm
(24–30in)

SPREAD
45cm (18in)

| Asteraceae/Compositae | |
|---|---|

## HELIOPSIS HELIANTHOIDES var. SCABRA 'Sommersonne'

**Habit** Upright, clump-forming. **Flowers** Large, single, daisy-like, in profusion in late summer. Rich yellow with a deep orange-yellow centre. **Leaves** Coarse, serrated, oval to lance-shaped. Dark green.
• NATIVE HABITAT Garden origin.
• CULTIVATION Easy to grow in fertile, well-drained soil, in full sun. A useful long-flowering plant for an autumn border. The cut flowers last well in water.
• PROPAGATION By division in autumn or spring.
• OTHER NAMES H. 'Summer Sun'.

☼ ◊
❀ ❀ ❀

HEIGHT
1–1.2m
(3–4ft)

SPREAD
60cm (2ft)

Asteraceae/Compositae

## *HELENIUM* 'Butterpat'

**Habit** Dense, branching, clump-forming.
**Flowers** Large, daisy-like, with reflexed ray
florets and a rounded disc, borne over long periods
in late summer. Rich deep yellow. **Leaves** Lance-
shaped, on stout stems. Dark green.
• NATIVE HABITAT Garden origin.
• CULTIVATION Easy to grow in any soil unless
waterlogged, in full sun. Divide and replant
regularly to maintain vigour. The flowers are
produced in great profusion and need an
unobtrusive, grow-through support to carry their
weight. A valuable long-flowering plant for a late
summer border. The rich, deep yellow flowers
associate particularly well with copper or bronze
foliage plants and with the deep mahogany-red
or bronze-marked flowers of *H*. 'Wyndley' or
*H*. 'Moerheim Beauty'. The flowers last well
in water when cut.
• PROPAGATION By division in spring or autumn.

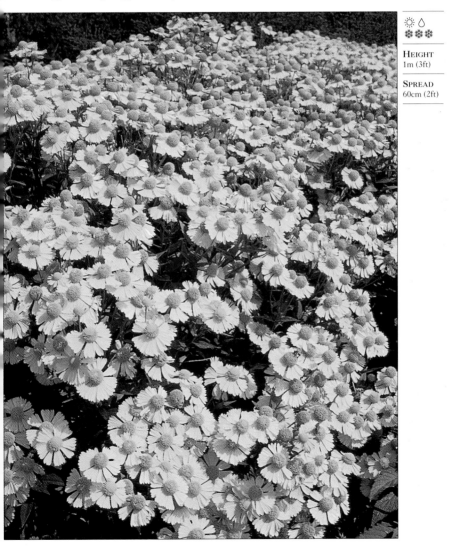

☼ ◊
❀ ❀ ❀

**HEIGHT**
1m (3ft)

**SPREAD**
60cm (2ft)

# DAYLILIES

Daylilies belong to the genus of perennials called *Hemerocallis*. As their name might suggest, they belong to the lily family, however, they are not true lilies, and their common name comes from the short-lived lily-like flowers, which usually last only a day.

Some daylilies are evergreen. They range in size from small, compact plants of just 30–38cm (12–15in) tall, to considerably larger plants of up to 1.5m (5ft). There is a wide range of modern cultivars available in a variety of colours from pale creamy-white through to yellow, vivid orange and red, pink and purple.

The flowers have a delicate appearance and some have coloured bands or streaks on the petals. Most daylilies produce flowers in succession over a period of four to six weeks during the summer months. The taller cultivars make elegant additions to a more formal herbaceous border. Some species of daylily and a few cultivars have a rich, strong fragrance.

Daylilies will thrive in most soils, but, for the best results, they should be planted in fertile, humus-rich soil that is moist but well-drained. Although they will tolerate some shade, the best blooms are produced by plants that receive direct sunlight for at least half the day. Protect the plants from slugs and snails, especially in spring.

The plants may be propagated by division in autumn or spring. Species come true from seed if they are grown in isolation. The seeds should be sown as soon as they are ripe. Young plants should be overwintered in frost-free conditions under glass.

Any abnormally swollen buds that appear in late spring or early summer should be picked off and discarded or burned, since this may be an indication that the plant is infected by *Hemerocallis* gall midges.

---

### H. 'Gentle Shepherd'
**Habit** Clump-forming.
**Flowers** From early to mid-summer. White with green throats and ruffled petals.
**Leaves** Semi-evergreen, strap-shaped. Light green.
• HEIGHT 70cm (28in).
• SPREAD 60cm (24in).

**H. 'Gentle Shepherd'**

☼ ◑ ❀ ❀ ❀

### H. 'Lullaby Baby'
**Habit** Vigorous, clump-forming.
**Flowers** Large, from early spring to mid-summer. Very pale pink petals with ruffled edges and green throats.
**Leaves** Semi-evergreen, strap-shaped. Mid-green.
• HEIGHT 50cm (20in).
• SPREAD 50cm (20in).

**H. 'Lullaby Baby'**

☼ ◑ ❀ ❀ ❀

### H. 'Siloam Virginia Henson'
**Habit** Low-growing, clump-forming.
**Flowers** Rounded, in early summer. Creamy-pink, ruffled petals, with rose-pink banding and green throats.
**Leaves** Broadly strap-shaped. Mid-green.
• HEIGHT 45cm (18in).
• SPREAD 65cm (26in).

**H. 'Siloam Virginia Henson'**

☼ ◑ ❀ ❀ ❀

### H. 'Scarlet Orbit'
**Habit** Low-growing, clump-forming.
**Flowers** Produced in mid-summer. Rich deep scarlet, revealing gold-flushed green throats as they open flat.
**Leaves** Semi-evergreen, luxuriant, strap-shaped. Mid-green.
• HEIGHT 50cm (20in).
• SPREAD 65cm (26in).

**H. 'Scarlet Orbit'**

☼ ◑ ❀ ❀ ❀

## H. 'Whisky on Ice'
**Habit** Clump-forming.
**Flowers** Rounded,
from early to mid-
summer. Very
distinctive combination
of amber, lemon and
paler creamy-yellow
with green throats.
**Leaves** Semi-
evergreen, luxuriant,
strap-shaped.
bluish-green.
HEIGHT 50cm (20in).
SPREAD 50cm (20in).

H. 'Whisky on Ice'

☼ ◐ ❄❄❄

## H. 'Stafford'
**Habit** Vigorous,
clump-forming.
**Flowers** Trumpet-
shaped, in succession
from mid- to late
summer. Glowing, rich
crimson with maroon
and yellow throats, each
petal with a narrow
yellow midrib.
**Leaves** Broadly strap-
shaped. Mid-green.
• HEIGHT 75cm (30in).
• SPREAD 60cm (24in).

H. 'Stafford'

☼ ◐ ❄❄❄

## H. 'Jolyene Nichole'
**Habit** Clump-forming.
**Flowers** Rounded, in
summer. Rose-pink with
ruffled petal margins.
**Leaves** Semi-evergreen,
luxuriant, strap-shaped.
blue-green.
HEIGHT 50cm (20in).
SPREAD 50cm (20in).

H. 'Jolyene Nichole'

☼ ◐ ❄❄❄

## H. 'Prairie Blue Eyes'
**Habit** Clump-forming.
**Flowers** Produced in
mid-summer. Maroon-
purple, with green
throats.
**Leaves** Semi-evergreen,
slender, strap-shaped..
Mid-green.
• HEIGHT 80cm (32in).
• SPREAD 90cm (3ft).

H. 'Prairie Blue Eyes'

☼ ◐ ❄❄❄

## H. 'Frank Gladney'
**Habit** Robust,
clump-forming.
**Flowers** Very large,
rounded, in summer.
Vivid coral-pink, with
golden throats and
black anthers.
**Leaves** Semi-evergreen,
broadly strap-shaped.
Mid-green.
• HEIGHT 60cm (24in).
• SPREAD 60cm (24in).

H. 'Frank Gladney'

☼ ◐ ❄❄❄

## H. 'Little Grapette'
**Habit** Vigorous,
clump-forming.
**Flowers** From early
spring to mid-summer.
Large, rich grape-purple,
with ruffled petal
margins, green throats
and darker purple eyes.
**Leaves** Semi-evergreen,
slender, strap-shaped.
Mid-green.
• HEIGHT 30–50cm
(12–20in).
• SPREAD 60cm (24in).

H. 'Little Grapette'

☼ ◐ ❄❄❄

## H. 'Super Purple'
**Habit** Vigorous, clump-forming.
**Flowers** Rounded, velvety petals with ruffled margins, produced in mid-summer. Red-purple, with lime-green throats.
**Leaves** Strap-shaped. Light green.
• HEIGHT 68cm (27in).
• SPREAD 65cm (26in).

*H. 'Super Purple'*

☼ ◊ ❄❄❄

## H. 'Brocaded Gown'
**Habit** Clump-forming.
**Flowers** Rounded, borne in summer. Creamy-white with ruffled petal margins.
**Leaves** Semi-evergreen, broadly strap-shaped. Mid-green.
• HEIGHT to 60cm (2ft).
• SPREAD to 60cm (2ft).

*H. 'Brocaded Gown'*

☼ ◊ ❄❄❄

## H. 'Marion Vaughan'
**Habit** Clump-forming.
**Flowers** Large, fragrant, trumpet-shaped, in succession in mid-summer. Lemon-yellow petals, each with a raised, white central stripe.
**Leaves** Strap-shaped. Mid-green.
• HEIGHT 1m (3ft).
• SPREAD 60cm (24in).

*H. 'Marion Vaughan'*

☼ ◊ ❄❄❄  ♇

## H. CITRINA
**Habit** Vigorous, clump-forming. **Flowers** Large, very fragrant, trumpet-shaped, opening at night in mid-summer and, each lasting a day. Rich lemon-yellow.
**Leaves** Strap-shaped. Dark green.
• HEIGHT 75cm (30in).
• SPREAD 75cm (30in).

*H. citrina*

☼ ◊ ❄❄❄

## H. LILIOASPHODELUS
**Habit** Robust, clump-forming, spreading.
**Flowers** Delicate, trumpet-shaped, very fragrant, each lasting 1–2 days and borne in late spring and early summer. Lemon- to chrome-yellow.
**Leaves** Strap-shaped. Mid-green.
• OTHER NAMES
H. flava.
• HEIGHT 60cm (24in) or more.
• SPREAD 60cm (24in).

*H. lilioasphodelus*

☼ ◊ ❄❄❄  ♇

## H. 'Corky'
**Habit** Clump-forming.
**Flowers** Trumpet-shaped, opening in late spring and early summer. Lemon-yellow with a brown petal reverse.
**Leaves** Slender, strap-shaped. Mid-green.
• HEIGHT 45cm (18in).
• SPREAD 45cm (18in).

*H. 'Corky'*

☼ ◊ ❄❄❄  ♇

## H. 'Cartwheels'
**Habit** Clump-forming.
**Flowers** Large, simple, produced in summer, opening widely at maturity. Rich, light golden-orange petals, slightly ruffled at the margin.
**Leaves** Strap-shaped. Mid-green.
• HEIGHT 75cm (30in).
• SPREAD 75cm (30in).

*H. 'Cartwheels'*

☼ ◊ ❄❄❄  ♇

**.' 'Hyperion'**
*abit* Clump-forming.
*lowers* Very fragrant,
y-like, in mid-summer.
ender, pale lemon-
ellow petals.
*eaves* Narrow, strap-
aped. Mid green.
HEIGHT 90cm (3ft).
SPREAD 90cm (3ft).

*H.* 'Hyperion'

☼ ◑ ❄❄❄

**H. 'Golden Chimes'**
*Habit* Clump-
forming, graceful.
*Flowers* Small,
delicate, trumpet-
shaped, each lasting
a day but borne in
succession from early
to mid-summer.
Golden-yellow with
a brown petal reverse.
*Leaves* Narrow, strap-
shaped. Mid green.
• HEIGHT 75cm (30in)
• SPREAD 60cm (24in)

*H.* 'Golden Chimes'

☼ ◑ ❄❄❄        ♈

**. 'Betty Woods'**
*labit* Robust,
preading,
ump-forming.
*lowers* Large, double,
eony-like, borne in mid-
nd late summer. Yellow.
*eaves* Evergreen,
rching, strap-shaped.
lid-green.
HEIGHT 65cm (26in).
SPREAD 60cm (24in).

*H.* 'Betty Woods'

☼ ◑ ❄❄❄

**H. 'Ruffled Apricot'**
*Habit* Slow-growing,
clump-forming.
*Flowers* Large, in mid-
summer. Deep apricot,
with ruffled petals, each
with a lavender-pink
midrib.
*Leaves* Stiff, strap-
shaped. Mid-green.
• HEIGHT 50cm (20in).
• SPREAD 65cm (26in).

*H.* 'Ruffled Apricot'

☼ ◑ ❄❄❄

**. FULVA
Green Kwanso'**
*Habit* Vigorous, clump-
r mound-forming.
*lowers* Large, double,
rumpet-shaped, in mid-
o late summer. Rich
awny-orange.
*eaves* Strap-shaped.
Light green.
OTHER NAMES
*.* 'Kwanzo Flore Pleno'.
HEIGHT 1m (3ft).
SPREAD 75cm (30in).

*H. fulva* 'Green
Kwanso'

☼ ◑ ❄❄❄

| Asteraceae/Compositae | |
|---|---|

## *ACHILLEA* 'Coronation Gold'  ☑

*Habit* Upright. *Flowers* Tiny, in large, flat heads, on slender, rigid stems during summer. Golden-yellow. *Leaves* Feathery, finely divided into oblong to lance-shaped segments. Silvery grey-green, hairy.
• NATIVE HABITAT Garden origin.
• CULTIVATION Grow in fertile, moisture-retentive, well-drained soil, in full sun. Divide and replant every third year to maintain vigour. The flower heads dry well and retain their herby fragrance.
• PROPAGATION By division in early spring or autumn.

☼ ◊
❀ ❀ ❀

HEIGHT
1m (3ft)

SPREAD
60cm (2ft)

| Acanthaceae | ZEBRA PLANT, SAFFRON SPIKE |
|---|---|

## *APHELANDRA SQUARROSA* 'Louisae'  ☾

*Habit* Erect. *Flowers* Tubular, 2-lipped, in dense spikes from the axils of yellow bracts, in late summer to autumn. Golden-yellow. *Leaves* Evergreen, oval, slightly wrinkled. Glossy, dark green with white veins and midrib.
• NATIVE HABITAT Mountains of tropical Americas.
• CULTIVATION Grow as a house or conservatory plant in cool climates, in humus-rich, well-drained soil in bright light, out of direct sun. Moisten soil with soft water. Apply liquid feed as flowers form.
• PROPAGATION By tip cuttings in spring.

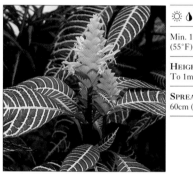

☼ ◐
Min. 13°C
(55°F)

HEIGHT
To 1m (3ft)

SPREAD
60cm (2ft)

| Asteraceae/Compositae | |
|---|---|

## *BERKHEYA MACROCEPHALA*

*Habit* Upright, sparsely branched. *Flowers* Daisy-like, with a spiny calyx beneath, borne on branching, spiny-leaved stems, throughout summer. Bright yellow with an orange-yellow centre. *Leaves* Narrowly oblong, deeply and irregularly lobed, spiny. Dark green.
• NATIVE HABITAT Damp, rocky grasslands in the Drakensberg Mountains, Natal.
• CULTIVATION Grow in fertile, moist but well-drained soil, in a warm, sunny, sheltered site.
• PROPAGATION By seed or division in spring.

☼ ◊
❀ ❀

HEIGHT
1m (3ft)

SPREAD
1m (3ft)

Asteraceae/Compositae

## *HELIOPSIS* 'Ballet Dancer'

**Habit** Upright, clump-forming. **Flowers** Large, double, daisy-like, with toothed petals, borne in profusion in late summer. Rich yellow with a deep orange-yellow centre. **Leaves** Coarse, serrated, oval to lance-shaped. Dark green.

• NATIVE HABITAT Garden origin.

• CULTIVATION Grow in any moderately fertile, well-drained soil in full sun. Will tolerate dry soils, but performs best on soils that do not become too dry in summer. A notably hardy, long-lived, undemanding and easily grown perennial. For best results lift and divide periodically and incorporate organic matter into the soil before replanting. This robust cultivar makes a valuable, long-flowering addition to the late summer and autumn border, where it associates particularly well with orange- and red-flowered plants. The cut flowers last moderately well in water.

• PROPAGATION By division in autumn or spring.

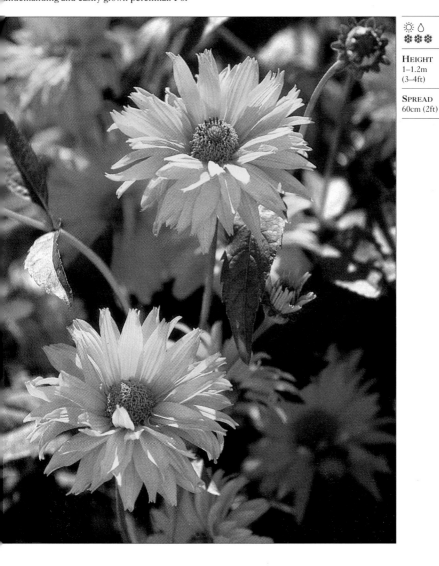

☼ ◊
❀ ❀ ❀

**HEIGHT**
1–1.2m
(3–4ft)

**SPREAD**
60cm (2ft)

| Asteraceae/Compositae | |
| --- | --- |

## ACHILLEA FILIPENDULINA 'Gold Plate' ♀

**Habit** Upright. **Flowers** Tiny, in large, flat heads, borne on rigid, leafy stems during summer. Deep yellow. **Leaves** Feathery, finely divided into oblong to lance-shaped segments. Greyish-green, densely hairy.
• NATIVE HABITAT Garden origin.
• CULTIVATION Grow in fertile, moisture-retentive, well-drained soil, in full sun. Divide and replant every third year to maintain vigour. The flower heads dry well and retain their colour and fragrance.
• PROPAGATION Division in early spring or autumn.

☼ ◊
❈ ❈ ❈

HEIGHT
1.2m (4ft)
or more

SPREAD
60cm (2ft)

| Malvaceae | DESERT MALLOW |
| --- | --- |

## SPHAERALCEA AMBIGUA

**Habit** Shrubby, much-branched. **Flowers** Mallow-like, broadly funnel-shaped, with 5 broad petals, produced singly in the leaf axils, from summer to first frosts. Coral-orange. **Leaves** Rounded, 3-lobed, soft and hairy. Grey-green.
• NATIVE HABITAT Dry, open habitats, from Utah to California, USA.
• CULTIVATION Grow in a warm, sunny, sheltered site, in fertile, well-drained soil.
• PROPAGATION By seed or division in spring.

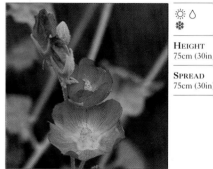

☼ ◊
❈

HEIGHT
75cm (30in

SPREAD
75cm (30in

| Asphodelaceae/Liliaceae | |
| --- | --- |

## KNIPHOFIA 'Royal Standard' ♀

**Habit** Upright, clump-forming. **Flowers** Small, narrowly tubular, borne on stout, upright stems in dense, terminal spikes, in late summer. Bright lemon-yellow, opening from scarlet-vermilion buds. **Leaves** Tough, narrow, linear, arching to form dense basal clumps. Mid-green.
• NATIVE HABITAT Garden origin.
• CULTIVATION Grow in full sun, in damp but well-drained soil. Needs ample moisture when in growth. Protect crowns in cold winter areas.
• PROPAGATION By division in spring.

☼ ◊
❈ ❈

HEIGHT
1–1.2m
(3–4ft)

SPREAD
60cm (2ft)

| Asphodelaceae/Liliaceae | |
| --- | --- |

## KNIPHOFIA THOMSONII var. SNOWDENII

**Habit** Upright, clump-forming. **Flowers** Small, pendent, narrowly tubular, borne on upright stems in open, terminal spikes, from mid-summer to first frosts. Coral-pink, yellowish on the inside. **Leaves** Tough, linear, forming basal clumps. Mid-green.
• NATIVE HABITAT Damp mountain grasslands in C. Africa.
• CULTIVATION Grow in damp but well-drained soil in full sun. Needs ample moisture during growth. Protect crowns in winter in cold areas.
• PROPAGATION By seed or division in spring.

☼ ◊
❈ ❈

HEIGHT
1m (3ft)

SPREAD
50cm (20in)

| Alstroemeriaceae/ Liliaceae | PERUVIAN LILY |
|---|---|

## *ALSTROEMERIA* Ligtu Hybrids  ☙

*Habit* Upright to slightly arching. *Flowers* Widely funnel-shaped, in summer. A range of rich and subtle pinks, yellows and orange, usually streaked and/or spotted with contrasting shades. *Leaves* Linear to narrowly lance-shaped, slightly fleshy, twisted. Mid-green.
• NATIVE HABITAT  Garden origin.
• CULTIVATION  Grow in fertile, moist, well-drained soil, in a warm, sunny site. Excellent for cutting. Provide a winter mulch of leafmould or similar.
• PROPAGATION  By division in early spring.

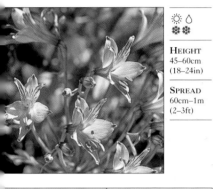

☼ ◊
❀ ❀

HEIGHT
45–60cm
(18–24in)

SPREAD
60cm–1m
(2–3ft)

| Asclepiadaceae | BUTTERFLY WEED |
|---|---|

## *ASCLEPIAS TUBEROSA*

*Habit* Upright, tuberous-rooted. *Flowers* Small, 5-horned, borne in dense, flat-topped clusters, over long periods in summer. Bright orange-red. *Leaves* Variable, usually lance-shaped and slightly fleshy. Light green.
• NATIVE HABITAT  Dry grasslands, E. and S. North America.
• CULTIVATION  Grow in deep, sandy, humus-rich and well-drained soil, in a warm, sunny site. It may take some time to become established.
• PROPAGATION  By seed or division in spring.

☼ ◊
❀ ❀

HEIGHT
to 75cm
(30in)

SPREAD
45cm (18in)

| Euphorbiaceae | |
|---|---|

## *EUPHORBIA GRIFFITHII* 'Fireglow'

*Habit* Upright, bushy, rhizomatous. *Flowers* Small, but surrounded by conspicuous, bright orange-red bracts, borne in terminal clusters in early summer. *Leaves* Smooth, linear to lance-shaped. Mid-green, with pale red-pink midribs.
• NATIVE HABITAT  Garden origin.
• CULTIVATION  Grow in fertile, humus-rich, moist but well-drained soil, in sun or light dappled shade. Good for borders and woodland gardens.
• PROPAGATION  By division in spring or early autumn, or by basal cuttings in spring or summer.

☼ ◊
❀ ❀ ❀

HEIGHT
to 1m (3ft)

SPREAD
50cm (20in)

| Caryophyllaceae | JERUSALEM CROSS, MALTESE CROSS |
|---|---|

## *LYCHNIS CHALCEDONICA*  ☙

*Habit* Upright, clump-forming. *Flowers* Small, cross-shaped, borne in dense, flat heads, at the ends of sturdy stems, in early summer. Brilliant vermilion. *Leaves* Oval, borne along the length of the flowering stem. Mid-green.
• NATIVE HABITAT  Scrub and woodland, W. Russia.
• CULTIVATION  Grow in fertile, moist but well-drained soil, in sun or light shade, sheltered from the wind. May need staking. Looks good alongside yellow-flowered and bronze-foliaged plants.
• PROPAGATION  Seed or division in autumn or spring.

☼ ◊
❀ ❀ ❀

HEIGHT
1–1.2m
(3–4ft)

SPREAD
30–45cm
(12–18in)

| Ranunculaceae | DOLL'S EYES, WHITE BANEBERRY |
|---|---|

## ACTAEA ALBA ♀

**Habit** Compact, clump-forming. **Flowers** Small, borne in fluffy, rounded heads, on slender stems, in early summer. White. **Fruits** Small, globose, toxic, white berries in late summer. **Leaves** Long-stalked, toothed, lobed. Fresh green.
• NATIVE HABITAT Woodlands of E. North America.
• CULTIVATION Grow in moist, leafy, humus-rich soil, in shade or semi-shade. Good for shady borders and woodland gardens.
• PROPAGATION Division in spring; seed in autumn.
• OTHER NAMES *A. pachypoda.*

| Scrophulariaceae | TURTLE-HEAD |
|---|---|

## CHELONE OBLIQUA

**Habit** Stiffly upright. **Flowers** Hooded, borne in stiff, erect, terminal spikes, in late summer and autumn. Lilac-pink. **Leaves** Lance-shaped, sharply toothed. Dark green.
• NATIVE HABITAT Damp woods and swamps, from Tennessee to Florida and Mississippi, USA.
• CULTIVATION Easy to grow in moist, well-drained, humus-rich soil, in sun or part-shade. A weather-resistant plant for a late summer border.
• PROPAGATION By soft tip cuttings in summer, or by seed or division in autumn or spring.

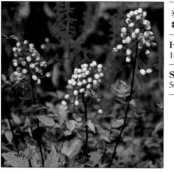

☀ ◊
❀ ❀ ❀

HEIGHT
1m (3ft)

SPREAD
50cm (20in)

☀ ◊
❀ ❀ ❀

HEIGHT
1m (3ft)

SPREAD
50cm (20in)

| Polygonaceae | |
|---|---|

## PERSICARIA CAMPANULATA

**Habit** Compact, creeping, stoloniferous. **Flowers** Tiny, bell-shaped, in branching, nodding heads on slender stems, from mid-summer to autumn. Pink or white. **Leaves** Oval, ribbed. Dark green and hairy, white to brownish-pink beneath.
• NATIVE HABITAT Damp forest, Himalayas.
• CULTIVATION Grow in cool, moist, fertile soil, in shade or semi-shade. An elegant perennial for damp borders and woodland gardens.
• PROPAGATION Seed or division in autumn or spring.
• OTHER NAMES *Polygonum campanulatum.*

☀ ◊
❀ ❀ ❀

HEIGHT
1m (3ft)

SPREAD
1m (3ft)

| Ranunculaceae | |
|---|---|

## *ANEMONE HUPEHENSIS*

**Habit** Vigorous, branching, stoloniferous. **Flowers** single, slightly cupped, borne in wiry-stemmed sprays from late summer to early autumn. White, soft pink or purplish-pink, darker on the reverse of the petals. **Leaves** More or less evergreen, deeply divided, with toothed leaflets. Dark green.
• NATIVE HABITAT Shady rocks and scrub, C. China.
• CULTIVATION Grow in any moderately fertile, well-drained soil, in sun or part-shade. An excellent perennial for a late summer border.
• PROPAGATION Seed or division in spring or autumn.

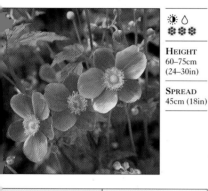

☀ ◐ ❀❀❀

**HEIGHT**
60–75cm
(24–30in)

**SPREAD**
45cm (18in)

| Convallariaceae/ Liliaceae | TOAD LILY |
|---|---|

## *TRICYRTIS FORMOSANA*

**Habit** Upright, rhizomatous. **Flowers** Spurred, lily-like, borne in open clusters, in early autumn. Yellow-throated, white to pink, heavily spotted with deep pinkish-mauve. **Leaves** Broadly lance-shaped, clasping stem. Glossy, deep green, dark-spotted.
NATIVE HABITAT Damp forest, Taiwan.
CULTIVATION Grow in moist, humus-rich soil, in a sheltered, sunny site, or in warm areas, in semi-shade. An unusual plant for borders or woodland gardens.
PROPAGATION Division in spring; seed in autumn.
OTHER NAMES *T. stolonifera*.

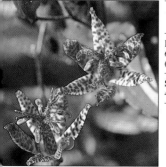

☀ ◐ ❀❀❀

**HEIGHT**
60cm–1m
(2–3ft)

**SPREAD**
45cm (18in)

| Asteraceae/Compositae | |
|---|---|

## *CHRYSANTHEMUM* 'Clara Curtis'

**Habit** Bushy, free-flowering. **Flowers** Large, flat, daisy-like, borne in profusion from summer to autumn. Clear pink, with yellow centres. **Leaves** Triangular-oval, divided into toothed and lobed segments. Dark bluish-green.
• NATIVE HABITAT Garden origin.
• CULTIVATION Grow in well-drained soil, in sun. Divide plants regularly to maintain vigour.
• PROPAGATION By division in spring.
• OTHER NAMES *C. rubellum* 'Clara Curtis', *Dendranthema zawadskii* 'Clara Curtis'.

☀ ◐ ❀❀❀

**HEIGHT**
75cm (30in)

**SPREAD**
45cm (18in)

# FLORISTS' CHRYSANTHEMUMS

Florists' chrysanthemums, which are now botanically classified under the genus *Dendranthema*, comprise the vast majority of chrysanthemums cultivated today. They are widely grown for their attractive and colourful flower heads, which make them popular for borders, cutting and exhibition.

Florists' chrysanthemums are grouped according to flowering season (early, mid- or late autumn), flower size and shape, and habit. They are further divided into disbudded and non-disbudded types.

**Disbudded types** – single, anemone-centred, incurved, intermediate and reflexed – have all but the crown bud removed. Exhibition plants are generally disbudded to leave about half the number of blooms per plant than garden plants.

**Non-disbudded types** – charm, pompon and spray types – produce several flowers per stem. **Charms** are rounded, dwarf plants bearing hundreds of star-shaped, single flowers. **Cascades** are similar but are trained into a variety of shapes. **Pompons** are also dwarf and bear 50 or more flower heads. **Sprays** are allowed to develop 4–5 stems, with at least 5 flowers per stem.

Most florists' chrysanthemums are half-hardy and should be lifted in autumn and overwintered in frost-free conditions. Some earlies are hardier and may not need lifting if kept dry. The lates need heat to flower and should be grown under cover at a minimum of 10°C (50°F). Grow in well-drained, neutral to slightly acid soil, enriched with well-rotted organic matter, in full sun. Insert supporting canes for tall cultivars at planting time and tie the stems in to the supports as growth proceeds. Water well during the growing season, and apply a balanced liquid fertilizer every 7–10 days.

Propagate by basal softwood cuttings in spring. Spray to control aphids, capsids, froghoppers, mildew and white rust.

INCURVED
Fully double, spherical flowers with incurved petals closing tightly over the crown.

FULLY REFLEXED
Fully double, almost spherical, with curved, pointed petals reflexing outwards and downwards, to touch the stem.

REFLEXED
Similar to fully reflexed, but with less strongly reflexed petals forming an umbrella-like or spiky outline.

INTERMEDIATE
Fully double, roughly spherical, with loosely incurving petals, either enclosing the crown or reflexing in the bottom half of the flower.

ANEMONE-CENTRED
Single, with a dome-shaped disc, up to half the diameter of the bloom, and an outer ring of up to 5 rows of flat, occasionally spoon-shaped petals at 90° to the stem.

SINGLE
Single, daisy-like flowers with a golden- or green-centred disc, and up to 5 rows of flat petals held at right angles to the stem, sometimes incurving or reflexing at their tips.

POMPON
Fully double, spherical or occasionally hemispherical, with tubular petals having flat, rounded tips.

SPOON-TYPE
Similar to single types, but with tubular petals expanding at their tips to form a spoon shape.

*C.* 'Pavilion'
*Habit* Upright.
*Flowers* Fully double,
spherical, to 18cm (7in)
across, with loosely
incurved petals,
produced in early
autumn. White.
  TIPS More suitable
for exhibition than for
garden use.
  HEIGHT 1.35m (4½ft).
  SPREAD 60–75cm
(2–2½ft).

*C.* 'Pavilion'
(Intermediate, Early)

☀ ◊ ❊                    ♈

*C.* 'Pennine Oriel'
*Habit* Upright.
*Flowers* Single, 9cm
(3½in) across, produced
in early autumn. Creamy-
white anemone-centre,
surrounded by about 5
rows of white petals with
slightly incurved margins.
  • TIPS May not need
lifting if kept dry. Good
for exhibition.
  • HEIGHT 1.2m (4ft).
  • SPREAD 60–75cm
(2–2½ft).

*C.* 'Pennine Oriel'
(Anemone-centred,
Spray, Early)

☀ ◊ ❊❊❊              ♈

*C.* 'Cloudbank'
*Habit* Upright.
*Flowers* Single,
anemone-centred,
7–9cm (3–3½in) across,
with about 5 rows of flat
petals, produced in late
autumn. White.
  HEIGHT 1.2m (4ft).
  SPREAD 75cm (2½ft).

*C.* 'Cloudbank'
(Anemone-centred,
Spray, Late)

☀ ◊ ❊

*C.* 'Alison Kirk'
*Habit* Upright.
*Flowers* Fully double,
spherical, 12–15cm
(5–6in) across, with
incurved petals, in early
autumn. Pure white.
  • TIPS More suitable for
exhibition than for
garden use.
  • HEIGHT 1.2m (4ft).
  • SPREAD 30–60cm
(1–2ft).

*C.* 'Alison Kirk'
(Incurved, Early)

☀ ◊ ❊                    ♈

*C.* 'Michael Fish'
*Habit* Upright.
*Flowers* Fully double,
spherical, to 15cm (6in)
across, with fairly tightly
incurved petals,
produced in early
autumn. White.
  • TIPS Suitable for
exhibition.
  • HEIGHT 1.2m (4ft).
  • SPREAD 60–75cm
(2–2½ft).

*C.* 'Michael Fish'
(Intermediate, Early)

☀ ◊ ❊

*C.* 'Duke of Kent'
*Habit* Upright.
*Flowers* Fully double,
to 25cm (10in) across,
with almost fully reflexed
petals, produced in late
autumn. White.
  • TIPS Suitable only for
exhibition. Grow under
cover. Needs warmth
to flower.
  • HEIGHT 1.5m (5ft).
  • SPREAD 30cm (1ft).

*C.* 'Duke of Kent'
(Reflexed, Late)

☀ ◊   Min. 10°C (50°F)

*C.* 'Dawn Mist'
*Habit* Upright.
*Flowers* Single,
8–9cm (3–3½in) across,
produced in early
autumn. About
5 rows of flat, very pale
pink petals, arranged
around a golden-
yellow disc.
  • TIPS May not need
lifting if kept dry.
  • HEIGHT 1.2m (4ft).
  • SPREAD 75cm–1m
(2½–3ft).

*C.* 'Dawn Mist'
(Single, Spray, Early)

☀ ◊ ❊❊❊❊

*C.* 'Salmon
Fairweather'
*Habit* Upright.
*Flowers* Fully double,
spherical, 14–15cm
(5½–6in) across, with
incurved petals, in late
autumn. Pale salmon-pink.
  • TIPS Suitable for
exhibition. Grow under
cover. Needs warmth
to flower.
  • HEIGHT 1–1.1m
(3–3½ft).
  • SPREAD to 75cm (2½ft).

*C.* 'Salmon
Fairweather'
(Incurved, Late)

☀ ◊   Min. 10°C (50°F)

## C. 'Roblush'
**Habit** Upright.
**Flowers** Fully double,
to 8cm (3in) across,
produced in late autumn.
Pale pink, reflexed,
petals with green-tinted
centres.
• TIPS Good for
exhibition. Grow under
cover. Needs warmth
to flower.
• HEIGHT 1.5m (5ft).
• SPREAD 75–1m
(2½–3ft).

**C. 'Roblush'**
(Reflexed, Spray,
Late)

☼ ◊   Min. 10°C (50°F)

## C. 'Marian Gosling'
**Habit** Upright. **Flowers**
Fully double, to 14cm
(5½in) across, with fully
reflexed petals,
produced in early
autumn. Pale pink.
• TIPS Good for
exhibition.
• HEIGHT 1.2–1.35m
(4–4½ft).
• SPREAD 60cm (2ft).

**C. 'Marian Gosling'**
(Reflexed, Early)

☼ ◊ ❄

## C. 'Dorridge Dream'
**Habit** Upright.
**Flowers** Fully double,
spherical, 12cm (5in)
across, with incurved
petals, produced in early
autumn. Rose-pink.
• TIPS Excellent for
exhibition. Grow under
cover. Needs warmth
to flower.
• HEIGHT 1.2m (4ft).
• SPREAD 60cm (2ft).

**C. 'Dorridge Dream'**
(Incurved, Early)

☼ ◊   Min. 10°C (50°F)

## C. 'Madeleine'
**Habit** Upright.
**Flowers** Fully double,
8cm (3in) across, with
reflexed petals, produced
in early autumn. Pink
• TIPS Good for
exhibition. May not
need lifting if kept dry.
• HEIGHT 1.2m (4ft).
• SPREAD 75cm–1m
(2½–3ft).

**C. 'Madeleine'**
(Reflexed, Spray,
Early)

☼ ◊ ❄❄❄           ⚡

## C. 'Ringdove'
**Habit** Dome-forming.
**Flowers** Single, to 2.5cm
(1in) across, produced in
late autumn. Deep pink
petals, arranged around
a greenish yellow disc.
• TIPS Excellent for
exhibition. Grow under
cover. Needs warmth
to flower.
• HEIGHT 1m (3ft).
• SPREAD 1m (3ft).

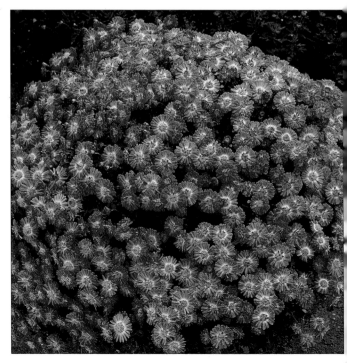

**C. 'Ringdove'**
(Single, Charm,
Late)

☼ ◊ Min. 10°C (50°F)

*C.* 'Brietner'
*Habit* Upright.
*Flowers* Fully double,
to 12cm (5in) across,
produced in early
autumn. Pink, reflexed
petals giving a spiky
outline.
• HEIGHT 1.1–1.2m
(3½–4ft).
• SPREAD to 75cm (2½ft).

*C.* 'Brietner'
(Reflexed, Early)

☼ ◊ ❀

*C.* 'Skater's Waltz'
*Habit* Upright.
*Flowers* Fully double,
spherical, 15–18cm
(6–7in) across, with
loosely incurved petals,
produced in early
autumn. Deep pink
with a paler reverse.
• TIPS Grow under cover.
Needs warmth to flower.
• HEIGHT 1. 5m (5ft).
• SPREAD 60–75cm
(2–2½ft).

*C.* 'Skater's Waltz'
(Intermediate, Early)

☼ ◊   Min. 10°C (50°F)

*C.* 'Pennine Flute'
*Habit* Upright.
*Flowers* Fully double,
5–8cm (2½–3in) across, in
early autumn. Pink, very
narrowly spoon-shaped
petals around a greenish-
yellow centre. Similar to
*C.* 'Pennine Jewel'.
• TIPS May not need
lifting if kept dry.
Good for exhibition.
• HEIGHT 1.2m (4ft).
• SPREAD 60–75cm
(2–2½ft).

*C.* 'Pennine Flute'
(Spoon-type, Spray,
Early)

☼ ◊ ❀❀❀   ♈

*C.* 'Yvonne Arnaud'
*Habit* Upright.
*Flowers* Fully double,
to 12cm (5in) across, with
reflexed petals, produced
in early autumn. Deep
pinkish-purple.
• HEIGHT 1.2m (4ft).
• SPREAD 60–75cm
(2–2½ft).

*C.* 'Yvonne Arnaud'
(Reflexed, Early)

☼ ◊ ❀   ♈

*C.* 'Talbot Jo'
*Habit* Upright.
*Flowers* Single, to 8cm
(3in) across, Produced
in early autumn. About
5 rows of flat, rich pink
petals surrounding the
greenish-gold disc.
• TIPS Good for
exhibition. May not
need lifting if kept dry.
• HEIGHT 1.5m (5ft).
• SPREAD 75cm–1m
(2½–3ft).

*C.* 'Talbot Jo'
(Single, Spray, Early)

☼ ◊ ❀❀❀

*C.* 'Purple
Pennine Wine'
*Habit* Upright.
*Flowers* Fully double,
to 8cm (3in) across,
with reflexed petals,
produced in early
autumn. Rich red-purple.
• TIPS Very good for
exhibition. May not
need lifting if kept dry.
• HEIGHT 1.2m (4ft).
• SPREAD 60–75cm
(2–2½ft).

*C.* 'Purple
Pennine Wine'
(Reflexed, Spray,
Early)

☼ ◊ ❀❀❀   ♈

*C.* 'Chippendale'
*Habit* Upright.
*Flowers* Fully double,
to 18cm (7in) across,
with fully reflexed
petals, produced in mid-
autumn. Pink with paler
reverse.
• TIPS Better suited
to exhibition than for
garden use.
• HEIGHT 1.2m (4ft).
• SPREAD 45cm (1½ft).

*C.* 'Chippendale'
(Reflexed, Mid-season)

☼ ◊ ❀

*C.* 'Maria'
*Habit* Upright, compact.
*Flowers* Small, fully
double, spherical, 4cm
(1½in) across, with
densely arranged,
tubular petals that
are flat at the tip,
produced in early
autumn. Pink.
• TIPS May not need
lifting if kept dry.
• HEIGHT 45cm (1½ft).
• SPREAD 30–60cm
(1–2ft).

*C.* 'Maria'
(Pompon, Early)

☼ ◊ ❀

## C. 'Cherry Chintz'
*Habit* Upright.
*Flowers* Fully double,
to 15cm (6in) across,
with fully reflexed
petals, produced in
early autumn. Red.
• TIPS Excellent for
exhibition.
• HEIGHT 1.2m (4ft).
• SPREAD 45cm (1½ft).

**C. 'Cherry Chintz'**
(Reflexed, Early)

## C. 'Rose Yvonne Arnaud'
*Habit* Upright.
*Flowers* Fully double,
to 12cm (5in) across, with
reflexed petals, produced
in early autumn. Deep
rose-pink. A sport of *C.*
'Yvonne Arnaud'.
• HEIGHT 1.2m (4ft).
• SPREAD 60–75cm
(2–2½ft).

**C. 'Rose Yvonne Arnaud'**
(Reflexed, Early)

## C. 'Sentry'
*Habit* Upright.
*Flowers* Fully double,
to 12cm (5in) across,
with fully reflexed
petals, produced in
early autumn. Red.
• TIPS Excellent for
exhibition.
• HEIGHT 1.2–1.35m
(4–4½ft).
• SPREAD 60–75cm
(2–2½ft).

**C. 'Sentry'**
(Reflexed, Early)

## C. 'George Griffiths'
*Habit* Upright.
*Flowers* Fully double,
to 14cm (5½in) across,
with fully reflexed
petals, produced in early
autumn. Dark red.
• TIPS Excellent for
exhibition.
• HEIGHT 1.2–1.35m
(4–4½ft).
• SPREAD 75cm (2½ft).

**C. 'George Griffiths'**
(Reflexed, Early)

## C. 'Redwing'
*Habit* Upright.
*Flowers* Single, to 8cm
(3in) across, produced in
early autumn. About 5
rows of flat red petals,
arranged around a golden
yellow disc.
• TIPS Suitable for
exhibition.
• HEIGHT 1.2–1.35m
(4–4½ft).
• SPREAD 60cm (2ft).

**C. 'Redwing'**
(Single, Spray, Early)

## C. 'Green Satin'
*Habit* Upright.
*Flowers* Fully double,
loosely spherical, 12cm
(5in) across, with loosely
incurved petals, in late
autumn. Green.
• TIPS Grow under cover.
Needs warmth to flower.
• HEIGHT 1.2m (4ft).
• SPREAD 60cm (2ft).

**C. 'Green Satin'**
(Intermediate, Late)

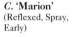 Min. 10°C (50°F)

## C. 'Marion'
*Habit* Upright.
*Flowers* Fully double,
8cm (3in) across, with
reflexed petals,
produced from late
summer. Pale yellow.
• TIPS May not need
lifting if kept dry.
• HEIGHT 1.2m (4ft).
• SPREAD 75cm (2½ft).

**C. 'Marion'**
(Reflexed, Spray,
Early)

## C. 'Discovery'
*Habit* Upright.
*Flowers* Fully double,
loosely spherical,
10–12cm (4–5in) across,
with loosely incurved
petals, in early autumn.
Pale yellow.
• HEIGHT 1.2m (4ft).
SPREAD 75cm (2½ft).

**C. 'Discovery'**
(Intermediate,
Early)

*C.* 'Marlene Jones'
*Habit* Upright.
*Flowers* Fully double,
loosely spherical, to
12–14cm (5–5⅛in) across,
with loosely incurved
petals, in early autumn.
Pale yellow.
• TIPS Good for
exhibition. May not
need lifting if kept dry.
• PROPAGATION
• HEIGHT 1m (3ft).
• SPREAD 60cm (2ft).

*C.* 'Marlene Jones'
(Intermediate, Early)

☼ ◊ ❀ ❀ ❀

*C.* 'Yellow
John Hughes'
*Habit* Upright.
*Flowers* Fully double,
spherical, 12–14cm
(5–5⅛in) across, with
incurved petals, in late
autumn. Yellow.
• TIPS Excellent for
exhibition. Grow under
cover. Needs warmth
to flower.
• HEIGHT 1.2m (4ft).
• SPREAD 60–75cm
(2–2½ft).

*C.* 'Yellow
John Hughes'
(Incurved, Late)

☼ ◊   Min. 10°C (50°F)

*C.* 'Primrose West
Bromwich'
*Habit* Upright.
*Flowers* Fully double, to
18cm (7in) or more
across, with fully reflexed
petals, produced in mid-
autumn. Pale yellow.
• TIPS Suitable only for
exhibition.
• HEIGHT 2.2m (7ft).
• SPREAD 45–60cm
(1½–2ft).

*C.* 'Primrose West
Bromwich'
(Reflexed, Mid-season)

☼ ◊ ❀

*C.* 'Edwin Painter'
*Habit* Upright.
*Flowers* Single, 14cm
(5⅛in) across, produced
in late autumn. About
5 rows of narrow, pointed,
yellow petals, arranged
around a central
green disc.
• TIPS Grow under cover.
Needs warmth to flower.
• HEIGHT 1.35–1.5m
(4½–5ft).
• SPREAD 75cm–1m
(2½–3ft).

*C.* 'Edwin Painter'
(Single, Late)

☼ ◊   Min. 10°C (50°F)

*C.* 'Pennine Jewel'
*Habit* Upright.
*Flowers* Fully double,
6–8cm (2½–3in) across,
with narrowly spoon-
shaped petals, produced
in early autumn. Pale
bronze petals arranged
around a golden-bronze
centre.
• TIPS Suitable for
exhibition. May not
need lifting if kept dry.
• HEIGHT 1.2m (4ft).
• SPREAD 60–75cm
(2–2½ft).

*C.* 'Pennine Jewel'
(Spoon-type, Spray,
Early)

☼ ◊ ❀ ❀ ❀

## C. 'Yellow Brietner'

**Habit** Upright.
**Flowers** Fully double, to 12cm (5in) across, with reflexed petals giving a spiky outline, produced in early autumn. Yellow. A sport of *C.* 'Brietner'.
• HEIGHT 1.1–1.2m (3½–4ft).
• SPREAD 75cm (2½ft).

**C. 'Yellow Brietner'**
(Reflexed, Early)

☼ ◊ ✽

## C. 'Pennine Alfie'

**Habit** Upright.
**Flowers** Fully double, 6–8cm (2½–3in) across, in early autumn. Pale bronze, spoon-shaped, petals, darker at the base, arranged around a golden-bronze centre.
• TIPS May not need lifting if kept dry.
• HEIGHT 1.2m (4ft).
• SPREAD 60–75cm (2–2½ft).

**C. 'Pennine Alfie'**
(Spoon-type, Spray, Early)

☼ ◊ ✽✽✽

## C. 'Golden Woolman's Glory'

**Habit** Upright.
**Flowers** Single, 18cm (7in) across, in late autumn. About 5 rows of narrow, pointed, deep golden-yellow petals, around a green disc.
• TIPS Excellent for exhibition. Grow under cover. Needs warmth to flower.
• HEIGHT 1.5m (5ft).
• SPREAD 1m (3ft).

**C. 'Golden Woolman's Glory'**
(Single, Late)

☼ ◊   Min. 10°C (50°F)

## C. 'Wendy'

**Habit** Upright.
**Flowers** Fully double, to 8cm (3in) across, produced in early autumn. Pale bronze, reflexed petals, darker towards the centre.
• TIPS May not need lifting if kept dry.
• HEIGHT 1.2m (4ft).
• SPREAD 60–75cm (2–2½ft).

**C. 'Wendy'**
(Reflexed, Spray, Early)

☼ ◊ ✽✽✽   ♟

## C. 'Sally Ball'

**Habit** Upright.
**Flowers** Single, 9cm (3½in) across, produced in early autumn. About 5 rows of flattish bronze petals around a yellow-bronze anemone-centre.
• TIPS Suitable for exhibition. May not need lifting if kept dry.
• HEIGHT 1.2m (4ft).
• SPREAD 75cm (2½ft).

**C. 'Sally Ball'**
(Anemone-centred, Spray Early)

☼ ◊ ✽✽✽

## C. 'Bronze Fairie'

**Habit** Upright, compact.
**Flowers** Small, fully double, spherical, 4cm (1½in) across, with densely arranged, tubular petals that are flat at the tip, produced in early autumn. Bronze.
• TIPS May not need lifting if kept dry.
• HEIGHT 30–60cm (2–2ft).
• SPREAD 60cm (2ft).

**C. 'Bronze Fairie'**
(Pompon, Early)

☼ ◊ ✽✽✽

## C. 'Bronze Yvonne Arnaud'

**Habit** Upright.
**Flowers** Fully double, to 12cm (5in) across, with reflexed petals, produced in early autumn. Bronze. A sport of *C.* 'Yvonne Arnaud'.
• HEIGHT 1.2m (4ft).
• SPREAD 60–75cm (2–2½ft).

**C. 'Bronze Yvonne Arnaud'**
(Reflexed, Early)

☼ ◊ ✽

## C. 'Salmon Fairie'

**Habit** Upright, compact.
**Flowers** Small, fully double, spherical, 4cm (1½in) across, with densely arranged, tubular petals that are flat at the tip, in early autumn. Salmon-orange. Similar to *C.* 'Bronze Fairie'.
• TIPS Grow under cover. Needs warmth to flower.
• HEIGHT 30–60cm (1–2ft).
• SPREAD 60cm (2ft).

**C. 'Salmon Fairie'**
(Pompon, Early)

☼ ◊   Min. 10°C (50°F)

## C. 'Rytorch'
*Habit* Upright.
*Flowers* Single, to 8cm
(3in) across, in late
autumn. About 5 rows of
flat, bronze-red petals,
with a ring of yellow
surrounding the greenish-
gold central disc.
  TIPS Good for exhibition.
Grow under cover. Needs
warmth to flower.
• HEIGHT 1.5m (5ft).
  SPREAD 75cm–1m
(2½–3ft).

*C.* 'Rytorch'
(Single, Spray, Late)

☼ ○  Min. 10°C (50°F)

## C. 'Bronze Hedgerow'
*Habit* Upright, robust.
*Flowers* Single, to
12cm (5in) across,
produced in late
autumn. Bronze, reflexed
petals around a green
central disc.
• TIPS Grow under cover.
Needs warmth to flower.
• HEIGHT 1.5m (5ft).
• SPREAD 75cm–1m
(2½–3ft).

*C.* 'Bronze Hedgerow'
(Single, Late)

☼ ○  Min. 10°C (50°F)

## C. 'Peach Margaret'
*Habit* Upright.
*Flowers* Fully double,
8–9cm (3–3½in) across,
with reflexed petals,
produced in early
autumn. Pale
salmon-pink.
• TIPS Excellent for
exhibition. May not need
lifting if kept dry.
• HEIGHT 1.2m (4ft).
• SPREAD to 75cm (2½ft).

*C.* 'Peach Margaret'
(Reflexed, Spray,
Early)

☼ ○ ✿✿✿

## C. 'Peach Brietner'
*Habit* Upright.
*Flowers* Fully double,
to 12cm (5in) across,
with fully reflexed petals,
giving a spiky outline,
produced in early
autumn. Peach-pink. A
sport of *C.* 'Brietner'.
• HEIGHT 1.1–1.2m
(3½–4ft).
• SPREAD to 75cm (2½ft).

*C.* 'Peach Brietner'
(Reflexed, Early)

☼ ○ ✿

## C. 'Salmon Margaret'
*Habit* Upright.
*Flowers* Fully double,
8–9cm (3–3½in) across,
with reflexed petals,
produced in early
autumn. Salmon.
Similar form to *C.*
'Peach Margaret'.
• TIPS May not need
lifting if kept dry.
• HEIGHT 1.2m (4ft).
• SPREAD to 75cm
(2½ft).

*C.* 'Salmon Margaret'
(Reflexed, Spray,
Early)

☼ ○ ✿✿✿       🏆

## C. 'Autumn Days'
*Habit* Upright.
*Flowers* Fully double,
loosely spherical, to 12cm
(5in) across, with loosely
incurved petals, in early
autumn. Bronze.
• HEIGHT 1.1–1.2m
(3½–4ft).
• SPREAD to 75cm (2½ft).

*C.* 'Autumn Days'
(Intermediate,
Early)

☼ ○ ✿

## C. 'Oracle'
*Habit* Upright.
*Flowers* Fully double,
spherical, to 12cm (5in)
across, with loosely
incurved petals,
produced in early
autumn. Pale bronze
• TIPS Good for
exhibition.
• HEIGHT 1.2m (4ft).
• SPREAD 60–75cm
(2–2½ft).

*C.* 'Oracle'
(Intermediate, Early)

☼ ○ ✿

## C. 'Buff Margaret'
*Habit* Upright.
*Flowers* Fully
double, 8–9cm
(3–3½in) across, with
reflexed petals,
produced in early
autumn. Pale bronze.
Similar form to
*C.* 'Peach Margaret'.
• TIPS May not need
lifting if kept dry.
• HEIGHT 1.2m (4ft).
• SPREAD to 75cm (2½ft).

*C.* 'Buff Margaret'
(Reflexed, Spray,
Early)

☼ ○ ✿✿✿

# MICHAELMAS DAISIES

Michaelmas daisies are invaluable late-flowering border plants from the genus *Aster*, grown for their profusion of daisy-like flower heads. They provide a useful source of colour in a late-summer or autumn display, and are generally good for cutting.

Grow in full sun or light shade in fertile, humus-rich, well-drained soil that remains reliably moist in summer. Provide twiggy or grow-through support for tall plants. Dead-head early-flowering cultivars.

Propagate by softwood cuttings in spring or by division in spring or autumn. Some Michaelmas daisies, particularly modern cultivars of *A. novi-belgii*, are susceptible to powdery mildew. Where this is a problem treat the plants regularly with a fungicide, or choose resistant cultivars.

**A. ERICOIDES**
**'White Heather'**
*Habit* Bushy.
*Flowers* Very small, daisy-like, long-lasting, borne in branching, wiry-stemmed sprays in late autumn. White ray florets surrounding a yellow disc.
*Leaves* Small, lance-shaped. Fresh green.
• TIPS Needs unobtrusive staking.
• HEIGHT 75cm (30in).
• SPREAD 50cm (20in).

*A. ericoides*
**'White Heather'**

☼ ◊ ✿✿✿

**A. LATERIFLORUS**
**'Delight'**
*Habit* Spreading.
*Flowers* Tiny, daisy-like, borne in dense sprays in autumn. White ray florets surrounding a central golden disc.
*Leaves* Small, narrowly lance-shaped. Dark green.
• TIPS Needs staking.
• HEIGHT 1.2m (4ft).
• SPREAD 1m (3ft).

*A. lateriflorus* 'Delight'

☼ ◊ ✿✿✿

**A. NOVAE-ANGLIAE**
**'Herbstschnee'**
*Habit* Vigorous, upright.
*Flowers* Daisy-like, single, borne in clusters in autumn. White with yellow centres.
*Leaves* Rough, lance-shaped. Dull green.
• TIPS May need staking.
• OTHER NAMES
*A.* 'Autumn Snow'.
• HEIGHT 75cm–1.1m (2½–3½ft).
• SPREAD to 60cm (2ft).

*A. novae-angliae*
**'Herbstschnee'**

☼ ◊ ✿✿✿

**A. NOVI-BELGII**
**'White Swan'**
*Habit* Vigorous, spreading.
*Flowers* Large, daisy-like, double, borne in dense sprays in autumn. Pure white ray florets.
*Leaves* Lance-shaped. Mid-green.
• TIPS May need staking.
• HEIGHT 1.2m (4ft).
• SPREAD 60cm (24in).

*A. novi-belgii*
**'White Swan'**

☼ ◊ ✿✿✿

**1.** *CORDIFOLIUS*
**'Silver Spray'**
*Habit* Lax, bushy,
upright.
*Flowers* Small, daisy-
like, borne in airy
sprays in autumn.
Pink-tinged white
ray florets, around
a yellow disc.
*Leaves* Lance-
shaped. Mid-green.
• TIPS Needs staking.
HEIGHT 1.2m (4ft).
SPREAD 1m (3ft).

*A. cordifolius*
**'Silver Spray'**

☼ ◊ ❊❊❊

**1.** *LATERIFLORUS*
**'Horizontalis'**
*Habit* Freely branching.
*Flowers* Tiny, borne in
branching sprays in
autumn. White,
sometimes pink-tinted
ray florets surrounding
a darker pink disc.
*Leaves* Small, lance-
shaped. Dark green.
• HEIGHT 60cm (24in).
• SPREAD 50cm (20in).

*A. lateriflorus*
**'Horizontalis'**

☼ ◊ ❊❊❊ ♆

**4.** *NOVI-BELGII*
**'Apple Blossom'**
*Habit* Vigorous,
spreading.
*Flowers* Daisy-like,
single, borne in dense
heads in autumn.
Soft pale pink ray
florets around a tiny
yellow disc.
*Leaves* Lance-shaped.
Mid-green.
• HEIGHT 90cm (3ft),
• SPREAD 60–75cm
(24–30in).

*A. novi-belgii*
**'Apple Blossom'**

☼ ◊ ❊❊❊

*A.* *NOVAE-ANGLIAE*
**'Harrington's Pink'**
*Habit* Vigorous, upright.
*Flowers* Daisy-like,
single, borne in
profuse clusters in
autumn. Bright clear
pink ray florets around
a yellow disc.
*Leaves* Rough-textured,
lance-shaped. Mid-green.
• TIPS May need staking.
• HEIGHT 1.2–1.5m
(4–5ft).
• SPREAD 60cm (24in).

*A. novae-angliae*
**'Harrington's Pink'**

☼ ◊ ❊❊❊ ♆

*A.* *NOVI-BELGII*
**'Lassie'**
*Habit* Vigorous,
spreading.
*Flowers* Large, daisy-
like, single, borne in
dense clusters in autumn.
Clear pink ray florets,
surrounding a golden
central disc.
*Leaves* Lance-shaped.
Mid-green.
• TIPS May need staking.
• HEIGHT 1.2m (4ft).
• SPREAD 75cm (30in).

*A. novi-belgii* **'Lassie'**

☼ ◊ ❊❊❊

*A.* *NOVAE-ANGLIAE*
**'Barr's Pink'**
*Habit* Vigorous, upright.
*Flowers* Daisy-like,
semi-double, borne in
profuse clusters in late
summer and autumn.
Bright, rose-pink ray
florets around a dark
pinkish-yellow disc.
*Leaves* Rough-textured,
lance-shaped. Mid-green.
• TIPS May need staking.
• HEIGHT 75cm (30in).
• SPREAD 60cm (24in).

*A. novae-angliae*
**'Barr's Pink'**

☼ ◊ ❊❊❊

*A.* *NOVI-BELGII*
**'Carnival'**
*Habit* Vigorous,
spreading.
*Flowers* Daisy-like,
double, borne in
dense clusters in
autumn. Cerise-red
ray florets obscure
the central disc.
*Leaves* Lance-shaped.
Dark green.
• HEIGHT 75cm (30in).
• SPREAD to 45cm
(18in).

*A. novi-belgii*
**'Carnival'**

☼ ◊ ❊❊❊

## A. *NOVI-BELGII* 'Royal Ruby'
*Habit* Vigorous, low-growing.
*Flowers* Large, daisy-like, semi-double, borne in dense clusters in autumn. Rich red ray florets, surrounding a yellow disc.
*Leaves* Lance-shaped. Mid-green.
• HEIGHT 45cm (18in).
• SPREAD 45cm (18in).

*A. novi-belgii* 'Royal Ruby'

☼ ◊ ❀❀❀

## A. *NOVI-BELGII* 'Patricia Ballard'
*Habit* Vigorous, spreading.
*Flowers* Large, daisy-like, semi-double, borne in dense heads in autumn. Pink ray florets, surrounding a small golden disc.
*Leaves* Lance-shaped. Mid-green.
• TIPS May need staking.
• HEIGHT 1.2m (4ft).
• SPREAD 75cm (30in).

*A. novi-belgii* 'Patricia Ballard'

☼ ◊ ❀❀❀

## A. *NOVI-BELGII* 'Freda Ballard'
*Habit* Vigorous, spreading.
*Flowers* Daisy-like, semi-double, borne in dense clusters in autumn. Rich rose-red ray florets, surrounding a golden central disc.
*Leaves* Lance-shaped. Mid-green.
• TIPS May need staking.
• HEIGHT 1.2m (4ft).
• SPREAD 50cm (20in).

*A. novi-belgii* 'Freda Ballard'

☼ ◊ ❀❀❀

## A. *NOVI-BELGII* 'Orlando'
*Habit* Vigorous, spreading.
*Flowers* Large, daisy-like, single, borne in dense clusters in autumn. Bright pink ray florets, surrounding a golden central disc.
*Leaves* Lance-shaped. Dark green.
• HEIGHT to 1m (3ft).
• SPREAD to 45cm (18in).

*A. novi-belgii* 'Orlando'

☼ ◊ ❀❀❀

## A. × *FRIKARTII* 'Mönch'
*Habit* Bushy.
*Flowers* Daisy-like, single, produced in profusion from late summer to autumn. Soft lavender-blue ray florets surrounding a greenish-yellow central disc.
*Leaves* Rough-textured, oblong. Dark green.
• HEIGHT 75cm (30in).
• SPREAD 45cm (18in).

*A. × frikartii* 'Mönch'

☼ ◊ ❀❀❀  ♛

## A. *NOVAE-ANGLIAE* 'Andenken an Alma Pötschke'
*Habit* Vigorous, upright.
*Flowers* Single, daisy-like, in clusters, in autumn. Bright cerise ray florets around a yellow disc.
*Leaves* Rough-textured, lance-shaped. Mid-green.
• OTHER NAMES A. 'Alma Potschke'.
• TIPS May need staking.
• HEIGHT 75cm (30in).
• SPREAD 60cm (24in).

*A. novae-angliae* 'Andenken an Alma Pötschke'

☼ ◊ ❀❀❀  ♛

## A. *NOVI-BELGII* 'Fellowship'
*Habit* Vigorous, spreading.
*Flowers* Large, daisy-like, double, borne in dense clusters in autumn. Clear deep pink ray florets.
*Leaves* Lance-shaped. Mid-green.
• TIPS May need staking.
• HEIGHT 1.2m (4ft).
• SPREAD 50cm (20in).

*A. novi-belgii* 'Fellowship'

☼ ◊ ❀❀❀

## A. *NOVI-BELGII* 'Jenny'
*Habit* Vigorous, spreading.
*Flowers* Daisy-like, double, borne in dense clusters in autumn. Red ray florets, surrounding a dark red central disc.
*Leaves* Lance-shaped. Mid-green.
• HEIGHT 45cm (18in).
• SPREAD 30cm (12in).

*A. novi-belgii* 'Jenny'

☼ ◊ ❀❀❀

**1. THOMSONII
'Nanus'**
**Habit** Compact,
upright.
**Flowers** Single, with
slender, pointed ray
florets. Pale lilac with a
central yellow disc.
**Leaves** Oval, coarsely
toothed. Mid-green.
**TIPS** Suitable for a
border front or large
rock garden.
**HEIGHT** 45cm (18in).
**SPREAD** 23cm (9in).

*A. thomsonii* 'Nanus'

☼ ◊ ❋❋❋

**A. NOVI-BELGII
'Marie Ballard'**
**Habit** Vigorous,
spreading.
**Flowers** Large, daisy-
like, single, borne in
dense clusters in
autumn. Clear pink ray
florets surrounding a
golden central disc.
**Leaves** Lance-shaped.
Mid-green.
• **HEIGHT** to 1m (3ft).
• **SPREAD** to 45cm
(18in).

*A. novi-belgii*
'Marie Ballard'

☼ ◊ ❋❋❋

**1. TURBINELLUS**
**Habit** Upright.
**Flowers** Small, single,
daisy-like, produced in
autumn. Pale violet ray
florets surrounding a
central yellow disc.
**Leaves** Narrowly lance-
shaped. Mid-green.
• **TIPS** Disease-resistant
and easy to grow.
**HEIGHT** 1.2m (4ft).
• **SPREAD** 60cm (2ft).

*A. turbinellus*

☼ ◊ ❋❋❋    ♉

**A. X FRIKARTII
'Wunder von Stäfa'**
**Habit** Bushy.
**Flowers** Daisy-like,
single, produced in
profusion from late
summer to autumn.
Lavender ray florets
surrounding a greenish-
yellow central disc.
**Leaves** Rough-
textured, oblong,
dark green.
• **HEIGHT** 75cm (30in).
• **SPREAD** 45cm (18in).

*A. x frikartii* '
'Wunder von Stäfa'

☼ ◊ ❋❋❋    ♉

**1. NOVI-BELGII
Professor
Anton Kippenburg'**
**Habit** Bushy, compact.
**Flowers** Daisy-like,
borne in large clusters in
autumn. Yellow disc
florets surrounded by
clear blue ray florets.
**Leaves** Narrowly lance-
shaped. Mid-green.
• **HEIGHT** 30cm (12in).
• **SPREAD** 45cm (18in).

*A. novi-belgii*
'Professor Anton
Kippenburg'

☼ ◊ ❋❋❋

## A. *AMELLUS* 'King George'

**Habit** Bushy.
**Flowers** Large, terminal, daisy-like, produced in autumn. Deep violet-blue ray florets around a central golden disc.
**Leaves** Rough, hairy, lance-shaped to oval. Mid-green.
• HEIGHT 50cm (20in).
• SPREAD 50cm (20in).

*A. amellus* 'King George'

☼ ◊ ✿✿✿   ⚜

## A. *NOVI-BELGII* 'Peace'

**Habit** Vigorous, spreading.
**Flowers** Large, daisy-like, single, borne in dense clusters in autumn. Mauve ray florets, surrounding a golden disc.
**Leaves** Lance-shaped. Mid-green.
• TIPS May need staking.
• HEIGHT 1.2m (4ft).
• SPREAD 75cm (30in).

*A. novi-belgii* 'Peace'

☼ ◊ ✿✿✿

## A. *LINOSYRIS*

**Habit** Upright, with unbranched stems.
**Flowers** Small, in wiry-stemmed clusters, in late summer and autumn. Golden-yellow. An unusual Michaelmas daisy with the disc florets forming the flowers rather than the ray florets.
**Leaves** Narrowly lance-shaped. Mid-green.
• OTHER NAMES
*A. linosyris* 'Goldilocks'.
• HEIGHT 60cm (24in).
• SPREAD 30cm (12in).

## A. *NOVI-BELGII* 'Royal Velvet'

**Habit** Vigorous, spreading. **Flowers** Large, daisy-like, single-double, borne in dense clusters in autumn. Rich deep violet ray florets, surrounding a yellow disc.
**Leaves** Lance-shaped. Mid-green.
• TIPS May need staking.
• HEIGHT 1.2m (4ft).
• SPREAD 75cm (30in).

*A. novi-belgii* 'Royal Velvet'

☼ ◊ ✿✿✿

## A. *NOVI-BELGII* 'Chequers'

**Habit** Vigorous, spreading.
**Flowers** Daisy-like, single, borne in dense clusters in autumn. Purple ray florets around a golden-yellow disc.
**Leaves** Lance-shaped. Mid-green.
• HEIGHT 90cm (3ft).
• SPREAD 60–75cm (24–30in).

*A. novi-belgii* 'Chequers'

☼ ◊ ✿✿✿

*A. linosyris* Goldilocks

☼ ◊ ✿✿✿

| Acanthaceae | |
|---|---|

## STROBILANTHES ATROPURPUREUS

**Habit** Upright, clump-forming. **Flowers** Curved, tubular, borne in many-flowered spikes, on branching stems, from summer to autumn. Dark violet-blue to purple. **Leaves** Soft, serrated, oval, long-stalked. Mid-green or yellowish-green.
  NATIVE HABITAT Scrub and forests, Himalayas.
  CULTIVATION Grow in fertile, moist but well-drained soil, in semi-shade, or in sun where soils remain reliably moist. Shelter from strong winds.
  PROPAGATION By seed, basal stem cuttings or division in spring.

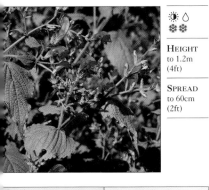

☼ ◊
❄ ❄

**HEIGHT**
to 1.2m
(4ft)

**SPREAD**
to 60cm
(2ft)

| Gentianaceae | WILLOW GENTIAN |
|---|---|

## GENTIANA ASCLEPIADEA  ♈

**Habit** Arching, clump-forming. **Flowers** Trumpet-shaped, borne in pairs in the leaf axils, towards the ends of arching stems, in late summer and autumn. Dark blue, spotted and striped on the inside. **Leaves** Lance-shaped. Fresh green.
• NATIVE HABITAT Woods and mountain meadows, from Europe to Turkey.
• CULTIVATION Grow in fertile, humus-rich, moist soil, in semi-shade, or in sun, in reliably moist soils.
• PROPAGATION By division in spring, or seed in autumn.

☼ ◊
❄ ❄ ❄

**HEIGHT**
to 90cm
(3ft)

**SPREAD**
to 60cm
(2ft)

| Asphodelaceae/Liliaceae | |
|---|---|

## KNIPHOFIA 'Percy's Pride'

**Habit** Upright, clump-forming. **Flowers** Small, narrowly tubular, borne on stout, upright stems in dense, narrow, terminal spikes, in autumn. Cream, tinted green or yellow. **Leaves** Tough, narrow, linear, arching to form dense basal clumps. Mid-green.
• NATIVE HABITAT Garden origin.
• CULTIVATION Grow in full sun, in damp, but well-drained soil. Needs ample moisture when in growth. Protect crowns in winter in cold areas.
• PROPAGATION By division in spring.

☼ ◊
❄ ❄

**HEIGHT**
1m (3ft)

**SPREAD**
50cm (20in)

| Hydrangeaceae | |
| --- | --- |

### KIRENGESHOMA PALMATA ♀

**Habit** Upright, clump-forming, rhizomatous.
**Flowers** Narrowly funnel-shaped, with fleshy
petals, borne in slender-stalked clusters in the
upper leaf axils, in late summer and autumn.
Creamy-yellow. **Leaves** Divided into shallow,
irregular, pointed lobes. Bright green.
• NATIVE HABITAT Mountain woodlands, Japan.
• CULTIVATION Grow in moist, humus-rich soil in
semi-shade. An exceptionally graceful plant for a
herbaceous or mixed border, or woodland garden.
• PROPAGATION Seed or division in autumn or spring.

☀ ◐
❀ ❀ ❀

HEIGHT
1m (3ft)

SPREAD
60cm (2ft)

| Asteraceae/Compositae | |
| --- | --- |

### HELENIUM 'Wyndley'

**Habit** Bushy, branching, clump-forming. **Flowers**
Large, daisy-like, produced over long periods in late
summer and autumn. Reflexed, red-streaked,
coppery-yellow ray florets around a rounded, brown
disc. **Leaves** Lance-shaped. Dark green.
• NATIVE HABITAT Garden origin.
• CULTIVATION Easily grown in almost any but
waterlogged soil, in full sun. A valuable long-
flowering plant for the late summer border. Divide
and replant regularly to maintain vigour.
• PROPAGATION By division in spring or autumn.

☀ ◐
❀ ❀ ❀

HEIGHT
60–75cm
(24–30in)

SPREAD
50cm (20in)

| Asphodelaceae/Liliaceae | |
| --- | --- |

### KNIPHOFIA CAULESCENS

**Habit** Upright, clump-forming. **Flowers** Small,
narrowly tubular, borne on upright stems in dense,
terminal spikes, in autumn. Yellow, opening from
salmon-red buds. **Leaves** Evergreen, tough, linear,
forming basal clumps. Blue-green.
• NATIVE HABITAT In peaty niches among damp
rocks, in the mountains of South Africa.
• CULTIVATION Grow in full sun, in damp but well-
drained soil. Needs ample moisture when in
growth. Protect crowns in winter in cold areas.
• PROPAGATION By seed or division in spring.

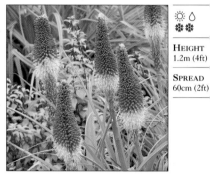

☀ ◐
❀ ❀

HEIGHT
1.2m (4ft)

SPREAD
60cm (2ft)

| Asphodelaceae/Liliaceae | |
| --- | --- |

### KNIPHOFIA 'Atlanta'

**Habit** Upright, clump-forming. **Flowers** Small,
tubular, borne on stout, upright stems in dense,
terminal spikes, in early autumn. Deep orange-red
and pale yellow. **Leaves** Grass-like, linear, arching
to form basal clumps. Mid-green.
• NATIVE HABITAT Garden origin.
• CULTIVATION Grow in full sun, in damp but
well-drained soil. Needs ample moisture when in
growth. Protect crowns in cold winter areas. Well-
suited to coastal gardens.
• PROPAGATION By division in spring.

☀ ◐
❀ ❀

HEIGHT
to 1m (3ft)

SPREAD
45cm (18in)

| Asphodelaceae/Liliaceae | |
|---|---|

## *KNIPHOFIA TRIANGULARIS* ♈

*Habit* Upright, clump-forming. *Flowers* Small, narrowly tubular, borne on upright stems in short terminal spikes, in autumn. Coral-orange. *Leaves* Narrow, linear, forming basal clumps. Mid-green.
NATIVE HABITAT Damp, peaty grasslands in the mountains of South Africa.
CULTIVATION Grow in full sun, in damp but well-drained soil. Needs ample moisture when in growth. Protect crowns in winter in cold areas.
PROPAGATION By seed or division in spring.
OTHER NAMES *K. galpinii* of gardens.

☼ ◊
❀❀

HEIGHT
1.2m (4ft)

SPREAD
60cm (2ft)

| Lamiaceae/Labiatae | |
|---|---|

## *SALVIA CONFERTIFLORA*

*Habit* Upright, woody-based. *Flowers* Tubular, 2-lipped, downy, in long, simple racemes, in late summer and autumn. Rich orange-vermilion. *Leaves* Large, oval, pointed. Bright green, clothed in tawny down beneath.
NATIVE HABITAT Brazil.
CULTIVATION Grow under glass in well-drained potting compost, or in full sun outdoors in a warm, sheltered site. Good for tubs in a cool conservatory.
PROPAGATION By seed in spring or softwood cuttings in summer.

☼ ◊
❀

HEIGHT
to 1.5m
(5ft)

SPREAD
60cm (2ft)

| Asteraceae/Compositae | |
|---|---|

## *HELENIUM* 'Moerheim Beauty'

*Habit* Upright, clump-forming. *Flowers* Large, daisy-like, borne on strong stems, in early autumn. Rich, dark orange-red ray florets surrounding a rounded, brown disc. *Leaves* Lance-shaped. Dark green.
• NATIVE HABITAT Garden origin.
• CULTIVATION Easily grown in almost any soil unless waterlogged, in full sun. A valuable long-flowering plant for a late summer border. Divide and replant regularly to maintain vigour.
• PROPAGATION By division in spring or autumn.

☼ ◊
❀❀❀

HEIGHT
1m (3ft)

SPREAD
60cm (2ft)

| Marantaceae | NEVER-NEVER PLANT |
|---|---|

## *CTENANTHE OPPENHEIMIANA* ♈
## 'Tricolor'

*Habit* Vigorous, bushy. *Flowers* Small, 3-petalled, borne in spikes, produced intermittently. White. *Leaves* Evergreen, leathery, lance-shaped. Green, irregularly blotched with creamy-white.
• NATIVE HABITAT Garden origin.
• CULTIVATION Grow as a house or conservatory plant in cool climates in moist, humus-rich, well-drained soil. Keep compost moist with tepid, soft water. Maintain even temperatures and humidity.
• PROPAGATION By division in spring.

☼ ◑

Min. 15°C
(59°F)

HEIGHT
1m (3ft)

SPREAD
1m (3ft)

| Lamiaceae/Labiatae | |
|---|---|

## *PLECTRANTHUS FORSTERI* 'Marginatus'

*Habit* Bushy, or semi-trailing. *Flowers* Small, tubular, borne irregularly. White to pale mauve. *Leaves* Aromatic, oval, 6 cm (2½in) long. Grey-green with scalloped, creamy-white margins.
• NATIVE HABITAT Garden origin.
• CULTIVATION Grow as a house or conservatory plant in cool climates, in moist soil, in sun or semi-shade. Water and feed regularly in growth.
• PROPAGATION By stem cuttings or division in spring or summer.
• OTHER NAMES *P. coleoides* 'Marginatus'.

☼ ◑

Min. 10°C
(50°F)

HEIGHT
60cm (2ft)

SPREAD
60cm (2ft)

| Araceae | CRYSTAL ANTHURIUM |
|---|---|

## *ANTHURIUM CRYSTALLINUM*

*Habit* Erect, tufted. *Flowers* Long-lasting, intermittent. Red-purple spathes, with a green spadix. *Leaves* Evergreen, to 45cm (18in) long and 30cm (12in) wide, heart-shaped at the base. Velvety dark green, with white or pale green veins.
• NATIVE HABITAT Tropical forest, Panama to Peru.
• CULTIVATION Grow as a house or conservatory plant in cool climates, in well-drained, peaty soil. Give bright light in winter; indirect sun in summer. Water freely in growth and maintain high humidity.
• PROPAGATION By division in spring.

☼ ◑

Min. 15°C
(59°F)

HEIGHT
75cm (30in)

SPREAD
60cm (24in)

| Acanthaceae | FRECKLE FACE, POLKA-DOT PLANT |
|---|---|

## *HYPOESTES PHYLLOSTACHYA* ♈

*Habit* Bushy, sub-shrubby. *Flowers* Small, tubular, intermittent. Lavender. *Leaves* Evergreen, oval, softly downy. Dark green, with irregular pink spots.
• NATIVE HABITAT South Africa, Madagascar, S.E. Asia.
• CULTIVATION Grow as a house or conservatory plant in cool climates, in fertile, well-drained soil in bright light. Water freely when in full growth.
• PROPAGATION By seed in spring or stem cuttings in spring or summer.
• OTHER NAMES *H. sanguinolenta* of gardens.

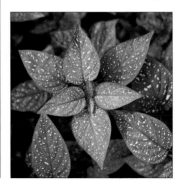

☼ ○

Min. 10°C
(50°F)

HEIGHT
75cm (30in)

SPREAD
75cm (30in)

| Araceae | |
|---|---|

## CALADIUM BICOLOR 'Pink Beauty'

**Habit** Tufted, tuberous-rooted. **Flowers** Tubular white spathes are produced in summer. **Leaves** Long-stalked, triangular. Dark green, mottled pink, with darker pink veins.

NATIVE HABITAT Garden origin.

CULTIVATION Grow as a house or conservatory plant in cool climates, in moist, humus-rich soil. Give bright light in winter; indirect sun in summer. Water freely in growth and maintain humidity. When leaves die, store tubers in a dark, frost-free place.

PROPAGATION By tubers when repotting in spring.

☀ ◐

Min. 19°C
(66°F)

HEIGHT
90cm (3ft)

SPREAD
90cm (3ft)

| Araceae | FLAMINGO FLOWER, TAIL FLOWER |
|---|---|

## ANTHURIUM ANDREANUM

**Habit** Erect. **Flowers** Long-lasting, produced intermittently. Bright red spathes with a red-tipped, yellow spadix. **Leaves** Evergreen, long-stalked, broadly oval, heart-shaped at the base. Dark green.

• NATIVE HABITAT Forest, Colombia, Ecuador.

• CULTIVATION Grow as a house or conservatory plant in cool climates, in moist, well-drained, peaty soil. Provide bright light in winter and indirect sun in summer. Water freely when in growth and maintain high humidity.

• PROPAGATION By division in spring.

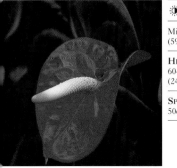

☀ ◐

Min. 15°C
(59°F)

HEIGHT
60–75cm
(24–30in)

SPREAD
50cm (20in)

| Lamiaceae/Labiatae | |
|---|---|

## SALVIA ELEGANS

**Habit** Upright, woody-based. **Flowers** Tubular, 2-lipped, in loose, branched racemes, in winter and spring. Scarlet. **Leaves** Oval to diamond-shaped, smooth or slightly downy. Mid-green.

• NATIVE HABITAT Mexico, Guatemala.

• CULTIVATION Grow in fertile, well-drained potting compost, under glass, or in similar soils outdoors, in full sun. Needs a warm, sheltered site. Good for tubs in a cool conservatory.

• PROPAGATION By seed in spring or softwood cuttings in summer.

☀ ◐
❄

HEIGHT
1.5m (5ft)
or more

SPREAD
60cm (2ft)

| Nepenthaceae | |
|---|---|

## NEPENTHES × HOOKERIANA

**Habit** Epiphytic, insectivorous. **Flowers** Pendent, pitcher-shaped, to 13cm (5in) long, with a spurred lid, long-lasting. Pale green, marked red-purple. **Leaves** Evergreen, lance-shaped. Dark green.

• NATIVE HABITAT Tropical forest, S.E. Asia.

• CULTIVATION Grow as a house or conservatory plant in cool climates in lattice pots in a damp mix of bark, perlite and peat moss. Maintain humidity.

• PROPAGATION By seed in spring, or stem cuttings in spring or summer.

• OTHER NAMES N. rafflesiana × ampullaria.

☀ ◐

Min. 18°C
(64°F)

HEIGHT
60–75cm
(24–30in)

SPREAD
60–75cm
(24–30in)

| Agavaceae | |
|---|---|

## PHORMIUM 'Dazzler'

**Habit** Upright, clump-forming. **Flowers**
Tubular, in large panicles, to 5m (15ft) high, in
summer. Dark red, borne on blue-purple stems.
**Leaves** Evergreen, stiff, sword-shaped, to 2m
(6ft) long, in basal clumps. Striped yellow,
salmon-pink, orange-red and bronze.
• NATIVE HABITAT Garden origin.
• CULTIVATION Grow in deep, fertile, humus-rich
soil, in a warm, sunny, sheltered site. Excellent for
coastal gardens and gravel plantings. This cultivar
combines a strongly architectural outline with

brilliantly coloured foliage. It is invaluable as
an accent plant in a herbaceous or mixed border,
providing strong contrasts of form against other
more softly rounded shapes. It is also useful as
a free-standing feature plant in a courtyard or
similar situation. Provide a dry winter mulch
in very cold areas.
• PROPAGATION By division in spring.

**HEIGHT**
2–2.5m
(6–8ft)

**SPREAD**
1m (3ft)

| Solanaceae | BUSH VIOLET |
|---|---|

## BROWALLIA SPECIOSA

**Habit** Bushy. **Flowers** Five-lobed, borne in profusion in summer or winter. Violet-blue with white eyes. **Leaves** Oval, pointed. Bright green.
• NATIVE HABITAT Tropical South America.
• CULTIVATION Grow as a house or conservatory plant in cool climates, in well-drained compost or soil, in sun or part-shade. Keep moist and feed when in flower. Encourage bushiness by pinching back young shoots. Often grown as a bedding annual.
• PROPAGATION By seed in spring or, for winter flowers, in late summer.

☀ ◊

Min.
10–15°C
(50–59°F)

**HEIGHT**
60–75cm
(24–30in)

**SPREAD**
45cm (18in)

| Araceae | |
|---|---|

## ALOCASIA CUPREA

**Habit** Upright, tufted, rhizomatous. **Flowers** Purple spathes produced intermittently. **Leaves** Oval, 30cm (12in) long, heart-shaped at base. Metallic, purple-green above, purple beneath.
• NATIVE HABITAT Tropical forest, Malaysia, Borneo.
• CULTIVATION Grow as a house or conservatory plant in cool climates, in semi-shade, with high humidity, in a mix of granulated bark, loam, sharp sand and charcoal.
• PROPAGATION By seed, stem cuttings, or division of the rhizomes in spring.

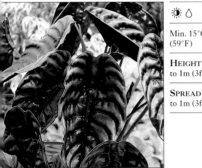

☀ ◊

Min. 15°C
(59°F)

**HEIGHT**
to 1m (3ft)

**SPREAD**
to 1m (3ft)

| Araceae | TANNIA |
|---|---|

## XANTHOSOMA SAGITTIFOLIUM

**Habit** Spreading, tufted, tuberous-rooted. **Flowers** Green spathes, to 20cm (8in) long, are produced intermittently. **Leaves** Broadly arrow-shaped, to 60cm (2ft) long. Glaucous, greyish-green.
• NATIVE HABITAT Cultivated for edible tubers in New World tropics, but natural range unknown.
• CULTIVATION Grow as a house or conservatory plant in cool climates, in moist, well-drained soil or compost, in semi-shade. Maintain high humidity.
• PROPAGATION By division or stem cuttings in spring or summer.

☀ ◊

Min. 15°C
(59°F)

**HEIGHT**
to 2m (6ft)
in flower

**SPREAD**
2m (6ft)
or more

| Asteraceae/Compositae | SILVER KING |
|---|---|

## ARTEMISIA LUDOVICIANA var. ALBULA

**Habit** Upright, bushy, stoloniferous. **Flowers** Tiny, in slender plumes, in summer. Grey-white. **Leaves** Evergreen, variable: entire and lance-shaped, or jaggedly toothed and broadly oval to elliptic. Silvery-white, densely hairy.
• NATIVE HABITAT Dry grassland, or light woodland, California, USA.
• CULTIVATION Grow in an open, sunny site, in well-drained soil. Cut back in spring for best foliage effects. Indispensable in a silver border.
• PROPAGATION By division in spring or autumn.

☀ ◊

**HEIGHT**
1.2m (4ft)

**SPREAD**
60cm (2ft)

| Gesneriaceae | |
|---|---|

### COLUMNEA MICROPHYLLA VARIEGATA

**Habit** Trailing. **Flowers** Tubular, hooded, borne singly in the leaf axils, in winter and spring. Scarlet, with yellow throats. **Leaves** Evergreen, oval to rounded. Grey-green, edged cream, often red-flushed beneath.
• NATIVE HABITAT Garden origin.
• CULTIVATION Grow as a house or conservatory plant in cool climates, in moist, well-drained soil or compost. Needs bright, indirect light and humidity. Keep drier in winter. Good for hanging baskets.
• PROPAGATION By tip cuttings after flowering.

Min. 15°C
(59°F)

HEIGHT
1m (3ft)
or more

SPREAD
indefinite

| Apiaceae/Umbelliferae | BAYONET PLANT, COMMON SPANIARD |
|---|---|

### ACIPHYLLA SQUARROSA

**Habit** Rosette-forming. **Flowers** Small, scented, in large, branching, candelabra-like spikes, to 2m (6ft) tall, in early summer. Yellow. **Leaves** Evergreen, rigid, bayonet-like, to 70cm (28in) long. Green or golden-green.
• NATIVE HABITAT Sub-alpine and mountain grassland, North and South Island, New Zealand.
• CULTIVATION Grow in full sun, in humus-rich, well-drained soil. Excellent architectural form, especially useful for planting in gravel.
• PROPAGATION By seed sown fresh or in spring.

HEIGHT
1–1.2m
(3–4ft)

SPREAD
1–1.2m
(3–4ft)

| Asparagaceae/Liliaceae | |
|---|---|

### ASPARAGUS DENSIFLORUS 'Sprengeri'

**Habit** Trailing, tuberous-rooted. **Flowers** Inconspicuous, borne in clusters in the leaf axils, in summer. Pink-tinted, white. **Fruits** Small, bright red berries, to 1cm (½in) across. **Leaves** Evergreen, small, flat, linear, leaf-like stems. Bright green.
• NATIVE HABITAT South Africa.
• CULTIVATION Grow as a house or conservatory plant in cool climates, in fertile, moist but well-drained soil or potting compost. Position in semi-shade, or in bright, indirect light.
• PROPAGATION By seed or division in spring.

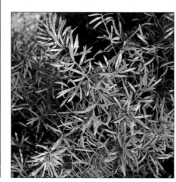

Min. 10°C
(50°F)

HEIGHT
to 1m (3ft)

SPREAD
50cm (20in)

| Asparagaceae/Liliaceae | |
|---|---|

**ASPARAGUS DENSIFLORUS 'Myers'** ♀
*Habit* Upright, tuberous-rooted. *Flowers*
inconspicuous, borne in axillary clusters in summer.
Pink-tinted, white. *Fruits* Small, bright red berries,
to 1cm (½in) across. *Leaves* Evergreen, needle-like,
borne in dense, cylindrical spikes. Dark green.
• NATIVE HABITAT Garden origin.
• CULTIVATION Grow as a house or conservatory
plant in cool climates. Place in fertile, moist but
well-drained soil or potting compost. Position in
semi-shade, or in bright, indirect light.
• PROPAGATION By seed or division in spring.

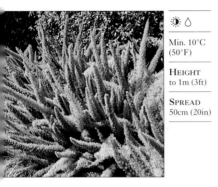

☀ ◊

Min. 10°C
(50°F)

HEIGHT
to 1m (3ft)

SPREAD
50cm (20in)

| Acanthaceae | MARBLE LEAF |
|---|---|

**PERISTROPHE HYSSOPIFOLIA
'Aureovariegata'**
*Habit* Bushy, sub-shrubby. *Flowers* Small, long-
tubed, 2-lipped, in clusters, in winter. Rose-pink.
*Leaves* Evergreen, lance-shaped, pointed. Dark
green with a central, creamy-yellow blotch.
• NATIVE HABITAT Garden origin.
• CULTIVATION Grow as a house or conservatory
plant in cool climates, in well-drained soil or
compost. Place in sun or part-shade. Water freely
in growth, less in winter. Attractive foliage plant.
• PROPAGATION Stem cuttings in spring or summer.

☀ ◊

Min. 15°C
(59°F)

HEIGHT
to 60cm
(2ft) or
more

SPREAD
1.2m (4ft)

| Zingiberaceae | |
|---|---|

**GLOBBA WINITII**
*Habit* Clump-forming, rhizomatous. *Flowers*
Small, tubular, in pendent sprays, intermittently.
Yellow, with large, reflexed, red-purple bracts.
*Leaves* Evergreen, lance-shaped, heart-shaped
at the base. Mid-green and slightly hairy beneath.
• NATIVE HABITAT Thailand.
• CULTIVATION Grow as a house or conservatory
plant in cool climates, in moist, well-drained,
humus-rich soil or compost. Needs high humidity;
water freely in growth, less when dormant in winter.
• PROPAGATION By division or seed in spring.

☀ ◊

Min. 18°C
(64°F)

HEIGHT
1m (3ft)

SPREAD
30cm (1ft)

| Strelitziaceae | BIRD-OF-PARADISE FLOWER |
|---|---|

**STRELITZIA REGINAE** ♀
*Habit* Clump-forming, palm-like. *Flowers* Short-
stemmed, beak-like, borne mainly in spring.
Orange and blue, enclosed in a boat-shaped, red-
edged bract. *Leaves* Evergreen, long-stalked,
oblong, to 70cm (28in) long. Bluish-green.
• NATIVE HABITAT South Africa.
• CULTIVATION Grow as a conservatory or house
plant in cool climates, in fertile, well-drained soil or
compost. Place in good light, but shade from hot
sun. Water freely in growth, sparingly in winter.
• PROPAGATION By seed or suckers in spring.

☀ ◊

Min.
5–10°C
(41–50°F)

HEIGHT
1m (3ft)
or more

SPREAD
75cm (30in)

| Berberidaceae | |
|---|---|

## EPIMEDIUM X YOUNGIANUM 'Niveum' ♚

**Habit** Compact, clump-forming. **Flowers** Small, cup-shaped, with or without spurs, borne in loose, branched clusters of 4–12, in late spring. White. **Leaves** Divided into 2–9 heart-shaped, serrated leaflets. Bright green, bronze on emergence.
• NATIVE HABITAT Garden origin.
• CULTIVATION Grow in moist but well-drained, humus-rich soil, in part-shade. Provides good ground cover in a damp, shady border. Cut away old foliage in late winter.
• PROPAGATION By division in spring or autumn.

☀ ◊
❀ ❀ ❀

**HEIGHT**
15–30cm
(6–12in)

**SPREAD**
30cm (12in)

| Boraginaceae | |
|---|---|

## PULMONARIA OFFICINALIS 'Sissinghurst White'

**Habit** Neat, clump-forming. **Flowers** Funnel-shaped, borne in terminal clusters in spring. Pure white. **Leaves** Semi-evergreen, long, elliptic. Mid-green with paler spotting.
• NATIVE HABITAT Garden origin.
• CULTIVATION Grow in fertile, humus-rich, moist but well-drained soil, in shade or semi-shade. Excellent for a woodland garden or shady border, especially beneath shrubs or trees.
• PROPAGATION By division in spring or autumn.

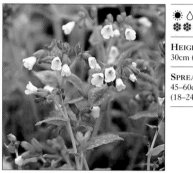

☀ ◊
❀ ❀ ❀

**HEIGHT**
30cm (12in)

**SPREAD**
45–60cm
(18–24in)

| Lamiaceae/Labiatae | |
|---|---|

## LAMIUM MACULATUM 'White Nancy' ♚

**Habit** Mat-forming. **Flowers** Small, hooded, 2-lipped, in dense, terminal, spike-like clusters, from late spring to summer. Pure white. **Leaves** Semi-evergreen, oval. Variegated silver-white.
• NATIVE HABITAT Garden origin.
• CULTIVATION Grow in cool, moist but well-drained soil, in full or part-shade. Excellent ground cover, but dislikes excessive winter wet.
• PROPAGATION By division in autumn or early spring, or by stem tip cuttings of non-flowering shoots in mid-summer.

☀ ◊
❀ ❀ ❀

**HEIGHT**
15cm (6in)

**SPREAD**
1m (3ft)

| Brassicaceae/Cruciferae | |
|---|---|

## PACHYPHRAGMA MACROPHYLLUM

**Habit** Spreading, rhizomatous. **Flowers** Small, 4-petalled, borne in dense, terminal clusters in spring. White. **Leaves** Large, oval, heart-shaped at the base, held on long stalks. Glossy, dark green.
• NATIVE HABITAT Moist, deciduous woodland, in the Caucasus, and N.E. Turkey.
• CULTIVATION Grow in moist, humus-rich soils in shade or semi-shade. Provides good ground cover.
• PROPAGATION By division or stem cuttings in late spring, or by seed in autumn.
• OTHER NAMES *Thlaspi macrophyllum*.

☀ ◊
❀ ❀ ❀

**HEIGHT**
to 30cm
(12in)

**SPREAD**
indefinite

| Trilliaceae/Liliaceae | |
|---|---|

## *TRILLIUM CERNUUM* f. *ALBUM*

*Habit* Clump-forming. *Flowers* Nodding,
3-petalled, borne in spring, beneath the leaves.
White, with maroon centres. *Leaves* Short-stalked,
rhombic, borne in terminal whorls of three, on
slender stems. Mid-green.
• NATIVE HABITAT Moist woods, E. North America.
• CULTIVATION Grow in moist, leafy, neutral to
acid soils, in full or part-shade. Excellent for a
woodland garden.
• PROPAGATION By division, after foliage dies
back in summer, or by seed in autumn.

HEIGHT
30–45cm
(12–18in)

SPREAD
30cm (12in)

| Lamiaceae/Labiatae | |
|---|---|

## *LAMIUM MACULATUM ALBUM*

*Habit* Mat-forming. *Flowers* Small, hooded,
2-lipped, borne in terminal, spike-like clusters, in
late spring and summer. Pure white. *Leaves* Semi-
evergreen, oval. Green with a silvery-white blotch.
• NATIVE HABITAT Garden origin.
• CULTIVATION Grow in cool, moist but well-
drained soil, in full or part-shade. Excellent ground
cover, but dislikes excessive winter wet.
• PROPAGATION By division in autumn or early
spring, or by stem tip cuttings of non-flowering
shoots in mid-summer.

HEIGHT
20cm (8in)

SPREAD
1m (3ft)

| Convallariaceae/ Liliaceae | LILY-OF-THE-VALLEY |
|---|---|

## *CONVALLARIA MAJALIS*

*Habit* Creeping, rhizomatous. *Flowers* Small,
very fragrant, pendent, bell-shaped, on arching
stems in late spring or early summer. Waxy white.
*Leaves* Narrowly oval. Mid- to dark green.
• NATIVE HABITAT Woodland, scrub and meadows,
in the mountains of northern temperate regions.
• CULTIVATION Grows best in moist, leafy soil,
in shade or semi-shade. Excellent for naturalizing
in a woodland garden or shady border.
• PROPAGATION By division after flowering or
in autumn.

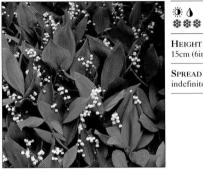

HEIGHT
15cm (6in)

SPREAD
indefinite

| Convallariaceae/ Liliaceae | FAIRY LANTERNS |
|---|---|

## *DISPORUM SMITHII*

*Habit* Spreading, clump-forming, rhizomatous.
*Flowers* Small, pendent, tubular-bell-shaped,
singly or in terminal clusters of 2–6, in spring.
White, tipped green. *Fruits* Oval, orange-red
berries, from late summer. *Leaves* Oval to lance-
shaped, heart-shaped at the base. Mid-green.
• NATIVE HABITAT Evergreen forests, coastal
mountains of W. North America.
• CULTIVATION Grow in cool, moist, humus-rich
soil in semi-shade. Good for woodland gardens.
• PROPAGATION Seed in autumn; division in spring.

HEIGHT
30–60cm
(12–24in)

SPREAD
60cm (24in)
or more

| Trilliaceae/Liliaceae | WAKE-ROBIN |
|---|---|

## *TRILLIUM GRANDIFLORUM*

*Habit* Clump-forming. *Flowers* Large,
3-petalled, borne above the leaves in spring. Pure
white, flushed pink with age. *Leaves* Large, oval
to almost circular, borne in terminal whorls of 3,
on slender stems. Mid-green.
• NATIVE HABITAT Moist woodlands and thickets,
in E. North America.
• CULTIVATION Grow in moist, leafy, neutral to
acid soils in full or part-shade. Excellent for a
peat terrace. This is the hardiest and most
rewarding of all the trilliums. In its double form

it is spectacular. For the most impressive
springtime display, do not overcrowd the plants
with other vigorous subjects, but allow them
enough space to spread. This perennial does
particularly well in the company of hostas, whose
foliage matures later in the season.
• PROPAGATION By division, after foliage dies
back in summer, or by seed in autumn.

HEIGHT
38cm (15in)

SPREAD
30cm (12in)

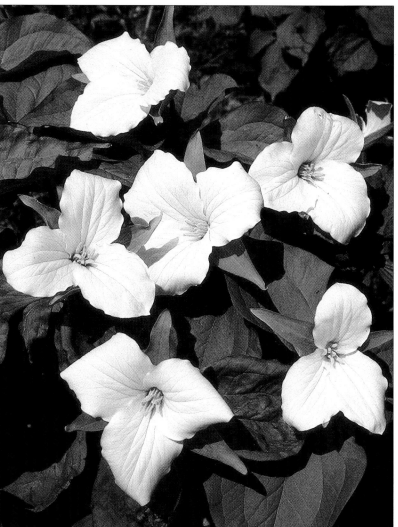

| Trilliaceae/Liliaceae | |
| --- | --- |

## *TRILLIUM OVATUM*

***Habit*** Clump-forming. ***Flowers*** Musk-scented, 3-petalled, borne above the leaves in spring. Pure white, fading to pink. ***Leaves*** Diamond-shaped, borne in terminal whorls of 3. Dark green, on slender red stems.
• NATIVE HABITAT Forest, W. North America.
• CULTIVATION Grow in moist, leafy, neutral to acid soils, in full or part-shade. Excellent for woodland gardens.
• PROPAGATION By division, after foliage dies back in summer, or by seed in autumn.

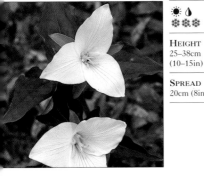

HEIGHT
25–38cm
(10–15in)

SPREAD
20cm (8in)

| Ranunculaceae | |
| --- | --- |

## *ADONIS BREVISTYLA*

***Habit*** Clump-forming, with stout, branching roots. ***Flowers*** Small, buttercup-like, borne singly at the ends of slender stems, in early spring. White, tinted blue on the petal reverse. ***Leaves*** Finely divided into flattened, pointed, lobes. Mid-green.
• NATIVE HABITAT Damp forest, scrub and rocky ravines, in Bhutan and W. China.
• CULTIVATION Grow in moist, humus-rich soil, in shade or semi-shade; shelter from cold, dry winds.
• PROPAGATION By fresh seed in late summer or by division after flowering.

HEIGHT
15–23cm
(6–9in)

SPREAD
15–23cm
(6–9in)

| Berberidaceae | HIMALAYAN MAY APPLE |
| --- | --- |

## *PODOPHYLLUM HEXANDRUM*

***Habit*** Clump-forming. ***Flowers*** Flattish, with 6 petals, borne singly at the ends of sturdy stems, in spring. White or pale pink. ***Fruits*** Fleshy, oval red berries, in summer. ***Leaves*** Divided into 3 lobes, unfurling fully after flowering. Dark green, mottled with brown.
• NATIVE HABITAT Scrub, forest and meadows, in the Himalayas and W. China.
• CULTIVATION Grow in moist, humus-rich soil.
• PROPAGATION Division in spring; seed in autumn.
• OTHER NAMES *P. emodi.*

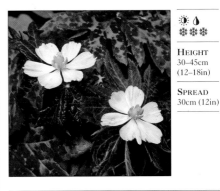

HEIGHT
30–45cm
(12–18in)

SPREAD
30cm (12in)

| Ranunculaceae | SNOWDROP, WINDFLOWER |
| --- | --- |

## *ANEMONE SYLVESTRIS*

***Habit*** Carpeting, rhizomatous. ***Flowers*** Fragrant, semi-pendent, cupped, borne singly or in pairs, on slender stems in spring and early summer. White, with yellow anthers. ***Leaves*** Divided and lobed. Mid-green, hairy beneath.
• NATIVE HABITAT Woods and rocky hills, C. and E. Europe to the Caucasus.
• CULTIVATION Grow in humus-rich, moist, well-drained soil. May be invasive where conditions suit.
• PROPAGATION By division in spring, by fresh seed in late summer, or by root cuttings in winter.

HEIGHT
30cm (12in)

SPREAD
30cm (12in)

| Trilliaceae/Liliaceae | |
|---|---|

## TRILLIUM CHLOROPETALUM 🏆

**Habit** Clump-forming. **Flowers** Fragrant, with 3 upright or incurved petals, borne above the leaves in spring. Purplish-pink to greenish-white. **Leaves** Diamond-shaped, borne in terminal whorls of 3, on red-green stems. Dark green, grey-marbled.
• NATIVE HABITAT Damp forests in California, USA.
• CULTIVATION Grow in moist, leafy, neutral to acid soils, in full or part-shade. Excellent for peat banks, woodland gardens, or shady borders.
• PROPAGATION By division, after foliage dies back in summer, or by seed in autumn.

☀️ ◐
❋❋❋

HEIGHT
30–45cm
(12–18in)

SPREAD
30–45cm
(12–18in)

| Berberidaceae | |
|---|---|

## EPIMEDIUM PUBIGERUM

**Habit** Dense, carpeting. **Flowers** Small, cup-shaped, borne in loose clusters of 12–35, in late spring. Yellow petals with creamy-white or pink inner sepals. **Leaves** Evergreen, divided into smooth, heart-shaped leaflets. Glossy, dark green.
• NATIVE HABITAT Woodland, Turkey, S.E. Europe.
• CULTIVATION Grow in moist, well-drained, humus-rich soil, in part-shade. Provides good ground cover in a shady border. May be damaged by late frosts. Cut away old foliage in late winter.
• PROPAGATION By division in spring or autumn.

☀️ ◐
❋❋❋

HEIGHT
45cm (18in)

SPREAD
45cm (18in)

| Saxifragaceae | |
|---|---|

## BERGENIA 'Silberlicht' 🏆

**Habit** Clump-forming. **Flowers** Small, open cup-shaped, borne in dense clusters, on sturdy stems in spring. White, often flushed pink. **Leaves** Evergreen, leathery, oval to rounded, toothed margins, in basal rosettes. Mid-green.
• NATIVE HABITAT Garden origin.
• CULTIVATION Grow in sun or semi-shade, in any well-drained soil. Best with some shelter from cold, dry winds to avoid foliage scorch.
• PROPAGATION Division in spring, after flowering.
• OTHER NAMES B. 'Silverlight'.

☀️ ◐
❋❋❋

HEIGHT
30cm (12in)

SPREAD
50cm (20in)

| Geraniaceae | |
|---|---|

## GERANIUM MACRORRHIZUM 🏆
## 'Ingwersen's Variety'

**Habit** Compact, carpeting, rhizomatous. **Flowers** Small, in pairs or umbels, in late spring and early summer. Soft rose-pink. **Leaves** Aromatic, semi-evergreen, divided into 5–7 deeply cut lobes. Mid-green, tinted red and bronze in winter.
• NATIVE HABITAT Mount Koprovnik, Montenegro.
• CULTIVATION Grow in almost any soil, in sun or semi-shade. Good weed-smothering ground cover.
• PROPAGATION By division in autumn or spring or by semi-ripe cuttings in summer.

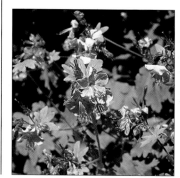

☀️ ◐
❋❋❋

HEIGHT
30cm (12in)

SPREAD
60cm (24in)

Saxifragaceae

## BERGENIA CILIATA

**Habit** Clump-forming. **Flowers** Small, open
cup-shaped, in dense clusters, in early spring.
White, fading to pink. **Leaves** Evergreen, large,
leathery, rounded, toothed, heart-shaped at the
base, fringed with bristles. Dark green, turning
red in autumn.
• NATIVE HABITAT Woods and rocky places, in
the Himalayas, from Afghanistan to S.E. Tibet.
• CULTIVATION Grow in sun or semi-shade, in a
cool position, in any well-drained soil. The best
results will be achieved if some shelter is given
from frost and wind. This perennial is not hardy
everywhere, and the leaves may be severely cut
back by hard frosts, although they will recover
speedily. A good idea is to plant in the proximity
of a small shrub by way of permanent protection.
• PROPAGATION By division in spring, after
flowering.

☼ ◊
❀ ❀

**HEIGHT**
30cm (12in)

**SPREAD**
50cm (20in)

Saxifragaceae

## BERGENIA 'Ballawley'

**Habit** Clump-forming. **Flowers** Small, open cup-shaped, borne in dense clusters, on sturdy, red stems, in spring. Bright crimson. **Leaves** Evergreen, leathery, oval to rounded, toothed, in basal rosettes. Mid-green, turning red in winter.
• NATIVE HABITAT Garden origin.
• CULTIVATION Grow in sun or semi-shade, in any well-drained soil. Best with some shelter from cold, dry winds to avoid foliage scorch.
• PROPAGATION By division in spring, after flowering.

HEIGHT
to 60cm
(24in)

SPREAD
60cm (24in)

Saxifragaceae

## BERGENIA CORDIFOLIA 'Purpurea'

**Habit** Clump-forming. **Flowers** Small, bell-shaped, borne in dense clusters, on sturdy red stem from late winter to early spring. Rose-pink. **Leave:** Evergreen, leathery, rounded, with wavy margins. Dark green, tinted purple, especially in winter.
• NATIVE HABITAT Garden origin.
• CULTIVATION Grow in sun or semi-shade, in any well-drained soil. This and its parent species are among the most cold- and heat-tolerant of bergenia Good for ground cover.
• PROPAGATION Division in spring, after flowering.

HEIGHT
50cm (20in

SPREAD
50cm (20in

Melanthiaceae/Liliaceae

## HELONIOPSIS ORIENTALIS

**Habit** Rosette-forming, rhizomatous. **Flowers** Small, narrow petalled, in nodding clusters, in late spring or early summer. Rose-pink. **Leaves** Evergreen, lance-shaped, in basal rosettes. Mid-green.
• NATIVE HABITAT Mountain woodland, scrub and meadows in Japan, Korea and Sakhalin Island.
• CULTIVATION Grow in moist but well-drained, humus-rich soil, in a cool, shady position.
• PROPAGATION By division in autumn, or by seed in autumn or spring.
• OTHER NAMES H. japonica.

HEIGHT
30cm (12in)

SPREAD
30cm (12in)

Leguminosae/
Papilionaceae

## LATHYRUS VERNUS 'Alboroseus'

**Habit** Bushy, clump-forming. **Flowers** Small, pea-like, borne in 3–15 flowered sprays, in spring. White and deep pink. **Leaves** Fern-like, divided into 2–4 pairs of pointed, oval leaflets. Mid-green.
• NATIVE HABITAT Species occurs in European scrub and woodland.
• CULTIVATION Grow in any well-drained soil, including poor stony soils, in sun or light shade. Dislikes root disturbance and may be slow to establish after transplanting.
• PROPAGATION By careful division in spring.

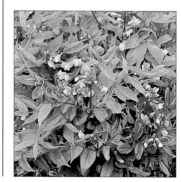

HEIGHT
30cm (12in)

SPREAD
30cm (12in

| Berberidaceae | |
|---|---|

## EPIMEDIUM GRANDIFLORUM 'Rose Queen' ♀

*Habit* Dense, clump-forming. *Flowers* Small, cup-shaped, spurred, on branching, wiry stems in spring. Deep pink. *Leaves* Divided into 2–3 smooth, thin, heart-shaped leaflets. Copper-tinted dark green.
NATIVE HABITAT Garden origin.
CULTIVATION Grow in moist but well-drained, humus-rich soil, in part-shade. Provides good ground cover in a shady border. May be damaged by wind and late frosts. Cut back old foliage in late winter.
PROPAGATION By division in spring or autumn.

☼ ◐
❀ ❀ ❀

HEIGHT
30cm (12in)

SPREAD
30cm (12in)

| Berberidaceae | |
|---|---|

## EPIMEDIUM X RUBRUM ♀

*Habit* Compact, carpeting, rhizomatous. *Flowers* Small, cup-shaped, in loose, branched clusters in spring. Crimson, with yellow spurs. *Leaves* Divided into heart-shaped, serrated leaflets. Mid-green, bronze-red on emergence and in autumn.
• NATIVE HABITAT Garden origin.
• CULTIVATION Grow in moist, well-drained, humus-rich soil, in part-shade. Cut back old foliage in late winter. Excellent ground cover in a damp, shady border or woodland garden.
• PROPAGATION By division in spring or autumn.

☼ ◐
❀ ❀ ❀

HEIGHT
30cm (12in)

SPREAD
20cm (8in)

| Lamiaceae/Labiatae | |
|---|---|

## LAMIUM MACULATUM

*Habit* Mat-forming, stoloniferous. *Flowers* Small, hooded, 2-lipped, borne in terminal, spike-like clusters, in mid spring. Mauve-pink. *Leaves* Semi-evergreen, oval, with a central, silver-white stripe.
• NATIVE HABITAT Woodland and meadows, from Europe and N. Africa to W. Asia.
• CULTIVATION Grow in moist but well-drained soil, in full or part-shade. Excellent ground cover.
• PROPAGATION By division in autumn or early spring, or by stem tip cuttings of non-flowering shoots in mid-summer.

☀ ◐
❀ ❀ ❀

HEIGHT
20cm (8in)

SPREAD
1m (3ft)

| Trilliaceae/Liliaceae | BIRTHROOT, SQUAWROOT |
|---|---|

## TRILLIUM ERECTUM ♀

*Habit* Clump-forming. *Flowers* Ill-scented, semi-nodding, with 3 petals, borne above the leaves in late spring. Maroon-purple. *Leaves* Broadly oval, in terminal whorls of 3. Mid-green.
• NATIVE HABITAT Damp woodlands, E. North America.
• CULTIVATION Grow in moist, leafy, neutral to acid soils in full or part-shade. Excellent for peat banks, woodland gardens or borders.
• PROPAGATION By division, after foliage dies back in summer, or by seed in autumn.

☀ ◐
❀ ❀ ❀

HEIGHT
30–45cm
(12–18in)

SPREAD
30cm (12in)

| Berberidaceae | |
|---|---|

## *EPIMEDIUM GRANDIFLORUM*
## 'Crimson Beauty'

*Habit* Dense, clump-forming. *Flowers* Small, cup-shaped, spurred, borne on wiry stems in spring. Crimson. *Leaves* Divided into 2–3 smooth, thin, heart-shaped leaflets. Copper-tinted dark green.
• NATIVE HABITAT Garden origin.
• CULTIVATION Grow in moist but well-drained, humus-rich soil, in part-shade. Provides good ground cover in a shady border. May be damaged by wind and late frosts. Cut back old foliage in late winter.
• PROPAGATION By division in spring or autumn.

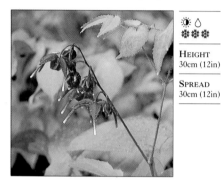

HEIGHT
30cm (12in)

SPREAD
30cm (12in)

| Berberidaceae | |
|---|---|

## *EPIMEDIUM GRANDIFLORUM* 'Lilafee'

*Habit* Dense, clump-forming. *Flowers* Small, cup-shaped, spurred, borne on branching, wiry stems in spring. Lavender-violet. *Leaves* Divided into 2–3 smooth, thin-textured, heart-shaped leaflets. Copper-tinted dark green.
• NATIVE HABITAT Garden origin.
• CULTIVATION Grow in moist but well-drained, humus-rich soil, in part-shade. Provides good ground cover in a shady border. May be damaged by wind and late frosts. Cut back old foliage in late winter.
• PROPAGATION By division in spring or autumn.

HEIGHT
30cm (12in)

SPREAD
30cm (12in)

| Trilliaceae/Liliaceae | TOADSHADE, WAKE-ROBIN |
|---|---|

## *TRILLIUM SESSILE*

*Habit* Clump-forming. *Flowers* Musk-scented, borne above the leaves in late spring. Has 3 maroon-brown petals and 3 brown-red sepals. *Leaves* Stemless, rounded, in terminal whorls of 3. Dark green, marked white, pale green or bronze.
• NATIVE HABITAT Woodland, E. North America.
• CULTIVATION Easily grown in moist, humus-rich, neutral to acid soils, in full or part-shade. Good for peat banks, woodland gardens or borders.
• PROPAGATION By division, after foliage dies back in summer, or by seed in autumn.

HEIGHT
30–38cm
(12–15in)

SPREAD
30–45cm
(12–18in)

| Berberidaceae | |
|---|---|

## *EPIMEDIUM ACUMINATUM*

*Habit* Tufted, creeping, clump-forming. *Flowers* Small, cup-shaped, with curved spurs, borne on branching, wiry stems, in spring or early summer. Pale violet-rose, yellow or white. *Leaves* Divided into 3 lance-shaped, long-pointed, spiny-toothed leaflets. Mid-green, tinted deep pink on emergence.
• NATIVE HABITAT Mountains of W. and C. China.
• CULTIVATION Grow in moist, well-drained, soil, in a shady border. Cut back old foliage in late winter.
• PROPAGATION By seed or division in spring or autumn.

HEIGHT
25–50cm
(10–20in)

SPREAD
30cm (12in)

Ranunculaceae

# ANEMONE NEMOROSA 'Robinsoniana'

**Habit** Carpeting, rhizomatous. **Flowers** Large, single, cup-shaped at first, opening flat, borne on red-tinted stems, in profusion in spring. Petals are pale lavender-blue with a creamy-grey petal reverse. **Leaves** Deeply divided into lance-shaped, toothed segments, dying down in mid-summer. Dark green.
  NATIVE HABITAT Garden origin.
  CULTIVATION Like all wood anemones, this perennial is excellent for a wild or woodland garden. It will naturalize with considerable ease in loose, moist, humus-rich soil in part-shade or dappled sunlight. It is also very attractive if planted at the foot of shrubs in a shrub border. The extended flowering period in early spring makes *A. nemorosa* 'Robinsoniana' one of the most popular of all the anemone cultivars.
• PROPAGATION By division in late summer.

HEIGHT
15cm (6in)

SPREAD
30cm (12in)
or more

| Ranunculaceae | |
|---|---|

## *ANEMONE NEMOROSA* 'Allenii' ♗

*Habit* Carpeting, rhizomatous. *Flowers* Large, single, cup-shaped, borne in profusion in spring. Pale lavender-blue, rich lilac on the reverse of the petals. *Leaves* Deeply divided into slender, toothed segments, dying down in mid-summer. Mid-green.
• NATIVE HABITAT Garden origin.
• CULTIVATION Grow in moist, humus-rich soil, in part-shade or dappled sunlight. Excellent for naturalizing in a woodland garden or shrub border.
• PROPAGATION By division in late summer.

☀ ◊
❋ ❋ ❋

HEIGHT
15cm (6in)

SPREAD
30cm (12in)
or more

| Paeoniaceae | |
|---|---|

## *GLAUCIDIUM PALMATUM* ♗

*Habit* Leafy, sparse-stemmed, stout-rooted. *Flowers* Large, cup-shaped, delicate, borne singly on slender stems, in late spring. Pale mauve. *Leaves* Paired, with 7–11 irregularly toothed lobes, borne at the ends of upright stems. Bright green.
• NATIVE HABITAT Mountain woodland, Japan.
• CULTIVATION Grow in moist but well-drained, humus-rich soil, in semi-shade or dappled sunlight, in a cool position with shelter from wind. Excellent for a woodland garden or cool, shady border.
• PROPAGATION By seed in autumn.

☀ ◊
❋ ❋ ❋

HEIGHT
50cm (20in)

SPREAD
50cm (20in)

| Geraniaceae | |
|---|---|

## *GERANIUM NODOSUM*

*Habit* Clump-forming, rhizomatous. *Flowers* Upright, funnel-shaped, borne in loose, open clusters throughout summer. Lilac or lilac-pink petals with dark-veins. *Leaves* Shiny, with 3–5 shallow, unevenly toothed lobes. Dark green.
• NATIVE HABITAT Woodland, in hills and mountains, from C. France to the Balkans.
• CULTIVATION Thrives in deep shade, even in poor, dry soils, but grows best in fertile, humus-ric soils. Suitable for a wild or woodland garden.
• PROPAGATION Seed or division in autumn or spri

☀ ◊
❋ ❋ ❋

HEIGHT
45cm (18in

SPREAD
45cm (18in

| Leguminosae/ Papilionaceae | SPRING VETCH |
|---|---|

## *LATHYRUS VERNUS*

*Habit* Bushy, clump-forming. *Flowers* Small, pea-like, borne in 3–15 flowered clusters in spring. Bright purple and blue with red veins. *Leaves* Fern-like, divided into 2–4 pairs of pointed, oval leaflets. Mid-green.
• NATIVE HABITAT Scrub and woodland in Europe.
• CULTIVATION Grow in well-drained soil, includin poor stony soils, in sun or light shade. Dislikes root disturbance and takes time to become established.
• PROPAGATION By seed in autumn or careful division in spring.

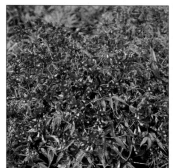

☀ ◊
❋ ❋ ❋

HEIGHT
30cm (12in

SPREAD
30cm (12in

**Brassicaceae/Cruciferae**

## CARDAMINE PENTAPHYLLOS

*Habit* Upright, spreading, rhizomatous. *Flowers* small, funnel-shaped, borne in clusters above the leaves, in spring. White or pale purple. *Leaves* Divided into 3–5 toothed, smooth leaflets. Dark green.

NATIVE HABITAT Mountain woodland, W. and C. Europe.

CULTIVATION Grow in moist but freely draining, preferably sandy, humus-rich soil, in cool conditions. Excellent for a woodland garden or damp, shady border. It grows particularly well in dappled shade beneath deciduous trees in more naturalistic areas of the garden, but is equally well-placed at the front of a border in more formal plantings. It is valued for its early flowering period and associates well with spring-flowering bulbs.

• PROPAGATION By seed or division in autumn.

• OTHER NAMES *Dentaria digitata, D. pentaphylla.*

HEIGHT
30–60cm
(12–24in)

SPREAD
45–60cm
(18–24in)

| Boraginaceae | |
|---|---|

### *PULMONARIA SACCHARATA*
**Habit** Clump-forming. **Flowers** Funnel-shaped, borne in terminal heads in spring. Pink then blue to blue-purple. **Leaves** Semi-evergreen, long, elliptic. Mid-green, variably spotted with white, and covered in fine hairs.
• NATIVE HABITAT Scrub and woodland, Europe.
• CULTIVATION Grow in fertile, humus-rich, moist but well-drained soil, in shade or semi-shade. Excellent for a woodland garden or shady border, especially beneath shrubs or trees.
• PROPAGATION Seed or division in spring or autumn.

**HEIGHT**
30cm (12in)

**SPREAD**
60cm (24in)

| Lamiaceae/Labiatae | |
|---|---|

### *LAMIUM ORVALA*
**Habit** Mound-forming, stoloniferous. **Flowers** Small, hooded, 2-lipped, in leafy, terminal, spike-like clusters, in late spring and early summer. Pink or purple-pink. **Leaves** Oval to diamond-shaped. Mid-green, sometimes with a central white stripe.
• NATIVE HABITAT Woodland margins, S.C. Europe
• CULTIVATION Grow in well-drained soil, in part-shade.
• PROPAGATION By seed or division in autumn or early spring, or by stem tip cuttings of non-flowering shoots in mid-summer.

**HEIGHT**
30cm (12in
or more

**SPREAD**
30cm (12in

| Polemoniaceae | |
|---|---|

### *POLEMONIUM REPTANS* 'Lambrook Mauve'
**Habit** Mound-forming, with a short rootstock. **Flowers** Funnel-shaped, to 2cm (¾in) long, borne in loose, terminal clusters, in late spring and early summer. Lilac-blue. **Leaves** Finely divided into 7–19 elliptic to lance-shaped leaflets. Mid-green.
• NATIVE HABITAT Garden origin.
• CULTIVATION Grow in reasonably fertile, humus-rich, well-drained soil. Although not generally recommended for a sunny situation, this plant is in fact quite accommodating and will tolerate woodland conditions in dappled sunlight or semi-shade. The leaves are generally evergreen and remain attractive for the greater part of the year. Excellent for herbaceous borders and cottage gardens.
• PROPAGATION By division in spring.
• OTHER NAMES *P. reptans* 'Lambrook Manor'.

**HEIGHT**
30–45cm
(12–18in)

**SPREAD**
30–45cm
(12–18in)

| Solanaceae | |
|---|---|

## SCOPOLIA CARNIOLICA

**Habit** Clump-forming, rhizomatous. **Flowers** Tubular to bell-shaped, variable, borne singly in the leaf axils, in early spring. Pale yellow to brownish-purple and yellow within. **Leaves** Coarse, oval to oblong, pointed. Mid-green.
NATIVE HABITAT Beech woods, in mountains, from C. and S.E. Europe to Russia.
CULTIVATION Grow in fertile, very well-drained soil, in shade or semi-shade. Good for a woodland garden or beneath shrubs in a border.
PROPAGATION Division in spring; seed in autumn.

HEIGHT
60cm (24in)

SPREAD
60cm (24in)

| Ranunculaceae | |
|---|---|

## HELLEBORUS PURPURASCENS

**Habit** Neat, clump-forming. **Flowers** Large, nodding, cup-shaped, in clusters of 2–4, in early spring. Deep purple-violet to maroon outside, sometimes green within. **Leaves** Deciduous, divided into 2–6 lance-shaped, coarsely toothed segments. Dark green.
• NATIVE HABITAT Mountain woodland, open grassland, often on sandy soils, in eastern C. Europe.
• CULTIVATION Grow in deep, fertile, moist but well-drained, humus-rich soil, in semi-shade.
• PROPAGATION By fresh seed or division in autumn.

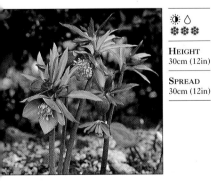

HEIGHT
30cm (12in)

SPREAD
30cm (12in)

| Scrophulariaceae | TOOTHWORT |
|---|---|

## LATHRAEA CLANDESTINA

**Habit** Spreading, rhizomatous, parasitic on willow or poplar roots. **Flowers** Hooded, tubular, 2-lipped, borne in short heads that emerge from soil level, in late winter and early spring. Purple. **Leaves** Reduced to pale, fleshy scales on the rhizomes.
• NATIVE HABITAT Damp woods and streamside meadows, S.W. Europe.
• CULTIVATION Grow in moist soil, in shade or dappled shade, at the roots of willow or poplar trees.
• PROPAGATION By fresh seed sown in moist soil, at the host tree roots, in late summer.

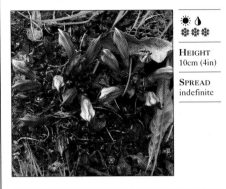

HEIGHT
10cm (4in)

SPREAD
indefinite

| Boraginaceae | |
|---|---|

## PULMONARIA ANGUSTIFOLIA
### 'Mawson's Variety'

**Habit** Clump- or mat-forming, rhizomatous. **Flowers** Funnel-shaped, borne in terminal clusters, in early spring. Intense clear blue, tinted red with age. **Leaves** Long, narrowly lance-shaped, finely hairy. Dark green and without spots.
• NATIVE HABITAT Garden origin.
• CULTIVATION Grow in fertile, humus-rich, moist, well-drained soil, in shade or semi-shade. Excellent for a woodland garden or shady border.
• PROPAGATION Seed or division in spring or autumn.

HEIGHT
23cm (9in)

SPREAD
23cm (9in)
often more

| Boraginaceae | BLUE BELLS, VIRGINIA COWSLIP |
|---|---|

## MERTENSIA PULMONARIOIDES ♇

**Habit** Clump-forming, summer-dormant. **Flowers** Pendent, tubular-bell-shaped, in hanging clusters in the leaf axils, in spring. Rich blue. **Leaves** Oval, dying down by mid-summer. Soft blue-green.
• NATIVE HABITAT Wet meadows and streambanks, North America.
• CULTIVATION Grow in moist, but well-drained, humus-rich soil, in shade, semi-shade, or in sun in reliably moist soil. Prone to slug damage.
• PROPAGATION Division in spring; seed in autumn.
• OTHER NAMES *M. virginica*.

☀ ◊
❄ ❄ ❄

HEIGHT
30–60cm
(12–24in)

SPREAD
30–45cm
(12–18in)

| Boraginaceae | |
|---|---|

## PULMONARIA SACCHARATA
### 'Frühlingshimmel'

**Habit** Clump-forming. **Flowers** Funnel-shaped, borne in terminal clusters, in spring. Pale sky blue with purple calyces. **Leaves** Semi-evergreen, long, elliptic. Mid-green spotted with white, finely hairy.
• NATIVE HABITAT Scrub and woodland, Europe.
• CULTIVATION Grow in fertile, humus-rich, moist but well-drained soil, in shade or semi-shade. Excellent for a woodland garden or shady border.
• PROPAGATION By division in spring or autumn.
• OTHER NAMES *P. saccharata* 'Spring Beauty'.

☀ ◊
❄ ❄ ❄

HEIGHT
30cm (12in)

SPREAD
60cm (24in)

| Boraginaceae | |
|---|---|

## BRUNNERA MACROPHYLLA
### 'Dawson's White'

**Habit** Clump-forming, rhizomatous. **Flowers** Small, in delicate panicles in spring. Bright blue, forget-me-not-like. **Leaves** Heart-shaped. Mid-green, irregularly edged with creamy-white.
• NATIVE HABITAT Garden origin.
• CULTIVATION Grow in moist, well-drained, humus-rich soil; shelter from wind to avoid leaf scorch. Good ground cover.
• PROPAGATION By division in spring or autumn.
• OTHER NAMES *B. macrophylla* 'Variegata'.

☀ ◊
❄ ❄ ❄

HEIGHT
45cm (18in)

SPREAD
60cm (24in)

| Papaveraceae | HAREBELL POPPY |
|---|---|

## MECONOPSIS QUINTUPLINERVIA ♇

**Habit** Mat-forming. **Flowers** Nodding, poppy-like, borne singly on strong, slender stems in late spring and early summer. Lavender-blue, darker at the base. **Leaves** Lance-shaped, in basal rosettes. Mid-green, clothed in rusty or golden hairs.
• NATIVE HABITAT Alpine meadows, Tibet, China.
• CULTIVATION Grow in moist, leafy soil, in a cool, sheltered site in dappled shade. Excellent for woodland or a peat bed. Dislikes warm conditions.
• PROPAGATION By fresh seed in late summer or by division after flowering.

☀ ◊ pH
❄ ❄ ❄

HEIGHT
30–45cm
(12–18in)

SPREAD
30cm (12in)

| Boraginaceae | |
| --- | --- |

## *BUGLOSSOIDES PURPUROCAERULEA*

*Habit* Ascending, spreading, rhizomatous.
*Flowers* Small, funnel-shaped, 5-lobed, in
terminal clusters, in early spring and early
summer. Red-purple at first, later turning deep
blue. *Leaves* Lance-shaped. Mid-green.
• NATIVE HABITAT Scrub, woodland edge,
usually on limestone, from W. Europe to Iran.
• CULTIVATION Grown in fertile, well-drained
soil in semi-shade or sun. This plant is ideally
suitable for a border or woodland garden. It is
a robust perennial of charming and delicate

appearance that associates well with smaller
species, and particularly with cultivars of
*Narcissus*. Where conditions suit, it will spread
to form colonies.
• PROPAGATION By seed or division in autumn
or spring.
• OTHER NAMES *Lithospermum purpureocaeruleum*.

HEIGHT
60cm (24in)

SPREAD
60cm (24in)

# PRIMULAS

Primulas are a genus of fully hardy to frost-tender annuals, biennials and perennials, some of which are evergreen. All have basal rosettes of leaves and tubular, bell-shaped, or flat (primrose-like) flowers. There are primulas to suit almost every garden situation, from rock garden, peat terrace and alpine house to herbaceous borders, watersides and bog gardens; a number are also grown as houseplants. Nearly all thrive best in climates with cool, moist summers.

Primulas are classified into a number of groups, of which the following are the most widely known and cultivated.

**Candelabra** primulas have tubular, flat-faced flowers in tiered whorls up the stem.

**Polyanthus** primulas have large clusters of flowers on stout stems and are often treated as biennials.

**Auricula** primulas include alpine, border and show auriculas. Their flattish flowers, which are borne in clusters above the leaves, often have a bright central ring or "paste". Show auriculas and some border auriculas have a waxy powder or "farina" on the leaves.

For ease of reference, their cultivation requirements may be grouped as follows.

1 – full sun and constantly moist soil
2 – full sun or part shade and moist, well-drained soil
3 – part shade and moist, well-drained soil
4 – part shade and well-drained, gritty loam
5 – full sun or part shade and alkaline soil
6 – part shade and gritty alkaline soil
7 – full or part shade and moist, peaty soil
8 – full sun and gritty, peaty soil
9 – part shade and gritty, peaty soil.

Propagate species by seed when fresh or in spring. Increase selected forms when dormant, either by division or root cuttings. Protect border perennials from slugs and snails, especially in damp situations.

---

**P. VULGARIS**
**'Gigha White'**
*Habit* Neat, clump-forming, floriferous.
*Flowers* Flat, singly amid the foliage in early spring. White, yellow-eyed.
*Leaves* Lance-shaped to oval, crinkled, toothed or scalloped. Fresh green.
• CULTIVATION 1or 3.
• HEIGHT 15–20cm (6–8in).
• SPREAD 15–20cm (6–8in).

*P. vulgaris*
**'Gigha White'**

☀ ◐ ❋ ❋ ❋

---

**P. 'Craddock White'**
*Habit* Clump-forming.
*Flowers* Fragrant, flat, upward-facing, in short-stemmed clusters in spring. Creamy-white.
*Leaves* Oval-oblong. Dark green with red veins.
• CULTIVATION 1 or 3.
• HEIGHT 8cm (3in).
• SPREAD 13cm (5in).

*P. 'Craddock White'*
(Polyanthus)

☀ ◐ ❋ ❋ ❋

---

**P. DENTICULATA**
**ALBA**
*Habit* Vigorous, upright, clump-forming.
*Flowers* Small, flat, in rounded heads, on strong stems in early to mid-spring. Yellow-eyed white.
*Leaves* Spoon-shaped, toothed. Bright green.
• CULTIVATION 1 or 3.
• HEIGHT 30–60cm (12–24in).
• SPREAD 30–45cm (12–18in).

*P. denticulata alba*

☀ ◐ ❋ ❋ ❋

---

**P. JAPONICA**
**'Postford White'**
*Habit* Clump-forming.
*Flowers* Small, tubular, in tiered whorls in early summer. White, spreading petal lobes, pink-eyed.
*Leaves* Oval or broadly spoon-shaped. Pale green.
• CULTIVATION 1 or 7. Good for a bog garden.
• HEIGHT 30–60cm (12–24in).
• SPREAD 30–45cm (12–18in).

*P. japonica*
**'Postford White'**
(Candelabra)

☀ ◐ ❋ ❋ ❋

## P. PULVERULENTA Bartley Hybrids
**Habit** Clump-forming.
**Flowers** Tubular, on white farinose stems, in tiered whorls in early summer. Pale pink with dark red-pink eye.
**Leaves** Lance-shaped to oval, toothed. Mid-green.
CULTIVATION 1 or 7.
HEIGHT 60cm–1m (2–3ft).
SPREAD 30–45cm (12–18in).

**P. pulverulenta Bartley Hybrids** (Candelabra)

## P. 'Iris Mainwaring'
**Habit** Neat, clump-forming.
**Flowers** Small, primrose-like, on short stems in early spring. Pale mauve, flushed red.
**Leaves** Oval to lance-shaped, toothed. Bright green.
• HEIGHT 15–20cm (6–8in).
• SPREAD 15–20cm (6–8in).

**P. 'Iris Mainwaring'**

## P. FARINOSA
**Habit** Compact, clump-forming.
**Flowers** Small, tubular, on short, sturdy stems in spring. White-eyed, with spreading, pink, occasionally white, petals.
**Leaves** Lance-shaped to oval, toothed. Mid-green, densely farinose.
• CULTIVATION 8.
• HEIGHT 15–30cm (6–12in).
• SPREAD 15cm (6in).

**P. farinosa** Bird's eye primrose

## P. VULGARIS subsp. SIBTHORPII
**Habit** Neat, clump-forming, floriferous.
**Flowers** Flat, singly, amid the foliage in early spring. Pink or purplish-pink with a yellowish-green eye.
**Leaves** Lance-shaped to oval, toothed. Fresh green.
• CULTIVATION 1 or 3.
• HEIGHT 15–20cm (6–8in).
• SPREAD 15–20cm (6–8in).

**P. vulgaris subsp. sibthorpii**

## P. ALLIONII
**Habit** Cushion- or rosette-forming.
**Flowers** Tubular, but flat-faced, on short stems from late winter to spring. Rose-pink, mauve or white.
**Leaves** Fleshy, lance-shaped to almost round, downy. Mid-green.
• CULTIVATION 5. Best in an alpine house.
• HEIGHT 8cm (3in).
• SPREAD 8–15cm (3–6in).

**P. allionii**

## P. MALACOIDES
**Habit** Clump-forming.
**Flowers** Small, single or double, in dense, tiered whorls in winter and early spring. Pink, purplish-pink or white.
**Leaves** Broadly oval, with shallow, toothed lobes, softly hairy. Pale green.
• CULTIVATION 4.
• HEIGHT 20–30cm (8–12in).
• SPREAD 20–30cm (8–12in).

**P. malacoides** Fairy primrose

Min. 5°C (41°F)

## P. ROSEA
**Habit** Clump-forming.
**Flowers** Flat, with heart-shaped, cleft petals, borne in short-stemmed clusters in spring. Glowing rose-pink with a yellow eye.
**Leaves** Lance-shaped to oval, toothed. Mid-green.
• CULTIVATION 1 or 7.
• HEIGHT 10–15cm (4–6in).
• SPREAD 15–20cm (6–8in).

**P. rosea**

## P. WARSHENEWSKIANA
**Habit** Very compact, clump-forming.
**Flowers** Tiny, flat, with spreading petal lobes, borne in small umbels in early spring. Bright pink, white-eyed.
**Leaves** Small, spoon-shaped. Dark green.
• CULTIVATION 8. Best in an alpine house.
• HEIGHT 2.5cm (1in).
• SPREAD 3.5–5cm (1½–2in).

**P. warshenewskiana**

## *P. CLUSIANA*
*Habit* Compact, clump-forming.
*Flowers* Tubular with spreading, heart-shaped deeply cleft petal lobes, borne in small clusters in spring. Pink, white-eyed.
*Leaves* Oval, leathery. Mid-green, grey-green beneath.
• CULTIVATION 8.
• HEIGHT 15–23cm (6–9in).
• SPREAD 15cm (6in).

*P. clusiana*

☀ ◐ ❀❀❀

## *P. SIEBOLDII*
*Habit* Spreading, clump-forming.
*Flowers* Flat, in heads above foliage in early summer. White-eyed pink, purple or white.
*Leaves* Oval to oblong with toothed lobes, soft, downy. Pale green.
• CULTIVATION 7.
• HEIGHT 15–20cm (6–8in).
• SPREAD 15–20cm (6–8in).

*P. sieboldii*

☀ ◐ ❀❀❀❀          ♈

## *P. PULVERULENTA*
*Habit* Upright, clump-forming.
*Flowers* Tubular, with spreading petal lobes, on white-farinose stems, in tiered whorls in early summer. Deep red with a dark purplish-red eye.
*Leaves* Oval to lance-shaped, toothed. Mid-green.
• CULTIVATION 1 or 7. Excellent for streamsides.
• HEIGHT 60cm–1m (2–3ft).
• SPREAD 30–45cm (12–18in).

*P. pulverulenta*
(Candelabra)

☀ ◐ ❀❀❀          ♈

## *P. SECUNDIFLORA*
*Habit* Clump-forming.
*Flowers* Pendent, funnel-shaped, in small clusters on long, farinose stems in summer. Reddish-purple.
*Leaves* Oblong to oval or lance-shaped, toothed. Mid-green.
• CULTIVATION 1 or 7. Good for a damp border.
• HEIGHT 30–45cm (12–18in).
• SPREAD 30cm (12in).

*P. secundiflora*

☀ ◐ ❀❀❀

## *P. JAPONICA* 'Miller's Crimson'
*Habit* Clump-forming.
*Flowers* Small, tubular, with spreading petal lobes, in tiered whorls in early summer. Crimson.
*Leaves* Oval, or broadly spoon-shaped. Pale green.
• CULTIVATION 1 or 7. Good for a bog garden.
• HEIGHT 30–60cm (12–24in).
• SPREAD 30–45cm (12–18in).

*P. japonica* 'Miller's Crimson' (Candelabra)

☀ ◐ ❀❀❀

## *P. VIALII*
*Habit* Clump-forming.
*Flowers* Small, tubular, borne in slender, conical spikes in late spring. Red in bud, opening purple.
*Leaves* Broadly lance-shaped to oblong, toothed. Soft, mid-green.
• CULTIVATION 1 or 3. Excellent for stream- and pond side, and damp borders. Short-lived.
• HEIGHT 30–45cm (12–18in).
• SPREAD 20–30cm (8–12in).

*P. vialii*

☀ ◐ ❀❀❀          ♈

## P. Cowichan
**Habit** Vigorous, rosette-forming.
**Flowers** Primrose-like, in long-stemmed, clusters in early spring. Red, blue, violet, or yellow.
**Leaves** Oval, crinkled. Bright to dark green.
• CULTIVATION 2.
• HEIGHT 10cm (4in).
• SPREAD 15–20cm (6–8in).

**P. Cowichan**
(Polyanthus)

☀ ◐ ✿✿✿

## P. NANA
**Habit** Rosette-forming.
**Flowers** Flat, singly on short stems in spring. Pale blue to pale mauve with a white eye.
**Leaves** Spoon-shaped, irregularly toothed or lobed. Pale green.
• CULTIVATION 8.
• OTHER NAMES
P. edgeworthii.
• HEIGHT 5–10cm (2–4in).
• SPREAD 10–15cm (4–6in).

**P. nana**

☀ ◐ pH ✿✿✿

## P. SONCHIFOLIA
**Habit** Rosette-forming.
**Flowers** Tubular, borne in dense umbels in spring. Spreading, blue-purple petal lobes edged with yellow.
**Leaves** Oval, serrated, lobed. Mid-green.
• CULTIVATION 8. Best in an alpine house.
• HEIGHT 20–30cm (8–12in).
• SPREAD 20–30cm (8–12in).

**P. sonchifolia**

☀ ◐ ✿✿✿

## P. PETIOLARIS
**Habit** Rosette-forming.
**Flowers** Tubular, borne in spring. Yellow-eyed, with spreading, toothed, satiny, purplish-pink petal lobes.
**Leaves** Small, oval, toothed. Mid-green.
• CULTIVATION 8. Best in an alpine house.
• HEIGHT 5–10cm (2–4in).
• SPREAD 10–15cm (4–6in).

**P. petiolaris**

☀ ◐ ✿✿✿

## P. MODESTA var. FAURIEAE
**Habit** Clump-forming.
**Flowers** Tubular, with heart-shaped petal lobes, borne in short-stemmed umbels in spring. Pinkish-purple, with a yellow-eye.
**Leaves** Elliptic to spoon-shaped, wavy, toothed. Mid-green, very farinose.
• CULTIVATION 8. Best in an alpine house.
• HEIGHT 5cm (2in).
• SPREAD 5cm (2in).

**P. modesta var. faurieae**

☀ ◐ ✿✿✿

## P. AURICULA 'Mark'
**Habit** Rosette-forming.
**Flowers** Flat, with rounded petals, produced in spring. Intense wine-purple, fading to pink at the margins, and with a pale creamy centre.
**Leaves** Oval, smooth. Vibrant green.
• CULTIVATION 2.
• HEIGHT 23–28cm (9–11in).
• SPREAD 15–23cm (6–9in).

**P. auricula 'Mark'**
(Alpine auricula)

☀ ◐ ✿✿✿

## P. AURICULA 'Adrian'
**Habit** Rosette-forming.
**Flowers** Flat, with rounded petals, borne from mid- to late spring. Light to dark purplish-blue, with a white centre.
**Leaves** Oval. Mid-green.
• CULTIVATION 2. Good for exhibition. Needs sharp drainage.
• HEIGHT 22–25cm (9–10in).
• SPREAD 15–20cm (6–8in).

**P. auricula 'Adrian'**
(Alpine auricula)

☀ ◐ ✿✿✿

## P. DENTICULATA
**Habit** Vigorous, upright, clump-forming.
**Flowers** Small, flat, in rounded heads, on strong stems in early to mid-spring. Lilac, purple or pink, with a yellow eye.
**Leaves** Oval, toothed. Bright green.
• CULTIVATION 1 or 3.
• HEIGHT 30–60cm (12–24in).
• SPREAD 30–45cm (12–18in).

**P. denticulata**
Drumstick primula

☀ ◐ ✿✿✿

### P. FLACCIDA
**Habit** Lax,
clump-forming.
**Flowers** Small, pendent,
broadly funnel-shaped,
farinose, in conical heads
in early summer.
Lavender or violet.
**Leaves** Oval, toothed.
Pale to mid-green.
• CULTIVATION 7 or 8.
• HEIGHT 15–30cm
(6–2in).
• SPREAD 15–23cm
(6–9in).

*P. flaccida*

☼ ◊ ❀❀❀          ♈

### P. MARGINATA
**Habit** Neat,
clump-forming.
**Flowers** Small, funnel-
shaped, in clusters in
early spring. Blue-lilac,
with a tiny white eye.
**Leaves** Oval to oblong,
toothed, slightly fleshy,
farinose. Mid-green.
• CULTIVATION 5.
• HEIGHT 10–15cm
(4–6in).
• SPREAD 10–20cm
(4–8in).

*P. marginata*

☼ ◊ ❀❀❀          ♈

### P. MARGINATA
### 'Linda Pope'
**Habit** Rosette-forming.
**Flowers** Flat, borne in
short-stemmed, umbel-
like clusters in spring.
White-eyed mauve-blue.
**Leaves** Narrowly oval,
toothed. Pale green,
covered with white farina.
• CULTIVATION 5.
Needs sharp drainage.
• HEIGHT 10–15cm
(4–6in).
• SPREAD 15–23cm (6–9in).

*P. marginata* 'Linda
Pope'
(Auricula)

☼ ◊ ❀❀❀          ♈

### P. WHITEI
### 'Sherriff's Variety'
**Habit** Clump-forming.
**Flowers** Tubular, in
neat heads in spring.
White- or creamy-eyed
pale purplish-blue.
**Leaves** Small, oval,
toothed. Mid-green.
• CULTIVATION 8.
• OTHER NAMES
*P. bhutanica.*
• HEIGHT 15cm (6in).
• SPREAD 15–23cm
(6–9in).

*P. whitei* 'Sherriff's
Variety'

☼ ◊ ❀❀❀

### P. AURICULA
### 'Margaret Martin'
**Habit** Rosette-forming.
**Flowers** Flat, borne in
mid- to late spring. Grey-
edged petals, flushed
black at the base, and
with a white central ring.
**Leaves** Spoon-shaped.
Grey-green, farinose.
• CULTIVATION 2.
Excellent for exhibition.
Needs sharp drainage.
• HEIGHT 20cm (8in).
• SPREAD 15cm (6in).

*P. auricula*
'Margaret Martin'
Show auricula

☼ ◊ ❀❀❀

### P. ALPICOLA
### var. LUNA
**Habit** Clump-forming.
**Flowers** Pendent, bell-
shaped, on long,
slender stems in early
summer. Soft sulphur-
yellow.
**Leaves** Oval to lance-
shaped. Mid-green.
• CULTIVATION 7.
• HEIGHT 15–60cm
(6–25in).
• SPREAD 15–30cm
(6–12in).

*P. alpicola* var. *luna*

☼ ◊ ❀❀❀

### P. FLORINDAE
**Habit** Clump-forming.
**Flowers** Sweetly
fragrant, pendent, bell-
shaped, in large, long-
stemmed heads in early
summer. Sulphur yellow.
**Leaves** Broadly oval,
toothed, shining.
Mid-green.
• CULTIVATION 1 or 7.
Good for a pondside,
damp border or bog
garden.
• HEIGHT 60cm–1m
(2–3ft).
• SPREAD 30–60cm
(1–2ft).

*P. florindae*
Giant Himalayan cowslip

☼ ◊ ❀❀❀          ♈

**P. VULGARIS**
**Habit** Neat,
clump-forming.
**Flowers** Flat, fragrant,
borne singly amid the
foliage in early spring.
Soft yellow.
**Leaves** Lance-shaped to
oval, toothed. Fresh green.
• CULTIVATION 1 or 3.
Good for a wild garden.
• HEIGHT 15–20cm
(6–8in).
• SPREAD 15–20cm
(6–8in).

*P. vulgaris*
Primrose

☀ ◊ ❀❀❀

**P. AURICULA**
**'Moonstone'**
**Habit** Rosette-forming.
**Flowers** Rounded,
double, produced in
profusion in spring. Pale
greenish-yellow.
**Leaves** Oval. Mid-green.
• CULTIVATION 2.
Best in an alpine house.
Needs good drainage.
• HEIGHT 23–25cm
(9–10in)!
• SPREAD 15–20cm
(6–8in).

*P. auricula*
**'Moonstone'**
(Border auricula)

☀ ◊ ❀❀❀

**P. PROLIFERA**
**Habit** Upright,
clump-forming.
**Flowers** Fragrant,
nodding, bell-shaped,
borne in tiered whorls
in summer. Yellow.
**Leaves** Oval, toothed.
Pale green.
• CULTIVATION 1 or 7.
• OTHER NAMES
*P. helodoxa.*
• HEIGHT 60cm–1m
(2–3ft).
• SPREAD 30–45cm
(12–18in).

*P. prolifera*
(Candelabra)

☀ ◊ ❀❀❀ ♈

**P. SIKKIMENSIS**
**Habit** Upright,
clump-forming.
**Flowers** Pendent,
funnel-shaped, borne in
long-stemmed clusters
in summer. Pale yellow.
**Leaves** Rounded to oval,
toothed. Pale green.
• CULTIVATION 1 or 7.
Good for a damp border.
• HEIGHT 45–75cm
(18–30in).
• SPREAD 30–45cm
(12–18in).

*P. sikkimensis*

☀ ◊ ❀❀❀

**P. ELATIOR**
**Habit** Clump-forming.
**Flowers** Small, fragrant,
tubular with spreading,
heart-shaped petal lobes,
borne in umbels in
spring. Yellow.
**Leaves** Oval to elliptic,
scalloped or irregularly
toothed. Bright green.
• CULTIVATION 1, 7 or 9.
Good in light woodland.
• HEIGHT 15–30cm
(6–12in).
• SPREAD 15cm (6in).

*P. elatior*
Oxlip

☀ ◊ ❀❀❀ ♈

**P. AURICULA**
**'Blairside Yellow'**
**Habit** Rosette-forming.
**Flowers** Small, slightly
funnel-shaped, borne in
short-stemmed clusters
in early spring. Golden-
yellow.
**Leaves** Tiny, rounded
to oval, in a dense basal
rosette. Pale green.
• CULTIVATION 2.
Needs sharp drainage.
• HEIGHT 2.5cm (1in).
• SPREAD 15cm (6in).

*P. auricula*
**'Blairside Yellow'**
(Alpine auricula)

☀ ◊ ❀❀❀

**P. KEWENSIS**
**Habit** Upright,
clump-forming.
**Flowers** Scented, tubular,
with heart-shaped petal
lobes, in whorls in late
winter and early spring.
Bright yellow.
**Leaves** Oval, toothed.
Pale green, white-farinose.
• CULTIVATION 4. Best
in a cool greenhouse.
• HEIGHT 30cm (12in).
• SPREAD 15–30cm
(6–12in).

*P. kewensis*

☀ ◊
Min. 5°C (41°F)   ♈

## P. VERTICILLATA
**Habit** Clump-forming.
**Flowers** Fragrant, bell-shaped, in tiered whorls in spring. Yellow.
**Leaves** Oval to lance-shaped, sharply serrated. Mid-green, farinose beneath.
• CULTIVATION 4. Best in a cold greenhouse.
• HEIGHT 20–25cm (8–10in).
• SPREAD 15–20cm (6–8in).

*P. verticillata*

☼ ◐ ❀

## P. BULLEYANA
**Habit** Upright, clump-forming.
**Flowers** Tubular with spreading petal lobes, borne in tiered whorls in early summer. Deep orange.
**Leaves** Oval to lance-shaped, toothed. Dark green.
• CULTIVATION 1 or 7.
• HEIGHT 60cm (24in).
• SPREAD 30cm (12in).

*P. bulleyana*
(Candelabra)

☼ ◐ ❀❀❀ 〔

## P. FORRESTII
**Habit** Clump-forming, with woody rhizomes.
**Flowers** Flat, in dense heads in late spring or early summer. Yellow with orange eyes.
**Leaves** Oval, wrinkled, toothed. Dark green.
• CULTIVATION 8. Needs sharp drainage.
• HEIGHT 15–23cm (6–9in).
• SPREAD 15–30cm (6–12in).

*P. forrestii*

☼ ◐ ❀❀❀

## P. AURICULA 'Janie Hill'
**Habit** Rosette-forming.
**Flowers** Flat, borne in mid- to late spring. Dark to golden brown. with a golden centre.
**Leaves** Oval. Mid-green.
• CULTIVATION 2. Good for exhibition. Needs sharp drainage.
• HEIGHT 23–25cm (9–10in).
• SPREAD 15–20cm (6–8in).

*P. auricula* 'Janie Hill'
(Alpine auricula)

☼ ◐ ❀❀❀

## P. VERIS
**Habit** Clump-forming.
**Flowers** Small, fragrant, funnel-shaped, in dense, stout-stemmed clusters in spring. Yellow.
**Leaves** Oval to lance-shaped, crinkled, toothed. Fresh green.
• CULTIVATION 1 or 3. Good to grow through turf.
• HEIGHT 15–20cm (6–8in).
• SPREAD 15–20cm (6–8in).

*P. veris*
Cowslip

☼ ◐ ❀❀❀ ♈

## P. 'Inverewe'
**Habit** Vigorous, upright, clump-forming.
**Flowers** Tubular with spreading lobes, borne in tiered whorls on long, floury stems in summer. Bright orange-red.
**Leaves** Coarse, oval to lance-shaped. Mid-green.
• CULTIVATION 1 or 7.
• HEIGHT 45–75cm (18–30in).
• SPREAD 30–45cm (12–18in).

*P. 'Inverewe'*
(Candelabra)

☼ ◐ ❀❀❀ 〔

## P. CHUNGENSIS
**Habit** Clump-forming.
**Flowers** Tubular with spreading petal lobes, borne in tiered whorls in early summer. Orange.
**Leaves** Elliptic to oblong, toothed and shallowly lobed. Mid-green.
• CULTIVATION 1 or 7.
• HEIGHT 60cm (24in).
• SPREAD 30cm (12in).

*P. chungensis*
(Candelabra)

☼ ◐ ❀❀❀

## P. Gold Laced Group
**Habit** Rosette-forming.
**Flowers** Small, flat, in heads from mid- to late spring. Dark red to almost black petals with a fine golden edge, yellow-centred.
**Leaves** Oval, wrinkled. Mid- to pale green.
• CULTIVATION 2 or 3.
• PROPAGATION By seed or division every year.
• HEIGHT 20cm (8in).
• SPREAD 25cm (10in).

*P. Gold Laced Group*
(Polyanthus)

☼ ◐ ❀❀❀

| Convallariaceae/ Liliaceae | |
|---|---|

## *DISPORUM SESSILE* 'Variegatum'

*Habit* Spreading, clump-forming, rhizomatous. *Flowers* Small, pendent, tubular-bell-shaped, borne singly or in clusters of 2–3 at ends of stems in spring. White, tipped green. *Leaves* Oval-lance-shaped, pleated. Striped green and white.
• NATIVE HABITAT Garden origin. Species occurs in wooded hills in Japan.
• CULTIVATION Grow in cool, moist, humus-rich soil, in semi-shade. Excellent for shady borders and woodland gardens.
• PROPAGATION By division in spring.

HEIGHT
45cm (18in)

SPREAD
30cm (12in)
or more

| Ranunculaceae | |
|---|---|

## *HELLEBORUS CYCLOPHYLLUS*

*Habit* Clump-forming. *Flowers* Small, nodding, cup-shaped, borne in clusters of up to 7, in early spring. Greenish-yellow, with prominent creamy-white stamens. *Leaves* Deciduous, palmately divided into 5–9 lance-shaped leaflets. Bright green.
• NATIVE HABITAT Woods, scrub, grassy hills, in Greece, S. Balkans, S. Bulgaria and Albania.
• CULTIVATION Grow in fertile, moist but well-drained soil, in sun or semi-shade.
• PROPAGATION By fresh seed or division in autumn.

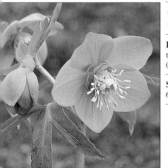

HEIGHT
to 60cm
(24in)

SPREAD
60cm (24in)

| Euphorbiaceae | |
|---|---|

## *EUPHORBIA CYPARISSIAS*

*Habit* Bushy, spreading, rhizomatous. *Flowers* Tiny, borne in rounded umbels, in late spring. Yellowish-green, with conspicuous lime-green bracts. *Leaves* Linear, smooth. Grey-green, sometimes flushed orange on poor soils.
• NATIVE HABITAT Dunes and dry, rocky meadows, in W. C. and S. Europe.
• CULTIVATION Grow in a warm, dry position in almost any well-drained soil. May be invasive.
• PROPAGATION By division or seed in spring or early autumn; by basal cuttings in spring or summer.

HEIGHT
30cm (12in)

SPREAD
30cm (12in)
or more

| Euphorbiaceae | |
|---|---|

## *EUPHORBIA AMYGDALOIDES* var. *ROBBIAE* ♟

**Habit** Creeping, rhizomatous. **Flowers** Tiny, in rounded, branching heads in spring. Yellowish-green with conspicuous yellow-green bracts. **Leaves** Spoon-shaped, in rosettes. Dark green.
• NATIVE HABITAT Woodland in Turkey.
• CULTIVATION Tolerates poor, dry soil, but best in moist, well-drained soil, in sun or part-shade. Good ground cover. Avoid contact with the irritant sap.
• PROPAGATION By division or seed in spring or early autumn; by basal cuttings in spring or summer.

☼ ◐
❀ ❀ ❀

**HEIGHT**
45–60cm
(18–24in)

**SPREAD**
60cm (24in)

| Saxifragaceae | |
|---|---|

## *TELLIMA GRANDIFLORA*

**Habit** Spreading, clump-forming. **Flowers** Small, bell-shaped, with fringed petals, borne in erect sprays, in late spring. Greenish-white or cream. **Leaves** Semi-evergreen, hairy, 3- to 7-lobed, kidney-shaped, heart-shaped at the base. Dark green, flushed purple.
• NATIVE HABITAT Coniferous woods of W. North America.
• CULTIVATION Grow in moist but well-drained soil in shade or semi-shade.
• PROPAGATION Seed or division in spring or autumn.

☼ ◐
❀ ❀ ❀

**HEIGHT**
60cm (24in)

**SPREAD**
60cm (24in)

| Euphorbiaceae | |
|---|---|

## *EUPHORBIA SEGUIERIANA*

**Habit** Bushy, clump-forming. **Flowers** Tiny, borne in large, terminal clusters over long periods, from late spring. Yellowish-green, with conspicuous, sulphurous yellow-green bracts. **Leaves** Narrow, lance-shaped, smooth. Bluish-green.
• NATIVE HABITAT Dry scrub, rocky hillsides, C. and W. Europe, east to the Caucasus and Siberia.
• CULTIVATION Grow in a warm, dry position in almost any well-drained soil.
• PROPAGATION By division or seed in spring or early autumn; by basal cuttings in spring or summer.

☼ ◐
❀ ❀

**HEIGHT**
45cm (18in)

**SPREAD**
45cm (18in)

| Valerianaceae | |
|---|---|

## *VALERIANA PHU* 'Aurea'

**Habit** Clump-forming, rhizomatous. **Flowers** Small, tubular, insignificant, borne in clusters in summer. White. **Leaves** Lance-shaped, some divided into leaflets. Bright golden-yellow in spring, turning lime-green and then mid-green by mid-summer.
• NATIVE HABITAT Species occurs on rocky hillsides, in Europe and the Caucasus. Garden origin.
• CULTIVATION Grow in any moderately fertile soil in sun.
• PROPAGATION By division in autumn.

☼ ◐
❀ ❀ ❀

**HEIGHT**
38cm (15in)

**SPREAD**
30–38cm
(12–15in)

Ranunculaceae

## *TROLLIUS* × *CULTORUM* 'Alabaster'

**Habit** Clump-forming. **Flowers** Rounded, almost globular, borne on sturdy, slender stems, above the leaves in late spring. Creamy-yellow, tinted pale green. **Leaves** Deeply divided into jagged-toothed leaflets, mostly in dense, basal clumps. Fresh green.

NATIVE HABITAT Garden origin.

• CULTIVATION Grow in moist, fertile, humus-rich soil in sun or part-shade. The native globe flower of Europe, *T. europaeus*, has long been in cultivation as a first-class border and pondside plant. A number of named cultivars have been introduced in recent years, usually of darker orange hues, so that *T.* × *cultorum* 'Alabaster' is an important introduction taking the colour down the other side of the spectrum into the paler shades. It plays a very useful role as a foil to other colours in the garden.

• PROPAGATION By division in early autumn.

HEIGHT
60cm (24in)

SPREAD
45cm (18in)

| Asteraceae/Compositae | GIANT BUTTERBURR |
|---|---|

## PETASITES JAPONICUS

**Habit** Spreading, rhizomatous. **Flowers** Tiny, daisy-like, in dense, rounded heads in early spring. Yellowish-white, cupped by pale green bracts.
**Leaves** Coarse, rounded, 80cm (32in) or more across, emerging after the flowers. Light green.
• NATIVE HABITAT Streambanks in woodland, Japan, Korea, China.
• CULTIVATION Grow in moist, humus-rich soil in sun or shade. Very invasive, but makes good ground cover by streambanks in large wild gardens.
• PROPAGATION By division in spring or autumn.

**HEIGHT**
60cm (24in)

**SPREAD**
1.5m (5ft)
or more

| Ranunculaceae | |
|---|---|

## ANEMONE × LIPSIENSIS

**Habit** Prostrate, carpeting, rhizomatous.
**Flowers** Large, single, cup-shaped, borne in profusion in spring. Pale yellow. **Leaves** Deeply divided into slender, toothed segments. Mid-green.
• NATIVE HABITAT Natural hybrid (*A. nemorosa* × *A. ranunculoides*) occurring in European woodland.
• CULTIVATION Grow in moist, humus-rich soil, in part-shade or dappled sunlight.
• PROPAGATION By division in late summer.
• OTHER NAMES *A. × seemannii.*

**HEIGHT**
15cm (6in)

**SPREAD**
30cm (12in)
or more

| Brassicaceae/Cruciferae | |
|---|---|

## CARDAMINE ENNEAPHYLLOS

**Habit** Upright, spreading, rhizomatous. **Flowers** Funnel-shaped, borne in nodding clusters above the leaves, in spring. Creamy-yellow. **Leaves** Divided into 2–6 pairs of coarsely toothed leaflets. Fresh green, bronzed when young.
• NATIVE HABITAT Mountain woodland in the eastern Alps and Carpathians to S. Italy.
• CULTIVATION Grow in moist but freely draining, preferably sandy, humus-rich soil, in cool condition
• PROPAGATION By seed or division in autumn.
• OTHER NAMES *Dentaria enneaphylla.*

**HEIGHT**
30–60cm
(12–24in)

**SPREAD**
45–60cm
(18–24in)

| Ranunculaceae | |
|---|---|

## ANEMONE RANUNCULOIDES

**Habit** Spreading, rhizomatous. **Flowers** Large, single, buttercup-like, borne in profusion in spring Deep yellow. **Leaves** Short-stalked, deeply divide into slender, toothed segments. Fresh green.
• NATIVE HABITAT Damp, deciduous woods and heathland, from N. Europe to W. Asia.
• CULTIVATION Grow in moist, humus-rich soil, in part-shade or dappled sunlight. Excellent for naturalizing in woodland gardens.
• PROPAGATION By division or fresh seed in late summer.

**HEIGHT**
20cm (8in)

**SPREAD**
20cm (8in)
or more

| Berberidaceae | |
| --- | --- |

## EPIMEDIUM DAVIDII

**Habit** Tufted, slowly creeping, clump-forming.
**Flowers** Small, cup-shaped, with curved spurs,
borne on branching, wiry stems, from spring to early
summer. Pale yellow. **Leaves** Divided into oval,
pointed leaflets. Mid-green, bluish-green beneath.
• NATIVE HABITAT Scrub and woodlands in the
mountains of W. Sichuan, China.
• CULTIVATION Grow in moist, humus-rich soil;
shelter from cold winds. For shady borders and
woodland gardens. Remove old leaves in late winter.
• PROPAGATION Seed or division in spring or autumn.

☀ ◐
❋ ❋

**HEIGHT**
30–50cm
(12–20in)

**SPREAD**
30cm (12in)

| Berberidaceae | |
| --- | --- |

## EPIMEDIUM × VERSICOLOR
## 'Neosulphureum'

**Habit** Compact, mound-forming. **Flowers** Small,
cup-shaped, short-spurred, borne in loose clusters
on branching stems, in spring. Pale yellow. **Leaves**
Divided into 3 heart-shaped, serrated leaflets.
Bright green, tinted red-purple on emergence.
• NATIVE HABITAT Garden origin.
• CULTIVATION Grow in moist, well-drained, humus-
rich soil, in part-shade. Provides good ground cover
in a shady border. Remove old leaves in late winter.
• PROPAGATION By division in spring or autumn.

☀ ◐
❋ ❋ ❋

**HEIGHT**
30cm (12in)

**SPREAD**
30cm (12in)

| Berberidaceae | |
| --- | --- |

## EPIMEDIUM PERRALDERIANUM

**Habit** Dense, carpeting. **Flowers** Small,
pendent, cupped, borne in loose, upright clusters,
in spring. Pale yellow with short brown spurs.
**Leaves** Evergreen or semi-evergreen, divided into
oval to rounded, sharply toothed leaflets. Glossy,
dark green, bronze when young.
• NATIVE HABITAT Scrub and oak woodland in the
mountains of Algeria.
• CULTIVATION Grow in moist, well-drained soil in
a sheltered site. Remove old leaves in late winter.
• PROPAGATION By division in spring or autumn.

☀ ◐
❋ ❋ ❋

**HEIGHT**
30cm (12in)

**SPREAD**
45cm (18in)

| Convallariaceae/ | BELLWORT, |
| --- | --- |
| Liliaceae | MERRY-BELLS |

## UVULARIA GRANDIFLORA    ♛

**Habit** Upright, clump-forming. **Flowers**
Pendulous, narrowly bell-shaped, borne on slender
stems in late spring or early summer. Yellow.
**Leaves** Lance-shaped, encircling the stem.
Bluish-green.
• NATIVE HABITAT Woodland, E. North America.
• CULTIVATION Grow in moist, well-drained,
humus-rich soil in dappled shade. Protect young
growth from slugs.
• PROPAGATION By division in early spring,
before flowering.

☀ ◐
❋ ❋ ❋

**HEIGHT**
45–60cm
(18–24in)

**SPREAD**
30cm (12in)

| Ranunculaceae | GLOBEFLOWER |
|---|---|

## *TROLLIUS EUROPAEUS*

**Habit** Clump-forming. **Flowers** Rounded, almost globular, borne on sturdy, slender stems, above the leaves in late spring. Lemon- to mid-yellow. **Leaves** Deeply divided into jagged-toothed leaflets, mostly in dense, basal clumps. Mid-green.
• NATIVE HABITAT Woodland streamsides and wet, shady meadows in Europe, Russia, North America.
• CULTIVATION Grow in moist, fertile, humus-rich soil, in sun or part-shade. Ideal if planted by water.
• PROPAGATION By seed in summer or autumn or by division in early autumn.

HEIGHT
60cm (24in)

SPREAD
45cm (18in)

| Ranunculaceae | |
|---|---|

## *TROLLIUS × CULTORUM* 'Earliest of All'

**Habit** Clump-forming. **Flowers** Rounded, almost globular, borne singly on sturdy, slender stems, above the leaves, in early spring. Butter-yellow. **Leaves** Deeply divided into jagged-toothed leaflets, mostly in dense, basal clumps. Fresh green.
• NATIVE HABITAT Garden origin.
• CULTIVATION Grow in moist, fertile, humus-rich soil in sun or part-shade. Excellent for pool- and streamsides and for damp borders.
• PROPAGATION By division in early autumn.

HEIGHT
60cm (24in)

SPREAD
45cm (18in)

| Euphorbiaceae | SPURGE |
|---|---|

## *EUPHORBIA POLYCHROMA*

**Habit** Rounded, clump-forming. **Flowers** Tiny, borne in terminal, flattened heads over long periods in spring. Yellowish-green, with conspicuous bright yellow bracts. **Leaves** Oval, softly hairy. Mid-green.
• NATIVE HABITAT Scrub and woodland, from C. and S.E. Europe to Turkey.
• CULTIVATION Grow in fertile, moist but well-drained soil, in sun or part-shade.
• PROPAGATION By division or seed in spring or early autumn; by basal cuttings in spring or summer
• OTHER NAMES *E. epithymoides*.

HEIGHT
45–60cm
(18–24in)

SPREAD
60cm (24in)

| Ranunculaceae | |
|---|---|

## *ADONIS VERNALIS*

**Habit** Clump-forming. **Flowers** Buttercup-like, borne singly at the ends of slender stems, in early spring. Shining yellow. **Leaves** Finely divided into slender, linear lobes. Mid-green.
• NATIVE HABITAT Dry, stony scrub and grassland, from Europe to Russia and Finland.
• CULTIVATION Grow in moist but very well-drained, humus-rich, preferably alkaline soil, in sun or semi-shade.
• PROPAGATION By fresh seed in late summer or by division after flowering.

HEIGHT
23–30cm
(9–12in)

SPREAD
23–30cm
(9–12in)

| Asteraceae/Compositae | |
|---|---|

## *DORONICUM* 'Miss Mason' ♟

**Habit** Low-growing, clump-forming, rhizomatous. **Flowers** Solitary, daisy-like, borne well above the foliage in mid- to late spring. Slender, bright yellow ray florets surrounding a golden-yellow disc. **Leaves** Heart-shaped, toothed. Dark green.
• NATIVE HABITAT Garden origin.
• CULTIVATION Grows best in moist but well-drained humus-rich soil, although it will do well in most soils. It needs a light, shady position and is particularly useful for woodland gardens. It is

also suitable for the front of a shady border, and the flowers are good for cutting. This is an excellent plant for early in the year, when a generous show of yellow daisies heralds the spring. Once established in favourable conditions, it will spread well.
• PROPAGATION By division in early autumn.

☀ ◊
❋ ❋ ❋

HEIGHT
45cm (18in)

SPREAD
60cm (24in)

| Ranunculaceae | |
|---|---|

## *ADONIS AMURENSIS*

**Habit** Clump-forming. **Flowers** Buttercup-like, borne singly in late winter and early spring. Shining yellow, with a bronze-tinted petal reverse. **Leaves** Finely divided into narrowly lance-shaped, toothed lobes. Mid-green.
• NATIVE HABITAT Mountain meadows, Manchuria, Japan, Korea.
• CULTIVATION Grow in moist but very well-drained, humus-rich soil, in sun or semi-shade.
• PROPAGATION By fresh seed in late summer or by division after flowering.

☀ ◊
❋ ❋ ❋

HEIGHT
30cm (12in)

SPREAD
23–30cm
(9–12in)

| Ranunculaceae | KING CUP, MARSH MARIGOLD |
|---|---|

## *CALTHA PALUSTRIS* ♟

**Habit** Marginal aquatic, clump-forming. **Flowers** Cup-shaped, 4cm (1½in) across, in long-stalked clusters in spring. Waxy, bright golden-yellow. **Leaves** Kidney-shaped, toothed, to 10cm (4in) across. Glossy, dark green.
• NATIVE HABITAT Marshes and streamsides, throughout most of the Northern Hemisphere.
• CULTIVATION Grow in full sun in wet soil by pond edges, or in shallow water to a depth of 23cm (9in).
• PROPAGATION By seed in autumn; by division in autumn or early spring.

☀ ◊
❋ ❋ ❋

HEIGHT
60cm (2ft)

SPREAD
45cm (18in)

| Papaveraceae | WELSH POPPY |
|---|---|

## MECONOPSIS CAMBRICA

**Habit** Spreading. **Flowers** Poppy-like, with
delicate petals, borne singly in spring and summer.
Lemon-yellow, golden-yellow, or rich orange.
**Leaves** Fern-like, deeply divided into irregular
lobes, mostly in basal clumps. Fresh green.
• NATIVE HABITAT Woodlands, mountain rocks
and old walls in W. Europe.
• CULTIVATION Grow in moist soil in sun, semi-
shade, or shade. Will naturalize in wild gardens.
• PROPAGATION By fresh seed in late summer or
division after flowering. Self-seeds freely.

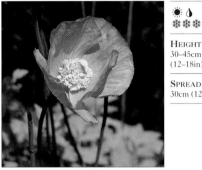

HEIGHT
30–45cm
(12–18in)

SPREAD
30cm (12in)

| Berberidaceae | |
|---|---|

## EPIMEDIUM × WARLEYENSE

**Habit** Clump- or mound-forming. **Flowers** Small,
cup-shaped, borne in loose clusters on wiry stems,
in spring. Coppery-orange and yellow. **Leaves**
Evergreen, oval, pointed, with few spiny teeth.
Light green, tinted red-purple on emergence.
• NATIVE HABITAT Garden origin.
• CULTIVATION Grow in moist, well-drained,
humus-rich soil, in part-shade. Provides good
ground cover in a shady border. Cut away old
foliage in late winter.
• PROPAGATION By division in spring or autumn.

HEIGHT
30cm (12in)

SPREAD
30cm (12in)

| Campanulaceae | |
|---|---|

## CAMPANULA ALLIARIIFOLIA

**Habit** Mound-forming. **Flowers** Nodding, bell-
shaped, borne in one-sided clusters throughout
summer. Creamy-white. **Leaves** Triangular, heart-
shaped at the base, roughly hairy. Mid-green.
• NATIVE HABITAT Damp cliffs, scrub and conifer
forests in the Caucasus and N. Turkey.
• CULTIVATION Grow in moist but well-drained
soil in sun or part-shade. Excellent for herbaceous
and mixed borders.
• PROPAGATION By basal cuttings in early summer;
by seed or division in spring or autumn.

HEIGHT
60cm (24in)

SPREAD
50cm (20in)

| Rubiaceae | SWEET WOODRUFF, WOODRUFF |
|---|---|

## *GALIUM ODORATUM*

***Habit*** Carpeting, rhizomatous. ***Flowers*** Tiny, 4-petalled, star-shaped, in terminal, clusters in early to mid-summer. White. ***Leaves*** Small, elliptic, in whorls of 6 up the stems. Glossy, bright green. Aromatic when dried.
• NATIVE HABITAT  Deciduous woods and hedgebanks in Europe and N. Africa.
• CULTIVATION  Grow in moist, well-drained soil, in semi-shade or sun. Good ground cover.
• PROPAGATION  Division in early spring or autumn.
• OTHER NAMES  *Asperula odoratum.*

HEIGHT
15cm (6in)

SPREAD
30cm (12in)
often more

| Ranunculaceae | |
|---|---|

## *ANEMONE RIVULARIS*

***Habit*** Clump-forming. ***Flowers*** Delicate, cup-shaped, borne on stiff, free-branching stems in summer. White, with a metallic blue tinge to the petal reverse and blue anthers. ***Leaves*** Deeply divided into toothed, cut lobes. Dark green.
• NATIVE HABITAT  Damp, mountain meadows and woodland clearings, from N. India to S.W. China.
• CULTIVATION  Grow in humus-rich, moist but well-drained soil, in sun or semi-shade.
• PROPAGATION  By seed in late summer or by careful division in spring.

HEIGHT
60cm (24in)

SPREAD
30cm (12in)

| Ranunculaceae | |
|---|---|

## *ANEMONE NARCISSIFLORA*

***Habit*** Clump-forming. ***Flowers*** Single, cup-shaped, borne in stiff-stemmed sprays in late spring and early summer. Widely spreading white petals, stained blue or pink on the reverse. ***Leaves*** Deeply divided into toothed, cut lobes. Dark green.
• NATIVE HABITAT  Damp, mountain meadows in Europe, Turkey, Russia, Japan and North America.
• CULTIVATION  Grow in humus-rich, moist but well-drained soil, in sun or semi-shade.
• PROPAGATION  By seed in late summer; by careful division in spring. A difficult plant to propagate.

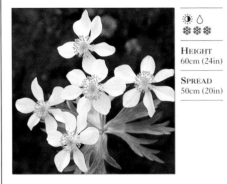

HEIGHT
60cm (24in)

SPREAD
50cm (20in)

| Asteraceae/Compositae | |
|---|---|

## *LEUCANTHEMUM × SUPERBUM* 'Esther Read'

***Habit*** Robust, clump-forming. ***Flowers*** Large, solitary, double, borne singly in summer. White. ***Leaves*** Coarse, lobed and toothed. Dark green.
• NATIVE HABITAT  Garden origin.
• CULTIVATION  Grow in moderately fertile, well-drained soil, in full sun. Suitable for cutting. Divide and replant every two years to maintain vigour.
• PROPAGATION  By division in spring or autumn.
• OTHER NAMES  *Chrysanthemum × superbum* 'Esther Read'.

HEIGHT
45cm (18in)

SPREAD
45cm (18in)

| Anthericaceae/Liliaceae | ST BERNARD'S LILY |
| --- | --- |

### *ANTHERICUM LILIAGO* 🏆

**Habit** Upright, fleshy-rooted. **Flowers** Small, trumpet-shaped, borne in long, spike-like heads, in early summer. White. **Leaves** Long, narrow, grass-like. Grey-green.
• NATIVE HABITAT Sunny meadows and scrub in mountains from S. Europe to S. Turkey.
• CULTIVATION Grow in fertile, well-drained soil, in full sun. Good for herbaceous borders and for cutting. May self-seed where conditions suit.
• PROPAGATION By division in spring or seed in autumn.

☀ ◌
❀ ❀ ❀

HEIGHT
45–60cm
(18–24in)

SPREAD
30cm (12in)

| Asteraceae/Compositae | |
| --- | --- |

### *ANTHEMIS PUNCTATA* subsp. 🏆
### *CUPANIANA*

**Habit** Carpeting, sub-shrubby. **Flowers** Small, single, daisy-like, borne singly on short stems in early summer. White with a yellow disc. **Leaves** Evergreen, finely cut. Silvery, turn green in winter.
• NATIVE HABITAT Cliffs and rocky places, Sicily.
• CULTIVATION Grow in well-drained soil, in a warm, sheltered site in full sun. Excellent for border edges. Cut back after flowering to maintain vigour.
• PROPAGATION By division in spring; basal cuttings in late summer, autumn, or spring.

☀ ◌
❀ ❀

HEIGHT
30cm (12in)

SPREAD
30cm (12in)
or more

| Asteraceae/Compositae | |
| --- | --- |

### *ANAPHALIS TRIPLINERVIS* var.
### *INTERMEDIA*

**Habit** Lax, spreading, clump-forming. **Flowers** Tiny, with papery petals, in dense clusters, in late summer and early autumn. White. **Leaves** Lance-shaped, densely hairy. Silvery grey-green.
• NATIVE HABITAT Woodland clearings, Himalayas.
• CULTIVATION Grow in any moderately fertile, well-drained, not too dry soil. Flowers dry well.
• PROPAGATION By seed in autumn, or by division in late winter or early spring.
• OTHER NAMES *A. nepalensis.*

☀ ◌
❀ ❀ ❀

HEIGHT
20–30cm
(8–12in)

SPREAD
30cm (12in)

| Asteraceae/Compositae | |
|---|---|

## ANAPHALIS NEPALENSIS var. MONOCEPHALA

**Habit** Compact, tuft-forming. **Flowers** Tiny, with papery petals, in dense, terminal, short-stemmed clusters, in late summer. White. **Leaves** Lance-shaped, densely hairy. Silver- or grey-green.
• NATIVE HABITAT Open habitats, Himalayas.
• CULTIVATION Grow in any moderately fertile, well-drained, not too dry soil. Flowers dry well.
• PROPAGATION By seed in autumn, or by division in late winter or early spring.
• OTHER NAMES *A. nubigena*.

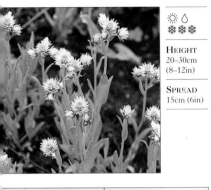

☀ ◊
❋ ❋ ❋

HEIGHT
20–30cm
(8–12in)

SPREAD
15cm (6in)

| Brassicaceae/Cruciferae | SEA KALE |
|---|---|

## CRAMBE MARITIMA

**Habit** Robust, mound-forming, with a woody rootstock. **Flowers** Small, sweetly scented, borne in large, rounded, branching heads, above the foliage in summer. White. **Leaves** Large, fleshy, with curled, wavy-margined lobes. Blue-green.
• NATIVE HABITAT Seaside shingle, on the coasts of N. Europe, the Baltic and the Black Sea.
• CULTIVATION Grow in well-drained, preferably sandy soil, in full sun. Excellent for coastal gardens.
• PROPAGATION By seed in autumn or spring; by root cuttings in winter.

☀ ◊
❋ ❋ ❋

HEIGHT
60cm (2ft)

SPREAD
60cm (2ft)

| Lamaceae/Labiatae | VARIEGATED APPLE MINT |
|---|---|

## MENTHA SUAVEOLENS 'Variegata'

**Habit** Dense, spreading, rhizomatous. **Flowers** Small, tubular, 2-lipped, seldom produced. White or pale pink. **Leaves** Apple-scented, rounded, wrinkled, softly woolly. Mid-green, heavily splashed with creamy-white.
• NATIVE HABITAT Garden origin.
• CULTIVATION Grow in any soil unless water-logged, in full sun or light shade. Less invasive than most mints and provides good foliage contrast in a herbaceous border. Leaves dry well for pot-pourri.
• PROPAGATION By division in spring or autumn.

☀ ◊
❋ ❋ ❋

HEIGHT
30–45cm
(12–18in)

SPREAD
60cm (24in)

| Apiaceae/Umbelliferae | VARIEGATED GROUND ELDER |
|---|---|

## AEGOPODIUM PODAGRARIA 'Variegatum'

**Habit** Vigorous, spreading. **Flowers** Tiny, insignificant, in small umbels in summer. White. **Leaves** Aromatic, divided into 3–9 oval, pointed, toothed leaflets. Greyish-green, variegated creamy-white.
• NATIVE HABITAT Garden origin.
• • CULTIVATION Grow in any soil unless water-logged, in sun or light shade. Good ground cover, but may be invasive, though less so than the green-leaved species. Dead-head to prevent seeding.
• PROPAGATION By division in spring or autumn.

☀ ◊
❋ ❋ ❋

HEIGHT
10–15cm
(4–6in)

SPREAD
Indefinite

| Saxifragaceae | |
|---|---|

## ASTILBE 'Irrlicht'

**Habit** Clump-forming. **Flowers** Tiny, in dense, feathery, tapering spires, in summer. White.
**Leaves** Divided into toothed, oval leaflets. Dark green.
• NATIVE HABITAT Garden origin.
• CULTIVATION Grow in moist, fertile, humus-rich soil, in sun or semi-shade. Good for damp borders, bog gardens or waterside plantings, associating well with *Hosta* and *Rodgersia*. Flower heads turn brown and die, persisting into winter unless dead-headed.
• PROPAGATION By division in spring or autumn.

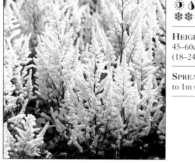

☼ ◗
❄ ❄ ❄

HEIGHT
45–60cm
(18–24in)

SPREAD
to 1m (3ft)

| Saxifragaceae | |
|---|---|

## ASTILBE 'Deutschland'

**Habit** Clump-forming. **Flowers** Tiny, in dense, feathery sprays, on strong stems, in summer. Creamy-white. **Leaves** Divided into toothed, oval leaflets. Dark green.
• NATIVE HABITAT Garden origin.
• CULTIVATION Grow in moist, fertile, humus-rich soil, in sun or semi-shade. Good for damp borders, bog gardens or waterside plantings. The flower heads turn brown and die, persisting into winter unless dead-headed.
• PROPAGATION By division in spring or autumn.

☼ ◗
❄ ❄ ❄

HEIGHT
to 60cm
(2ft)

SPREAD
to 1m (3ft)

| Saxifragaceae | |
|---|---|

## HEUCHERA CYLINDRICA 'Greenfinch'

**Habit** Dense, clump- or carpet-forming. **Flowers** Tiny, bell-shaped, borne in graceful spikes on long, slender, hairy stems, in summer. Pale green.
**Leaves** Evergreen, rounded, lobed, wavy-edged, in dense basal rosettes. Dark green.
• NATIVE HABITAT Garden origin.
• CULTIVATION Grow in moist but well-drained soil, in sun or semi-shade. Good ground cover in a herbaceous border or woodland garden.
• PROPAGATION By division in autumn or spring, using young, outer portions of the crown.

☼ ◊
❄ ❄ ❄

HEIGHT
45–60cm
(18–24in)

SPREAD
50cm (20in)

| Saxifragaceae | |
|---|---|

## TIARELLA TRIFOLIATA

**Habit** Spreading, clump-forming. **Flowers** Tiny, star-shaped, borne in slender, open spires on upright stems, from early to mid-summer. White to pale pink. **Leaves** Semi-evergreen, 3-lobed, each lobe further divided and toothed. Dark green.
• NATIVE HABITAT Streambanks in damp woods in W. North America.
• CULTIVATION Grow in moist but well-drained soil in shade or semi-shade.
• PROPAGATION By seed or division in spring or autumn.

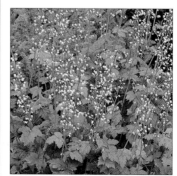

☼ ◊
❄ ❄ ❄

HEIGHT
30cm (12in)

SPREAD
30cm (12in)

| Commelinaceae | |
|---|---|

## TRADESCANTIA × ANDERSONIANA 'Osprey' ♈

**Habit** Clump-forming. **Flowers** 3-petalled, borne in succession throughout summer. Pure white, with blue-purple stamens, surrounded by two leaf-like, green bracts. **Leaves** Slightly fleshy, narrowly lance-shaped, borne on jointed stems. Mid-green.
• NATIVE HABITAT Garden origin.
• CULTIVATION Grow in moist, well-drained soil, in sun or light shade. A long-flowering plant for a herbaceous border. Protect young growth from slugs.
• PROPAGATION By division in spring or autumn.

☀ ◐
❀ ❀ ❀

HEIGHT
to 60cm
(24in)

SPREAD
45cm (18in)

| Caryophyllaceae | |
|---|---|

## GYPSOPHILA 'Rosenschleier' ♈

**Habit** Mound-forming, with trailing stems. **Flowers** Tiny, double, in airy sprays, in summer. White then very pale pink. **Leaves** Slightly fleshy, narrowly lance-shaped. Blue-green.
• NATIVE HABITAT Garden origin (*G. paniculata* × *G. repens* 'Rosea').
• CULTIVATION Grows best in deep, moderately fertile, well-drained soil. Resents disturbance. The flowers dry well for winter arrangements.
• PROPAGATION By grafting in winter.
• OTHER NAMES *G.* 'Veil of Roses', *G.* 'Rosy Veil'.

☀ ◐
❀ ❀ ❀

HEIGHT
30cm (12in)

SPREAD
to 1m (3ft)

| Geraniaceae | |
|---|---|

## GERANIUM CLARKEI 'Kashmir White'

**Habit** Clump- or carpet-forming, rhizomatous. **Flowers** Cup-shaped, borne in open clusters throughout summer. White, with lilac or lilac-pink veined petals. **Leaves** Deeply cut into 7 dissected, lobes. Dark green.
• NATIVE HABITAT A selection of the species which occurs in alpine meadows in Kashmir.
• CULTIVATION Grow in fertile, humus-rich, moist but well-drained soils, in sun or light shade.
• PROPAGATION By division in autumn or spring.
• OTHER NAMES *G. pratense* 'Kashmir White'.

☀ ◐
❀ ❀ ❀

HEIGHT
45–60cm
(18–24in)

SPREAD
45–60cm
(18–24in)

| Gesneriaceae | |
|---|---|

## STREPTOCARPUS CAULESCENS

**Habit** Upright, clump-forming. **Flowers** Small, tubular, intermittently on long stalks in the leaf axils, through the year. White or violet, with violet stripes. **Leaves** Fleshy, narrowly oval. Dark green.
• NATIVE HABITAT Tanzania, Kenya.
• CULTIVATION Grow as a house or conservatory plant in cool climates, in moist, humus-rich soil or compost. Requires bright indirect light and high humidity. Avoid wetting the leaves when watering.
• PROPAGATION By seed in spring, division after flowering, or by tip cuttings in spring or summer.

☀ ◐

Min.
10–15°C
(50–59°F)

HEIGHT
to 45cm
(18in) or
more

SPREAD
to 45cm
(18in) or
more

Geraniaceae

## GERANIUM RENARDII

*Habit* Compact, mound-forming. *Flowers* Single, borne in open clusters above the foliage in early to mid-summer. White or blue-tinted, with maroon-purple veins. *Leaves* Rounded, wrinkled and softly hairy, with 5–7 toothed, shallow lobes. Sage-green.
• NATIVE HABITAT Cliffs and rocky meadows in the Caucasus mountains.
• CULTIVATION Grow in well-drained soil in full sun. This perennial can play a valuable double role in the border. Its attractively marked flowers provide summer interest, while its neat form and foliage act as a subtle foil for other more vibrant coloured herbaceous plants at the front of the border. The leaves also look good in a silver- or grey-leaved border.
• PROPAGATION By seed or division in autumn or spring.

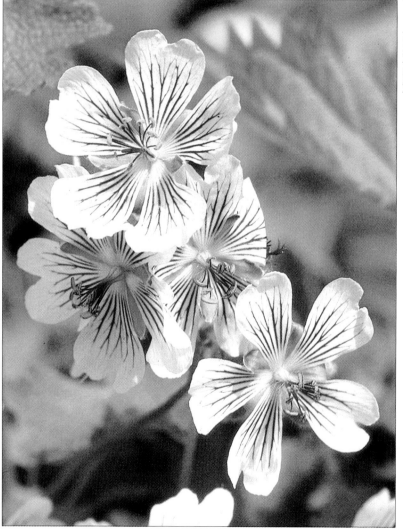

☼ ◊
❀ ❀ ❀

**HEIGHT**
30cm (12in)

**SPREAD**
30cm (12in)

| Acanthaceae | |
|---|---|

## RUELLIA DEVOSIANA

**Habit** Bushy, sub-shrubby. **Flowers** Tubular, borne singly in the leaf axils, in spring and summer. White, tinged and striped mauve. **Leaves** Evergreen, broadly lance-shaped. Dark green and pale-veined above, purple beneath.
• NATIVE HABITAT  Forest margins, Brazil.
• CULTIVATION  Grow as a house or conservatory plant in cool climates, in moist but well-drained soil or compost. Site in partial shade and maintain high humidity.
• PROPAGATION  By stem cuttings or seed in spring.

Min. 15°C
(59°F)

HEIGHT
45cm (18in)
or more

SPREAD
45cm (18in)
or more

| Asteraceae/Compositae | |
|---|---|

## OSTEOSPERMUM 'Whirligig'

**Habit** Clump-forming, woody-based. **Flowers** Large, single, daisy-like, with spoon-shaped petals, during summer. White above, powder-blue to chalky-grey beneath, with dark blue-grey central discs. **Leaves** Evergreen, aromatic, long, narrow, toothed and serrated. Dark grey-green.
• NATIVE HABITAT  Garden origin.
• CULTIVATION  Grow in well-drained soil in full sun. Overwinter young plants in frost-free conditions.
• PROPAGATION  By cuttings of non-flowering shoots in mid-summer.

HEIGHT
60cm (24in)

SPREAD
30–45cm
(12–18in)

| Iridaceae | |
|---|---|

## DIPLARRHENA MORAEA

**Habit** Clump-forming, tufted, rhizomatous. **Flowers** Small, scented, iris-like, borne on wiry stems in early summer. Has 3 rounded, white petals and yellow and purple centres. **Leaves** Long, narrow, strap-shaped, Mid-green.
• NATIVE HABITAT  Damp, mountain grassland in Tasmania and S.E. Australia.
• CULTIVATION  Grow in a warm, sunny, sheltered site, in humus-rich, sandy, well-drained soil that remains moist during summer. Protect from frost.
• PROPAGATION  By seed or division in spring.

HEIGHT
45cm (18in)

SPREAD
23cm (9in)

| Saxifragaceae | |
|---|---|

## HEUCHERA MICRANTHA var. DIVERSIFOLIA 'Palace Purple'

**Habit** Dense, clump- or carpet-forming. **Flowers** Tiny, bell-shaped, borne in graceful, open sprays, on slender, dark-purple stems in summer. White. **Leaves** Evergreen, with toothed and cut lobes, in dense basal clumps. Metallic, dark purple-red.
• NATIVE HABITAT  Garden origin.
• CULTIVATION  Grow in moist, well-drained soil, in sun or semi-shade. Provides good ground cover.
• PROPAGATION  By division in autumn or spring, using young, outer portions of the crown.

HEIGHT
45–60cm
(18–24in)

SPREAD
50cm (20in)

| Lamiaceae/Labiatae | BASTARD BALM |
|---|---|

## *MELITTIS MELISSOPHYLLUM*

**Habit** Upright, clump-forming. **Flowers** Tubular, 2-lipped, borne in whorls in the axils of leafy spikes, in summer. White, purple or pink, with a purple lower lip. **Leaves** Aromatic, oval, finely scalloped and hairy. Mid- to bright green.
• NATIVE HABITAT Mountain woodland and scrub, from W.C. and S. Europe to the Ukraine.
• CULTIVATION Grow in fertile, well-drained soil, in light shade. Suitable for a wildflower border.
• PROPAGATION By seed in autumn, or by division in spring or autumn.

☼ ◊
❀ ❀ ❀

HEIGHT
30cm (12in)

SPREAD
30cm (12in)

| Asteraceae/Compositae | DUSTY MILLER, SILVER LACE |
|---|---|

## *TANACETUM PTARMICIFLORUM*

**Habit** Shrubby, clump-forming. **Flowers** Small, daisy-like, to 2.5cm (1in) across, borne in dense heads in summer. White. **Leaves** Very finely divided and downy. Silver-grey.
• NATIVE HABITAT Canary Islands.
• CULTIVATION Grow in full sun, in any moderately fertile, well-drained soil. Good for a border front, as edging, in gravel plantings and for containers. Excellent as a filler in a silver border. May be grown as an annual. Protect from frost.
• PROPAGATION By seed or stem cuttings in spring.

☼ ◊
❀

HEIGHT
To 50cm
(20in)

SPREAD
50cm (20in)

| Apiaceae/Umbelliferae | |
|---|---|

## *ASTRANTIA MAJOR* subsp. *INVOLUCRATA*

**Habit** Clump-forming. **Flowers** A dome of tiny, greenish-pink florets, surrounded by long, papery, white and pink, green-tipped bracts, borne in summer and autumn. **Leaves** Divided into 3–5 coarsely toothed lobes. Dark green.
• NATIVE HABITAT Meadows and woodland in the mountains of C. and E. Europe.
• CULTIVATION Grow in any fertile, well-drained soil in sun. Flowers are good for cutting and drying.
• PROPAGATION By division in spring or fresh seed in late summer.

☼ ◊
❀ ❀ ❀

HEIGHT
60cm (24in)

SPREAD
45cm (18in)

| Apiaceae/Umbelliferae | |
|---|---|

## *ASTRANTIA MAJOR*

**Habit** Clump-forming. **Flowers** A dome of tiny, greenish-pink florets, with a star-shaped collar of papery white, pink and green bracts beneath, borne throughout summer and autumn. **Leaves** Divided into 3–5 coarsely toothed lobes. Mid-green.
• NATIVE HABITAT Meadows and woodland in the mountains of C. and E. Europe.
• CULTIVATION Grow in any fertile, well-drained soil in sun. Flowers are good for cutting and drying.
• PROPAGATION By division in spring or fresh seed in late summer.

☼ ◊
❀ ❀ ❀

HEIGHT
60cm (24in)

SPREAD
45cm (18in)

Scrophulariaceae

# *MIMULUS* 'Andean Nymph'

**Habit** Spreading, mat-forming. **Flowers**
Snapdragon-like, tubular with spreading lobes,
freely produced throughout summer. Rose-pink,
tipped creamy-yellow and spotted deep pink at
the throat. **Leaves** Broadly oval, toothed.
Bright green.

• NATIVE HABITAT  Garden origin, Chile.
  CULTIVATION  Grow in moist soil in full sun. In
cold areas, overwinter young plants in frost-free
conditions as insurance against winter losses.
Although it has a tendency to be rather short-lived,
this is an extremely useful and colourful plant
for the edge of a pond or stream where it can be
mixed with complementary water plants. In
particular, the pink flowers match perfectly the
pink tones in the leaves of the variegated
*Houttuynia cordata* 'Chameleon'.

• PROPAGATION  By division in spring or softwood
cuttings in late summer.

**HEIGHT**
23cm (9in)

**SPREAD**
25cm (10in)

| Saxifragaceae | |
|---|---|

## × *HEUCHERELLA TIARELLOIDES* ♥

*Habit* Dense, carpet-forming, stoloniferous.
*Flowers* Tiny, bell-shaped, borne in feathery, long-stemmed sprays in early summer. Pink. *Leaves* Evergreen, rounded, with a lobed, toothed and scalloped margin, in dense basal clumps. Mid-green.
• NATIVE HABITAT Garden origin.
• CULTIVATION Grow in moist but well-drained soil, in sun or semi-shade. Good for ground cover at the front of a herbaceous border.
• PROPAGATION By division in autumn or spring, using young, outer portions of the crown.

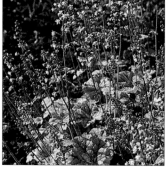

☀: ◐ ◊
❀ ❀ ❀

HEIGHT
45cm (18in)

SPREAD
45cm (18in)

| Saxifragaceae | |
|---|---|

## × *HEUCHERELLA ALBA* 'Bridget Bloom'

*Habit* Dense, clump-forming, stoloniferous.
*Flowers* Tiny, bell-shaped, in feathery, long-stemmed sprays, intermittently from early summer until autumn. Soft rose-pink. *Leaves* Evergreen, lobed, in dense basal clumps. Mid-green.
• NATIVE HABITAT Garden origin.
• CULTIVATION Grow in moist well-drained soil, in sun or semi-shade. Good ground cover at the front of a herbaceous border.
• PROPAGATION By division in autumn or spring, using young, outer portions of the crown.

☀: ◐ ◊
❀ ❀ ❀

HEIGHT
45cm (18ir

SPREAD
30cm (12ir

| Apiaceae/Umbelliferae | |
|---|---|

## *ASTRANTIA MAXIMA* ♥

*Habit* Mat- or clump-forming. *Flowers* A dome of tiny, rose-pink florets with a star-shaped collar of papery, greenish-pink bracts beneath, borne during summer and autumn. *Leaves* Divided into 3 coarsely toothed lobes. Mid-green.
• NATIVE HABITAT Woods and damp meadows, from S. Europe to the Caucasus.
• CULTIVATION Grow in any fertile, well-drained soil in sun. Flowers are good for cutting and drying.
• PROPAGATION By division in spring or fresh seed in late summer.

☀: ◊
❀ ❀ ❀

HEIGHT
60cm (24in)

SPREAD
30cm (12in)

| Asteraceae/Compositae | |
|---|---|

## *ERIGERON* 'Charity'

*Habit* Robust, clump-forming. *Flowers* Daisy-like, borne in profusion over long periods in summer. Slender, pale lilac-pink ray florets around a greenish-yellow disc. *Leaves* Lance-shaped to spoon-shaped. Mid-green.
• NATIVE HABITAT Garden origin.
• CULTIVATION Grow in moderately fertile, well-drained soil in sun. A valuable addition to the summer border, noted for its long flowering period.
• PROPAGATION By division in spring or early autumn, or by softwood cuttings in early summer.

☀: ◊
❀ ❀ ❀

HEIGHT
60cm (24in)

SPREAD
60cm (24in

Papaveraceae

## *DICENTRA* 'Spring Morning'

**Habit** Hummock-forming. ***Flowers*** Small, pendent, narrowly heart-shaped, borne on fleshy, arching stems, in late spring and summer. Pink. ***Leaves*** Fern-like, deeply cut. Bright greyish-green.

• NATIVE HABITAT Garden origin.
• CULTIVATION Grow in humus-rich, moist but well-drained soil, in semi-shade. A beautiful plant for a shady herbaceous border or woodland garden. Thrives best and flowers for longer periods in cool shaded conditions, but will tolerate part-day sun where soil remains reliably moist during the growing season. Valued for the neat hummocks of finely divided foliage and elegant sprays of flowers, it associates well with ferns and makes an attractive feature when planted with other dicentras with darker flowers, such as *D.* 'Bacchanal'.

• PROPAGATION By division when dormant in late winter.

**HEIGHT**
30cm (12in)

**SPREAD**
30cm (12in)

| Geraniaceae | |
|---|---|

## GERANIUM ENDRESSII ♀

**Habit** Compact, carpeting, rhizomatous. **Flowers** Single, cup-shaped, borne in profusion throughout summer. Rose-pink. **Leaves** Semi-evergreen, with 5 broadly toothed, deeply cut lobes. Mid- to bright green.
• NATIVE HABITAT Damp habitats in the Pyrenees.
• CULTIVATION Grow in moist, well-drained soil, in full sun. Excellent for herbaceous borders, cottage gardens, and with old-fashioned roses.
• PROPAGATION By seed or division in autumn or spring.

☀ ◊
❀ ❀ ❀

HEIGHT
45cm (18in)

SPREAD
60cm (24in)

| Geraniaceae | |
|---|---|

## GERANIUM ASPHODELOIDES

**Habit** Mound-forming. **Flowers** Small, delicate, star-shaped, on very slender stems, throughout summer. White, or pale to dark pink, with darker veins. **Leaves** Mostly basal, divided into 5 or 7 lobes. Mid-green.
• NATIVE HABITAT Woods and meadows, from S. Europe to Turkey and N. Iran.
• CULTIVATION Grow in moderately fertile, well-drained soil, in sun or light shade. Suitable for borders, or a cottage or wildflower garden.
• PROPAGATION Seed or division in spring or autumn.

☀ ◊
❀ ❀ ❀

HEIGHT
to 60cm
(24in)

SPREAD
60cm (24in)

| Geraniaceae | |
|---|---|

## GERANIUM × OXONIANUM
## 'Wargrave Pink' ☙

**Habit** Dense, carpeting. **Flowers** Small, cup-shaped, borne in profusion throughout summer. Bright salmon-pink. **Leaves** Semi-evergreen, with 5 deeply cut, toothed lobes. Mid-green.
• NATIVE HABITAT Garden origin.
• CULTIVATION Grow in any soil unless waterlogged, in sun or light shade. Excellent weed-smothering ground cover. Also suitable for the front of herbaceous borders and for cottage gardens.
• PROPAGATION By division in autumn or spring.

☀ ◊
❀ ❀ ❀

HEIGHT
45cm (18in)

SPREAD
60cm (24in)

| Rosaceae | JAPANESE BURNET |
|---|---|

## SANGUISORBA OBTUSA

**Habit** Clump-forming, rhizomatous. **Flowers** Tiny, in dense, slightly arching, "bottle-brush" spikes, borne above the foliage in mid-summer. Rose-crimson. **Leaves** Divided, with 13–17 oval or elliptic leaflets. Grey-green, blue-green beneath.
• NATIVE HABITAT Alpine meadows, Japan.
• CULTIVATION Tolerates semi-shade. Grow in fertile, moist, but well-drained soil. Good for damp borders, woodland gardens and waterside plantings
• PROPAGATION By division in spring or seed in autumn.

☀ ◊
❀ ❀ ❀

HEIGHT
1–1.2m
(3–4ft)

SPREAD
60cm (2ft)

| Scrophulariaceae | |
|---|---|

## DIASCIA RIGESCENS ♟

**Habit** Trailing, mat-forming. **Flowers** Spurred, flat-faced, in dense, upright spikes throughout summer. Salmon-pink. **Leaves** Heart-shaped, toothed. Mid-green.
• NATIVE HABITAT Damp forest margins and grassland in South Africa.
• CULTIVATION Grow in fertile, humus-rich, moist but well-drained soil, in full sun. Is excellent for a rock garden, border front or raised bed.
• PROPAGATION By fresh seed or softwood cuttings in spring, or semi-ripe cuttings in summer.

☼ ◊
❀ ❀

**HEIGHT**
23cm (9in)

**SPREAD**
to 30cm
(12in)

| Scrophulariaceae | |
|---|---|

## DIASCIA VIGILIS ♟

**Habit** Prostrate. **Flowers** Flat, outward-facing, short-spurred, in loose, upright spires throughout summer. Clear pink. **Leaves** Narrowly oval, toothed. Pale green.
• NATIVE HABITAT Damp, rocky places and scrub in the Drakensberg mountains and W. Lesotho.
• CULTIVATION Grow in fertile, humus-rich, moist but well-drained soil, in full sun. Is excellent for a border front or raised bed.
• PROPAGATION By fresh seed or softwood cuttings in spring, or semi-ripe cuttings in summer.

☼ ◊
❀ ❀

**HEIGHT**
30–40cm
(12–16in)

**SPREAD**
60cm (24in)

| Caryophyllaceae | FLOWER OF JOVE |
|---|---|

## LYCHNIS FLOS-JOVIS

**Habit** Upright, clump-forming. **Flowers** Variable, borne in terminal, rounded clusters, in mid-summer. Soft rose-pink, purplish-pink or scarlet. **Leaves** Lance- to spoon-shaped. Grey-green, white-hairy.
• NATIVE HABITAT Dry, sub-alpine slopes in the European Alps.
• CULTIVATION Grow in well-drained, not too fertile soil, in full sun. Suitable for the front of a herbaceous border or for cottage gardens.
• PROPAGATION By division or seed in autumn or spring.

☼ ◊
❀ ❀ ❀

**HEIGHT**
45cm (18in)

**SPREAD**
45cm (18in)

| Caryophyllaceae | ALPINE CATCHFLY |
|---|---|

## LYCHNIS VISCARIA

**Habit** Upright, clump-forming. **Flowers** Small, sticky, star-shaped, borne in dense, upright, spike-like heads, in early summer. Bright reddish-purple. **Leaves** Oval to lance-shaped, sticky-hairy beneath. Mid-green.
• NATIVE HABITAT Dry, rocky hills and cliffs, from Europe to W. Asia.
• CULTIVATION Grow in well-drained, not too fertile soil, in full sun. Suitable for the front of a herbaceous border and for cottage gardens.
• PROPAGATION Seed or division in autumn or spring.

☼ ◊
❀ ❀ ❀

**HEIGHT**
30cm (12in)
or more

**SPREAD**
30–45cm
(12–18in)

| Geraniaceae | |
|---|---|

## GERANIUM MACRORRHIZUM

**Habit** Compact, carpeting, rhizomatous. **Flowers** Small, in pairs or clusters, in early summer. Magenta-pink, soft rose-pink or white. **Leaves** Aromatic, semi-evergreen, divided into 5–7 deeply cut lobes. Mid-green, tinted red and bronze in autumn.
• NATIVE HABITAT Scrub, woodland and screes in the mountains of S. Europe.
• CULTIVATION Grow in almost any moist or dry soil, in sun or semi-shade. Makes excellent ground cover.
• PROPAGATION By seed or division in autumn or spring, or by semi-ripe cuttings in summer.

☼ ◊
✳ ✳ ✳

**HEIGHT**
30–38cm
(12–15in)

**SPREAD**
60cm (24in)
or more

| Polygonaceae | |
|---|---|

## PERSICARIA MACROPHYLLA

**Habit** Clump-forming, spreading, rhizomatous. **Flowers** Tiny, borne in dense, sometimes nodding, cylindrical spikes, on strong, slender stems, in mid-summer. Rich rose-pink. **Leaves** Lance-shaped. Blue-green.
• NATIVE HABITAT Alpine meadows, Himalayas.
• CULTIVATION Grow in moist, fertile soil. Vigorous and long-flowering specimen for a moist border.
• PROPAGATION Seed or division in spring or autumn.
• OTHER NAMES *P. sphaerostachya, Polygonum macrophyllum, Polygonum sphaerostachyum.*

☼ ◊
✳ ✳ ✳

**HEIGHT**
45–60cm
(18–24in)

**SPREAD**
30cm (12in)
often more

| Asteraceae/Compositae | |
|---|---|

## OSTEOSPERMUM JUCUNDUM ⏳

**Habit** Clump-forming, woody-based. **Flowers** Large, single, daisy-like, borne in profusion in late summer. Soft pink, dark-eyed. **Leaves** Evergreen, lance-shaped, toothed and serrated. Mid-green.
• NATIVE HABITAT Mountain rocks and damp grassland, often at high altitudes, in South Africa.
• CULTIVATION Grow in well-drained soil in sun.
• PROPAGATION By seed in spring or by cuttings of non-flowering shoots in mid-summer.
• OTHER NAMES *O. barberiae, Dimorphotheca barberiae.*

☼ ◊
✳ ✳

**HEIGHT**
30cm (12in)

**SPREAD**
30cm (12in)

| Asteraceae/Compositae | |
|---|---|

## CENTAUREA HYPOLEUCA 'John Coutts'

**Habit** Upright, clump-forming. **Flowers** Large, cornflower-like, borne on branching stems from early to mid-summer. Deep bright pink with paler centres. **Leaves** Deeply divided into lobed and cut, slightly hairy segments. Green, densely white-hairy beneath.
• NATIVE HABITAT Garden origin.
• CULTIVATION Grow in any well-drained soil, including poor soils, in full sun. Good for the front of a herbaceous border and for cottage gardens.
• PROPAGATION By division in spring or autumn.

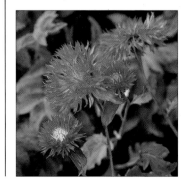

☼ ◊
✳ ✳ ✳

**HEIGHT**
60cm (24in)

**SPREAD**
45cm (18in)

| Lamiaceae/Labiatae | |
|---|---|

## PHYSOSTEGIA VIRGINIANA 'Vivid' ♀

**Habit** Upright, rhizomatous. **Flowers** Tubular, hooded, 2-lipped, in erect spikes, in late summer. Dark lilac-pink. **Leaves** Toothed, elliptic or lance-shaped. Mid-green.
• NATIVE HABITAT Garden origin.
• CULTIVATION Grow in moist, humus-rich, fertile soil, in sun. The flowers have hinged stalks that stay fixed when moved, hence the species common name of obedient plant. Suitable for herbaceous borders. The flowers are good for cutting.
• PROPAGATION By division in spring.

☼ ◑
❀ ❀ ❀

**HEIGHT**
30–60cm
(12–24in)

**SPREAD**
30–60cm
(12–24in)

| Geraniaceae | |
|---|---|

## ERODIUM MANESCAVII

**Habit** Mound-forming. **Flowers** Geranium-like, in loose clusters of 5–20, throughout summer. Deep magenta-pink with darker blotches. **Leaves** Divided into deeply cut, toothed leaflets. Blue-green.
• NATIVE HABITAT Alpine meadows, Pyrenees.
• CULTIVATION Grow in moist but well-drained soil, in a warm, sunny site. Good for the front of a herbaceous border and for gravel plantings.
• PROPAGATION By semi-ripe cuttings in summer, or by seed in autumn or spring.

☼ ◌
❀ ❀

**HEIGHT**
45cm (18in)

**SPREAD**
60cm (24in)

| Melastomataceae | SPANISH-SHAWL |
|---|---|

## HETEROCENTRON ELEGANS

**Habit** Mat-forming, dense, creeping. **Flowers** Small, 4-petalled, profusely in summer and autumn. Magenta to mauve. **Leaves** Evergreen, small, oval to oblong, bristly to downy. Mid-green.
• NATIVE HABITAT Mexico, Guatemala, Honduras.
• CULTIVATION Grow as a house or conservatory plant in cool climates, in well-drained soil or compost in full sun. Suitable for inside borders and pots, or for sunny banks outside in frost-free areas.
• PROPAGATION By softwood or stem tip cuttings in late winter or early spring.

☼ ◌

Min. 5°C
(41°F)

**HEIGHT**
5cm (2in)

**SPREAD**
indefinite

| Bignoniaceae | |
| --- | --- |

## INCARVILLEA MAIREI

**Habit** Compact, clump-forming. **Flowers**
Trumpet-shaped, on short stems in early summer;
stems elongate after flowering. Purplish-pink, grey-
white or yellow within. **Leaves** Divided into pairs
of oval to oblong leaflets. Mid- to dark green.
• NATIVE HABITAT Dry, stony slopes, Himalayas.
• CULTIVATION Grow in deep, sandy, very well-
drained soil, in full sun. Protect young growth
from slugs. Mulch crowns with dry bracken litter
or similar in winter.
• PROPAGATION By seed in autumn or spring.

☀ ◊
❀ ❀ ❀

**HEIGHT**
30cm (12in)

**SPREAD**
30cm (12in)

| Asteraceae/Compositae | BUTTON SNAKEWORT |
| --- | --- |

## LIATRIS SPICATA

**Habit** Upright, clump-forming. **Flowers** Small,
in dense, upright, cylindrical spikes, borne on stiff
stems in late summer. Bright purplish-pink.
**Leaves** Narrow, grass-like, borne in basal
tufts. Mid-green.
• NATIVE HABITAT Damp meadows and marshes,
E. North America.
• CULTIVATION Grow in fertile, moist, well-drained
soil, in full sun. Cut flowers last well in water.
• PROPAGATION By division in spring.
• OTHER NAMES L. callilepis.

☀ ◊
❀ ❀ ❀

**HEIGHT**
60cm (24in)

**SPREAD**
30cm (12in)

| Saxifragaceae | |
| --- | --- |

## BOYKINIA JAMESII

**Habit** Rhizomatous, mound-forming. **Flowers**
Open, bell-shaped, 2.5cm (1in) across, borne
in long-stalked sprays in early summer. Spoon-
shaped, cherry-carmine petals with a green eye.
**Leaves** Kidney-shaped, 2.5cm (1in) wide,
leathery, in basal rosettes. Bright green.
• NATIVE HABITAT Moist, shady mountain
habitats in northwest USA.
• CULTIVATION Needs moist but well-drained,
humus-rich, neutral to acid soil. Suits a shady
niche in a rock garden. It is also an excellent

plant for the alpine house, and responds well to
generous applications of liquid fertilizer. It rarely
sets seed in cultivation.
• PROPAGATION Division in spring, or seed in
autumn.
• OTHER NAMES Telesonix jamesii.

☀ ◊ pH
❀ ❀ ❀

**HEIGHT**
60cm (24in)

**SPREAD**
30cm (12in)

| Geraniaceae | |
|---|---|

## *GERANIUM* 'Ann Folkard'

*Habit* Clump-forming, with a short, creeping rootstock. *Flowers* Single, cup-shaped, borne in great profusion in mid-summer. Bright magenta-pink, with dark veins and black centres. *Leaves* Rounded, divided into 7 deeply cut lobes. Bright yellowish-green leaves turning red in autumn.
• NATIVE HABITAT Garden origin.
• CULTIVATION This geranium is easily grown in any moderately fertile, well-drained soil, in full sun or part-shade. It is well-suited for inclusion in a herbaceous border and makes a very attractive addition to an informal cottage-style garden. This is one of the most reliable and attractive of the more recently introduced hardy geraniums and is widely available.
• PROPAGATION Many geraniums are easily propagated by division, but each plant of *G.* 'Ann Folkard' forms just one rootstock that defies division. It is therefore best propagated by cuttings taken of sideshoots in summer.

☼ ◊
❀ ❀ ❀

**HEIGHT**
50cm (20in)

**SPREAD**
1m (36in)

| Gesneriaceae | |
|---|---|

## *ACHIMENES* 'Little Beauty'

*Habit* Bushy. *Flowers* Large, funnel-shaped, in summer. Deep pink with a yellow eye. *Leaves* Oval, toothed. Glossy, bluish-green.
• NATIVE HABITAT Garden origin.
• CULTIVATION Grow as a house or conservatory plant in cool climates, in well-drained, humus-rich potting compost. Site in bright, indirect light. Water freely when in growth. Dry out after flowering and store rhizomes in frost-free conditions over winter.
• PROPAGATION By division of rhizomes in spring, or by stem cuttings in summer.

☼ ◊

Min. 10°C
(50°F)

**HEIGHT**
25cm (10in)

**SPREAD**
30cm (12in)

| Scrophulariaceae | |
|---|---|

## *MIMULUS LEWISII* ♛

*Habit* Creeping, upright. *Flowers* Snapdragon-like, tubular with spreading lobes, borne singly in the leaf axils, in summer. Deep rose-pink, paler and spotted deep pink at the throat. *Leaves* Lance-shaped with wavy-toothed margins. Mid-green.
• NATIVE HABITAT By streamsides in the mountains of W. North America.
• CULTIVATION Tolerates dry soils but best in moist or wet soil, in full sun. Good for a bog garden.
• PROPAGATION By seed or division in spring or softwood cuttings in late summer.

☼ ◊
❀ ❀

**HEIGHT**
60cm (24in)

**SPREAD**
45cm (18in)

# CARNATIONS AND PINKS

Carnations and pinks belong to the genus *Dianthus*. They are widely grown both for their attractive, often spicy-scented flowers, and their silvery, grey- or blue-green leaves.

The single, double, or semi-double flowers, which come in almost every colour except blue and green, may be "selfs", all of one colour; "fancies" with contrasting stripes, flakes, or ticks; "picotee" with petals edged in a contrasting colour to the usually white or yellow ground; or "laced" in which the centre of each petal has a zone of a contrasting colour.

Carnations and pinks are divided here into the following groups:

**Border carnations** have an upright habit and flower prolifically once in mid-summer. Each stem bears 5 or more, often scented flowers. Grow in a border, or for cutting and exhibition.

**Perpetual-flowering carnations** are grown under glass for cutting and exhibition. They bloom all year, and are usually disbudded to leave one terminal bud per stem. Spray forms have the central bud removed to leave 4–5 flowers per stem

**Old-fashioned pinks** are grown in borders for their clove-scented flowers, produced in mid-summer.

**Modern pinks** have clove-scented flowers, produced in flushes in summer. They are excellent for borders or cutting.

Carnations and pinks need an open position in full sun, and humus-rich, well-drained, neutral and alkaline soil. All except the perpetual-flowering carnations are hard

Carnations and pinks can be propagated from cuttings of non-flowering shoots in summer for hardy perennials, and in late winter under glass for half-hardy perennials Propagate border carnations after flowering by layering. This involves wounding and pinning down the stems of non-flowering sideshoots to encourage new roots to form.

## D. 'Mrs. Sinkins'

*Habit* Clump-forming.
*Flowers* Heavily scented, fully-double, with fringed petals, borne in profusion in mid-summer. White.
*Leaves* Evergreen, linear. Grey-green.
• TIPS A sturdy and reliable old cultivar.
• HEIGHT 30cm (12in).
• SPREAD 23–30cm (9–12in).

**D. 'Mrs. Sinkins'**
(Old-fashioned pink)

## D. 'Haytor'

*Habit* Clump-forming.
*Flowers* Clove-scented, semi-double with fringed petals, in clusters of 4–6, in several flushes through summer. White.
*Leaves* Evergreen, linear, Grey-green.
• CULTIVATION Excellent for cutting.
• HEIGHT 30–45cm (12–18in).
• SPREAD 23–30cm (9–12in).

**D. 'Haytor'**
(Modern pink)

## D. 'Musgrave's Pink'

*Habit* Clump-forming.
*Flowers* Scented, single, profusely, in mid-summer. White with a green eye.
*Leaves* Evergreen, linear. Grey-green.
• TIPS A very old and reliable cultivar.
• OTHER NAMES
*D.* 'Charles Musgrave', *D.* 'Green Eyes'.
• HEIGHT 30cm (12in).
• SPREAD 23–30cm (9–12in).

**D. 'Musgrave's Pink'**
(Old-fashioned pink)

## D. 'White Ladies'

*Habit* Clump-forming.
*Flowers* Very fragrant, fully double, borne in profusion in mid-summer. Fringed white petals flushed green at the base.
*Leaves* Evergreen, linear. Grey-green.
• HEIGHT 30–45cm (12–18in).
• SPREAD 23–30cm (9–12in).

**D. 'White Ladies'**
(Old-fashioned pink)

## D. 'Nives'
**Habit** Neat.
**Flowers** Fully double,
to 10cm (4in) across,
produced throughout
the year but mainly in
summer. White.
**Leaves** Evergreen,
linear. Blue-green.
TIPS Needs staking.
HEIGHT 1–1.5m
(3–5ft).
SPREAD 30cm (1ft).

**D. 'Nives'**
(Perpetual-flowering
carnation)

☀ ◊ ❄

## D. 'Eva Humphries'
**Habit** Clump-forming.
**Flowers** Scented, semi-
double, to 8cm (3in)
across, in clusters of up
to 5, in mid-summer.
White petals finely
edged with purple.
**Leaves** Evergreen,
linear. Blue-green.
HEIGHT 75cm (2½ft).
SPREAD 30cm (1ft).

**D. 'Eva Humphries'**
(Border carnation)

☀ ◊ ❄❄❄

## D. 'Dad's Favourite'
**Habit** Clump-forming.
**Flowers** Scented, semi-
double, borne in
profusion in mid-
summer. White with
red and chocolate-
brown lacing.
**Leaves** Evergreen,
linear. Grey-green.
OTHER NAMES
D. 'A.J. Macsel'.
HEIGHT 30–45cm
(12–18in).
SPREAD 23–30cm
(9–12in).

## D. 'Fair Folly'
**Habit** Clump-forming.
**Flowers** Clove-scented,
single, in clusters of 4–5, in
mid-summer only. Dusky
pink to purple, each petal
with 2 white splashes.
**Leaves** Evergreen,
linear. Grey-green.
• OTHER NAMES
D. 'Constance Finnis'.
• HEIGHT 30–45cm
(12–18in).
• SPREAD 23–30cm
(9–12in).

**D. 'Fair Folly'**
(Old-fashioned pink)

☀ ◊ ❄❄❄

## D. 'Gran's Favourite'
**Habit** Clump-forming.
**Flowers** Scented,
semi-double, borne
in profusion in mid-
summer. White with
deep raspberry-
pink lacing.
**Leaves** Evergreen,
linear. Grey-green.
• HEIGHT 30–45cm
(12–18in).
• SPREAD 23–30cm
(9–12in).

**D. 'Gran's Favourite'**
(Modern laced pink)

☀ ◊ ❄❄❄   ⚆

**D. 'Dad's Favourite'**
(Old-fashioned pink)

☀ ◊ ❄❄❄

### D. 'Alice'
*Habit* Clump-forming.
*Flowers* Clove-scented,
semi-double, borne in
clusters of 4–6, in
several flushes
throughout summer.
Ivory-white petals
with a bold crimson eye.
*Leaves* Evergreen,
linear. Grey-green.
• HEIGHT 30–45cm
(12–18in).
• SPREAD 23–30cm
(9–12in).

**D. 'Alice'**
(Modern pink)

☼ ◊ ❀❀❀

### D. 'London Brocade'
*Habit* Clump-forming.
*Flowers* Clove-scented,
fully double, in clusters
of 4–5, in profusion in
mid-summer. Crimson-
laced, pink petals.
*Leaves* Evergreen,
linear. Grey-green.
• TIPS Excellent for cut-
ting.
• HEIGHT 30–45cm
(12–18in).
• SPREAD 23–30cm
(9–12in).

**D. 'London Brocade'**
(Old-fashioned pink)

☼ ◊ ❀❀❀

### D. 'London Delight'
*Habit* Clump-forming.
*Flowers* Scented, semi-
double, borne in
profusion in mid-
summer. Lavender petals
laced with purple.
*Leaves* Evergreen,
linear. Grey-green.
• HEIGHT 30cm (12in).
• SPREAD 23–30cm
(9–12in).

### D. 'Prudence'
*Habit* Clump-forming,
spreading. *Flowers* Well-
scented, semi-double,
borne in profusion in
mid-summer. Palest
pink, laced with
red-purple.
*Leaves* Evergreen,
linear. Grey-green.
• HEIGHT 30cm (12in).
• SPREAD 23–30cm
(9–12in) or more.

**D. 'Prudence'**
(Old-fashioned pink)

☼ ◊ ❀❀❀

### D. 'Forest Treasure'
*Habit* Clump-forming.
*Flowers* Scented,
double, to 8cm
(3in).across, in clusters of
up to 5, in mid-summer.
White petals splashed
with reddish-purple.
*Leaves* Evergreen,
linear. Blue-green.
• HEIGHT 75cm (2½ft).
• SPREAD 30cm (1ft).

**D. 'Forest Treasure'**
(Border carnation)

☼ ◊ ❀❀❀

**D. 'London Delight'**
(Old-fashioned pink)

☼ ◊ ❀❀❀

## D. 'Pierrot'

**Habit** Neat –
needs support.
**Flowers** Fully double, to
10cm (4in) across, all year
but mainly in summer.
Pale rose-lavender petals,
finely edged with purple.
**Leaves** Evergreen,
linear. Blue-green.
• OTHER NAMES
D. 'Pink Calypso'.
• HEIGHT 1–1.5m
(3–5ft).
• SPREAD 30cm (1ft).

**D. 'Pierrot'**
(Perpetual-flowering
carnation)

☼ ◊ ❀

## D. 'Emile Paré'

**Habit** Clump-forming.
**Flowers** Small, scented,
semi-double, borne in
dense clusters, in mid-
summer. Salmon-pink.
**Leaves** Evergreen,
linear. Mid-green.
• HEIGHT 30–45cm
(12–18in).
• SPREAD 23–30cm
(9–12in).

**D. 'Emile Paré'**
(Old-fashioned pink)

☼ ◊ ❀ ❀ ❀

## D. 'Doris'

**Habit** Clump-forming.
**Flowers** Clove-scented,
fully double, in clusters
of 4–6, in profuse flushes
throughout summer.
Pale pink with a darker
salmon-pink ring at the
centre.
**Leaves** Evergreen,
linear, grey-green.
• HEIGHT 30–45cm
(12–18in).
• SPREAD 23–30cm
(9–12in).

**D. 'Doris'**
(Modern pink)

☼ ◊ ❀ ❀ ❀       ⚲

## D. 'Monica Wyatt'

**Habit** Clump-forming.
**Flowers** Strongly clove-
scented, fully double,
in clusters of 4–6, in
several flushes through
summer. Cyclamen-pink
with a magenta eye.
**Leaves** Evergreen,
linear. Grey-green.
• HEIGHT 30–45cm
(12–18in).
• SPREAD 23–30cm
(9–12in).

**D. 'Monica Wyatt'**
(Modern pink)

☼ ◊ ❀ ❀ ❀       ⚲

## D. 'Pink Calypso'

**Habit** Neat –
needs support.
**Flowers** Fully double,
to 10cm (4in) across,
produced all year round
but mainly in summer.
Strong, clear pink petals.
**Leaves** Evergreen,
linear. Blue-green.
• OTHER NAMES
D. 'Truly Yours'.
• HEIGHT 1–1.5m
(3–5ft).
• SPREAD 30cm (1ft).

**D. 'Pink Calypso'**
(Perpetual-flowering
carnation)

☼ ◊ ❀

## D. 'Valda Wyatt'

**Habit** Clump-forming.
**Flowers** Strongly clove-
scented, fully double,
borne in clusters of
4–6, in several flushes
throughout summer.
Rose-lavender.
**Leaves** Evergreen,
linear. Grey-green.
• HEIGHT 30–45cm
(12–18in).
• SPREAD 23–30cm
(9–12in).

**D. 'Valda Wyatt'**
(Modern pink)

☼ ◊ ❀ ❀ ❀       ⚲

## D. 'Becky Robinson'

**Habit** Clump-forming.
**Flowers** Clove-scented,
semi-double, borne in
clusters of 4–6, in
several flushes
throughout summer.
Rose-pink petals laced
with ruby-red.
**Leaves** Evergreen,
linear. Grey-green.
• TIPS Good for
exhibition.
• HEIGHT 30–45cm
(12–18in).
• SPREAD 23–30cm
(9–12in).

**D. 'Becky Robinson'**
(Modern laced pink)

☼ ◊ ❀ ❀ ❀       ⚲

**D. 'Pink Jewel'**
*Habit* Clump-forming.
*Flowers* Clove-scented,
semi-double, in several
flushes throughout
summer. Pink.
*Leaves* Evergreen,
linear, Grey-green.
• TIPS Very floriferous
and excellent for rock
gardens.
• HEIGHT 10–15cm
(4–6in).
• SPREAD 23–30cm
(9–12in).

**D. 'Pink Jewel'**
(Modern pink)

☼ ◊ ✻✻✻

**D. 'Joy'**
*Habit* Clump-forming.
*Flowers* Clove-scented,
fully double, borne in
clusters of 4–6, in several
flushes throughout
summer. Rich pink.
*Leaves* Evergreen,
linear. Grey-green.
• TIPS Excellent for
cutting.
• HEIGHT 30–45cm
(12–18in).
• SPREAD 23–30cm
(9–12in).

**D. 'Joy'**
(Modern pink)

☼ ◊ ✻✻✻

**D. 'Houndspool Ruby'**
*Habit* Clump-forming.
*Flowers* Clove-scented,
fully double, in clusters of
4–6, in profuse flushes in
summer. Ruby-pink, with
a darker ring at the centre.
*Leaves* Evergreen, linear.
Grey-green.
• OTHER NAMES *D.*
'Ruby', *D.* 'Ruby Doris'.
• HEIGHT 30–45cm
(12–18in).
• SPREAD 23–30cm
(9–12in).

**D. 'Houndspool Ruby'**
(Modern pink)

☼ ◊ ✻✻✻        ♛

**D. 'Christopher'**
*Habit* Clump-forming.
*Flowers* Lightly clove-
scented, fully double,
borne in clusters of 4–6, in
several flushes in summer.
Bright salmon-red.
*Leaves* Evergreen, linear.
Grey-green.
• TIPS Excellent for
cutting.
• HEIGHT 30–45cm
(12–18in).
• SPREAD 23–30cm
(9–12in).

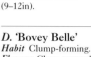

**D. 'Christopher'**
(Modern pink)

☼ ◊ ✻✻✻

**D. 'Bovey Belle'**
*Habit* Clump-forming.
*Flowers* Clove-scented,
fully double, borne in
clusters of 4–6, in several
flushes throughout
summer. Bright
purplish-pink.
*Leaves* Evergreen,
linear. Grey-green.
• TIPS Good for cutting.
• HEIGHT 30–45cm
(12–18in).
• SPREAD 23–30cm
(9–12in).

**D. 'Bovey Belle'**
(Modern pink)

☼ ◊ ✻✻✻

**D. 'Laced Monarch'**
*Habit* Clump-forming.
*Flowers* Fully double,
to 5cm (2in) across, in
profusion, in mid-
summer. Pink, with
maroon-red lacing.
*Leaves* Evergreen,
linear. Blue-green.
• HEIGHT 30–45cm
(12–18 in).
• SPREAD 23–30cm
(9–12in).

**D. 'Laced Monarch'**
(Modern laced pink)

☼ ◊ ✻

**D. 'Astor'**
*Habit* Neat.
*Flowers* Scented, fully
double, to 10cm (4in)
across, produced
throughout the year
but mainly in summer.
Scarlet.
*Leaves* Evergreen,
linear. Blue-green.
• TIPS Needs staking.
• HEIGHT 1–1.5m (3–5ft).
• SPREAD 30cm (1ft).

**D. 'Astor'**
(Perpetual-flowering
carnation)

☼ ◊ ✻

## D. 'Nina'
**Habit** Neat.
**Flowers** Fully double,
to 10cm (4in) across,
produced throughout
the year but mainly in
summer. Crimson, with
neatly arranged, smooth-
edged petals.
**Leaves** Evergreen,
linear. Blue-green.
TIPS Needs staking.
• HEIGHT 1–1.5m
(3–5ft).
• SPREAD 30cm (1ft).

**D. 'Nina'**
(Perpetual-flowering
carnation)

☀ ◊ ❄

## D. 'Bookham Perfume'
**Habit** Clump-forming.
**Flowers** Scented, semi-
double, to 8cm (3in)
across, borne on short,
stiff stems in clusters of
up to 5, in mid-summer.
Crimson.
**Leaves** Evergreen,
linear. Blue-green.
• HEIGHT 75cm (2½ft).
• SPREAD 30cm (1ft).

**D. 'Bookham Perfume'**
(Border carnation)

☀ ◊ ❄ ❄ ❄

## D. 'Brympton Red'
**Habit** Clump-forming.
**Flowers** Single, in
profusion in mid-
summer. Bright crimson
with darker shading.
**Leaves** Evergreen,
linear. Grey-green.
• HEIGHT 30cm (12in).
• SPREAD 23–30cm
(9–12in).

**D. 'Brympton Red'**
(Old-fashioned pink)

☀ ◊ ❄ ❄ ❄

## D. 'Lavender Clove'
**Habit** Vigorous, clump-
forming. **Flowers**
scented, semi-double, to
8cm (3in) across, borne
on long stems in clusters
of up to 5, in mid-
summer. Dusky
lavender-grey.
**Leaves** Evergreen,
linear. Blue-green.
• HEIGHT 75cm (2½ft).
• SPREAD 30cm (1ft).

**D. 'Lavender Clove'**
(Border carnation)

☀ ◊ ❄ ❄ ❄

## D. 'Bookham Fancy'
**Habit** Clump-forming.
**Flowers** Scented, semi-
double, to 8cm (3in)
across, borne on short,
stiff stems in clusters of
up to 5, in mid-summer.
Bright yellow, edged
and flecked carmine-
purple.
**Leaves** Evergreen,
linear. Blue-green.
• HEIGHT 75cm (2½ft).
• SPREAD 30cm (1ft).

**D. 'Bookham Fancy'**
(Border carnation)

☀ ◊ ❄ ❄ ❄

## D. 'Happiness'
**Habit** Clump-forming.
**Flowers** Scented, semi-
double, to 8cm (3in)
across, in clusters of up
to 5, in mid-summer.
Yellow petals, striped
scarlet-orange.
**Leaves** Evergreen,
linear. Blue-green.
• HEIGHT 75cm (2½ft).
• SPREAD 30cm (1ft).

**D. 'Happiness'**
(Border carnation)

☀ ◊ ❄ ❄ ❄

## D. 'Clara'
**Habit** Neat – needs
support.
**Flowers** Fully double,
to 10cm (4in). across,
produced throughout
the year but mainly in
summer. Yellow; flecked
with salmon-red.
**Leaves** Evergreen, linear.
Blue-green.
• HEIGHT 1–1.5m (3–5ft).
• SPREAD 30cm (1ft).

**D. 'Clara'**
(Perpetual-flowering
carnation)

☀ ◊ ❄

## D. 'Crompton Princess'
**Habit** Neat.
**Flowers** Fully double,
to 10cm (4in) across,
produced throughout
the year but mainly in
summer. Pure white.
**Leaves** Evergreen, linear.
Blue-green.
• TIPS Needs staking.
• HEIGHT 1–1.5m (3–5ft).
• SPREAD 30cm (1ft).

**D. 'Crompton Princess'**
(Perpetual-flowering
carnation)

☀ ◊ ❄

### D. 'Cream Sue'
*Habit* Neat.
*Flowers* Fully double, to 10cm (4in) across, produced throughout the year but mainly in summer. Rich cream.
*Leaves* Evergreen, linear. Blue-green.
• TIPS Needs staking.
• HEIGHT 1–1.5m (3–5ft).
• SPREAD 30cm (1ft).

**D. 'Cream Sue'**
(Perpetual-flowering carnation)

☼ ◊ ❄

### D. 'Valencia'
*Habit* Neat.
*Flowers* Fully double, to 10cm (4in) across, produced throughout the year but mainly in summer. Golden-orange petals.
*Leaves* Evergreen, linear. Blue-green.
• TIPS Needs staking.
• HEIGHT 1–1.5m (3–5ft).
• SPREAD 30cm (1ft).

**D. 'Valencia'**
(Perpetual-flowering carnation)

☼ ◊ ❄

### D. 'Borello'
*Habit* Neat.
*Flowers* Fully double, to 10cm (4in) across, produced throughout the year but mainly in summer. Yellow.
*Leaves* Evergreen, linear. Blue-green.
• TIPS Needs staking.
• HEIGHT 1–1.5m (3–5ft).
• SPREAD 30cm (1ft).

**D. 'Borello'**
(Perpetual-flowering carnation)

☼ ◊ ❄

### D. 'Raggio di Sole'
*Habit* Neat.
*Flowers* Fully double, to 10cm (4in) across, produced throughout the year but mainly in summer. Bright orange petals.
*Leaves* Evergreen, linear. Blue-green.
• TIPS Needs staking.
• HEIGHT 1–1.5m (3–5ft).
• SPREAD 30cm (1ft).

**D. 'Raggio di Sole'**
(Perpetual-flowering carnation)

☼ ◊ ❄

### D. 'Golden Cross'
*Habit* Clump-forming.
*Flowers* Scented, double, to 8cm (3in) across, in clusters of up to 5, in mid-summer. Yellow.
*Leaves* Evergreen, linear. Blue-green.
• HEIGHT 75cm (2½ft).
• SPREAD 30cm (1ft).

**D. 'Golden Cross'**
(Border carnation)

☼ ◊ ❄ ❄ ❄

### D. 'Christine Hough'
*Habit* Clump-forming.
*Flowers* Scented, semi-double, to 8cm (3in) across, in clusters of up to 5, in mid-summer. Apricot petals overlaid and streaked with dark pink.
*Leaves* Evergreen, linear. Blue-green.
• HEIGHT 75cm (2½ft).
• SPREAD 30cm (1ft).

**D. 'Christine Hough'**
(Border carnation)

☼ ◊ ❄ ❄ ❄

### D. 'Aldridge Yellow'
*Habit* Clump-forming.
*Flowers* Semi-double, to 8cm (3in) across, borne in clusters of up to 5, in mid-summer. Clear yellow.
*Leaves* Evergreen, linear. Blue-green.
• HEIGHT 75–110cm (2½–3½ft).
• SPREAD 30cm (1ft).

**D. 'Aldridge Yellow'**
(Border carnation)

☼ ◊ ❄ ❄ ❄

### D. 'Albisola'
*Habit* Neat.
*Flowers* Fully double, to 10cm (4in) across, produced throughout the year but mainly in summer. Clear tangerine-orange.
*Leaves* Evergreen, linear. Blue-green.
• TIPS Needs staking.
• HEIGHT 1–1.5m (3–5ft).
• SPREAD 30cm (1ft).

**D. 'Albisola'**
(Perpetual-flowering carnation)

☼ ◊ ❄

| Gesneriaceae | |
|---|---|

## SINNINGIA 'Red Flicker'

**Habit** Low-growing, tuberous-rooted. **Flowers** Large, fleshy, funnel-shaped, borne on short stems, in summer. Pinkish-red. **Leaves** Large, oval, in basal rosettes. Bluish-green.

NATIVE HABITAT Garden origin.

CULTIVATION In cool climates, grow as a house or conservatory plant in moist, peaty soil or compost. Site in bright light, water freely and keep humid. Overwinter dried tubers in frost-free conditions.

PROPAGATION By division of tubers or by stem cuttings in late spring or summer.

☀ ◐
Min. 15°C (59°F)

**HEIGHT**
to 30cm (12in)

**SPREAD**
45cm (18in)

| Bignoniaceae | |
|---|---|

## INCARVILLEA DELAVAYI

**Habit** Clump-forming. **Flowers** Trumpet-shaped, borne in few-flowered clusters at the ends of sturdy stems, in early summer. Pinkish-red. **Leaves** Divided into pairs of oval to oblong segments, in basal clumps. Mid- to dark green.

• NATIVE HABITAT Scrub and grassland, in the mountains of S.W. China.
• CULTIVATION Grow in deep, sandy, moist, well-drained soil, in full sun. Protect young growth from slugs. Mulch crowns with dry bracken litter in winter.
• PROPAGATION By seed in autumn or spring.

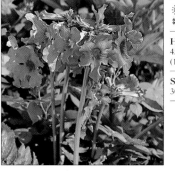

☀ ◌
❅ ❅ ❅

**HEIGHT**
45–60cm (18–24in)

**SPREAD**
30cm (12in)

| Verbenaceae | |
|---|---|

## VERBENA 'Sissinghurst'                    ♈

**Habit** Mat-forming. **Flowers** Small, brilliant, borne in rounded heads, on lax stems, throughout summer. Magenta-pink. **Leaves** Oval to lance-shaped, cut and toothed. Mid-green.

NATIVE HABITAT Garden origin.

CULTIVATION Grow in fertile, well-drained soil, in full sun. Overwinter young plants in frost-free conditions. The low, mat-forming habit suits the front of a mixed or herbaceous border or edging for paths and borders. V. 'Sissinghurst' is also excellent for planting in hanging baskets, large window boxes or tubs for patio decoration. The brilliant magenta-pink flowers associate well with deep blue and purple flowers and are especially beautiful in combinations with grey- or silver-leaved plants. The cut flowers last well in water.
• PROPAGATION By stem cuttings in late summer or autumn.

☀ ◌
❅

**HEIGHT**
15–20cm (6–8in)

**SPREAD**
45cm (18in)

| Rosaceae | |
|---|---|

## *POTENTILLA NEPALENSIS* 'Miss Willmott' ♀

*Habit* Clump-forming. *Flowers* Open cup-shaped, on slender, branching stems, throughout summer. Pink, with cherry-red centres. *Leaves* Palmately divided into 5 toothed leaflets. Mid-green.
• NATIVE HABITAT Garden origin.
• CULTIVATION Grow in any moderately fertile, well-drained soil, in sun or light shade. Good for the front of a herbaceous border and for cottage gardens.
• PROPAGATION By division in spring or autumn. Seed comes reasonably true; sow in autumn.

☼ ◊
✽ ✽ ✽

HEIGHT
50cm (20in)

SPREAD
60cm (24in)

| Commelinaceae | |
|---|---|

## *TRADESCANTIA* X *ANDERSONIANA* 'Purewell Giant' ♀

*Habit* Clump-forming. *Flowers* 3-petalled, borne in succession throughout summer. Red-purple, surrounded by two leaf-like, green bracts. *Leaves* Slightly fleshy, narrowly lance-shaped, borne on jointed stems. Mid-green.
• NATIVE HABITAT Garden origin.
• CULTIVATION Grow in fertile, moist but well-drained soil, in sun or light shade. Protect young growth from slugs.
• PROPAGATION By division in spring or autumn.

☼ ◊
✽ ✽ ✽

HEIGHT
to 60cm
(24in)

SPREAD
45cm (18in)

| Caryophyllaceae | |
|---|---|

## *LYCHNIS VISCARIA* 'Splendens Plena' ♀

*Habit* Upright, clump-forming. *Flowers* Small, double, borne in dense, spike-like heads, in early summer. Bright magenta-pink. *Leaves* Oval to lance-shaped, sticky-hairy beneath. Mid-green.
• NATIVE HABITAT The species occurs on dry, rocky hills and cliffs, from Europe to W. Asia.
• CULTIVATION Grow in well-drained, not too fertile soil, in full sun. Suitable for the front of a herbaceous border and for cottage gardens.
• PROPAGATION By division in autumn or spring.
• OTHER NAMES *L. viscaria* 'Flore Pleno'.

☼ ◊
✽ ✽ ✽

HEIGHT
45cm (18in)

SPREAD
45cm (18in)

| Papaveraceae | |
|---|---|

## *DICENTRA* 'Stuart Boothman' ♀

*Habit* Tufted, clump-forming. *Flowers* Small, pendent, narrowly heart-shaped, borne on arching stems, over long periods in late spring and summer. Carmine-pink. *Leaves* Fern-like, very finely cut. Dark grey-green.
• NATIVE HABITAT Garden origin.
• CULTIVATION Grow in humus-rich, moist, well-drained soil, in semi-shade. Suitable for a shady herbaceous border or woodland garden.
• PROPAGATION By division in late winter.
• OTHER NAMES *D.* 'Boothman's Variety'.

☼ ◊
✽ ✽ ✽

HEIGHT
45cm (18in)

SPREAD
30cm (12in)

Crassulaceae

## *EDUM* 'Ruby Glow'

**Habit** Clump-forming. **Flowers** Small, borne in dense, flattened heads on leafy stems, in profusion from late summer to autumn. Rich ruby-red. **Leaves** Fleshy, oval. Purple-grey.
NATIVE HABITAT Garden origin.
CULTIVATION Grow in fertile, well-drained soil, with adequate moisture during summer, in full sun. The nectar-rich flowers are very attractive to bees, butterflies and other beneficial insects. This perennial's handsome leaves and flowers and formal habit make it an excellent choice for softening the front of a mixed or herbaceous border; associates especially well with grey- or silver-leaved plants. It is also suitable for a raised bed, or the top of a wall or terrace, where it is given room to sprawl over the edge.
• PROPAGATION By division in spring.
• OTHER NAMES *Hylotelephium* 'Ruby Glow'.

☀ ◊
❋ ❋ ❋

HEIGHT
30–45cm
(12–18in)

SPREAD
30–45cm
(12–18in)

| Caryophyllaceae | |
|---|---|

## LYCHNIS CORONARIA

**Habit** Upright, clump-forming, often short-lived. **Flowers** Small, profuse, in open, grey-stemmed sprays, throughout summer. Bright magenta-pink to rose-crimson. **Leaves** Oval to lance-shaped, densely hairy, mostly in basal clumps. Silver-grey.
• NATIVE HABITAT Scrub, woodland, rocky slopes, from S.E. Europe to Iran and Turkestan.
• CULTIVATION Grow in well-drained soil, in full sun. Suitable for a herbaceous, especially silver border or a cottage garden. Self-seeding may pose a problem.
• PROPAGATION Seed or division in spring.

HEIGHT
45–60cm
(18–24in)

SPREAD
45cm (18in)

| Euphorbiaceae | |
|---|---|

## EUPHORBIA DULCIS 'Chameleon'

**Habit** Upright, rhizomatous. **Flowers** Tiny, borne in branching, slender-stemmed heads in early summer. Yellowish-green, with conspicuous purple-flushed, yellow-green bracts. **Leaves** Oblong to lance-shaped. Dark purple, tinted red in autumn.
• NATIVE HABITAT Garden origin.
• CULTIVATION Grow in moist, well-drained soil, in part-shade or sun. Avoid contact with irritant sa
• PROPAGATION By division in spring or early autumn, or by basal cuttings in spring or summer.

HEIGHT
45–60cm
(18–24in)

SPREAD
60cm (24

| Leguminosae/ Papilionaceae | CORAL GEM PARROTS BEAK |
|---|---|

## LOTUS BERTHELOTII

**Habit** Trailing. **Flowers** Large, beak- or claw-like, in clusters, in summer. Orange-red to scarlet or purple. **Leaves** Finely divided into linear or thread-like segments, on silvery stems. Silver-hairy.
• NATIVE HABITAT Canary Islands, Cape Verde Islands, Tenerife.
• CULTIVATION In cooler climates, grow as a house or conservatory plant in freely draining, sandy compost. Site in full sun. Excellent in a hanging basket.
• PROPAGATION By scarified seed in spring, or by semi-ripe cuttings in summer.

Min. 5°C
(41°F)

HEIGHT
30cm (12in)

SPREAD
indefinite

| Saxifragaceae | |
|---|---|

## ASTILBE 'Fanal'

**Habit** Clump-forming. **Flowers** Tiny, deep in neat, feathery, tapering spires, on strong stems, in summer. Crimson-red. **Leaves** Divided into toothed, oval, leaflets. Dark green.
• NATIVE HABITAT Garden origin.
• CULTIVATION Grow in moist, fertile, humus-ric soil, in sun or semi-shade. Good for damp borders bog gardens or waterside plantings. The flower heads dry and turn brown, persisting into winter unless dead-headed.
• PROPAGATION By division in spring or autumn.

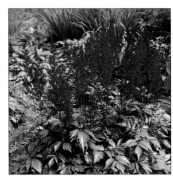

HEIGHT
60cm (2f

SPREAD
to 1m (3f

| Gesneriaceae | |
|---|---|

## SINNINGIA 'Switzerland'

**Habit** Low-growing, tuberous-rooted. **Flowers** Large, fleshy, funnel-shaped, in summer. Scarlet, with ruffled, white-rimmed petals. **Leaves** Large, oval, velvety, in basal rosettes. Dark green.
NATIVE HABITAT Garden origin.
CULTIVATION In cool climates, grow as a house or conservatory plant in moist, peaty soil or compost. Site in bright light, water freely and keep humid. Overwinter dried tubers in frost-free conditions.
PROPAGATION By division of tubers or by stem cuttings in late spring or summer.

Min. 15°C
(59°F)

HEIGHT
to 30cm
(12in)

SPREAD
45cm (18in)

| Papaveraceae | |
|---|---|

## DICENTRA 'Bacchanal'

**Habit** Spreading, rhizomatous. **Flowers** Small, pendent, narrowly heart-shaped, on fleshy, arching stems, in late spring and summer. Very dark red. **Leaves** Fern-like, deeply cut. Fresh green.
NATIVE HABITAT Garden origin.
CULTIVATION Grow in humus-rich, moist but well-drained soil, in semi-shade. An exceptionally dark-flowered cultivar and a beautiful plant for a shady herbaceous border or woodland garden.
PROPAGATION By division when dormant in late winter.

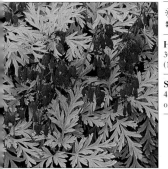

HEIGHT
30–45cm
(12–18in)

SPREAD
45cm (18in)
or more

| Saxifragaceae | |
|---|---|

## HEUCHERA 'Red Spangles'

**Habit** Dense, clump-forming. **Flowers** Small, bell-shaped, in open spikes on slender, dark red stems, in early summer and again in late summer. Crimson-scarlet. **Leaves** Evergreen, heart-shaped, with toothed, rounded, lobes. Purplish-green.
• NATIVE HABITAT Garden origin.
• CULTIVATION Grow in moist, well-drained soil, in sun or semi-shade. Provides good ground cover.
• PROPAGATION By division in autumn or spring, using young, outer portions of the crown.

HEIGHT
30cm (12in)

SPREAD
30cm (12in)

Gesneriaceae

## *SMITHIANTHA* 'Orange King'

*Habit* Bushy, upright, with tuber-like rhizomes.
*Flowers* Pendent, tubular, borne in summer and
autumn. Orange-red, spotted red within and with
yellow lips. *Leaves* Large, oval and heart-shaped
at the base, scalloped, velvety. Emerald green,
veined dark reddish-purple.
• NATIVE HABITAT Garden origin.
• CULTIVATION Grow as a house or conservatory
plant in cool climates and place in bright, indirect
light. The plant benefits from space where air can
circulate freely. Feed and water generously when

in growth, gradually reducing water after
flowering and, in winter, kept almost dry until
the spring repotting takes place. Suitable for a
herbaceous border in tropical gardens, in well-
drained, humus-rich soil.
• PROPAGATION By division of rhizomes in
early spring.

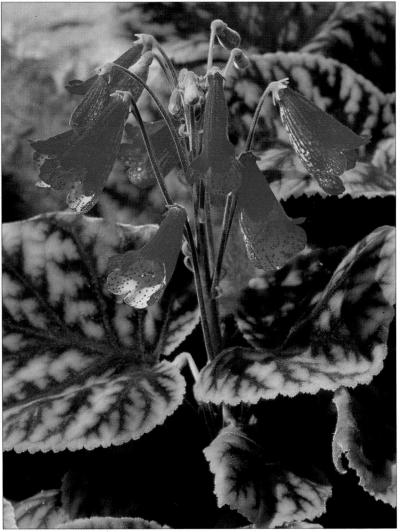

Min. 15°C
(59°F)

HEIGHT
to 60cm
(24in)

SPREAD
to 60cm
(24in)

| Caryophyllaceae | |
|---|---|

## *LYCHNIS* × *ARKWRIGHTII* 'Vesuvius'

*Habit* Upright, clump-forming. *Flowers* Small, cross-shaped, in flat heads, at the ends of sturdy stems, in early summer. Brilliant orange-scarlet. *Leaves* Oval, borne along the length of the flowering stem. Dark bronze-green.
• NATIVE HABITAT Garden origin
• CULTIVATION Grow in fertile, moist, well-drained soil, in sun or light shade; shelter from wind. Looks good with yellow-flowered and bronze-leaved plants.
• PROPAGATION By division in autumn or spring.
• OTHER NAMES *L.* × *haageana* 'Vesuvius'.

☀ ◊
❀❀❀

HEIGHT
45cm (18in)

SPREAD
30cm (12in)

| Rosaceae | |
|---|---|

## *POTENTILLA* 'William Rollison'

*Habit* Clump-forming. *Flowers* Saucer-shaped, semi-double, on slender, branching stems, throughout summer. Deep orange, flushed scarlet. *Leaves* Palmate, strawberry-like. Dark green.
• NATIVE HABITAT Garden origin.
• CULTIVATION Grow in any moderately fertile, well-drained soil, in sun or light shade. A valuable long-flowering plant, suitable for the front of herbaceous borders and cottage gardens.
• PROPAGATION By division in spring or autumn.

☀ ◊
❀❀❀

HEIGHT
45cm (18in)

SPREAD
45cm (18in)

| Rosaceae | |
|---|---|

## *POTENTILLA* 'Gibson's Scarlet'

*Habit* Clump-forming. *Flowers* Saucer-shaped, on slender, borne on branching stems, throughout summer. Brilliant scarlet. *Leaves* Palmate, strawberry-like. Dark green.
• NATIVE HABITAT Garden origin.
• CULTIVATION Grow in any moderately fertile, well-drained soil, in sun or light shade. A valuable long-flowering perennial, suitable for the front of a herbaceous border and for cottage gardens.
• PROPAGATION By division in spring or autumn.

☀ ◊
❀❀❀

HEIGHT
45cm (18in)

SPREAD
45cm (18in)

| Papaveraceae | |
|---|---|

## *PAPAVER* 'Fireball'

*Habit* Spreading, clump-forming. *Flowers* Pompon-like, fully double, with narrow, satiny, petals, on wiry stems, in summer. Orange-scarlet. *Leaves* Narrowly lance-shaped, doubly toothed, dying back after flowering. Green, bristly-hairy.
• NATIVE HABITAT Garden origin.
• CULTIVATION Grow in well-drained, fertile soil, in full sun. A reliable, long-lived perennial for the front of a herbaceous border and cottage gardens.
• PROPAGATION By root cuttings in winter, or by division in autumn.

☀ ◊
❀❀❀

HEIGHT
40cm (16in)

SPREAD
30cm (12in)

| Rosaceae | |
|---|---|

## POTENTILLA ATROSANGUINEA

**Habit** Clump-forming. **Flowers** Open cup-shaped, borne on finely hairy, branching stems, throughout summer. Dark red. **Leaves** Divided into 3 neatly scalloped leaflets. Mid-green, often silvery beneath.
• NATIVE HABITAT Grassy slopes, Himalayas.
• CULTIVATION Grow in any moderately fertile, cool, moist but well-drained soil, in sun or light shade. Good for the front of a herbaceous border and for cottage gardens.
• PROPAGATION By seed or division in spring or autumn.

☼ ◊
❀ ❀ ❀

HEIGHT
50cm (20in)

SPREAD
60cm (24in)

| Asphodelaceae/Liliaceae | |
|---|---|

## KNIPHOFIA 'Strawberries and Cream'

**Habit** Upright, clump-forming. **Flowers** Small, narrowly tubular, borne on slender, upright stems in terminal spikes, in late summer. Creamy-white, opening from pinkish-red buds. **Leaves** Grass-like, narrowly linear, arching to form basal clumps. Mid-green.
• NATIVE HABITAT Garden origin.
• CULTIVATION Grow in full sun, in moist but well-drained soil. Needs ample moisture when in growth. Mulch crowns in cold winter areas.
• PROPAGATION By division in spring.

☼ ◊
❀ ❀

HEIGHT
60cm (24in)

SPREAD
45cm (18in)

| Asteraceae/Compositae | |
|---|---|

## GAILLARDIA 'Dazzler'

**Habit** Lax, open. **Flowers** Large, daisy-like, borne singly on lax stems, over a long period in summer. Yellow-tipped, bright orange-red petals, around an orange-red disc. **Leaves** Soft, lance-shaped, toothed and lobed. Mid- to dark green.
• NATIVE HABITAT Garden origin.
• CULTIVATION Grow in light, well-drained, not too fertile soil, in sun. Needs staking, but provides brilliant, long-lasting colour in a summer border.
• PROPAGATION By root cuttings in winter.
• OTHER NAMES *Gaillardia* x *grandiflora* 'Dazzler'.

☼ ◊
❀ ❀ ❀

HEIGHT
60cm (24in)

SPREAD
50cm (20in)

| Scrophulariaceae | |
|---|---|

## MIMULUS 'Royal Velvet'

**Habit** Compact. **Flowers** Snapdragon-like, tubular with spreading lobes, freely produced throughout summer. Mahogany red with golden-yellow, mahogany-speckled throats. **Leaves** Broadly oval, toothed. Mid-green.
• NATIVE HABITAT Garden origin.
• CULTIVATION Grow in moist soil in full sun. In cold areas, overwinter young plants in frost-free conditions as insurance against winter losses.
• PROPAGATION By division in spring or softwood cuttings in late summer.

☼ ◊
❀

HEIGHT
30cm (12in)

SPREAD
23cm (9in)

| Polemoniaceae | |
|---|---|

## *POLEMONIUM CARNEUM*

**Habit** Clump-forming, slow-spreading. **Flowers** Small, bell- to cup-shaped, in loose clusters, in early summer. Pink or lilac-pink. **Leaves** Finely divided into 11–19 elliptic to oval leaflets. Mid-green.
• NATIVE HABITAT Scrub and grassland in the coastal hills of California.
• CULTIVATION Tolerates dry soils. Grows best in humus-rich, sharply drained soil, in a warm, sunny, sheltered site. Suitable for herbaceous borders.
• PROPAGATION By seed or division in spring.

☼ ◊
❋ ❋ ❋

HEIGHT
45cm (18in)

SPREAD
45cm (18in)

| Zingiberaceae | |
|---|---|

## *KAEMPFERIA PULCHRA*

**Habit** Tufted, rhizomatous. **Flowers** Small, in short spikes from the centre of tufts of foliage during summer. Lilac-pink. **Leaves** Aromatic, elliptic. Dark green variegated with pale green, bronze and silver.
• NATIVE HABITAT Thailand, Malaysia.
• CULTIVATION In cool climates, grow as a house or conservatory plant in moist, humus-rich soil or compost. Maintain high humidity. Water freely when in growth. Withhold water as leaves begin to yellow and keep dry during dormancy.
• PROPAGATION By division in late spring.

◑ ◊
Min. 18°C
(64°F)

HEIGHT
15cm (6in)

SPREAD
30cm (12in)

| Alliaceae/Liliaceae | |
|---|---|

## *TULBAGHIA VIOLACEA*

**Habit** Vigorous, clump-forming. **Flowers** Small, star-shaped, borne in terminal clusters, in late summer and autumn. Lilac-purple or lilac-pink. **Leaves** Semi-evergreen, linear, in basal clumps. Glaucous green.
• NATIVE HABITAT Eastern Cape, Transvaal, South Africa.
• CULTIVATION Grow in well-drained soil, in a warm, sheltered site, in full sun. Suitable for the front of a herbaceous border or the base of a warm wall.
• PROPAGATION By division or seed in spring.

☼ ◊
❋

HEIGHT
45–60cm
(18–24in)

SPREAD
30cm (12in)

| Gesneriaceae | FALSE AFRICAN VIOLET |
|---|---|

## *STREPTOCARPUS SAXORUM* ♈

**Habit** Rounded, clump-forming. **Flowers** Small, tubular, with long-stalks, in leaf axils, in late summer. Lilac with a white tube. **Leaves** Softly hairy, fleshy, elliptic to oval. Dark bluish-green.
• NATIVE HABITAT Tanzania, Kenya.
• CULTIVATION Grow as a house or conservatory plant in cool climates, in moist, humus-rich soil. Site in bright, indirect light, with high humidity. Avoid wetting the leaves when watering.
• PROPAGATION By seed in spring, by division after flowering, or by tip cuttings in spring or summer.

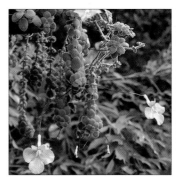

◑ ◊
Min.
10–15°C
(50–59°F)

HEIGHT
30cm (12in)
or more

SPREAD
30cm (12in)
or more

| Asteraceae/Compositae | |
|---|---|

## *ERIGERON* 'Dignity'

*Habit* Robust, clump-forming. *Flowers* Daisy-like, borne in profusion over long periods in summer. Slender, pink-violet ray florets around a greenish-yellow disc. *Leaves* Lance- to spoon-shaped. Mid-green.
• NATIVE HABITAT Garden origin.
• CULTIVATION Grow in moderately fertile, well-drained soil in sun. A valuable addition to a summer border, noted for its long flowering period.
• PROPAGATION By division in spring or early autumn, or by softwood cuttings in early summer.

☼ ◊
❀ ❀ ❀

HEIGHT
45cm (18in)

SPREAD
45cm (18in)

| Verbenaceae | |
|---|---|

## *VERBENA RIGIDA* ⚲

*Habit* Stiffly upright or spreading, tuberous-rooted. *Flowers* Small, borne in dense spikes, in late summer. Purple to magenta. *Leaves* Coarse, oblong, toothed, mostly along the stems. Mid-green.
• NATIVE HABITAT Argentina, Brazil.
• CULTIVATION Grow in moderately fertile, well-drained soil, in a warm, sunny, sheltered site. Mulch with dry bracken litter in cold winter areas.
• PROPAGATION By division of tubers or seed in autumn, or, in cold areas, in spring.
• OTHER NAMES *V. venosa*.

☼ ◊
❀

HEIGHT
45–60cm
(18–24in)

SPREAD
30cm (12in)

| Commelinaceae | |
|---|---|

## *TRADESCANTIA* X *ANDERSONIANA* 'Purple Dome'

*Habit* Clump-forming. *Flowers* 3-petalled, in succession through summer. Rich purple, each surrounded by two leaf-like, green bracts. *Leaves* Slightly fleshy, narrowly lance-shaped, borne on jointed stems. Mid-green.
• NATIVE HABITAT Garden origin.
• CULTIVATION Grow in fertile, moist but well-drained soil, in sun or light shade. Protect young growth from slugs. Good for a herbaceous border.
• PROPAGATION By division in spring or autumn.

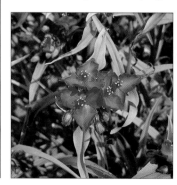

☼ ●
❀ ❀ ❀

HEIGHT
to 60cm
(24in)

SPREAD
45cm (18in)

## *POLEMONIUM PULCHERRIMUM*

*Habit* Clump-forming, upright. *Flowers* Small, bell- to cup-shaped, borne in dense, terminal clusters, in late spring and summer. Purple-blue with white or yellow throats. *Leaves* Finely divided into 11–37 elliptic to oval leaflets. Mid-green.

• NATIVE HABITAT Scrub and grassland, N.W. America.

• CULTIVATION Grow in reasonably fertile, humus-rich, well-drained soil, in full sun. The elegantly divided foliage and profusion of attractive flowers produced over long periods in summer, make this an ideal perennial for the front of a herbaceous or mixed border. It is more compact and lower-growing than the more commonly seen *P. caeruleum* and is also suitable for the larger rock garden. In its native regions it is also used in a wildflower garden.

• PROPAGATION By seed or division in spring.

☼ ◊
❄ ❄ ❄

HEIGHT
50cm (20in)

SPREAD
30cm (12in)

| Asteraceae/Compositae | |
|---|---|

## ERIGERON 'Serenity'

**Habit** Robust, clump-forming. **Flowers** Daisy-like, borne in profusion over long periods in summer. Slender, violet ray florets around a greenish-yellow disc. **Leaves** Lance- to spoon-shaped. Mid-green.
• NATIVE HABITAT Garden origin.
• CULTIVATION Grow in moderately fertile, well-drained soil in sun. Suitable for a summer border and valued for its long flowering period. Needs some support.
• PROPAGATION By division in spring or early autumn, or by softwood cuttings in early summer.

☼ ◊
❋ ❋ ❋

**HEIGHT**
60cm (24in)

**SPREAD**
60cm (24in)

| Boraginaceae | |
|---|---|

## MOLTKIA DOERFLERI

**Habit** Upright, rhizomatous. **Flowers** Small, tubular to funnel-shaped, in few-flowered, terminal clusters in early summer. Purplish-pink. **Leaves** Small, lance-shaped, clothed in tiny bristles pressed closely against the surface. Bright green.
• NATIVE HABITAT Rocky places in Albania.
• CULTIVATION Grow in very well-drained soil in a warm, sheltered site. Suitable for the front of a Mediterranean-type border, or for the crevices of a sunny wall.
• PROPAGATION By seed in autumn.

☼ ◊
❋ ❋

**HEIGHT**
to 50cm (20in)

**SPREAD**
25cm (10in)

| Asteraceae/ Compositae | PERENNIAL CORNFLOWER |
|---|---|

## CENTAUREA MONTANA

**Habit** Clump-forming, rhizomatous. **Flowers** Large, cornflower-like, borne on lax stems from early to mid-summer. Purple, blue, white, or pink. **Leaves** Lance-shaped, soft. Greyish-green, white-hairy beneath at first.
• NATIVE HABITAT Woodland and subalpine meadows, in the mountains of Europe.
• CULTIVATION Grow in moist but well-drained soil, in full sun or light shade. Good for the front of herbaceous borders and for cottage gardens.
• PROPAGATION Seed or division in spring or autumn.

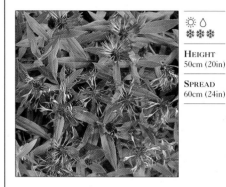

☼ ◊
❋ ❋ ❋

**HEIGHT**
50cm (20in)

**SPREAD**
60cm (24in)

| Geraniaceae | |
|---|---|

## GERANIUM HIMALAYENSE 'Gravetye' ♀

**Habit** Clump-forming. **Flowers** Large, cup-shaped, in long-stemmed clusters in summer. Clear violet-blue, with a reddish petal base and white eye. **Leaves** Deeply divided into 7 overlapping, lobed and toothed segments. Mid- to bright green.
• NATIVE HABITAT Garden origin.
• CULTIVATION Tolerates dry soils. Grow in any well-drained, fertile soil, in sun or light shade. Good for cottage gardens and herbaceous or mixed borders.
• PROPAGATION By division in autumn or spring.
• OTHER NAMES *G. grandiflorum* var. *alpinum*.

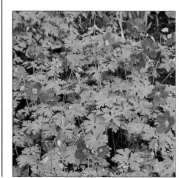

☼ ◊
❋ ❋ ❋

**HEIGHT**
30cm (12in)

**SPREAD**
60cm (24in)

Lamiaceae/Labiatae

## STACHYS MACRANTHA 'Superba'

**Habit** Clump-forming, spreading. **Flowers**
Tubular, hooded, 2-lipped, borne in dense,
whorled, upright spikes, in mid-summer. Purple-
violet. **Leaves** Soft, heart-shaped, wrinkled and
roughly hairy. Mid-green.
• NATIVE HABITAT Garden origin.
• CULTIVATION Grow in any moderately fertile,
well-drained soil, in sun or light shade. A hardy,
easily grown and undemanding perennial that
spreads slowly to form dense clumps of foliage.
It makes an attractive display at the front of a
herbaceous border where its spreading habit
helps soften any straight lines. It is also suitable
for cottage gardens and other informal plantings.
The flowers are attractive to bees. This is a useful
perennial for underplanting or edging borders of
old-fashioned shrub roses, since it flowers when
many of these are at their peak. Pink- or white-
flowered variants are also available (*S. macrantha*
'Rosea', *S. macrantha* 'Nivea'). The cut flowers
last well in an indoor display.
• PROPAGATION By division in autumn or spring.

☼ ◊
❄ ❄ ❄

**HEIGHT**
30–45cm
(12–18in)

**SPREAD**
30–60cm
(12–24in)

| Commelinaceae | |
| --- | --- |

## *TRADESCANTIA* × *ANDERSONIANA* 'Isis' ♕

*Habit* Clump-forming. *Flowers* Three-petalled, borne in succession throughout summer. Deep blue, surrounded by two leaf-like, green bracts. *Leaves* Slightly fleshy, narrowly lance-shaped, borne on jointed stems. Mid-green.
• NATIVE HABITAT Garden origin.
• CULTIVATION Grow in fertile, moist but well-drained soil, in sun or light shade. An excellent, long-flowering plant for herbaceous borders. Protect young growth from slugs.
• PROPAGATION By division in spring or autumn.

☼ ◊
❈ ❈ ❈

HEIGHT
to 60cm
(24in)

SPREAD
45cm (18in)

| Campanulaceae | BALLOON FLOWER |
| --- | --- |

## *PLATYCODON GRANDIFLORUS* ♕

*Habit* Clump-forming. *Flowers* Large, bell-shaped, opening from balloon-shaped buds, in summer. Grey-blue or blue-violet. *Leaves* Elliptic to lance-shaped, neatly toothed. Bluish-green.
• NATIVE HABITAT Grassy slopes, in the hills and mountains of N. China, E. Siberia and Japan.
• CULTIVATION Grow in fertile, moist, well-drained soil, in sun or light shade. Excellent for herbaceous borders. Foliage emerges rather late in spring.
• PROPAGATION By seed in autumn, or by basal cuttings of non-flowering shoots in summer.

☼ ◊
❈ ❈ ❈

HEIGHT
45–60cm
(18–24in)

SPREAD
30–45cm
(12–18in)

| Geraniaceae | |
| --- | --- |

## *GERANIUM* × *MAGNIFICUM* ♕

*Habit* Clump-forming, stoloniferous. *Flowers* Large, cup-shaped, borne in few-flowered clusters in early summer. Rich violet-blue with darker veins. *Leaves* Hairy, divided into 9–11 rounded, overlapping lobes. Greyish-green.
• NATIVE HABITAT Long cultivated, origin unknown.
• CULTIVATION Tolerant of exposed sites. Grow in any well-drained, fertile soil, in light shade, or in full sun for more prolific flowering. Excellent for cottage gardens and herbaceous borders.
• PROPAGATION By division in autumn or spring.

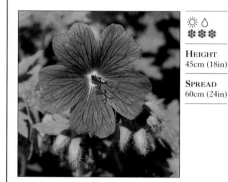

☼ ◊
❈ ❈ ❈

HEIGHT
45cm (18in)

SPREAD
60cm (24in)

| Geraniaceae | |
| --- | --- |

## *GERANIUM* 'Johnson's Blue' ♕

*Habit* Vigorous, clump-forming. *Flowers* Large, cup-shaped, borne in few-flowered clusters, throughout summer. Deep lavender-blue. *Leaves* Deeply divided into 7–9 narrow, further lobed and divided segments. Bright green.
• NATIVE HABITAT Garden origin.
• CULTIVATION Grow in any well-drained, fertile soil, in light shade or in full sun. Excellent for cottage gardens and herbaceous or mixed borders, associating well with old-fashioned roses.
• PROPAGATION By division in autumn or spring.

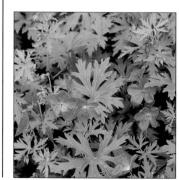

☼ ◊
❈ ❈ ❈

HEIGHT
30cm (12in)

SPREAD
60cm (24in)

| Geraniaceae | |
|---|---|

## GERANIUM HIMALAYENSE

**Habit** Clump-forming. **Flowers** Large, cup-shaped, in long-stemmed clusters, in summer. Deep violet-blue, white-eyed. **Leaves** Deeply divided into 7 toothed segments. Mid- to bright green.
• NATIVE HABITAT  Forest clearings, scrub and grassy slopes, in the Himalayas.
• CULTIVATION  Tolerates dry soils. Grow in well-drained, fertile soil, in sun or light shade. Suited to cottage garden or herbaceous or mixed border.
• PROPAGATION  By division in autumn or spring.
• OTHER NAMES  *G. grandiflorum.*

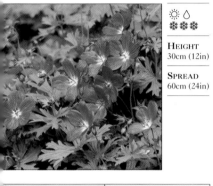

☀ ◊
❀ ❀ ❀

**HEIGHT**
30cm (12in)

**SPREAD**
60cm (24in)

| Dipsacaceae | |
|---|---|

## SCABIOSA CAUCASICA 'Clive Greaves' ♀

**Habit** Clump-forming. **Flowers** Borne on strong, wiry stems, throughout summer. Lavender-blue petals arranged around a domed, pincushion-like centre. **Leaves** Lower leaves lance-shaped, in basal clumps, stem leaves pinnately divided. Grey-green.
• NATIVE HABITAT  Garden origin.
• CULTIVATION  Grow in moderately fertile, well-drained, preferably alkaline soil, in full sun. Excellent for cutting. Suitable for herbaceous borders and cottage gardens.
• PROPAGATION  By division in spring or autumn.

☀ ◊
❀ ❀ ❀

**HEIGHT**
45–60cm
(18–24in)

**SPREAD**
45–60cm
(18–24in)

| Asteraceae/Compositae | STOKES' ASTER |
|---|---|

## STOKESIA LAEVIS

**Habit** Rosette-forming, upright. **Flowers** Cornflower-like, produced freely during summer at the ends of hairy, leafy stems. Lavender-blue, purple-blue, or occasionally white. **Leaves** Elliptic to narrowly lance-shaped, forming winter-green rosettes. Mid-green,
• NATIVE HABITAT  Moist pine woods, S.E. North America.
• CULTIVATION  Grow in moist but well-drained, sandy, preferably slightly acid soil, in full sun.
• PROPAGATION  Seed or division in spring or autumn.

☀ ◊
❀ ❀ ❀

**HEIGHT**
30–45cm
(12–18in)

**SPREAD**
30–45cm
(12–18in)

| Polemoniaceae | JACOB'S LADDER |
|---|---|

## POLEMONIUM CAERULEUM

**Habit** Clump-forming, upright. **Flowers** Small, cup-shaped, in dense, terminal clusters, in summer. Lavender-blue. **Leaves** Finely divided into 17–27 lance-shaped leaflets. Mid- to bright green.
• NATIVE HABITAT Scrub and grassland, from N. and C. Europe to Siberia, the Himalayas and W. North America.
• CULTIVATION Grow in fertile, humus-rich, moist, well-drained soil, in full sun. Suited to herbaceous borders and cottage gardens. Self-seeds freely.
• PROPAGATION By seed or division in spring.

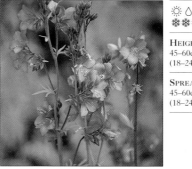

☼ ◊
❋❋❋

HEIGHT
45–60cm
(18–24in)

SPREAD
45–60cm
(18–24in)

| Geraniaceae | |
|---|---|

## GERANIUM ERIANTHUM

**Habit** Mound-forming. **Flowers** Saucer-shaped, 5-petalled, mainly in early summer, but often again later in the season. Pale to deep blue-violet with darker veins. **Leaves** Divided into 7–9 deeply lobed and toothed segments. Dark green.
• NATIVE HABITAT Scrub, sub-alpine meadows and coastal grasslands in E. Siberia, Japan, Alaska and W. Canada.
• CULTIVATION Grow in well-drained soil in sun or light shade. Good for a border or cottage garden.
• PROPAGATION Seed or division in spring or autumn.

☼ ◊
❋❋❋

HEIGHT
50cm (20in)

SPREAD
50cm (20in)

| Asteraceae/Compositae | BLUE CUPIDONE, CUPID'S DART |
|---|---|

## CATANANCHE CAERULEA 'Major' ✂

**Habit** Clump-forming. **Flowers** Small, daisy-like, opening from silvery, papery, oval buds and borne on wiry stems in summer. Lavender-blue, **Leaves** Narrow, linear, in basal clumps. Bluish-green.
• NATIVE HABITAT Species occurs in dry grasslands of S.W. Europe.
• CULTIVATION Grow in well-drained, preferably sandy soil, in full sun. Ideal for a herbaceous border but propagate regularly to maintain vigorous stock. Flowers and buds dry well for winter arrangements.
• PROPAGATION By root cuttings in winter.

☼ ◊
❋❋❋

HEIGHT
45–60cm
(18–24in)

SPREAD
30cm (12in)

| Plumbaginaceae | |
|---|---|

## LIMONIUM PLATYPHYLLUM 'Blue Cloud'

**Habit** Clump-forming. **Flowers** Tiny, borne in diffuse, airy sprays on branching stems, in late summer. Bluish-mauve. **Leaves** Leathery, spoon-shaped, in basal rosettes. Dark green.
• NATIVE HABITAT Species occurs in dry grassland, from S.E. Europe to S. Russia.
• CULTIVATION Grow in well-drained, sandy soil, in full sun. Flowers are good for cutting and drying.
• PROPAGATION By division in spring or root cuttings in winter.
• OTHER NAMES L. latifolium 'Blue Cloud'.

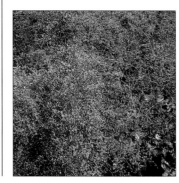

☼ ◊
❋❋❋

HEIGHT
30cm (12in
often more

SPREAD
45cm (18in

| Lamiaceae/Labiatae | CATMINT |

## NEPETA X FAASSENII

**Habit** Mound-forming. **Flowers** Small, tubular,
-lipped, borne in loose spike-like clusters,
throughout summer. Soft lavender-blue. **Leaves**
aromatic, toothed, oblong-oval, finely hairy.
Grey-green.

NATIVE HABITAT Garden origin.

CULTIVATION Grow in well-drained, preferably
alkaline soil, in full sun. Good for softening the
edge of a dry, sunny herbaceous border, where it
will attract bees, butterflies and other beneficial
insects. Cut back hard after the first flush of
flowers to encourage a second flush later in the
season. Cats are attracted to the aromatic foliage
and may roll on the plant and crush it. They can
be deterred by inserting prickly twigs into the
base of the clump. The leaves and flowers dry
well for pot-pourri.

• PROPAGATION By division in spring or by
stem tip or softwood cuttings in summer.

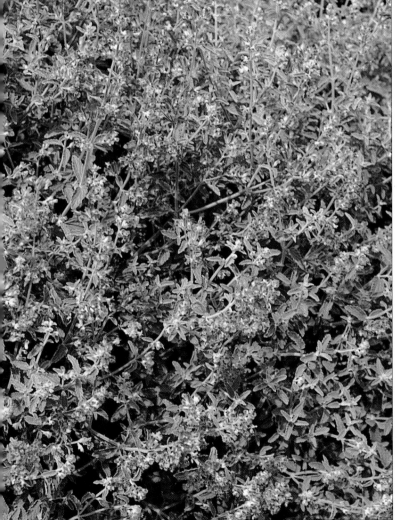

☼ ◊
❀ ❀ ❀

HEIGHT
45cm (18in)

SPREAD
45cm (18in)

| Ranunculaceae | FALSE ANEMONE |
| --- | --- |

## ANEMONOPSIS MACROPHYLLA

**Habit** Clump-forming, rhizomatous. **Flowers** Nodding, waxy, anemone-like, borne in open clusters on wiry stems in late summer. **Leaves** Fern-like, finely divided leaflets. Dark, glossy green.
• NATIVE HABITAT Mountain woodland in Japan.
• CULTIVATION Grow in moist, humus-rich, preferably acid soil, in a shady, sheltered site. Excellent for a shaded herbaceous border or woodland garden.
• PROPAGATION By division in spring or fresh seed in late summer.

☀ ◐ ◊
❊ ❊ ❊

**HEIGHT**
45–60cm
(18–24in)

**SPREAD**
50cm (20in)

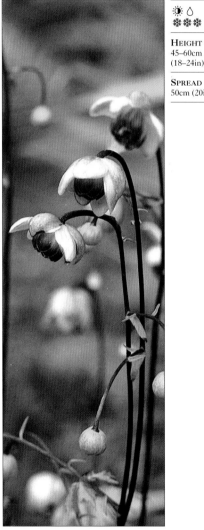

| Campanulaceae | |
| --- | --- |

## CAMPANULA 'Burghaltii'

**Habit** Mound-forming. **Flowers** Nodding, funnel-shaped, borne on erect, wiry stems in summer. Pale lavender-grey, opening from amethyst buds. **Leaves** Oval, soft, leathery. Mid-green.
• NATIVE HABITAT Garden origin.
• CULTIVATION Grow in moist but well-drained soil, in sun or part-shade. Provide support. Excellent for herbaceous and mixed borders. Cut flowers last reasonably well in water.
• PROPAGATION By basal cuttings in early summer or by division in spring or autumn.

☀ ◊
❊ ❊ ❊

**HEIGHT**
60cm (24in)

**SPREAD**
30cm (12in)

| Apiaceae/Umbelliferae | |
| --- | --- |

## ERYNGIUM BOURGATII

**Habit** Upright, clump-forming. **Flowers** Tiny, in dense, rounded heads amidst long, slender, spiny metallic blue-purple bracts, from mid- to late summer. Purplish-blue. **Leaves** Rounded, much divided into spiny, leathery leaves. Dark green with silvery venation.
• NATIVE HABITAT Rocky places, in the Pyrenees.
• CULTIVATION Grow in moderately fertile, freely draining soil, in full sun. Flowers dry well.
• PROPAGATION By seed in autumn, by division in spring, or by root cuttings in winter.

☀ ◊
❊ ❊ ❊

**HEIGHT**
45–60cm
(18–24in)

**SPREAD**
30cm (12in)

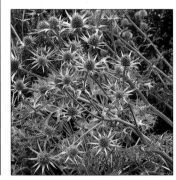

| Boraginaceae | |
| --- | --- |

## MERTENSIA SIMPLICISSIMA

**Habit** Procumbent, clump-forming. **Flowers** Small, tubular, blue, on low stems in early summer. **Leaves** Fleshy, rounded to spoon-shaped. Pale blue-grey.
• NATIVE HABITAT  Coastal sand and shingle, Japan.
• CULTIVATION  Grow in sharply drained soils, with added grit or sand, in full sun. Shelter from dry wind to avoid foliage scorch. Good for coastal gardens.
• PROPAGATION  By seed or division in autumn or spring.
• OTHER NAMES  *M. asiatica*, *M. maritima* subsp. *asiatica*.

☼ ◊
❀ ❀ ❀

**HEIGHT**
30cm (12in)

**SPREAD**
30cm (12in)

| Apocynaceae | |
| --- | --- |

## AMSONIA ORIENTALIS ♟

**Habit** Clump-forming, subshrubby. **Flowers** Small, star-shaped, borne in open, terminal sprays in summer. Pale grey-blue. **Leaves** Narrowly oval, borne all along the stems. Greyish-green or green.
• NATIVE HABITAT  Grassy places, Greece to Turkey.
• CULTIVATION  Grow in any fertile, well-drained soil, in sun or light shade. Leave undisturbed after planting.
• PROPAGATION  By division in spring, by softwood cuttings in summer, or by seed in autumn.
• OTHER NAMES  *Rhazya orientalis*.

☼ ◊
❀ ❀ ❀

**HEIGHT**
45–60cm
(18–24in)

**SPREAD**
30–45cm
(12–18in)

| Scrophulariaceae | DIGGER SPEEDWELL |
| --- | --- |

## PARAHEBE PERFOLIATA ♟

**Habit** Clump-forming, subshrubby, woody-based. **Flowers** Small, narrowly funnel-shaped, borne in slender, branching, clusters in early summer. Blue-violet. **Leaves** Oval, leathery, clasping and circling the stems. Glaucous, greyish-green.
• NATIVE HABITAT  Mountains of S.E. Australia.
• CULTIVATION  Grow in well-drained soil, in a warm, sheltered site. Good for a raised bed, sunny herbaceous border, or sprawling through low shrubs.
• PROPAGATION  Semi-ripe cuttings in early summer.
• OTHER NAMES  *Veronica perfoliata*.

☼ ◊
❀ ❀

**HEIGHT**
45–60cm
(18–24in)

**SPREAD**
45cm (18in)

| Apiaceae/Umbelliferae | |
| --- | --- |

## ERYNGIUM VARIIFOLIUM

**Habit** Upright, rosette-forming. **Flowers** Tiny, in dense, conical heads above long, slender, spiny, silvery-white bracts, in late summer. Grey-blue. **Leaves** Oval, heart-shaped, scalloped. Dark green, veined and marbled with white.
• NATIVE HABITAT  Rocky mountains of N. Africa.
• CULTIVATION  Grow in moderately fertile, freely draining soil, in full sun. Flowers are good for drying.
• PROPAGATION  By seed in autumn, by division in spring, or by root cuttings in winter.

☼ ◊
❀ ❀ ❀

**HEIGHT**
45cm (18in)

**SPREAD**
25cm (10in)

Linaceae

## *LINUM NARBONENSE*

*Habit* Clump-forming. *Flowers* Small, cup- or
bowl-shaped, borne in few-flowered clusters on
short, slender stems, from early to mid-summer.
Pale to azure blue. *Leaves* Small, linear-lance-
shaped. Greyish-green.
• NATIVE HABITAT Dry hills, around the
Mediterranean.
• CULTIVATION Grow in well-drained, moderately
fertile soil, in a warm, sunny site. Valued for its
long flowering season, the clear blues of its silk-
textured blooms and its airy, twiggy habit, it is

suitable for a herbaceous border particularly those
with a Mediterranean theme. Although usually
deciduous, in mild areas it may remain evergreen.
Seed-raised plants yield an attractive range of
blues that are especially effective if planted in
drifts. This perennial tends to be short-lived, so
propagate regularly.
• PROPAGATION By seed in autumn.

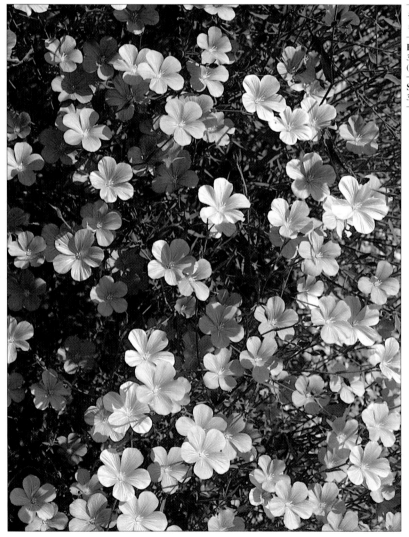

☼ ◊
❀ ❀ ❀

**HEIGHT**
30–60cm
(12–24in)

**SPREAD**
30cm (12in)

| Scrophulariaceae | |
|---|---|

## *VERONICA GENTIANOIDES* ♟

**Habit** Mat-forming. **Flowers** Small, 4-lobed, borne in slender, upright spikes, in early summer. Pale blue, occasionally dark blue or white. **Leaves** Lance-shaped to oval, in basal clumps. Glossy dark green.
• NATIVE HABITAT Woods and meadows, in mountains from the Caucasus to S.W. Asia.
• CULTIVATION Grow in moist but well drained soil, in full sun or light shade. Excellent for the edge of a border.
• PROPAGATION Seed or division in spring or autumn.

☀ ◊
✿ ✿ ✿

**HEIGHT**
45cm (18in)

**SPREAD**
45cm (18in)
or more

| Boraginaceae | |
|---|---|

## *SYMPHYTUM* 'Goldsmith'

**Habit** Robust, clump-forming, rhizomatous.
**Flowers** Pendent, tubular, in short, paired clusters, from spring to early summer. Blue, white and pink. **Leaves** Coarse, hairy, oval to lance-shaped. Dark green, edged and splashed with gold and cream.
• NATIVE HABITAT Garden origin.
• CULTIVATION Grow in moist soil in sun or shade. Is less invasive than the species. Cut back after first flowering to produce a second flush of bloom.
• PROPAGATION By division in spring.
• OTHER NAMES *S. ibericum* 'Jubilee'.

☀ ◊
✿ ✿ ✿

**HEIGHT**
30cm (12in)

**SPREAD**
45cm (18in)
or more

| Apocynaceae | |
|---|---|

## *AMSONIA TABERNAEMONTANA*

**Habit** Clump-forming. **Flowers** Small, star-shaped, borne in open, terminal clusters, in summer. Pale blue. **Leaves** Narrowly oval to oval. Greyish-green or green.
• NATIVE HABITAT Damp grasslands of E. North America.
• CULTIVATION Grow in fertile, moist but well-drained soil, in sun or light shade. Leave undisturbed after planting.
• PROPAGATION By division in spring, by softwood cuttings in summer, or by seed in autumn.

☀ ◊
✿ ✿ ✿

**HEIGHT**
45–60cm
(18–24in)

**SPREAD**
30–45cm
(12–18in)

| Boraginaceae | CHATHAM ISLAND FORGET-ME-NOT |
|---|---|

## *MYOSOTIDIUM HORTENSIA*

**Habit** Clump-forming. **Flowers** Small, forget-me-not-like, in dense, rounded clusters, in summer. Blue. **Leaves** Evergreen, fleshy, kidney- to heart-shaped, deeply ribbed, glossy. Bright green.
• NATIVE HABITAT Rocky and sandy coastlines of the Chatham Islands (New Zealand).
• CULTIVATION Grow in well-drained, humus-rich soil in part-shade, with shelter from wind. Good for coastal gardens. A seaweed mulch is beneficial.
• PROPAGATION By fresh seed in autumn or division in spring. Not an easy plant.

☼ ◊
❄ ❄

**HEIGHT**
45–60cm
(18–24in)

**SPREAD**
60cm (24in)

| Geraniaceae | |
|---|---|

## *GERANIUM WALLICHIANUM* 'Buxton's Variety' ♀

**Habit** Clump-forming, spreading. **Flowers** Large, cup-shaped, from mid-summer to autumn. White-centred, blue or blue-purple. **Leaves** Divided into 5 toothed, lobes. Mid- to bright green, white-flecked.
• NATIVE HABITAT A selected form of garden origin.
• CULTIVATION Grow in well-drained, soil, in sun or light shade. Good for a cottage garden or border.
• PROPAGATION Division in autumn or spring.
• OTHER NAMES G. 'Buxton's Blue'.

☼ ◊
❄ ❄ ❄

**HEIGHT**
30cm (12in)

**SPREAD**
60cm (24in)

| Lamiaceae/Labiatae | |
|---|---|

## *SALVIA CACALIIFOLIA* ♀

**Habit** Upright, rhizomatous. **Flowers** Tubular, 2-lipped, in branched, spiky clusters, in late summer. Deep blue. **Leaves** Diamond-shaped, glossy. Dark green.
• NATIVE HABITAT Mexico, Guatemala.
• CULTIVATION Grow as a house or conservatory plant in cool climates, in well-drained potting compost. If grown outdoors, place in fertile, humus-rich soil in full sun.
• PROPAGATION By seed in spring or softwood cuttings in summer.

☼ ◊

Min. 5°C
(41°F)

**HEIGHT**
45cm (18in)

**SPREAD**
45cm (18in)

| Lamiaceae/Labiatae | |
|---|---|

## *SALVIA PATENS* ♀

**Habit** Upright, branching. **Flowers** Hooded, tubular, 2-lipped, borne in whorls in long, spike-like clusters, in late summer. Intense bright blue or pale blue. **Leaves** Sticky-hairy, oval to diamond-shaped. Mid-green.
• NATIVE HABITAT Scrub and rocks in Mexico.
• CULTIVATION Grow in well-drained soil, in full sun. Excellent for borders, bedding and for patio tubs. Protect young plants from frost in winter.
• PROPAGATION By seed in spring or by softwood cuttings in mid-summer.

☼ ◊
❄

**HEIGHT**
45–60cm
(18–24in)

**SPREAD**
45cm (18in)

| Asteraceae/Compositae | ROMAN WORMWOOD |
| --- | --- |

## ARTEMISIA PONTICA ♀

**Habit** Vigorous, upright. **Flowers** Tiny, in slender, nodding plumes, in summer. Grey-white. **Leaves** Aromatic, feathery, divided into finely hairy, linear, segments, arranged all along the upright stems. Silvery grey-green.
• NATIVE HABITAT Dry, grassy and rocky hillsides, in central and eastern Europe.
• CULTIVATION Grow in well-drained soil, in full sun. Invaluable in a silver border and excellent for colour and texture contrasts in a herbaceous border.
• PROPAGATION Division or seed in spring or autumn.

☼ ◊
✿ ✿ ✿

HEIGHT
60cm (24in)

SPREAD
20cm (8in)
often more

| Polygonaceae | |
| --- | --- |

## PERSICARIA VIRGINIANA
### 'Painter's Palette'

**Habit** Mound-forming. **Flowers** Seldom produced in cultivation. **Leaves** Oval to elliptic. Green, banded with maroon-brown, splashed and striped ivory-yellow and pink-tinted over all.
• NATIVE HABITAT Garden origin.
• CULTIVATION Grow in moist but well-drained soil, with wind shelter. Good foliage contrast in a border.
• PROPAGATION By division in autumn or spring.
• OTHER NAMES *Tovara virginiana* 'Painter's Palette', *Polygonum virginianum* 'Painter's Palette'.

☼ ◊
✿ ✿ ✿

HEIGHT
60cm (24in)

SPREAD
60cm (24in)

| Rosaceae | |
| --- | --- |

## ALCHEMILLA CONJUNCTA

**Habit** Clump-forming. **Flowers** Tiny, star-shaped, in many-branched clusters, in mid-summer. Greenish-yellow. **Leaves** Circular, with 7–9 segments joined at the base, with teeth almost hidden by silky hair. Blue-green above, silver below.
• NATIVE HABITAT Sub-alpine meadows and rocky streamsides, in the Jura and S.W. Alps.
• CULTIVATION Grow in moist, well-drained soil, in an open sunny site. Often confused with *A. alpina*.
• PROPAGATION By seed or division in spring or autumn.

☼ ◊
✿ ✿ ✿

HEIGHT
30cm (12in)

SPREAD
30cm (12in)

| Rosaceae | LADY'S MANTLE |
| --- | --- |

## ALCHEMILLA MOLLIS ♀

**Habit** Clump-forming, vigorous. **Flowers** Tiny, star-shaped, in rounded, open sprays throughout summer. Bright greenish-yellow. **Leaves** Circular, with 9–11 rounded, neatly toothed lobes. Soft green.
• NATIVE HABITAT Streambanks, meadows and forests, in the eastern Carpathians and Caucasus.
• CULTIVATION Grow in moist, well-drained soil, in an open sunny site. Suitable for herbaceous borders, gravel and paving crevice plantings. Flowers dry well for winter arrangements. Self-seeds freely.
• PROPAGATION Seed or division in spring or autumn.

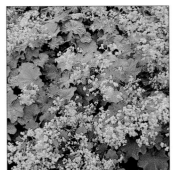

☼ ◊
✿ ✿ ✿

HEIGHT
30cm (12in)

SPREAD
30cm (12in)

# HOSTAS

Hostas, also known as plantain lilies, are grown primarily for their luxuriant and decorative foliage, which provides a wide range of colours and textural contrasts in a herbaceous border. Many hostas also produce attractive spike-like heads of bell-, trumpet-shaped, or tubular flowers, which rise gracefully above the foliage in mid-summer. Some flowers are strongly fragrant.

Hostas are suitable for many situations from damp, shady borders and poolsides to containers. The large clump-forming species provide excellent ground cover.

Grow in moist but well-drained, humus-rich, neutral soil, in partial shade, but take care to protect the leaves against slug and snail damage.

Propagate by division in early spring.

---

### H. *UNDULATA* var. *UNIVITTATA*
**Habit** Vigorous, clump-forming.
**Flowers** Trumpet-shaped, in long spikes above the foliage in mid-summer. Pale mauve.
**Leaves** Narrowly oval, twisted at the tip, to 15cm (6in) long. Mid-green, with a narrow creamy-white, central blotch.
• HEIGHT 45cm (1½ft).
• SPREAD 60cm (2ft).

*H. undulata* **var.** *univittata*

☀ ◑ ❄❄❄ ♇

---

### H. *DECORATA*
**Habit** Slow-growing, stoloniferous.
**Flowers** Trumpet-shaped, in dense heads in mid-summer. Violet.
**Fruits** Large, oval, glossy brown seed heads.
**Leaves** Oval, tapering, 15cm (6in) long. Dark green with neat, narrow, white margins.
• HEIGHT 45cm (1½ft).
• SPREAD 1m (3ft).

*H. decorata*

☀ ◑ ❄❄❄

---

### H. *CRISPULA*
**Habit** Slow-growing, clump-forming.
**Flowers** Trumpet-shaped, borne above the foliage in early summer. Pale mauve.
**Leaves** Large, oval to heart-shaped, with wavy margins, tips twisted. Dark green, white edged.
• TIPS May be damaged by late frosts.
• HEIGHT 75cm (2½ft).
• SPREAD 1m (3ft).

*H. crispula*

☀ ◑ ❄❄❄ ♇

---

### H. *UNDULATA* var. *ALBOMARGINATA*
**Habit** Clump-forming.
**Flowers** Trumpet-shaped, in spikes well above foliage in mid-summer. Pale violet.
**Leaves** Lance-shaped to oval, round-tipped. Mid-green, with a cream edge extending down the stalk.
• OTHER NAMES *H. undulata* 'Albomarginata'.
• HEIGHT 75cm (2½ft).
• SPREAD 1m (3ft).

*H. undulata* **var.** *albomarginata*

☀ ◑ ❄❄❄

---

### H. 'Ginko Craig'
**Habit** Low-growing, clump-forming.
**Flowers** Bell-shaped, borne in tall spikes above the foliage in late summer. Deep violet.
**Leaves** Small, lance-shaped. Dark green with a fine white edge.
• TIPS Good for a border edge.
• HEIGHT to 30cm (1ft).
• SPREAD 30–45cm (1–1½ft).

*H. 'Ginko Craig'*

☀ ◑ ❄❄❄

---

### H. 'Shade Fanfare'
**Habit** Vigorous, clump-forming, free-flowering.
**Flowers** Trumpet-shaped, in many spikes in summer. Lavender.
**Leaves** Medium, to 12cm (5in) long, heart-shaped. Pale green, with cream margins; pale green becomes yellow in sun.
• TIPS For sun or partial shade.
• HEIGHT 45cm (1½ft).
• SPREAD 75cm (2½ft).

*H. 'Shade Fanfare'*

☀ ◑ ❄❄❄ ♇

## H. 'Ground Master'
**Habit** Low-growing, clump-forming.
**Flowers** Trumpet-shaped. borne above the foliage in late summer. Violet-purple.
**Leaves** Narrow, lance-shaped. Mid-green, edged with a broad creamy-white band.
• TIPS Good for the border front.
• HEIGHT 30cm (12in).
• SPREAD 45cm (18in).

*H.* 'Ground Master'

☼ ◊ ❀❀❀

## H. 'Regal Splendor'
**Habit** Clump-forming.
**Flowers** Trumpet-shaped, borne in tall spikes in summer. Lilac.
**Leaves** Large, to 30cm (12in) long, arching. Dark greyish-blue with an irregular cream or creamy-white edge.
• HEIGHT 1m (3ft).
• SPREAD 1m (3ft).

*H.* 'Regal Splendor'

☼ ◊ ❀❀❀

## H. SIEBOLDIANA var. ELEGANS
**Habit** Robust, clump-forming, slow-growing.
**Flowers** Bell-shaped, borne just above the foliage in early summer. Very pale lilac.
**Leaves** Large, heart-shaped, deeply ribbed, puckered. Bluish-green.
• TIPS Leaves become dull green in sun.
• HEIGHT 1m (3ft).
• SPREAD 1.5m (5ft).

*H. sieboldiana*
var. *elegans*

☼ ◊ ❀❀❀ ♛

## H. ROHDEIFOLIA
**Habit** Upright, clump-forming.
**Flowers** Trumpet-shaped, in erect heads, in summer. Pale mauve with a purple stripe.
**Leaves** Erect, lance-shaped, pointed, to 18cm (7in) long, veined. Glossy bluish-green, usually with a fine yellow edge.
• HEIGHT to 1m (3ft).
• SPREAD to 1m (3ft).

*H. rohdeifolia*

☼ ◊ ❀❀❀

## H. 'Halcyon'
**Habit** Robust, clump-forming.
**Flowers** Trumpet-shaped, in dense spikes just above foliage in mid-summer. Violet-mauve.
**Leaves** Heart-shaped, pointed, to 15cm (6in) long. Grey-blue, turning muddy green in sun.
• TIPS Heavy rain may spoil leaves.
• HEIGHT 30cm (1ft).
• SPREAD 1m (3ft).

*H.* 'Halcyon'

☼ ◊ ❀❀❀ ♛

## H. 'Snowden'
**Habit** Clump-forming.
**Flowers** Trumpet-shaped, in tall spikes in summer. White, tinged green.
**Leaves** Large, to 30cm (12in) long, narrowly heart-shaped, pointed, slightly corrugated. Grey-blue, maturing to greyish-green.
• HEIGHT 1m (3ft).
• SPREAD 1m (3ft).

*H.* 'Snowden'

☼ ◊ ❀❀❀

## H. 'Krossa Regal'
**Habit** Forms a vase-shaped clump.
**Flowers** Trumpet-shaped, in tall, wavy spikes in summer. Pale lilac.
**Leaves** Very large, to 45cm (18in) long, gracefully arching, ribbed. Grey-blue.
• TIPS Makes an excellent specimen plant.
• HEIGHT 1m (3ft).
• SPREAD 1m (3ft).

*H.* 'Krossa Regal'

☼ ◊ ❀❀❀ ♛

## H. 'Blue Wedgwood'
**Habit** Slow-growing, clump-forming.
**Flowers** Bell-shaped, borne above the foliage in mid-summer. Pale lavender.
**Leaves** Medium, to 18cm (7in) long, broadly triangular, lightly puckered, with rippled margins. Blue-grey.
• HEIGHT 23cm (9in).
• SPREAD 45cm (1½ft).

*H.* 'Blue Wedgwood'

☼ ◊ ❀❀❀

## H. SIEBOLDIANA

**Habit** Robust, clump-forming, slow-growing.
**Flowers** Bell-shaped, borne just above the foliage in early summer. Very pale lilac.
**Leaves** Large, to 38cm (15in) long, heart-shaped, deeply ribbed and puckered. Bluish grey-green.
• TIPS Best in semi-shade or shade. Leaves become dull green in sun.
• HEIGHT 1m (3ft).
• SPREAD 1.5m (5ft).

*H. sieboldiana*

☀ ◑ ❀❀❀

## H. TOKUDAMA f. AUREONEBULOSA

**Habit** Slow-growing, clump-forming.
**Flowers** Trumpet-shaped, just above foliage in mid-summer. Pale lilac-grey.
**Leaves** Cup-shaped, puckered. Cloudy yellow at the centre, glaucous blue at the edge.
• OTHER NAMES H. tokudama 'Variegata'.
• HEIGHT 45cm (1½ft).
• SPREAD 75cm (2½ft).

*H. tokudama f. aureonebulosa*

☀ ◑ ❀❀❀

## H. 'Love Pat'

**Habit** Vigorous, clump-forming.
**Flowers** Trumpet-shaped, borne in spikes in summer. Pale lilac.
**Leaves** To 15cm (6in) long, rounded, cupped, deeply puckered. Deep glaucous blue.
• HEIGHT 60cm (2ft).
• SPREAD 60cm (2ft).

*H. 'Love Pat'*

☀ ◑ ❀❀❀   ♛

## H. 'Hadspen Blue'

**Habit** Slow-growing, mound-forming.
**Flowers** Trumpet-shaped, in short spikes in mid-summer. Lavender.
**Leaves** Heart-shaped, to 15cm (6in) long, smooth and closely veined. Deep glaucous blue.
• TIPS Good for a smaller border, or where space is limited.
• HEIGHT 30cm (12in).
• SPREAD 30cm (12in).

*H. 'Hadspen Blue'*

☀ ◑ ❀❀❀

## H. TARDIFLORA

**Habit** Clump-forming.
**Flowers** Trumpet-shaped, in dense heads just above foliage in late summer and early autumn. Lilac-purple.
**Leaves** Erect, lance-shaped to narrowly elliptic, to 15cm (6in) long, thick textured. Glossy dark green.
• HEIGHT 30cm (1ft).
• SPREAD 75cm (2½ft).

*H. tardiflora*

☀ ◑ ❀❀❀

## H. PLANTAGINEA

**Habit** Clump-forming.
**Flowers** Fragrant, trumpet-shaped, long-tubed, in late summer and early autumn. White.
**Leaves** Heart-shaped, to 28cm (11in) long, conspicuously veined. Glossy yellow-green.
• TIPS Grows well in sun.
• HEIGHT 60cm (2ft).
• SPREAD 1.2m (4ft).

*H. plantaginea*
August lily

☀ ◑ ❀❀❀

## H. VENTRICOSA

**Habit** Clump-forming.
**Flowers** Bell-shaped, borne in racemes above the foliage in late summer. Deep purple.
**Leaves** Heart-shaped, to 24cm (10in) long, slightly wavy-edged. Glossy dark green.
• TIPS Usually comes true from seed.
• HEIGHT 70cm (28in).
• SPREAD 1m (3ft) or more.

*H. ventricosa*

☀ ◑ ❀❀❀   ♛

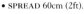

### *H.* 'Tall Boy'
*Habit* Upright,
clump-forming.
*Flowers* Trumpet-
shaped, borne on tall
stems 1.2m (4ft) or more
in height, in late summer.
Rich lilac.
*Leaves* Oval to broadly
lance-shaped, long-
pointed. Dull green.
• TIPS Good by the
edge of water.
• HEIGHT 60cm (2ft).
• SPREAD 60cm (2ft).

*H.* 'Tall Boy'

☀ ◑ ❋❋❋

### *H.* 'Royal Standard'
*Habit* Upright,
clump-forming.
*Flowers* Trumpet-shaped,
fragrant, in tall spikes,
opening on summer
evenings. Pure white.
*Leaves* Large, to 25cm
(10in) long, rather stiff,
broadly oval, ribbed.
Glossy bright green.
• TIPS Grows well in
full sun.
• HEIGHT 60cm (2ft).
• SPREAD 1.2m (4ft).

*H.* 'Royal Standard'

☀ ◑ ❋❋❋          ⚍

### *H.* 'Honeybells'
*Habit* Rapidly growing,
lax, clump-forming.
*Flowers* Bell-shaped,
fragrant, in late summer.
White, streaked violet.
*Leaves* Large, to 25cm
(10in) long, oval, blunt-
tipped, veined, smooth,
slightly wavy-edged.
Light green.
• TIPS Very tolerant
of sun.
• HEIGHT 1m (3ft).
• SPREAD 60cm (2ft).

*H.* 'Honeybells'

☀ ◑ ❋❋❋          ⚍

### *H. VENUSTA*
*Habit* Vigorous,
mat-forming.
*Flowers* Trumpet-
shaped, borne well
above the foliage in
mid-summer. Purple.
*Leaves* Small, oval to
lance-shaped. Matt, mid-
to dark olive green.
• TIPS Good ground
cover.
• HEIGHT 5cm (2in).
• SPREAD to 30cm
(12in).

*H. venusta*

☀ ◑ ❋❋❋          ⚍

### *H. LANCIFOLIA*
*Habit* Arching,
clump-forming.
*Flowers* Trumpet-
shaped, borne above
foliage in late summer
and autumn. Deep violet.
*Leaves* Narrowly lance-
shaped, to 17cm (7in)
long, thin-textured.
Glossy dark green.
• TIPS Needs shade or
semi-shade.
• HEIGHT 45cm (1½ft).
• SPREAD 75cm (2½ft).

*H. lancifolia*

☀ ◑ ❋❋❋          ⚍

### *H.* 'August Moon'
*Habit* Clump-forming.
*Flowers* Trumpet-
shaped, borne above
foliage in mid-summer.
Pale grey-mauve.
*Leaves* Large, to 25cm
(10in) long, broadly oval,
slightly corrugated.
Pale golden-yellow
with a faint glaucous
bloom.
• TIPS Tolerates full sun.
• HEIGHT 60cm (2ft).
• SPREAD 1m (3ft).

*H.* 'August Moon'

☀ ◑ ❋❋❋

### *H.* 'Blue Skies'
*Habit* Slow-growing,
clump-forming.
*Flowers* Bell-shaped,
in dense spikes.
Palest lavender to
nearly white.
*Leaves* Small, heart-
shaped, abruptly tipped,
smooth. Dark bluish-
green.
• TIPS Grow in dappled
shade.
• HEIGHT to 23cm (9in).
• SPREAD 30cm (12in).

*H.* 'Blue Skies'

☀ ◑ ❋❋❋

## H. 'Frances Williams'
**Habit** Slow-growing, but robust, clump-forming.
**Flowers** Trumpet-shaped, borne just above foliage in early summer. Very pale lavender.
**Leaves** Large, to 38cm (15in) long, heart-shaped, deeply ribbed, puckered. Bluish grey, with a broad, irregular yellow edge.
• HEIGHT 1m (3ft).
• SPREAD 1m (3ft)..

*H.* 'Frances Williams'

☀ ◐ ❄❄❄    ♈

## H. MONTANA 'Aureomarginata'
**Habit** Clump-forming.
**Flowers** Trumpet-shaped, in tall heads in mid-summer. Pale violet.
**Leaves** Large, with prominent veins. Dark glossy green, gold-edged.
• TIPS Comes up early can be damaged by frost.
• OTHER NAMES *H.* 'Aureomarginata'.
• HEIGHT 1.1m (3½ft).
• SPREAD 1m (3ft).

*H. montana* 'Aureomarginata'

☀ ◐ ❄❄❄

## H. FORTUNEI var. ALBOPICTA
**Habit** Vigorous, clump-forming.
**Flowers** Trumpet-shaped, in early summer. Pale violet.
**Leaves** Oval to heart-shaped. Creamy-yellow, with irregular mid-green margins; the centres fade to pale green.
• OTHER NAMES
*H. fortunei* 'Albopicta',
*H.* 'Aureomaculata'.
• HEIGHT 75cm–1m (2½–3ft).
• SPREAD 1m (3ft).

*H. fortunei* var. *albopicta*

☀ ◐ ❄❄❄    ♈

## H. FORTUNEI var. AUREOMARGINATA
**Habit** Clump-forming.
**Flowers** Trumpet-shaped, violet, in mid-summer.
**Leaves** Oval to heart-shaped. Mid-green with irregular creamy-yellow edges.
• TIPS Tolerates sun.
• HEIGHT 75cm–1m (2½–3ft).
• SPREAD 1m (3ft).

*H. fortunei* var. *aureomarginata*

☀ ◐ ❄❄❄    ♈

## H. 'Golden Tiara'
**Habit** Neat, rapidly growing, clump-forming.
**Flowers** Trumpet-shaped, borne in tall heads, in mid-summer, and sometimes repeating. Lavender-purple.
**Leaves** Broadly heart-shaped, to 15cm (6in) long. Dark green with irregular, chartreuse-yellow edges.
• HEIGHT 15cm (6in).
• SPREAD 30cm (12in).

*H.* 'Golden Tiara'

☀ ◐ ❄❄❄    ♈

## H. VENTRICOSA 'Aureomarginata'
**Habit** Clump-forming.
**Flowers** Bell-shaped, borne above foliage in late summer. Deep purple.
**Leaves** Heart-shaped, to 24cm (10in) long. Glossy dark green, with irregular, creamy-white, wavy edge.
• OTHER NAMES
*H. ventricosa* 'Variegata'.
• HEIGHT 70cm (28in).
• SPREAD 1m (3ft) or more.

*H. ventricosa* 'Aureomarginata'

☀ ◐ ❄❄❄    ♈

## H. 'Piedmont Gold'
**Habit** Slow-growing, clump-forming.
**Flowers** Trumpet-shaped, in summer. Pale lavender.
**Leaves** Large, heart-shaped, to 25cm (10in) long, smooth, with slightly fluted margins. Bright golden-yellow.
• TIPS Best in light shade.
• HEIGHT 60cm (2ft).
• SPREAD 75cm (2½ft).

*H.* 'Piedmont Gold'

☀ ◐ ❄❄❄

**H. 'Wide Brim'**
*Habit* Vigorous,
clump-forming.
*Flowers* Trumpet-
shaped, borne in
abundant spikes in
summer. Pale lavender.
*Leaves* Medium, to
18cm (7in) long, ribbed
and puckered. Dark
green with a broad,
irregular, creamy-
white margin.
• HEIGHT 75cm (2½ft).
• SPREAD 75cm (2½ft).

*H.* 'Wide Brim'

☼ ◑ ❄❄❄　　　♉

**H. 'Birchwood
Parky's Gold'**
*Habit* Vigorous,
clump-forming.
*Flowers* Bell-shaped,
in profusion. Lavender.
*Leaves* Small, wavy,
heart-shaped. Chartreuse
on unfurling, becoming
bright yellow.
• TIPS Dense ground
cover. Ideal for woodland
gardens.
• HEIGHT 45cm (18in).
• SPREAD 75m (30in).

*H.* 'Birchwood
Parky's Gold'

☼ ◑ ❄❄❄

**H. VENTRICOSA var.
AUREOMACULATA**
*Habit* Clump-forming.
*Flowers* Bell-shaped, in
racemes above foliage in
late summer. Deep purple.
*Leaves* Heart-shaped, to
24cm (10in) long, slightly
wavy-edged. Glossy dark
green with irregular,
central creamy-yellow
markings.
• HEIGHT 70cm (28in).
• SPREAD 1m (3ft)
or more.

*H. ventricosa* var.
*aureomaculata*

☀ ◑ ❄❄❄

**H. SIEBOLDIANA
f. KABITAN**
*Habit* Clump-forming,
stoloniferous.
*Flowers* Small, trumpet-
shaped, in tall spikes in
early summer. Mid-violet.
*Leaves* Lance-shaped,
thin-textured, ruffled.
Greenish-yellow, with a
narrow, dark green edge.
• OTHER NAMES
*H.* 'Kabitan'.
• HEIGHT to 30cm (1ft).
• SPREAD 60cm (2ft).

*H. sieboldiana*
f. *kabitan*

☼ ◑ ❄❄❄

**H. 'Gold Standard'**
*Habit* Vigorous,
clump-forming.
*Flowers* Trumpet-shaped,
borne above leaves in mid-
summer. Violet.
*Leaves* Large, oval to
heart-shaped, 25cm
(10in) long, pale green,
then pale yellow, turning
golden with age, with a
narrow, irregular, darker
green margin.
• HEIGHT 75cm (2½ft).
• SPREAD 1m (3ft).

*H.* 'Gold Standard'

☼ ◑ ❄❄❄

**H. 'Golden Prayers'**
*Habit* Upright,
clump-forming.
*Flowers* Funnel-shaped,
borne in dense heads in
mid-summer. White,
suffused with lavender.
*Leaves* To 15cm (6in)
long, heart-shaped,
cupped and puckered.
Bright golden-yellow.
• TIPS Suited to a rock
garden.
• HEIGHT 15cm (6in).
• SPREAD 30cm (12in).

*H.* 'Golden Prayers'

☼ ◑ ❄❄❄

**H. 'Sum and
Substance'**
*Habit* Vigorous,
clump-forming.
*Flowers* Trumpet-
shaped, in tall spikes
in late summer. Pale
lavender.
*Leaves* Very large, to
45cm (18in) long, heart-
shaped, thick-textured,
smooth, ribbed. Glossy
golden green.
• HEIGHT 1m (3ft).
• SPREAD 1m (3ft).

*H.* 'Sum and
Substance'

☼ ◑ ❄❄❄　　　♉

| Lamiaceae/Labiatae | |
|---|---|

### *STACHYS BYZANTINA* 'Primrose Heron'

***Habit*** Mat-forming. ***Flowers*** Small, tubular, 2-lipped, in white-woolly, upright spikes, in summer. Pink. ***Leaves*** Evergreen, thick, oblong to spoon-shaped or elliptic, densely white-woolly, mainly in basal rosettes. Yellow-green beneath the hairs.
• NATIVE HABITAT Garden origin.
• CULTIVATION Grow in well-drained soil, ideally in a hot, sunny site. Good for ground cover and border edging, especially in a silver border.
• PROPAGATION By division in spring.

☼ ◊
❀ ❀ ❀

HEIGHT
30–38cm
(12–15in)

SPREAD
60cm (2ft)

| Sarraceniaceae | TRUMPETS, YELLOW PITCHER PLANT |
|---|---|

### *SARRACENIA FLAVA*  ♈

***Habit*** Upright, rhizomatous, insectivorous. ***Flowers*** Musk-scented, nodding, to 10cm (4in) across, from late spring to early summer. Yellow or greenish-yellow. ***Leaves*** Modified to form erect, hooded, trumpet-shaped pitchers, 30–100cm (1–3ft) tall. Yellow green, veined maroon.
• NATIVE HABITAT Pinelands, E. North America.
• CULTIVATION Grow as a house or conservatory plant in cool climates, on damp peat or moss, in sun or part-shade. Keep slightly drier in winter.
• PROPAGATION By seed in spring.

☼ ◗

Min. 5°C
(41°F)

HEIGHT
45cm (18in)

SPREAD
45cm (18in)

| Iridaceae | |
|---|---|

### *SISYRINCHIUM STRIATUM*

***Habit*** Upright, tuft-forming. ***Flowers*** Small, slightly cupped, borne in sturdy, upright spikes in summer. Creamy-yellow, striped purple. ***Leaves*** Evergreen or semi-evergreen, long, lance-shaped, in basal, fan-shaped clumps. Blue-green.
• NATIVE HABITAT Scrub, woods, Chile, Argentina.
• CULTIVATION Grow in moist, well-drained soil, in sun, at the border front, or in gravel plantings.
• PROPAGATION By division in early spring, or by seed in autumn. Self-seeds freely.
• OTHER NAMES *Phaiophleps nigricans.*

☼ ◊
❀ ❀ ❀

HEIGHT
45–60cm
(18–24in)

SPREAD
30cm (12in)

| Lamiaceae/Labiatae | GOLDEN MARJORAM |
|---|---|

## ORIGANUM VULGARE 'Aureum' ♟

**Habit** Mat-forming, woody-based. **Flowers** Tiny, 2-lipped, in short spikes in summer, but only occasionally produced. Lavender-mauve. **Leaves** Very aromatic, rounded-oval. Golden-yellow on emergence, pale greenish-yellow at maturity.
• NATIVE HABITAT Garden origin. Species occurs in open woodland and dry grassland, in Europe.
• CULTIVATION Grow in well-drained, alkaline soil, in full sun. Good for border fronts and sunny banks.
• PROPAGATION By division in spring, or cuttings of non-flowering shoots in early summer.

☀ ◊
❋❋❋

HEIGHT
8cm (3in)

SPREAD
indefinite

| Rosaceae | |
|---|---|

## FILIPENDULA ULMARIA 'Aurea'

**Habit** Clump-forming, upright. **Flowers** Tiny, in feathery plumes, on branching stems, in mid-summer. Creamy-white. **Leaves** Aromatic, divided into 3–5 pairs of oval-oblong leaflets. Golden, turning pale creamy-green.
• NATIVE HABITAT Species occurs by streambanks and in damp meadows from Europe to N.W. China.
• CULTIVATION Grow in moist soils, in partial shade; leaves scorch in full sun. Excellent for a foliage border.
• PROPAGATION By division in autumn or winter.

◐ ◊
❋❋❋

HEIGHT
30cm (1ft)

SPREAD
30cm (1ft)

| Asphodelaceae/Liliaceae | |
|---|---|

## KNIPHOFIA 'Little Maid' ♟

**Habit** Upright, clump-forming. **Flowers** Small, narrowly tubular, borne on upright stems in dense, terminal spikes, over long periods in late summer. Creamy-yellow, opening from pale green buds. **Leaves** Grass-like, narrowly linear, arching to form basal clumps. Mid-green.
• NATIVE HABITAT Garden origin.
• CULTIVATION Grow in full sun, in moist, well-drained soil. Needs ample moisture when in growth. Mulch crowns in cold winter areas.
• PROPAGATION By division in spring.

☀ ◊
❋❋

HEIGHT
60cm (24in)

SPREAD
45cm (18in)

---

Asteraceae/Compositae

## OSTEOSPERMUM 'Buttermilk'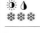

**Habit** Clump-forming, woody-based. **Flowers**
Large, single, daisy-like, borne on slender, sturdy
stems throughout summer. Pale yellow petals
surround a dark reddish-brown central disc.
**Leaves** Evergreen, aromatic, long, narrow,
and serrated. Grey-green.
• NATIVE HABITAT Garden origin.
• CULTIVATION Grow in fertile, well-drained soil, in
full sun. Protect young plants from frost in winter.
• PROPAGATION By cuttings of non-flowering
shoots in mid-summer.

☼ ◊
❄

HEIGHT
60cm (24in)

SPREAD
30cm (12in)

---

Polemoniaceae

## POLEMONIUM PAUCIFLORUM

**Habit** Clump-forming, slow-spreading. **Flowers**
Nodding, long-tubed, with spreading petal lobes,
in loose clusters, in late summer. Pale yellow,
flushed red. **Leaves** Finely divided into 11–25
elliptic to lance-shaped leaflets. Mid-green.
• NATIVE HABITAT Mountain streamsides, Arizona
and N. Mexico.
• CULTIVATION Grow in humus-rich, moist, well-
drained soil, in a sheltered site in sun or part-shade.
Suitable for a herbaceous border. Self-seeds freely.
• PROPAGATION By seed or division in spring.

☼ ◊
❄❄❄

HEIGHT
30–45cm
(12–18in)

SPREAD
45cm (18in)

---

Asteraceae/Compositae

## ACHILLEA 'Taygetea'

**Habit** Upright. **Flowers** Tiny, in large, flat heads,
borne on rigid, leafy stems during summer. Pale
lemon-yellow. **Leaves** Feathery, finely divided
into oblong to lance-shaped finely hairy segments.
Silver-grey.
• NATIVE HABITAT Garden origin.
• CULTIVATION Grow in well-drained soil, in full
sun. Excellent for a silver border. Divide and replan
every third year to maintain vigour. The flower
heads dry well and retain their colour and fragrance
• PROPAGATION Division in early spring or autumn.

☼ ◊
❄❄❄

HEIGHT
60cm (24in

SPREAD
50cm (20in

---

Asteraceae/Compositae

## x SOLIDASTER LUTEUS

**Habit** Clump-forming. **Flowers** Small, daisy-like,
borne in slender-stemmed, branched heads, from
mid-summer to autumn. Bright creamy-yellow.
**Leaves** Lance-shaped to elliptic. Mid-green.
• NATIVE HABITAT A natural hybrid of
garden origin.
• CULTIVATION Grow in any fertile, well-drained
soil, in full sun. A valuable, long-flowering
perennial for a late summer border.
• PROPAGATION By division in spring or autumn.
• OTHER NAMES x S. hybridus.

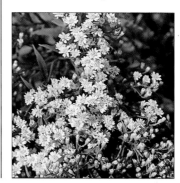

☼ ◊
❄❄❄

HEIGHT
60cm (24in

SPREAD
75cm (30in

| Asteraceae/Compositae | |
|---|---|

## *ACHILLEA* 'Moonshine' ♈

**Habit** Upright. **Flowers** Tiny, in large, flat heads, borne on rigid, leafy, grey stems during summer. Bright yellow. **Leaves** Feathery, finely divided into linear to lance-shaped segments, densely hairy. Silvery grey-green.
• NATIVE HABITAT Garden origin.
• CULTIVATION Grow in fertile, well-drained soil, in full sun. Excellent for a silver border. Divide and replant every second or third year to maintain vigour. The flower heads dry well for arrangements.
• PROPAGATION Division in early spring or autumn.

☼ ◊
❀ ❀ ❀

**HEIGHT**
45–60cm
(18–24in)

**SPREAD**
50cm (20in)

| Brassicaceae/Cruciferae | VARIEGATED WINTER CRESS |
|---|---|

## *BARBAREA VULGARIS* 'Variegata'

**Habit** Lax, rosette-forming. **Flowers** Small, 4-petalled, in branching heads, in early summer. Silvery-yellow. **Leaves** Basal leaves have 2–5 pairs of lateral lobes; stem leaves simple. Glossy green, blotched cream.
• NATIVE HABITAT Species occurs in damp hedges and ditches, throughout Europe. Garden origin.
• CULTIVATION Grow in moist but well-drained soil, in full sun or part-shade. Suitable for a cottage garden or wild garden. Self-seeds freely.
• PROPAGATION By division in spring or autumn.

☼ ◊
❀ ❀ ❀

**HEIGHT**
25–45cm
(10–18in)

**SPREAD**
to 23cm
(9in)

| Asteraceae/Compositae | |
|---|---|

## *ACHILLEA* 'Schwellenburg'

**Habit** Low-growing, spreading. **Flowers** Tiny, in large, flat heads, borne on rigid, leafy stems during summer. Lemon-yellow. **Leaves** Feathery, finely divided into oblong to lance-shaped segments, hairy. Greyish-green.
• NATIVE HABITAT Garden origin.
• CULTIVATION Grow in fertile, moisture-retentive, well-drained soil, in full sun. Divide and replant every third year to maintain vigour. The flower heads dry well for winter decoration.
• PROPAGATION Division in early spring or autumn.

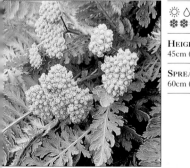

☼ ◊
❀ ❀ ❀

**HEIGHT**
45cm (18in)

**SPREAD**
60cm (24in)

| Asteraceae/Compositae | |
|---|---|

## *HELICHRYSUM* 'Schweffellicht'

**Habit** Clump-forming, tufted. **Flowers** Tiny, papery, borne in dense heads on upright stems, from mid- to late summer. Orange-tinted, pale sulphur-yellow. **Leaves** Narrowly lance-shaped, softly and densely woolly-hairy. Silver-green.
• NATIVE HABITAT Garden origin.
• CULTIVATION Grow in light, well-drained, fertile soil, in full sun. Excellent for the front of a silver border. Cut flowers dry well for winter arrangements.
• PROPAGATION By division in spring.
• OTHER NAMES *H.* 'Sulphur Light'.

☼ ◊
❀ ❀

**HEIGHT**
40–60cm
(16–24in)

**SPREAD**
30cm (12in)

| Rosaceae | |
|---|---|

## *POTENTILLA RECTA* 'Warrenii'

**Habit** Clump-forming. **Flowers** Open cup-shaped, borne in open, branching clusters, through summer. Rich golden-yellow. **Leaves** Divided into 5–7 lance-shaped, serrated, finely hairy leaflets. Green.
• NATIVE HABITAT Garden origin.
• CULTIVATION Grow in any moderately fertile, moist but well-drained soil, in sun or light shade. Good for a cottage garden, or the front of a herbaceous border.
• PROPAGATION By division in spring or autumn.
• OTHER NAMES *P. recta* 'Macrantha'.

☼ ◊
❁ ❁ ❁

HEIGHT
50cm (20in)

SPREAD
60cm (24in)

| Asteraceae/Compositae | |
|---|---|

## *GAILLARDIA ARISTATA*

**Habit** Upright, open clump-forming. **Flowers** Large, daisy-like, borne singly on slender, sturdy stems, over long periods in summer. Rich yellow, with an orange-red centre. **Leaves** Aromatic, soft, lance-shaped, entire, toothed, or lobed. Mid-green.
• NATIVE HABITAT Dry meadows and prairies, W. North America.
• CULTIVATION Grow in light, well-drained soil, in sun. Needs staking and may be short-lived.
• PROPAGATION By seed in spring or autumn, or by root cuttings in winter.

☼ ◊
❁ ❁ ❁

HEIGHT
60cm (24in)

SPREAD
50cm (20in)

| Scrophulariaceae | |
|---|---|

## *CALCEOLARIA BIFLORA*

**Habit** Mat-forming, rhizomatous. **Flowers** Small, pouched, borne in loose clusters of 2–8, on slender stems in summer. Yellow. **Leaves** Variable, softly hairy, oval-lance-shaped to diamond-shaped, in basal rosettes. Dark green.
• NATIVE HABITAT Chile and Argentina.
• CULTIVATION Grow in moist but well-drained, humus-rich soil, in part-shade. Suitable for a peat bed, shady border front, or rock garden.
• PROPAGATION By seed in autumn or spring, or by division in spring.

☼ ◊
❁ ❁ ❁

HEIGHT
30cm (12in)

SPREAD
15cm (6in)
or more

| Ranunculaceae | |
|---|---|

## *RANUNCULUS CONSTANTINOPOLITANUS* 'Plenus'

**Habit** Clump-forming. **Flowers** Double, pompon-like, borne on short stems above the foliage, in early summer. Yellow, with a green centre. **Leaves** Divided into 3 deeply toothed lobes. Dark green.
• NATIVE HABITAT Species occurs in damp meadows, from Europe to N. Africa and W. Asia.
• CULTIVATION Grow in moist, fertile soil, in sun or part-shade. Suitable for a border or cottage garden.
• PROPAGATION By division in spring or autumn.
• OTHER NAMES *R. bulbosus* 'Speciosus'.

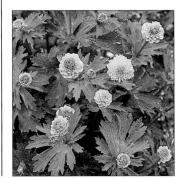

☼ ◊
❁ ❁ ❁

HEIGHT
50cm (20in)

SPREAD
30cm (12in)

Onagraceae

## *OENOTHERA FRUTICOSA* 'Fyrverkeri'

**Habit** Clump-forming. **Flowers** Fragrant, cup-shaped, in upright or ascending spikes, from mid-to late summer. Bright yellow. **Leaves** Broadly lance-shaped to broadly oval. Glossy mid-green, flushed purple, on red-tinted stems.

NATIVE HABITAT Garden origin.

CULTIVATION Grow in light, preferably sandy, well-drained soil, in full sun. It is good for the front of a warm, sunny herbaceous border and is suitable for rock and cottage gardens. Although the individual flowers are not long-lived, there are sufficient numbers to give a continuous display of colour towards the end of the season. Valued also for its handsome glossy foliage and purple-tinted young leaves that contrast beautifully with the red stems. It associates particularly well with bronze- or copper-leaved plants.

• PROPAGATION By division in autumn or spring, or by softwood cuttings in late spring.

• OTHER NAMES *O. fruticosa* 'Fireworks', *O. tetragona* 'Fireworks'.

**HEIGHT**
30–38cm
(12–15in)

**SPREAD**
30–38cm
(12–15in)

| Scrophulariaceae | YELLOW MUSK |
|---|---|

## *MIMULUS LUTEUS*

*Habit* Creeping, upright. *Flowers* Snapdragon-like, tubular with spreading lobes, borne in the leaf axils throughout summer. Bright yellow, with occasional dark red or purple-red spots. *Leaves* Broadly oval, toothed, finely hairy. Mid-green.
• NATIVE HABITAT By streamsides and in wet places; Chile, but naturalized elsewhere.
• CULTIVATION Grow in moist or wet soil, in full sun. Good for a bog garden, streambank, or pondside.
• PROPAGATION By seed or division in spring or softwood cuttings in late summer.

HEIGHT
30cm (12in)

SPREAD
30cm (12in)

| Papaveraceae | LAMPSHADE POPPY |
|---|---|

## *MECONOPSIS INTEGRIFOLIA*

*Habit* Rosette-forming, short-lived perennial or biennial. *Flowers* Large, poppy-like, with satiny petals, borne in branched clusters on long, bristly stems, in late spring and early summer. Pale yellow. *Leaves* Large, lance-shaped to oval. Pale green, clothed in downy, orange-red hairs.
• NATIVE HABITAT Tibet, Upper Burma, W. China.
• CULTIVATION Grow in moist, humus-rich soils, in semi-shade or shade, in a cool, sheltered site. Excellent for a peat bed or woodland garden.
• PROPAGATION By fresh seed in late summer.

HEIGHT
45–60cm
(18–24in)

SPREAD
60cm (24in)

| Rosaceae | |
|---|---|

## *GEUM* 'Lady Stratheden'

*Habit* Clump-forming. *Flowers* Double, cup-shaped, borne on arching, branching stems, over long periods in summer. Clear, bright yellow. *Leaves* Large, lobed, heart-shaped at the base. Mid-green.
• NATIVE HABITAT Garden origin.
• CULTIVATION Grow in moist but well-drained soil, in sun. An easily grown herbaceous border plant, valued for its long flowering period.
• PROPAGATION By division in spring or autumn. Seed sown in spring comes reasonably true.

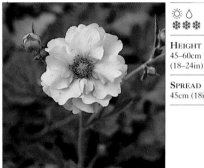

HEIGHT
45–60cm
(18–24in)

SPREAD
45cm (18in)

| Rosaceae | |
|---|---|

## *POTENTILLA MEGALANTHA*

*Habit* Clump-forming. *Flowers* Open cup-shaped, borne singly on slender stems, in profusion in summer. Rich yellow. *Leaves* Large, palmate, with 3 softly hairy leaflets. Soft green.
• NATIVE HABITAT Meadows and woodland, Japan.
• CULTIVATION Grow in any moderately fertile, moist but well-drained soil, in sun or light shade. Good for the front of herbaceous borders and cottage gardens.
• PROPAGATION By seed or division in spring or autumn.

HEIGHT
20cm (8in)

SPREAD
15cm (6in)

| Asteraceae/Compositae | YELLOW OX-EYE |
| --- | --- |

## BUPHTHALMUM SALICIFOLIUM

**Habit** Upright, spreading. **Flowers** Daisy-like, borne singly on sturdy, leafy stems throughout summer. Clear yellow, with narrow, widely spaced ray florets around a darker yellow disc. **Leaves** Lance-shaped to linear-lance-shaped, toothed or entire. Mid-green.
• NATIVE HABITAT Damp, stony places, C. Europe.
• CULTIVATION Grow in moist, well-drained soil, in sun or light shade. May need staking. Spreads on fertile soils. Good for wild or cottage gardens.
• PROPAGATION Seed or division in spring or autumn.

☀ ◊
❀ ❀ ❀

**HEIGHT**
60cm (2ft)

**SPREAD**
1m (3ft)

| Asteraceae/Compositae | |
| --- | --- |

## BIDENS FERULIFOLIA

**Habit** Clump-forming, spreading, short-lived. **Flowers** Starry, 4cm (1½in) across, in profusion, from mid-spring to first frosts. Golden-yellow. **Leaves** Very finely divided, fennel-like. Fresh green.
• NATIVE HABITAT Grassland and waste ground in southern USA, Mexico, Guatemala.
• CULTIVATION Grow in sun, in well-drained soil. Good for a border, gravel plantings, hanging basket and other containers. May be grown as an annual.
• PROPAGATION Seed, division, or stem cuttings in spring.

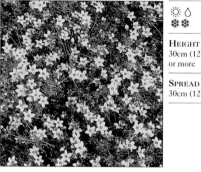

☀ ◊
❀ ❀

**HEIGHT**
30cm (12in)
or more

**SPREAD**
30cm (12in)

| Asteraceae/Compositae | |
| --- | --- |

## GAZANIA RIGENS var. UNIFLORA

**Habit** Mat-forming. **Flowers** Daisy-like, with pointed, borne singly on short stems, in early summer. Yellow-orange or yellow ray florets around yellow disc. **Leaves** Spoon-shaped or divided, smooth. Dark green above, silvery-white beneath.
NATIVE HABITAT South Africa.
CULTIVATION Tolerant of dry soils and salt-laden winds. Suitable for containers. Treat as an annual in cool areas. Grow in well-drained soil in a warm, sunny, sheltered site.
PROPAGATION By seed or division in spring.

☀ ◊
❀

**HEIGHT**
23cm (9in)

**SPREAD**
20–30cm
(8–12in)

| Crassulaceae | |
| --- | --- |

## SEDUM AIZOON 'Euphorbioides'

**Habit** Clump-forming, rhizomatous. **Flowers** Small, star-shaped, borne in dense, slightly rounded heads, over long periods in summer. Dark yellow, opening from red buds. **Leaves** Fleshy, oblong-lance-shaped. Bluish-green.
• NATIVE HABITAT Species occurs on dry hills, in scrub and on rocky streambanks, in N. Asia.
• CULTIVATION Grow in fertile, moist but well-drained soil, in sun or light shade.
• PROPAGATION By division in spring or autumn.
• OTHER NAMES S. aizoon 'Aurantiacum'.

☀ ◊
❀ ❀ ❀

**HEIGHT**
45cm (18in)

**SPREAD**
45cm (18in)

| Ranunculaceae | DOUBLE MEADOW BUTTERCUP |
|---|---|

## RANUNCULUS ACRIS 'Flore Pleno'

**Habit** Clump-forming. **Flowers** Double, pompon-like, borne on sturdy, slender, branching stems, in late spring and early summer. Golden-yellow, with a less pronounced green centre than *R. constantinopolitanus* 'Plenus'. **Leaves** Deeply cut and lobed. Mid- to dark green.
• NATIVE HABITAT Said to have occurred naturally in damp pastures, in northern England. Grown in gardens since the 16th century.
• CULTIVATION Grow in moist, fertile soil, in sun or part-shade. Valued for its dark foliage and wiry

stems topped by neat, shining, golden-yellow, pompon-like blooms, it is a charming plant that is happy in the wilder parts of the garden in damp borders, cottage gardens and bog gardens. It often benefits from gentle support by way of branches placed discreetly around the clump. Unlike its parent species, the meadow buttercup, *R. acris*, this variant does not self-seed or produce runners and it is unlikely to spread invasively.
• PROPAGATION By division in spring or autumn.

☼ ◊
❄ ❄ ❄

HEIGHT
45–60cm
(18–24in)

SPREAD
45–60cm
(18–24in)

| Tropaeoleaceae | |
| --- | --- |

## *TROPAEOLUM POLYPHYLLUM*

**Habit** Prostrate, trailing. **Flowers** Spurred, short trumpet-shaped, singly on long stalks in the leaf axils; in summer. Bright yellow. **Leaves** Divided into 5- to 7 or more, rounded lobes. Grey-green.
• NATIVE HABITAT Chile, Argentina.
• CULTIVATION Grow in very well-drained soil, in sun. Suitable for sunny banks, or raised beds and very effective when allowed to cascade over a sunny wall. Dies back completely after flowering. Needs to be planted deeply to be successful.
• PROPAGATION By seed in spring.

**HEIGHT** 5–8cm (2–3in) or more

**SPREAD** 1m (3ft)

| Rosaceae | |
| --- | --- |

## *POTENTILLA* 'Yellow Queen'

**Habit** Clump-forming. **Flowers** Open cup-shaped, semi-double, borne on slender stems, in profusion in mid-summer. Bright yellow. **Leaves** Divided into 3 finely hairy, neatly toothed leaflets. Dark green, usually silvery beneath.
• NATIVE HABITAT Garden origin.
• CULTIVATION Grow in any moderately fertile, moist but well-drained soil, in sun or light shade. Good for the front of herbaceous or mixed borders and cottage gardens.
• PROPAGATION By division in spring or autumn.

**HEIGHT** to 60cm (24in) or more

**SPREAD** 45cm (18in)

| Asteraceae/Compositae | |
| --- | --- |

## *COREOPSIS LANCEOLATA*

**Habit** Bushy, clump-forming. **Flowers** Daisy-like, with toothed, ray florets, borne on branching stems, in profusion throughout summer. Bright yellow with a golden-yellow centre. **Leaves** Narrowly lance-shaped, spoon-shaped to linear, all along the flowering stems. Mid-green.
• NATIVE HABITAT Central and southeast USA.
• CULTIVATION Easily grown in any fertile, well-drained soil, in full sun. Good for the summer border; the cut flowers last very well in water.
• PROPAGATION Seed or division in spring or autumn.

**HEIGHT** 45cm (18in)

**SPREAD** 30cm (12in)

| Asteraceae/Compositae | |
| --- | --- |

## *HIERACIUM LANATUM*

**Habit** Clump- or rosette-forming. **Flowers** Small, dandelion-like, borne on wiry, branching, grey-hairy stems, in summer. Bright yellow. **Leaves** Broad, lance-shaped, densely white-felted, in large basal rosettes. Grey.
• NATIVE HABITAT Limestone rocks and cliffs in the Alps and Jura mountains.
• CULTIVATION Grow in sharply drained, preferably alkaline and not too fertile soil, in full sun. Excellent for planting on a sunny wall or raised bed.
• PROPAGATION Seed or division in spring or autumn.

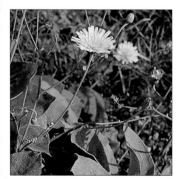

**HEIGHT** 30–45cm (12–18in)

**SPREAD** 30cm (12in)

| Asteraceae/Compositae | |
|---|---|

## *COREOPSIS VERTICILLATA*

**Habit** Bushy, rhizomatous. **Flowers** Star-shaped, daisy-like, borne on branching stems, in profusion throughout summer. Bright golden-yellow. **Leaves** Finely divided into hair-like segments. Bright green.
• NATIVE HABITAT Dry woodland clearings, E. North America.
• CULTIVATION Tolerant of dry soils. Easily grown in any fertile, well-drained soil, in full sun. Good for a summer border; the cut flowers last very well in water. Divide regularly to maintain vigour.
• PROPAGATION By seed or division in spring.

HEIGHT
40–60cm
(16–24in)

SPREAD
30cm (12in)

| Balsaminaceae | |
|---|---|

## *IMPATIENS REPENS*

**Habit** Creeping, stem-rooting. **Flowers** 5-petalled, with a large, finely hairy spur, in summer. Rich yellow. **Leaves** Evergreen, small, scalloped, kidney-shaped. Mid-green.
• NATIVE HABITAT Sri Lanka, India.
• CULTIVATION Grow as a house or conservatory plant in cool climates in moist, well-drained potting compost. If grown outdoors site in full sun. Provides very effective ground cover in a border.
• PROPAGATION By seed or stem cuttings in spring or summer.

Min. 10°C
(50°F)

HEIGHT
to 5cm
(2in)

SPREAD
indefinite

| Brassicaceae/Cruciferae | |
|---|---|

## *ERYSIMUM* 'Moonlight'

**Habit** Mat-forming. **Flowers** Small, 4-petalled, borne in dense, terminal clusters, in succession throughout summer. Pale yellow. **Leaves** Evergreen, narrowly lance-shaped. Grey-green.
• NATIVE HABITAT Garden origin.
• CULTIVATION Grow in poor, gritty, well-drained soil, in a sheltered site, in full sun. Is often short-lived, so propagate regularly. Good for the front of a border, sunny bank, or rock garden.
• PROPAGATION By softwood cuttings in summer.
• OTHER NAMES *Cheiranthus* 'Moonlight'.

HEIGHT
15cm (6in)

SPREAD
20cm (8in)

| Asteraceae/ Compositae | |
|---|---|

## *ERIOPHYLLUM LANATUM*

**Habit** Clump- or cushion-forming. **Flowers** Star-shaped, daisy-like, usually borne singly on slender, sturdy stems, in profusion over long periods in summer. Bright yellow. **Leaves** Dense, finely divided. Silvery-grey, white-woolly beneath.
• NATIVE HABITAT Dry scrub, in the foothills and mountains of W. North America.
• CULTIVATION Grow in sharply drained, not too fertile soil, in full sun.
• PROPAGATION By seed or division in spring.

HEIGHT
30cm (12in)

SPREAD
30cm (12in)

| Asteraceae/Compositae | |
|---|---|

## *INULA ENSIFOLIA*

*Habit* Clump-forming. *Flowers* Daisy-like, with slender, ray florets, borne on slender, wiry stems, in late summer. Bright yellow with a golden disc. *Leaves* Small, lance-shaped to elliptic. Mid-green.
• NATIVE HABITAT Scrub and grasslands, E. Europe and eastern C. Europe.
• CULTIVATION Grow in any moist but well-drained soil, in sun or light shade. May spread rapidly. Suitable for borders and wild or woodland gardens.
• PROPAGATION By seed or division in spring or autumn.

☼ ◊
❀ ❀ ❀

HEIGHT
30cm (12in)

SPREAD
30cm (12in)

| Rosaceae | |
|---|---|

## *GEUM* 'Borisii'

*Habit* Clump-forming. *Flowers* Single, cup-shaped, borne on hairy, slender, branching stems, over long periods in summer. Bright orange. *Leaves* Large, irregularly lobed. Pale to mid-green.
• NATIVE HABITAT Damp meadows, Balkans, N. Turkey.
• CULTIVATION Grow in moist but well-drained soil, in sun. An easily grown herbaceous border plant, associating well with blue- or yellow-flowered perennials.
• PROPAGATION By division in spring or autumn.

☼ ◊
❀ ❀ ❀

HEIGHT
30cm (12in)

SPREAD
30cm (12in)

| Scrophulariaceae | |
|---|---|

## *CALCEOLARIA* 'John Innes'

*Habit* Clump-forming, stoloniferous. *Flowers* Small, pouched, borne in loose, slender-stemmed clusters, in late spring and summer. Yellow, freckled red-brown. *Leaves* Evergreen, broadly oval, in basal clumps. Mid-green.
• NATIVE HABITAT Garden origin.
• CULTIVATION Grow in moist but well-drained, humus-rich soil, in sun or light shade. Suitable for a peat bed, border front, or rock garden.
• PROPAGATION By division in spring.

◑ ◊
❀ ❀

HEIGHT
15–20cm
(6–8in)

SPREAD
25–30cm
(10–12in)

| Crassulaceae | |
|---|---|

## *RHODIOLA HETERODONTA*

*Habit* Clump-forming. *Flowers* Small, borne in dense, slightly rounded heads on leafy stems, in late spring and early summer. Orange-red to purple, sometimes greenish beneath. *Leaves* Fleshy, oval, toothed. Bluish-green.
• NATIVE HABITAT Dry, rocky places, Afghanistan to Nepal.
• CULTIVATION Grow in well-drained soil in sun.
• PROPAGATION By division from spring to mid-summer, or by seed in autumn or spring.
• OTHER NAMES *Sedum heterodontum.*

☼ ◊
❀ ❀ ❀

HEIGHT
45cm (18in)

SPREAD
25cm (10in)

| Liliaceae<br>Convallariaceae | TOAD LILY |
|---|---|

## *TRICYRTIS HIRTA ALBA*

*Habit* Upright, rhizomatous. *Flowers* Large,
spurred, bell-shaped, borne in the upper leaf axils,
in late summer and early autumn. White, usually
spotted deep purple. *Leaves* Lance-shaped, hairy
and stem-clasping. Mid-green.
• NATIVE HABITAT Damp, shady rocks, Japan.
• CULTIVATION Grow in moist, humus-rich, fertile
soil, in a sheltered site, in sun, or in warm areas,
in semi-shade. Good for woodland gardens.
• PROPAGATION By division in spring or seed
in autumn.

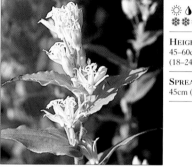

HEIGHT
45–60cm
(18–24in)

SPREAD
45cm (18in)

| Iridaceae | |
|---|---|

## *SCHIZOSTYLIS COCCINEA* 'Sunrise'

*Habit* Clump-forming, rhizomatous. *Flowers*
Large, shallowly cup-shaped, in upright spikes, in
early autumn. Clear pink. *Leaves* Long, narrowly
sword-shaped, ribbed, in basal clumps. Mid-green.
• NATIVE HABITAT Garden origin.
• CULTIVATION Grow in fertile, moist but well-
drained soil, in full sun. Divide and replant
regularly to maintain vigour. Excellent for front
border placement and for pondside plantings
above water level. Cut flowers last well in water.
• PROPAGATION By division in spring.

HEIGHT
60cm (24in)

SPREAD
23–30cm
(9–12in)

| Crassulaceae | ICE-PLANT |
|---|---|

## *SEDUM SPECTABILE* 'Brilliant'

*Habit* Clump-forming. *Flowers* Small, bright
borne in dense, flattened heads on leafy stems, in
profusion from late summer to autumn. Rose-pink.
*Leaves* Fleshy, oval-elliptic. Grey-green.
• NATIVE HABITAT Garden origin.
• CULTIVATION Grow in fertile, well-drained soil,
with adequate moisture during summer, in full
sun. Excellent for the border front and very
attractive to bees and butterflies.
• PROPAGATION By division in spring.
• OTHER NAMES *Hylotelephium spectabile* 'Brilliant'.

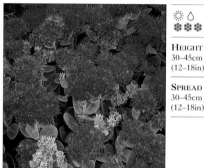

HEIGHT
30–45cm
(12–18in)

SPREAD
30–45cm
(12–18in)

| Polygonaceae | |
|---|---|

## *PERSICARIA MILLETII*

*Habit* Clump-forming, spreading, rhizomatous.
*Flowers* Tiny, borne in dense, broadly cylindrical
spikes, on strong, slender stems, in summer and
autumn. Deep rose-crimson. *Leaves* Linear-lance-
shaped to oblong. Dark green.
• NATIVE HABITAT Alpine scrub, rocks, Himalayas.
• CULTIVATION Grow in any moist, fertile soil, in
sun or semi-shade. A vigorous and long-flowering
specimen for a damp border.
• PROPAGATION Seed or division in spring or autumn.
• OTHER NAMES *Polygonum milletii.*

HEIGHT
60cm (24in)

SPREAD
60cm (24in)
often more

| Asteraceae/Compositae | |
|---|---|

## SENECIO PULCHER

**Habit** Upright. **Flowers** Large, daisy-like, borne in loose, few-flowered, terminal clusters, in late summer and autumn. Bright purplish-pink ray florets around a golden-yellow disc. **Leaves** Leathery, elliptic, scalloped or lobed, hairy. Dark green.
• NATIVE HABITAT S. Brazil, Uruguay, Argentina.
• CULTIVATION Grow in light, well-drained soil, in full sun, in a warm, sheltered site. The strongly coloured flowers associate well with silver-leaved plants.
• PROPAGATION By seed or division in spring.

☼ ◊
❅

HEIGHT
45–60cm
(18–24in)

SPREAD
50cm (20in)

| Convallariaceae/<br>Liliaceae | LILY TURF |
|---|---|

## LIRIOPE MUSCARI

**Habit** Spreading, tufted, tuberous-rooted. **Flowers** Small, rounded bell-shaped, in dense, upright, spikes in autumn. Lavender or purple-blue. **Leaves** Evergreen, strap-shaped. Glossy dark green.
• NATIVE HABITAT Woodlands of China and Japan.
• CULTIVATION Tolerates dry soils and shade, but flowers best in sun. Grow in fertile, humus-rich, moist but well-drained soil. Provide shelter from strong winds to avoid foliage scorch.
• PROPAGATION By division in spring or seed in autumn.

☼ ◊
❆ ❆ ❆

HEIGHT
30cm (12in)

SPREAD
45cm (18in)

| Gesneriaceae | |
|---|---|

## CHIRITA LAVANDULACEA

**Habit** Upright. **Flowers** Funnel-shaped, in the leaf axils, from spring to autumn, if sown in succession. White tube, with lavender-blue petal lobes. **Leaves** Evergreen, downy, to 20cm (8in) long. Pale green.
• NATIVE HABITAT Tropical Asia.
• CULTIVATION Grow as a house or conservatory plant in cool climates. Site in moist soil, in bright, indirect light, with high humidity. Avoid wetting the leaves when watering.
• PROPAGATION By tip cuttings in summer, or by seed, if available, in late winter or spring.

◑ ◊

Min. 15°C
(59°F)

HEIGHT
60cm (24in)

SPREAD
60cm (24in)

| Asteraceae/Compositae | CAPE DANDELION |
|---|---|

## ARCTOTHECA CALENDULA

**Habit** Mound-forming, carpeting. **Flowers** Daisy-like, borne from late spring to autumn. Yellow ray florets around a darker yellow disc. **Leaves** Divided or entire. Mid- to dark green, roughly hairy above, white-downy beneath.
• NATIVE HABITAT South Africa, naturalized in C. Portugal, S.W. Spain.
• CULTIVATION Grow as a house or conservatory plant in cool climates. Site in full light. Grow outdoors only where there is no danger of frost.
• PROPAGATION By seed or division in spring.

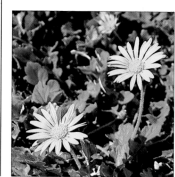

☼ ◊

Min. 5°C
(41°F)

HEIGHT
30cm (12in)

SPREAD
30cm (12in)

# BEGONIAS

Begonias form a varied genus of plants that provide flowers, foliage and attractive habit all year round. Because they are mostly tropical or subtropical, in cool climates they are grown as houseplants or in the conservatory, where the trailing types are well-suited to hanging baskets.

All begonias need light, well-drained and neutral to slightly acid soil or compost, with bright but indirect light. Water more when in full growth, and less in winter. Feed in late spring and summer at every other watering. Repot every spring.

The more commonly cultivated begonias are grouped as follows.

**Cane-stemmed** – frost tender, grown mainly for their attractive assymetrical heart-shaped leaves. Take leaf, tip or stem cuttings in spring or summer.

**Rex-Cultorum** – grown for their foliage. Keep at 21–24°C (70–75°F). Take leaf or rhizome cuttings in summer.

**Rhizomatous** – grown for their foliage and/or flowers, keep at around 19°C (66°F) and water from below. Take leaf cuttings in spring or rhizome cuttings in summer.

**Semperflorens** – grown for clusters of rounded flowers. Plant out when danger of frost has passed. Sow seed or take basal cuttings in spring.

**Shrub-like** – grown for their foliage and habit. Keep humid and provide bright light in winter to enhance leaf colour. Pinching out growing tips makes them bushier. Sow ripe seed or take leaf, stem or tip cuttings.

**Tuberous** (the Tuberhybrida Group in particular) – grown for exhibition, as pot plants, or for summer beds. Start tubers in spring, and remove all flower buds until at least 3 pairs of leaves show. Sow seed in spring, or take stem cuttings in summer

**Winter-flowering** – grown for their bronze-green leaves and profusion of winter flowers. Keep humid. Take basal cuttings.

---

*B.* **'Billie Langdon'**
*Habit* Upright, tuberous.
*Flowers* Double, to 18cm (7in) across, produced in profusion throughout summer. Pure white, with broad, veined petals, and a rose-bud centre.
*Leaves* Oval, to 20cm (8in) long. Rich green.
• HEIGHT 60cm (24in).
• SPREAD 45cm (18in).

*B.* **'Billie Langdon'**
(Tuberhybrida Group)

☀ ◊
Min. 10°C (50°F)

---

*B. ALBOPICTA*
*Habit* Fast-growing.
*Flowers* Pendent, small, single, in clusters in late summer. Green-white.
*Leaves* Evergreen, oval-lance-shaped, 8cm (3in) long, with wavy margins. Green, silver-spotted above, pale green beneath.
• TIPS Pinch out tips to encourage bushy growth.
• HEIGHT 60–100cm (2–3ft).
• SPREAD 30cm (12in).

*B. albopicta*
(Cane-stemmed)
Guinea-wing begonia
☀ ◊
Min. 10°C (50°F)

---

*B. FOLIOSA*
*Habit* Shrubby, with pendent stems.
*Flowers* Small, to 1.5cm (½in) across, single, produced from autumn to spring. White.
*Leaves* Evergreen, oval, notched, to 8mm (⅜in) long, in two ranks along the stems. Dark green.
• TIPS Prone to whitefly. Needs light and humidity.
• HEIGHT 45cm (18in).
• SPREAD 30cm (12in).

*B. foliosa*
(Shrub-like)
Fern begonia
☀ ◊
Min. 10°C (50°F)

---

*B. OLSONIAE*
*Habit* Compact, upright.
*Flowers* Single, to 3cm (1¼in) across, on arching stems above the foliage, year-round. Pale pink or white.
*Leaves* Evergreen, obliquely oval to rounded, 12–20cm (5–8in) long. Satiny, bronze-green with prominent creamy-white veins, brown-red beneath.
• HEIGHT 22cm (9in).
• SPREAD 30cm (12in).

*B. olsoniae*
(Shrub-like)
☀ ◊
Min. 10°C (50°F)

## B. *MANICATA*

**Habit** Upright,
then arching.
**Flowers** Single, 1.5cm
(½in) across, in small
clusters above the foliage
in late winter. Pink.
**Leaves** Evergreen,
obliquely heart-shaped,
15cm (6in) long. Glossy
light green, with a fringe
of red bristles below the
leaf base.
• TIPS Grow under glass
in cool climates in partial
shade and in well-drained
soil. Pot up small
plantlets during the
growing season.
• HEIGHT 60cm (24in).
• SPREAD 35cm (14in).

*B. manicata*
(Rhizomatous)

☼ ◊
Min. 10°C (50°F)

## B. *SCHARFFII*

**Habit** Upright, shrubby.
**Flowers** Single, prolific,
in clusters, to 5cm (2in)
across, from autumn to
summer. Pink-white.
**Leaves** Obliquely oval,
to 25cm (10in) long. Dark
metallic grey-green, red-
tinted beneath.
• OTHER NAMES
*B. haageana.*
• HEIGHT 60cm–1.2m
(2–4ft).
• SPREAD 60cm (2ft).

*B. scharffii*
(Shrub-like)

☼ ◊
Min. 10°C (50°F)

## B. 'Weltoniensis'

**Habit** Shrub-like.
**Flowers** Single, to 3cm
(1¼in) across, in profuse
sprays from early summer
to mid-autumn. Pink.
**Leaves** Oval, shallowly
lobed, with toothed
margins. Apple-green
with purple-red veins.
• HEIGHT 30–45cm
(12–18in).
• SPREAD 30cm (12in).

*B. 'Weltoniensis'*
(Shrub-like)
Grapevine begonia
☼ ◊
Min. 10°C (50°F)

## B. 'Ingramii'

**Habit** Shrubby, upright,
slender-stemmed.
**Flowers** Single, to 3cm
(1¼in) across, more or less
continuously throughout
the year. Deep pink.
**Leaves** Evergreen, oval-
lance-shaped, toothed,
7–8cm (3in) long. Bright
green.
• HEIGHT 75cm (30in).
• SPREAD 45cm (18in).

*B. 'Ingramii'*
(Shrub-like)

☼ ◊
Min. 10°C (50°F)

## B. *METALLICA*

**Habit** Upright.
**Flowers** Single, to
3.5cm (1½in) across,
in autumn. Pink,
red-hairy.
**Leaves** Evergreen,
obliquely oval-heart-
shaped, 18cm (7in) long.
Dark green, red-hairy,
with a bright metallic
sheen and sunken, dark
red veins.
• HEIGHT 90cm (3ft).
• SPREAD 60cm (2ft).

*B. metallica*
(Shrub-like)
Metallic-leaf begonia
☼ ◊
Min. 10°C (50°F)

## B. 'Merry Christmas'

**Habit** Upright,
rhizomatous.
**Flowers** Single, to 1cm
(½in) across, sparse, from
autumn to early winter.
Pale rose-pink.
**Leaves** Obliquely heart-
shaped, 15–20cm (6–8in)
long. Satiny bright red
with a broad emerald-
green outer band and a
velvety, deep red-pink
centre, sometimes edged
with grey.
• OTHER NAMES
*B. 'Ruhrtal'.*
• HEIGHT 25–30cm
(10–12in).
• SPREAD 25–30cm
(10–12in).

*B. 'Merry Christmas'*
(Rex Cultorum)

☼ ◊
Min. 10°C (50°F)

### . 'Roy Hartley'
**Habit** Upright, tuberous.
**Flowers** Double, to
5cm (6in) across, with
lightly serrated petals,
profusely throughout
summer. Soft pink,
tinted salmon-pink.
**Leaves** Oval, to 15cm
(6in) long. Rich green.
• TIPS Depth of flower
colour depends on light
intensity.
HEIGHT 60cm (24in).
SPREAD 45cm (18in).

**B. 'Roy Hartley'**
(Tuberhybrida Group)

☼ ◊
Min. 10°C (50°F)

### . × CORALLINA 'Lucerna'
**Habit** Vigorous, upright.
**Flowers** Single, to 4cm
(1½in) across, in clusters,
in summer. Rose-pink.
**Leaves** Evergreen, oval,
20–35cm (8–14in) long.
Olive-green, heavily
spotted silver above,
dark red beneath.
OTHER NAMES
. 'Lucerna'.
HEIGHT 2–2.2m (6–7ft).
SPREAD 35cm (14in).

**B. × corallina 'Lucerna'**
(Cane-stemmed)

☼ ◊
Min. 10°C (50°F)

### . 'Red Ascot'
**Habit** Dense,
branching.
**Flowers** Single, to 2cm
(¾in) across, produced
from the leaf axils in
profusion in summer.
Crimson-red.
**Leaves** Evergreen,
rounded, to 8cm (3in)
across, waxy and fleshy.
Emerald-green, paler
beneath.
HEIGHT 15cm (6in).
SPREAD 15cm (6in).

**B. 'Red Ascot'**
(Semperflorens Cultorum)

☼ ◊
Min. 7°C (45°F)

### . 'Organdy'
**Habit** Dense,
branching.
**Flowers** Single, to 2cm
(¾in) across, produced
from leaf axils profusely
in summer. Shades of
red, pink and white,
**Leaves** Evergreen,
rounded, to 8cm (3in)
long, waxy and fleshy.
Green-bronze, paler
beneath.
• HEIGHT 15cm (6in).
• SPREAD 15cm (6in).

**B. 'Organdy'**
(Semperflorens Cultorum)

☼ ◊
Min. 7°C (45°F)

### B. 'Flamboyant'
**Habit** Low, bushy,
compact, and tuberous.
**Flowers** Single, 5cm
(2in) across, produced in
profuse clusters in
summer. Deep cerise
to red.
**Leaves** Heart-shaped,
to 15cm (6in) long.
Rich green.
• TIPS Tolerates
full sun.
• HEIGHT 17cm (7in).
• SPREAD 15cm (6in).

**B. 'Flamboyant'**
(Tuberhybrida Group:
Multiflora)

☼ ◊
Min. 10°C (50°F)

### B. 'Helen Lewis'
**Habit** Upright.
**Flowers** Single, to 1cm
(½in) across, sparsely
hairy, in early summer.
Creamy-white.
**Leaves** Obliquely oval,
15–20cm (6–8in) long,
silky. Dark wine-red with
a broad, irregular silver
band towards the margins.
• HEIGHT 45–60cm
(18–24in).
• SPREAD 45–60cm
(18–24in).

**B. 'Helen Lewis'**
(Rex Cultorum)

☼ ◊
Min. 10°C (50°F)

### B. 'Duartei'
**Habit** Upright.
**Flowers** Single, to 1cm
(½in) across, sparse, in late
winter/early spring. Pink.
**Leaves** Obliquely heart-
shaped, to 17cm (7in)
long, spirally twisted.
Red-hairy, dark green,
with silver-grey streaks
and almost black edges.
• HEIGHT 45–60cm
(18–24in).
• SPREAD 45–60cm
(18–24in).

**B. 'Duartei'**
(Rex Cultorum)

☼ ◊
Min. 10°C (50°F)

### B. 'Thurstonii'
**Habit** Upright.
**Flowers** Single, to
1.5–2cm (½–¾in) across,
relatively insignificant,
and sparsely produced
in summer. Pink.
**Leaves** Evergreen,
oval, taper-pointed,
15cm (6in) long, glossy.
Green, deeply veined,
rich red-brown
beneath.
• HEIGHT 2m (6ft).
• SPREAD 45cm (18in).

**B. 'Thurstonii'**
(Shrub-like)

☼ ◊
Min. 10°C (50°F)

*B. SERRATIPETALA*
**Habit** Trailing.
**Flowers** Single, 2–3cm
(¾–1¼in) across produced
sparsely year-round.
Deep pink.
**Leaves** Evergreen,
obliquely oval, 8cm (3in)
long, deeply serrated,
with waved margins.
Dark bronze-green, with
raised, deep pink spots.
• TIPS Prefers moderate
humidity, with fairly
dry roots.
• HEIGHT 45cm (18in).
• SPREAD 45cm (18in).

*B. serratipetala*
(Shrub-like)

☼ ◊
Min. 13°C (55°F)

*B.* 'Orpha C. Fox'
**Habit** Upright.
**Flowers** Single, to 3cm
(1¼in) across, in clusters,
mainly in summer.
Rose-pink.
**Leaves** Evergreen, oval,
15cm (6in) long. Grey-
green, splashed silver and
maroon beneath.
• HEIGHT 90cm (36in).
• SPREAD 30cm (12in).

*B.* 'Orpha C. Fox'
(Cane-stemmed)

☼ ◊
Min. 10°C (50°F)

*B.* 'Silver Queen'
**Habit** Upright.
**Flowers** Small, single, to
1.5–2cm (½–¾in) across,
relatively insignificant, in
autumn. Pink.
**Leaves** Evergreen, oval,
20cm (8in) long. Silver,
with metallic purple
centres that become dull
purple in bright light.
• HEIGHT 30cm (12in).
• SPREAD 45cm (18in)

*B.* 'Silver Queen'
(Rex Cultorum)

☼ ◊
Min. 10°C (50°F) ♥

*B. PUSTULATA*
'Argentea'
**Habit** Creeping.
**Flowers** Single, small, in
clusters in summer. White.
**Leaves** Oval, 15cm (6in)
long. Dark green, finely
hairy, with blisters, and
silvery markings.
• OTHER NAMES
*B.* 'Silver'.
• HEIGHT 15–20cm
(6–8in).
• SPREAD 20–25cm
(8–10in).

*B. pustulata* 'Argentea'
(Rhizomatous)

☼ ◊
Min. 13°C (55°F)

*B. MASONIANA*
**Habit** Upright to arching.
**Flowers** Single, to 2cm
(¾in) across, freely in
summer. Green-white.
**Leaves** Evergreen,
obliquely oval-heart-
shaped, to 20cm (8in)
long, warty. Dark green,
red-hairy, with a brown
cross-shaped central mark.
• OTHER NAMES
*B.* 'Iron Cross'.
• HEIGHT 50cm (20in).
• SPREAD 45cm (18in).

*B. masoniana*
(Rhizomatous)
Iron-cross begonia
☼ ◊
Min. 13°C (55°F)

*B. BOWERAE*
**Habit** Creeping.
**Flowers** Single, about
1.5–2cm (½–¾in) across,
produced freely in winter.
White, tinted pink.
**Leaves** Evergreen, oval,
2.5cm (1in) long. Bright
green, marked chocolate-
brown, and fringed with
fine hairs.
• HEIGHT 25cm (10in).
• SPREAD 18cm (7in).

*B. bowerae*
(Rhizomatous)
Eyelash begonia
☼ ◊
Min. 10°C (50°F)

*B. MANICATA*
'Crispa'
**Habit** Upright, then
arching. **Flowers** Single,
small, 1.5cm (½in) across,
in clusters in late winter.
Deep pink.
**Leaves** Evergreen,
obliquely heart-shaped,
15cm (6in) long. Glossy
light green, with crested
margins, and a fringe of
red bristles at the base.
• HEIGHT 60cm (24in).
• SPREAD 35cm (14in).

*B. manicata* 'Crispa'
(Rhizomatous)

☼ ◊
Min. 10°C (50°F)

**B. 'Norah Bedson'**
*Habit* Bushy, upright.
*Flowers* Single, about
.5–2cm (½–¾in) across,
in early spring. Pink.
*Leaves* Evergreen, oval,
taper-pointed, to 5cm
(2in) long. Bright green,
mottled chocolate-brown,
splashed red beneath.
HEIGHT 23cm (9in).
SPREAD 25cm (10in).

**B. 'Norah Bedson'**
(Rhizomatous)
☀ ◊
Min. 10°C (50°F)

**B. 'Oliver Twist'**
*Habit* Bushy, upright.
*Flowers* Single, about
.5–2cm (½–¾in) across,
in winter or early
spring. Pink.
*Leaves* Evergreen, oval,
15–30cm (6–12in) long,
ruffled and crested. Pale
to mid-green, with brown
markings along the veins.
HEIGHT 45cm (18in).
SPREAD 25cm (10in).

**B. 'Oliver Twist'**
(Rhizomatous)
☀ ◊
Min. 10°C (50°F)

**B. PRISMATOCARPA**
*Habit* Creeping.
*Flowers* Single, to 1.5cm
(⅝in) across, year-round.
Yellow.
*Leaves* Evergreen,
obliquely oval, 2–3 lobed,
3cm (1¼in) long. Shining
bright green.
• TIPS Suited to a
terrarium.
HEIGHT 15–20cm
(6–8in).
SPREAD 20–25cm
(8–10in).

**B. prismatocarpa**
(Rhizomatous)
☀ ◊
Min. 16°C (62°F)

**B. NELUMBIIFOLIA**
*Habit* Upright. *Flowers*
single, 1.5cm (⅝in)
across, sparsely produced
in branching clusters in
late winter. Greyish-
white.
*Leaves* Evergreen,
peltate, rounded, to
30cm (12in) across.
Green, fringed at the
margins, hairy
beneath.
HEIGHT 45cm (18in).
SPREAD 60cm (24in).

**B. nelumbiifolia**
(Rhizomatous)
Lily-pad begonia
☀ ◊
Min. 10°C (50°F)

**B. 'Apricot Cascade'**
*Habit* Pendent,
tuberous.
*Flowers* Double, to 7cm
(3in) across, with serrated
petals, profusely from
summer to autumn. Pale
apricot-orange.
*Leaves* Oval, to 20cm
(8in) long. Emerald-green.
• TIPS Grow indoors in
cool climates. Good for
hanging baskets.
• HEIGHT 60cm (24in).
• SPREAD 60cm (24in).

**B. 'Apricot Cascade'**
(Tuberhybrida Group:
Pendula)
☀ ◊
Min. 10°C (50°F)

**B. 'Can-Can'**
*Habit* Upright, tuberous.
*Flowers* Double, to
18cm (7in) across, in
profusion through
summer. Rich yellow, the
serrated petals having a
heavy red-picotee
margin.
*Leaves* Oval, to 20cm
(8in) long. Rich green.
• HEIGHT 90cm (36in).
• SPREAD 45cm (18in).

**B. 'Can-Can'**
(Tuberhybrida Group)
☀ ◊
Min. 10°C (50°F)

**B. 'Orange Rubra'**
*Habit* Slow-growing.
*Flowers* Single, 2–3cm
(¾–1¼in) across, in
panicles year-round.
Vivid orange.
*Leaves* Evergreen,
lance-shaped, 12cm
(5in) long. Emerald-
green, sometimes silver-
spotted.
• TIPS Stake and pinch
out for a bushy plant.
• HEIGHT 60cm (24in).
• SPREAD 45cm (18in).

**B. 'Orange Rubra'**
(Cane-stemmed)
☀ ◊
Min. 10°C (50°F)

**B. SUTHERLANDII**
*Habit* Trailing, tuberous.
*Flowers* Single, to 2.5cm
(1in) across, in sprays
through summer. Orange,
*Leaves* Oval-lance-
shaped, to 15cm (6in) long,
serrated. Bright green with
red veins and margins.
• TIPS Good for hanging
baskets. Susceptible to
mildew.
• HEIGHT 45cm–1m
(18in).
• SPREAD indefinite.

**B. sutherlandii**
(Tuberous)
☀ ◊
Min. 10°C (50°F)

| Araceae | |
|---|---|

## *SPATHIPHYLLUM FLORIBUNDUM* 'Mauna Loa'

*Habit* Compact, tufted, rhizomatous. *Flowers* Fragrant, produced intermittently and irregularly. Each flower is formed by a fleshy, white spadix surrounded by a large, white spathe. *Leaves* Large, lance-shaped to elliptic, glossy. Dark green.
• NATIVE HABITAT Garden origin. Species occurs in damp tropical forests in Central America, the Philippines and Indonesia.
• CULTIVATION Grow as a house or conservatory plant in cool climates. Site in bright, indirect light, providing shade from the summer sun. It is essential for maximum flower production to maintain humidity: water freely when in growth and keep drier in winter. The growing medium should be equal parts of leafmould and bark with loam added. The addition of pieces of charcoal will ensure this mixture is kept "sweet". The requirements for high humidity are more easily met in a greenhouse or conservatory. In the home, keep humid by standing the plant's pot on a saucer of pebbles kept permanently wet.
• PROPAGATION By division in spring or summer.

☀ ◐

Min. 15°C
(59°F)

**HEIGHT**
45–60cm
(18–24in)

**SPREAD**
45–60cm
(18–24in)

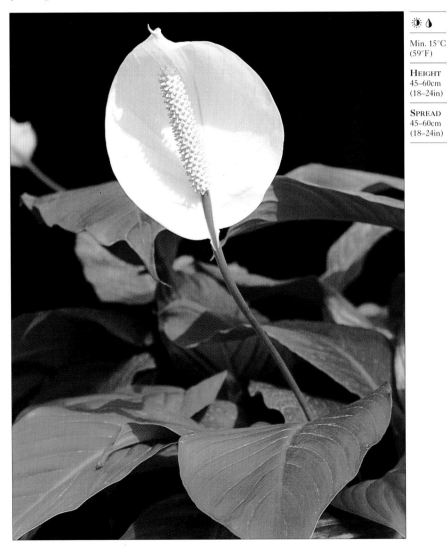

| Gesneriaceae | LACE FLOWER |
|---|---|

## EPISCIA DIANTHIFLORA

**Habit** Prostrate, creeping, stoloniferous. **Flowers** Small, broadly tubular, with fringed petals. White. **Leaves** Evergreen, thick, elliptic to oval, toothed, velvety. Dark green.
• NATIVE HABITAT Tropical Costa Rica and Mexico.
• CULTIVATION Grow as a house or conservatory plant in cool climates in well-drained compost or soil, in bright indirect light. Water freely during growth.
• PROPAGATION By division, by removal of rooted stems, or by stem cuttings in summer.
• OTHER NAMES *Alsobia dianthiflora.*

Min. 15°C (59°F)
HEIGHT 10cm (4in)
SPREAD indefinite

| Commelinaceae | |
|---|---|

## TRADESCANTIA FLUMINENSIS 'Albovittata'

**Habit** Vigorous, trailing, with rooting stems. **Flowers** Tiny, 3-petalled, produced intermittently. White. **Leaves** Evergreen, broadly oval to lance-shaped. Bluish-green with broad, white stripes.
• NATIVE HABITAT Garden origin.
• CULTIVATION Grow as a house or conservatory plant in cool climates. Feed and water freely when in growth. Cut straggly stems back in spring.
• PROPAGATION By tip cuttings in spring, summer, or autumn.

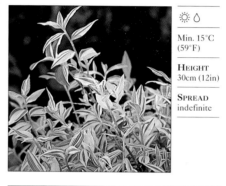

Min. 15°C (59°F)
HEIGHT 30cm (12in)
SPREAD indefinite

| Acanthaceae | |
|---|---|

## HEMIGRAPHIS REPANDA

**Habit** Prostrate, with spreading, rooting stems. **Flowers** Tiny, tubular, borne intermittently. White. **Leaves** Narrowly lance-shaped, toothed, scalloped, or lobed, satiny. Greyish-green, flushed red-purple above and darker purple beneath.
• NATIVE HABITAT Tropical Malaysia.
• CULTIVATION In cool climates grow as a house or conservatory plant in well-drained soil or compost. Protect from hot sun. Water freely during growth; less in winter. Cut back straggly growth in spring.
• PROPAGATION By stem cuttings in summer.

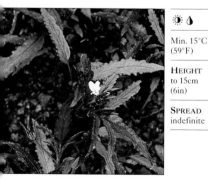

Min. 15°C (59°F)
HEIGHT to 15cm (6in)
SPREAD indefinite

| Lamiaceae/Labiatae | VARIEGATED GROUND IVY |
|---|---|

## GLECHOMA HEDERACEA 'Variegata'

**Habit** Mat-forming, rhizomatous. **Flowers** Insignificant, produced in summer. Mauve or white. **Leaves** Evergreen, toothed, oval, heart-shaped at the base. Green, marbled with white and silver-grey.
• NATIVE HABITAT Garden origin.
• CULTIVATION Grow in moist but well-drained soil, in sun or shade. Excellent ground cover, but may be invasive. Also suitable for hanging baskets and other containers.
• PROPAGATION By division in spring or autumn, or by softwood cuttings in spring.

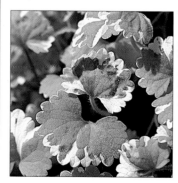

HEIGHT 15cm (6in)
SPREAD indefinite

| Ranunculaceae | LENTEN ROSE |

## *HELLEBORUS ORIENTALIS* white

**Habit** Clump-forming. **Flowers** Nodding, cup-shaped, borne in clusters of 1–4 in late winter and early spring. White, sometimes with darker spots. **Leaves** Evergreen (deciduous in cold winters) divided into 7–10 segments. Light to dark green.
• NATIVE HABITAT Scrub, woodland edge, in grass, from N.E. Greece, N. and N.E. Turkey to the Caucasus.
• CULTIVATION Grow in fertile, heavy, moist but well-drained soil, in a sunny or semi-shaded site, with shelter from cold winds. Particularly suited to woodland gardens, but also excellent in a shady herbaceous border or beneath deciduous shrubs. It associates particularly well with snowdrops (*Galanthus* species) and makes an attractive feature when planted with the pink and purple colour forms of the species (see pages 280 and 284).
• PROPAGATION By fresh seed, or division in autumn.

☀ ◊
❋ ❋ ❋

**HEIGHT**
45cm (18in)

**SPREAD**
45cm (18in)

| Commelinaceae | |
| --- | --- |

## TRADESCANTIA FLUMINENSIS 'Aurea' ♔

**Habit** Vigorous, trailing, with rooting stems.
**Flowers** Tiny, 3-petalled, produced intermittently.
**Leaves** Evergreen, broadly oval to lance-shaped.
Green with irregular, creamy-white stripes.
• NATIVE HABITAT Garden origin.
• CULTIVATION Grow as a house or conservatory
plant in cool climates. Cut straggly stems in spring.
• PROPAGATION By tip cuttings in spring, summer
or autumn.
• OTHER NAMES T. fluminensis 'Variegata'.
T. albiflora 'Variegata'.

☼ ◊

Min. 15°C
(59°F)

**HEIGHT**
30cm (12in)

**SPREAD**
indefinite

| Acanthaceae | SILVER-NET LEAF |
| --- | --- |

## FITTONIA VERSCHAFFELTII ♔
## var. ARGYRONEURA

**Habit** Creeping, stem-rooting. **Flowers** Small, in
spikes, produced occasionally, but best removed as
they appear. White. **Leaves** Evergreen, oval to
elliptic. Emerald green, net-veined with white.
• NATIVE HABITAT Tropical Peru.
• CULTIVATION Grow as a house or conservatory
plant in cool climates. Needs high humidity.
Water freely during growth; less in winter.
• PROPAGATION Division or stem cuttings in summer.
• OTHER NAMES F. argyroneura.

☼ ♦

Min. 15°C
(59°F)

**HEIGHT**
15cm (6in)

**SPREAD**
indefinite

| Piperaceae | EMERALD-RIPPLE PEPPER |
| --- | --- |

## PEPEROMIA CAPERATA

**Habit** Bushy, upright. **Flowers** Minute, densely
clustered in upright spikes, produced irregularly.
Creamy-white. **Leaves** Evergreen, heart-shaped,
with pink leaf stalks, sunken veins and a wrinkled
surface. Dark green.
• NATIVE HABITAT Origin uncertain, probably Brazil.
• CULTIVATION Grow as a house or conservatory
plant in cool climates. Best in peaty soil or potting
compost. Water moderately, less in winter.
• PROPAGATION By division, seed, or leaf or stem
cuttings in spring or summer.

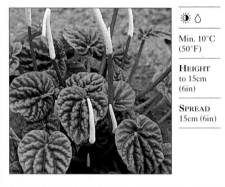

◑ ◊

Min. 10°C
(50°F)

**HEIGHT**
to 15cm
(6in)

**SPREAD**
15cm (6in)

| Anthericaceae/Liliaceae | SPIDER PLANT |
| --- | --- |

## CHLOROPHYTUM COMOSUM 'Vittatum' ♔

**Habit** Tufted, rosette-forming, forming plantlets
at the nodes of stems. **Flowers** Tiny, star-shaped,
borne intermittently on slender, white stems. White.
**Leaves** Evergreen, long, narrow, lance-shaped.
Green with a central white stripe.
• NATIVE HABITAT Garden origin.
• CULTIVATION Grow as a house or conservatory
plant in cool climates. Site in bright, indirect light.
Water freely when in growth, otherwise sparingly.
• PROPAGATION Divide, or pot up young plantlets
at any time except during winter.

◑ ◊

Min. 5°C
(41°F)

**HEIGHT**
30cm (12in)

**SPREAD**
30cm (12in)

| Convallariaceae/ Liliaceae | |
|---|---|

## ASPIDISTRA ELATIOR 'Variegata' ♟

**Habit** Clump-forming, rhizomatous. **Flowers** Small, inconspicuous, usually borne in late winter at soil level. Green or purplish. **Leaves** Evergreen, oval to lance-shaped, on long stalks, glossy. Dark green, with irregular, longitudinal, creamy stripes.
• NATIVE HABITAT Garden origin.
• CULTIVATION Grow as a house or conservatory plant in cool climates. Tolerant of a wide range of growing conditions but best in fertile, well-drained soil in full shade. Full sun will scorch the foliage.
• PROPAGATION By division in spring.

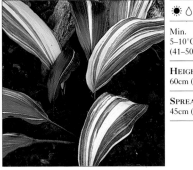

☀ ◊

Min.
5–10°C
(41–50°F)

HEIGHT
60cm (24in)

SPREAD
45cm (18in)

| Ranunculaceae | CHRISTMAS ROSE |
|---|---|

## HELLEBORUS NIGER ♟

**Habit** Clump-forming. **Flowers** Nodding, cup-shaped, borne singly or in clusters of 2–3, in winter and early spring. White. **Leaves** Evergreen (deciduous in cold winters) divided into 7–9 segments, toothed at the tip. Dark green.
• NATIVE HABITAT Mountain woodland, open grassland, C. Europe (Alps).
• CULTIVATION Grow in deep, fertile, moist but well-drained, preferably alkaline soil, in sun or semi-shade, with shelter from cold wind.
• PROPAGATION Fresh seed, or division in autumn.

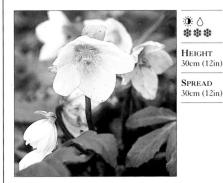

☀ ◊
❋ ❋ ❋

HEIGHT
30cm (12in)

SPREAD
30cm (12in)

| Ranunculaceae | |
|---|---|

## HELLEBORUS NIGER 'Potter's Wheel'

**Habit** Clump-forming. **Flowers** Nodding, cup-shaped, rounded, borne singly or in clusters of 2–3, in winter and early spring. White, larger than the species and with a distinct green eye. **Leaves** Evergreen (deciduous in cold winters) divided into 7–9 segments. Dark green.
• NATIVE HABITAT Garden origin.
• CULTIVATION Grow in deep, fertile, moist but well-drained soil, preferably alkaline, with shelter from cold wind.
• PROPAGATION By division in autumn.

☀ ◊
❋ ❋ ❋

HEIGHT
30cm (12in)

SPREAD
30cm (12in)

| Ranunculaceae | |
|---|---|

## HELLEBORUS × STERNII 'Boughton Beauty'

**Habit** Clump-forming, compact. **Flowers** Nodding, cup-shaped, borne in terminal clusters, in winter and early spring. Pale lime-green, tinged rose-pink. **Leaves** Evergreen (deciduous in cold winters) divided into segments. Dark greyish-green often veined grey or silver and pink-tinted.
• NATIVE HABITAT Garden origin.
• CULTIVATION Grow in deep, moist, well-drained soil, preferably alkaline, with shelter from cold wind
• PROPAGATION By division in autumn.

☀ ◊
❋ ❋

HEIGHT
45cm (18in)

SPREAD
45cm (18in)

Poaceae/Graminae

## *OPLISMENUS AFRICANUS* 'Variegatus'

**Habit** Creeping, stem-rooting grass.
**Flowers** Inconspicuous, borne intermittently.
**Leaves** Evergreen, narrowly lance-shaped to oval, wavy-margined. Green, striped white and often tinted pink.
• NATIVE HABITAT Garden origin. The species originates in shady tropical forests.
• CULTIVATION Grow as a house or conservatory plant in cool climates. Does best in fertile, moist but well-drained soil, in bright, indirect light or part-shade. Water pot-grown plants freely when in full growth and apply a balanced liquid fertilizer once a month; keep drier in winter. In frost-prone areas its trailing habit makes it especially suitable for hanging baskets. It is also useful for underplanting in a conservatory border. In warmer regions, use in a mixed or herbaceous border, or site where it can trail over terrace walls or similar.
• PROPAGATION By division of rooted stems in spring.
• OTHER NAMES *O. hirtellus* 'Variegatus'.

Min. 15°C
(60°F)

**HEIGHT**
20cm (8in)
or more

**SPREAD**
indefinite

| Ranunculaceae | |
| --- | --- |

### *HELLEBORUS × STERNII*

*Habit* Clump-forming. *Flowers* Nodding, cup-shaped, borne in terminal clusters, in winter and early spring. Pale green, tinged pink or purple-brown. *Leaves* Evergreen (deciduous in cold winters) divided into segments. Dark greyish-green often veined grey or silver.
• NATIVE HABITAT Garden origin.
• CULTIVATION Grow in deep, fertile, moist but well-drained, preferably alkaline soil, in sun or semi-shade. Provide shelter from cold wind.
• PROPAGATION By division in autumn.

☀ ◌
❄ ❄

HEIGHT
45cm (18in)

SPREAD
45cm (18in)

| Ranunculaceae | LENTEN ROSE |
| --- | --- |

### *HELLEBORUS ORIENTALIS* subsp. *GUTTATUS*

*Habit* Clump-forming. *Flowers* Nodding, cup-shaped, borne in clusters of 1–4 in late winter and early spring. White or cream, spotted red-purple. *Leaves* Evergreen (deciduous in cold winters) divided into 7–10 segments. Light to dark green.
• NATIVE HABITAT Garden origin.
• CULTIVATION Grow in fertile, heavy, moist but well-drained soil, in sun or semi-shade. Provide shelter from cold wind. Good for woodland gardens.
• PROPAGATION By division in autumn.

☀ ◌
❄ ❄ ❄

HEIGHT
45cm (18in)

SPREAD
45cm (18in)

| Ranunculaceae | LENTEN ROSE |
| --- | --- |

### *HELLEBORUS ORIENTALIS* pink

*Habit* Clump-forming. *Flowers* Nodding, cup-shaped, borne in clusters of 1–4 in late winter and early spring. Pink, sometimes with darker spots. *Leaves* Evergreen (deciduous in cold winters) divided into 7–10 segments. Green.
• NATIVE HABITAT Scrub, woodland edge, from N.E. Greece, N. and N.E. Turkey to the Caucasus.
• CULTIVATION Grow in fertile, heavy, moist but well-drained soil, in sun or semi-shade, with shelter from cold wind. Good for woodland gardens.
• PROPAGATION Fresh seed, or division in autumn.

☀ ◌
❄ ❄ ❄

HEIGHT
45cm (18in)

SPREAD
45cm (18in)

| Gesneriaceae | |
| --- | --- |

### *STREPTOCARPUS* 'Nicola'

*Habit* Upright, rosette-forming. *Flowers* Small, semi-double, funnel-shaped, borne intermittently in small, long-stalked clusters. Deep rose-pink. *Leaves* Evergreen, fleshy, strap-shaped, wrinkled. Dark green.
• NATIVE HABITAT Garden origin.
• CULTIVATION Grow as a house or conservatory plant in cool climates. Needs high humidity. Water freely when in growth; avoid wetting leaves.
• PROPAGATION By division after flowering, or by leaf cuttings in spring or summer.

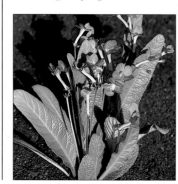

☀ ◌

Min.
10–15°C
(50–59°F)

HEIGHT
25cm (10in)

SPREAD
50cm (20in)

| Commelinaceae | SILVER INCH PLANT |
|---|---|

## TRADESCANTIA ZEBRINA ♀

**Habit** Trailing, with rooting stems. **Flowers** Tiny, 3-petalled, borne intermittently. Pink or violet-blue. **Leaves** Evergreen, oval-oblong, fleshy. Purple-tinted, bluish-green, with 2 broad silvery bands.
• NATIVE HABITAT Tropical Mexico.
• CULTIVATION Grow as a house or conservatory plant in cool climates. Feed and water freely when in growth; avoid wetting the foliage.
• PROPAGATION By tip cuttings in spring, summer, or autumn.
• OTHER NAMES T. pendula, T. zebrina pendula.

☼ ◊

Min. 15°C
(59°F)

HEIGHT
15cm (6in)

SPREAD
indefinite

| Gesneriaceae | FLAME VIOLET |
|---|---|

## EPISCIA CUPREATA

**Habit** Prostrate, creeping, stoloniferous. **Flowers** Small, tubular, borne intermittently. Scarlet with a yellow throat. **Leaves** Evergreen, small, thick, downy and wrinkled. Purple-tinted with silver veins.
• NATIVE HABITAT Colombia, Venezuela, Brazil.
• CULTIVATION In cool climates, grow as a house or conservatory plant in moist, well-drained soil or compost. Site in bright, indirect light, with shade from summer sun. Water freely when in full growth.
• PROPAGATION By division, by removal of rooted stems, or by stem cuttings in summer.

☼ ◊

Min. 15°C
(59°F)

HEIGHT
10cm (4in)

SPREAD
indefinite

| Asteraceae/Compositae | BARBERTON DAISY |
|---|---|

## GERBERA JAMESONII

**Habit** Upright. **Flowers** Large, long-stemmed, daisy-like, borne from summer to winter. Variably coloured from white, yellow and orange, to dark red. **Leaves** Evergreen, oblong-spoon-shaped, jaggedly divided. Dark green.
• NATIVE HABITAT South Africa, Swaziland.
• CULTIVATION Grow in sandy soil or compost in sun. Protect from frost in well-ventilated conditions. Good for cool conservatories. Cut flowers last well.
• PROPAGATION By seed in autumn or spring, or by heel cuttings from sideshoots in summer.

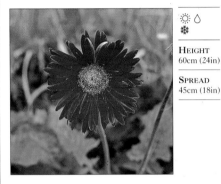

☼ ◊
❄

HEIGHT
60cm (24in)

SPREAD
45cm (18in)

| Saxifragaceae | |
|---|---|

## TELLIMA GRANDIFLORA 'Rubra'

**Habit** Spreading, clump-forming. **Flowers** Small, bell-shaped, in erect clusters, in late spring. Greenish-white, with pink-fringed petals. **Leaves** Semi-evergreen, hairy, 3- to 7-lobed, heart-shaped. Dark green, flushed red-purple.
• NATIVE HABITAT Species occurs in coniferous woods of W. North America.
• CULTIVATION Grow in moist but well-drained soil in shade or semi-shade.
• PROPAGATION By division at any time.
• OTHER NAMES T. grandiflora 'Purpurea'.

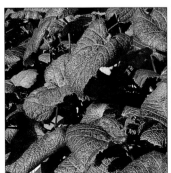

☼ ◊
❄ ❄ ❄

HEIGHT
60cm (24in)

SPREAD
60cm (24in)

# AFRICAN VIOLETS

African violet is the common name for the genus *Saintpaulia*. These small, evergreen, rosette-forming perennials may be grown as summer bedding in warm, humid climates, or as attractive, indoor pot plants.

Grow in loamless potting compost in bright, indirect light at a temperature of 13–15°C (55–59°F). Keep the compost moist but not waterlogged and avoid splashing the foliage when watering. In summer, feed with dilute liquid fertilizer every 10 days. Provide high humidity by standing the plant on a saucer of pebbles, topped up with soft water. Repot every other year in spring.

Propagate by leaf cuttings in summer and root in a mix of equal parts peat and sand at 18–21°C (64–70°F). Sow seed in early spring at 18–21°C (64–70°F).

## S 'Garden News'
**Habit** Stemless, rosette-forming.
**Flowers** Fully double, with frilled petals, borne in clusters of 2–8, throughout the year. Pure white.
**Leaves** Evergreen, almost round, to 8cm (3in) long, slightly scalloped and finely hairy. Bright green.
• HEIGHT to 10cm (4in).
• SPREAD to 25cm (10in).

*S.* '**Garden News**'

☀ ◊
Min. 15°C (59°F)

## S. 'Fancy Pants'
**Habit** Stemless, rosette-forming.
**Flowers** Single, produced year-round, in clusters of 2–8. Pure white petals with red-frilled edges, surrounding a yellow eye.
**Leaves** Evergreen, almost round, to 8cm (3in). long, slightly scalloped and finely hairy. Mid-green.
• HEIGHT to 10cm (4in).
• SPREAD to 25cm (10in).

*S.* '**Fancy Pants**'

☀ ◊
Min. 15°C (59°F)

## S. 'Miss Pretty'
**Habit** Stemless, rosette-forming.
**Flowers** Large, single, in clusters of 2–8, all year. White, pink-frilled petals.
**Leaves** Evergreen, almost round, to 8cm (3in) long, slightly scalloped and finely hairy. Pale green.
• HEIGHT to 10cm (4in).
• SPREAD to 25cm (10in).

*S.* '**Miss Pretty**'

☀ ◊
Min. 15°C (59°F).

## S. 'Pip Squeak'
**Habit** Stemless, rosette-forming.
**Flowers** Small, to 1cm (½in) across, single, bell-shaped, 5-lobed, produced singly or in pairs, well above the foliage, throughout the year. Pale pink.
**Leaves** Evergreen, oval, 1–2cm (½–¾in) long, unscalloped, deep green.
• HEIGHT 8cm (3in).
• SPREAD 10cm (4in).

*S.* '**Pip Squeak**'

☀ ◊
Min. 15°C (59°F)

## S. 'Rococo Pink'
**Habit** Stemless, rosette-forming.
**Flowers** Fully double, in clusters of 2–8, throughout the year. Iridescent pink.
**Leaves** Evergreen, almost round, to 8cm (3in) long, slightly scalloped and finely hairy. Dark green, edged with emerald green with a small, pale area at base of leaf blade.
• HEIGHT to 10cm (4in).
• SPREAD to 25cm (10in).

*S.* '**Rococo Pink**'

☀ ◊
Min. 15°C (59°F)

### . 'Colorado'
*abit* Stemless,
sette-forming.
*lowers* Single, borne
 clusters of 2–8,
roughout the year.
rilled, magenta petals
ith a yellow eye.
*eaves* Evergreen,
most round, to 8cm
in) long, slightly
alloped and finely
airy. Dark green.
HEIGHT to 10cm (4in).
SPREAD to 25cm
0in).

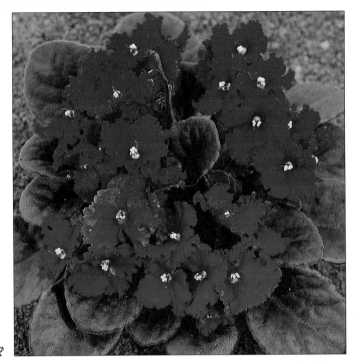

. 'Colorado'

☀ ◑
1in.15°C (59°F) 🏆

### . 'Kristi Marie'
*Habit* Stemless,
osette-forming.
*Flowers* Semi-double,
orne in clusters of 2–8,
hroughout the year.
Dusky red petals, finely
dged with white.
*Leaves* Evergreen,
lmost round, to 8cm
3in) long, slightly
calloped and finely hairy.
Dark green.
• HEIGHT to 10cm (4in).
• SPREAD to 25cm (10in).

S. 'Kristi Marie'

☀ ◑
Min.15°C (59°F) 🏆

### S. 'Bright Eyes'
*Habit* Stemless,
rosette-forming.
*Flowers* Single, borne
in clusters of 2–8,
throughout the year.
Deep violet-blue
with a yellow eye.
*Leaves* Evergreen,
almost round, to 8cm
(3in) long, slightly
scalloped and finely
hairy. Dark green.
• HEIGHT to 10cm (4in).
• SPREAD to 25cm (10in).

S. 'Bright Eyes'

☀ ◑
Min.15°C (59°F) 🏆

### S. 'Porcelain'
*Habit* Stemless,
osette-forming.
*Flowers* Semi-double,
orne in clusters of 2–8,
he year.
White petals, edged with
ich purple-blue.
*Leaves* Evergreen,
lmost round, to 8cm
3in). long, slightly
calloped and finely
airy. Dark green.
• HEIGHT to 10cm (4in).
• SPREAD to 25cm (10in).

S. 'Porcelain'

☀ ◑
Min.15°C (59°F).

### S. 'Delft'
*Habit* Stemless,
rosette-forming.
*Flowers* Semi-double,
borne in clusters of 2–8,
throughout the year.
Slightly frilled, violet-blue
petals, with a yellow eye.
*Leaves* Evergreen,
almost round, to 8cm
(3in). long, slightly
scalloped and finely hairy.
Dark green.
• HEIGHT to 10cm (4in).
• SPREAD to 25cm (10in).

S. 'Delft'

☀ ◑
Min.15°C (59°F) 🏆

| Ranunculaceae | LENTEN ROSE |
|---|---|

## *HELLEBORUS ORIENTALIS* purple

*Habit* Clump-forming. *Flowers* Nodding, cup-shaped, borne in clusters of 1–4 in late winter and early spring. Purple, sometimes with darker spots. *Leaves* Evergreen (deciduous in cold winters) divided into 7–10 segments. Green.
• NATIVE HABITAT Scrub, or woodland edge, from N.E. Greece, N. and N.E. Turkey to the Caucasus.
• CULTIVATION Grow in fertile, heavy, moist but well-drained soil, in sun or semi-shade. Provide shelter from cold wind. Good for woodland gardens.
• PROPAGATION Fresh seed, or division in autumn.

☀ ◐
❋ ❋ ❋

HEIGHT
45cm (18in)

SPREAD
45cm (18in)

| Acanthaceae | MOSAIC PLANT, PAINTED NET-LEAF |
|---|---|

## *FITTONIA VERSCHAFFELTII*

*Habit* Creeping, stem-rooting. *Flowers* Small, in 4-angled spikes produced occasionally. White, with overlapping green bracts. Remove flowers as they appear. *Leaves* Evergreen, oval to elliptic, olive-green, net-veined with ruby red or scarlet.
• NATIVE HABITAT Tropical Peru.
• CULTIVATION Grow as a house or conservatory plant in cool climates. Needs high humidity. Water freely when in full growth; less in winter. Cut back straggly growth in spring.
• PROPAGATION Division or stem cuttings in summer

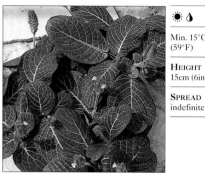

☀ ◐

Min. 15°C
(59°F)

HEIGHT
15cm (6in)

SPREAD
indefinite

| Agavaceae/Phormiaceae | |
|---|---|

## *PHORMIUM TENAX* 'Bronze Baby'

*Habit* Upright, clump-forming, dwarf. *Flowers* Tubular, in branched heads, borne on red-purple stems, occasionally in summer. Dull dark red. *Leaves* Evergreen, stiff, sword-shaped, in basal clumps. Bronze-tinted, red-purple.
• NATIVE HABITAT Garden origin.
• CULTIVATION Grow in deep, fertile, humus-rich soil, in a warm, sunny, sheltered site. Excellent for coastal gardens. Suitable for raised beds, gravel plantings and the front of a border.
• PROPAGATION By division in spring.

☀ ◐
❋ ❋

HEIGHT
45–60cm
(18–24in)

SPREAD
45–60cm
(18–24in)

| Convallariaceae/ Liliaceae | |
|---|---|

## *OPHIOPOGON PLANISCAPUS* 'Nigrescens'

*Habit* Spreading, clump-forming. *Flowers* Small, tubular, in upright clusters, in summer. White or lilac. *Fruits* Berry-like, small. Dull blue. *Leaves* Evergreen, linear, grass-like. Purple-black.
• NATIVE HABITAT Garden origin; species originates in Japanese woodlands.
• CULTIVATION Grow in humus-rich, well-drained soil, in sun or semi-shade. Good ground cover; can be used as a low-maintenance grass substitute.
• PROPAGATION By division in spring.

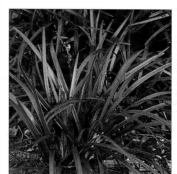

☀ ◐
❋ ❋ ❋

HEIGHT
23cm (9in)

SPREAD
30cm (12in
or more

| Commelinaceae | |
|---|---|

## TRADESCANTIA PALLIDA 'Purple Heart' ♀

**Habit** Trailing, with rooting stems. **Flowers** Tiny, 3-petalled, borne singly at the stem tips in summer. Pink or pink-and-white. **Leaves** Evergreen, elliptic to lance-shaped, slightly fleshy. Dark purple.
NATIVE HABITAT Tropical E. Mexico.
CULTIVATION In cool climates, grow as a house or conservatory plant. Grow in well-drained compost or soil in bright, indirect light. Water freely in growth.
PROPAGATION By tip cuttings in spring, summer, or autumn.
OTHER NAMES *Setcreasea purpurea.*

☼ ◊

Min. 15°C
(59°F)

**HEIGHT**
15cm (6in)

**SPREAD**
indefinite

| Commelinaceae | |
|---|---|

## TRADESCANTIA SILLAMONTANA ♀

**Habit** Upright. **Flowers** Tiny, 3-petalled, borne at the stem tips in summer. Bright purplish-pink. **Leaves** Evergreen, elliptic-oval, stem-clasping. Green, flushed purple-red, white-hairy.
• NATIVE HABITAT Tropical N.E. Mexico.
• CULTIVATION Grow as a house or conservatory plant in cool climates. Feed and water freely when in growth; avoid wetting leaves.
• PROPAGATION By tip cuttings in spring, summer, or autumn.

☼ ◊

Min.
10–15°C
(50–59°F)

**HEIGHT**
30cm (12in)

**SPREAD**
30cm (12in)

| Lamiaceae/Labiatae | |
|---|---|

## AJUGA REPTANS 'Atropurpurea'

**Habit** Carpet-forming, stoloniferous. **Flowers** Small, 2-lipped, tubular, in short, whorled spikes in spring. Blue. **Leaves** Evergreen, oblong to spoon-shaped, in rosettes, glossy. Dark bronze-purple.
• NATIVE HABITAT Garden origin.
• CULTIVATION Tolerates sun or shade and most soils, but grows best in fertile, moist but well-drained soil. Invaluable for border edging and as ground cover beneath shrubs and robust perennials. Spreads freely in good, moist soils.
• PROPAGATION By division in spring.

☼ ◊
❄ ❄ ❄

**HEIGHT**
15cm (6in)

**SPREAD**
1m (3ft)

| Urticaceae | WATERMELON BEGONIA |
|---|---|

## PELLIONIA REPENS ♀

**Habit** Creeping, with rooting stems. **Flowers**
Insignificant. **Leaves** Evergreen, broadly oval,
scalloped. Soft grey green at the centre, edged
with purplish-brown.
• NATIVE HABITAT Vietnam to Malaysia and Burma.
• CULTIVATION Grow as a house or conservatory
plant in cool climates. Needs a humid atmosphere.
• PROPAGATION Separate rooted stems or take
stem cuttings in spring or summer.
• OTHER NAMES *P. daveauana, Elatostema
daveauana, E. repens.*

☼ ◐

Min. 15°C
(59°F)

HEIGHT
10cm (4in)

SPREAD
indefinite

| Ranunculaceae | |
|---|---|

## HELLEBORUS TORQUATUS 'Dido'

**Habit** Clump-forming. **Flowers** Nodding or held
horizontally, double, cup-shaped, borne in clusters
in late winter and early spring. Purple outside, lime-
green within. **Leaves** Deciduous, emerging with
or after the flowers, divided into 10–30 narrow,
segments. Dark green.
• NATIVE HABITAT Garden origin.
• CULTIVATION Grow in fertile, heavy, moist but
well-drained soil, in sun or semi-shade, in a site with
shelter from cold wind. Good for woodland gardens.
• PROPAGATION By division in autumn.

☼ ◐
✿ ✿ ✿

HEIGHT
40–45cm
(16–18in)

SPREAD
45cm (18in)

| Scrophulariaceae | MEXICAN FOXGLOVE, MEXICAN VIOLET |
|---|---|

## TETRANEMA ROSEUM

**Habit** Rosette-forming. **Flowers** Nodding,
trumpet-shaped, shallowly lobed, mostly in summ
but intermittently throughout the year. Lilac to
mauve with darker markings. **Leaves** Evergreen,
stalkless, broadly oval, slightly leathery. Dark gree
• NATIVE HABITAT Damp, shady habitats in Mexic
• CULTIVATION Grow as a house or conservatory
plant in cool climates. Needs a humid, draught-fre
atmosphere. Take care not to overwater.
• PROPAGATION By division or seed in spring.
• OTHER NAMES *T. mexicanum.*

☼ ◐

Min. 13°C
(55°F)

HEIGHT
to 20cm
(8in)

SPREAD
30cm (12ir

| Lamiaceae/Labiatae | |
|---|---|

## AJUGA REPTANS 'Multicolor'

**Habit** Carpet-forming, stoloniferous. **Flowers**
Small, 2-lipped, tubular, in short, whorled spikes ir
spring. Blue. **Leaves** Evergreen, spoon-shaped, in
basal rosettes. Dark green, marked cream and pink
• NATIVE HABITAT Garden origin.
• CULTIVATION Tolerates sun or shade and most
soil types. Good for border edging and as ground
cover beneath shrubs and robust perennials.
• PROPAGATION By division in spring.
• OTHER NAMES *A. reptans* 'Rainbow', *A. reptans*
'Tricolor'

☼ ◐
✿ ✿ ✿

HEIGHT
12cm (5in)

SPREAD
45cm (18in

| Gesneriaceae | |
|---|---|

## *STREPTOCARPUS* 'Constant Nymph'

*Habit* Upright, rosette-forming. *Flowers* Small, funnel-shaped, borne intermittently in small clusters. Purple-blue with dark veins and yellow throats. *Leaves* Evergreen, fleshy, strap-shaped, wrinkled. Dark green.
• NATIVE HABITAT Garden origin.
• CULTIVATION Grow as a house or conservatory plant in cool climates. Needs high humidity. Water freely during growth; avoid wetting leaves.
• PROPAGATION By division after flowering, or by leaf cuttings in spring or summer.

Min.
10–15°C
(50–59°F)

HEIGHT
25cm (10in)

SPREAD
50cm (20in)

| Commelinaceae | PUSSY EARS |
|---|---|

## *CYANOTIS SOMALIENSIS*

*Habit* Creeping, with rooting shoots. *Flowers* Small, stemless, 3-petalled, in the leaf axils, in winter and spring. Purplish-blue. *Leaves* Evergreen, fleshy, narrowly oblong, with round-pointed tips, glossy, densely hairy, and fringed with long hairs beneath. Dark green.
• NATIVE HABITAT Uncertain, probably Somalia.
• CULTIVATION Grow as a house or conservatory plant in cool climates, in humus-rich, well-drained potting compost. Water moderately, less in winter.
• PROPAGATION Tip cuttings from spring to autumn.

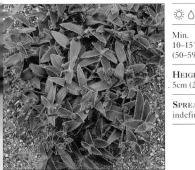

Min.
10–15°C
(50–59°F)

HEIGHT
5cm (2in)

SPREAD
indefinite

| Marantaceae | HERRINGBONE PLANT |
|---|---|

## *MARANTA LEUCONEURA* var. *ERYTHRONEURA*

*Habit* Low-growing, rhizomatous. *Flowers* Small, 3-petalled, in an upright spike, year-round. White or violet. *Leaves* Evergreen, oblong, velvety. Black-green, with red veins and lime-green midrib zone.
• NATIVE HABITAT Garden origin.
• CULTIVATION Grow as a house or conservatory plant in cool climates. Needs constant humidity and a draught-free position. Good for a terrarium.
• PROPAGATION By division in spring or summer, or stem cuttings in summer.

Min. 15°C
(59°F)

HEIGHT
to 30cm
(12in)

SPREAD
to 30cm
(12in)

| Dracaenaceae | |
|---|---|

## *SANSEVIERIA TRIFASCIATA* 'Hahnii'

*Habit* Upright, stemless, rosette-forming and rhizomatous. *Flowers* Small, but seldom produced. Pale green. *Leaves* Evergreen, stiff, erect, broadly lance-shaped, with a pointed tip. Banded horizontally with dark green, pale green and white.
• NATIVE HABITAT Garden origin.
• CULTIVATION Grow as a house or conservatory plant in cool climates, in any moderately fertile potting compost. Water moderately when in growth. A tough and adaptable plant.
• PROPAGATION By division in summer.

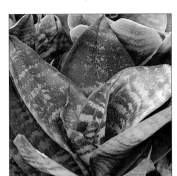

Min.
10–15°C
(50–59°F)

HEIGHT
15–30cm
(6–12in)

SPREAD
10cm (4in)

| Marantaceae | CATHEDRAL WINDOWS, PEACOCK PLANT |
|---|---|

## CALATHEA MAKOYANA

**Habit** Clump-forming. **Flowers** Tubular, in short, dense spikes, produced intermittently. White with purple lobes. **Leaves** Evergreen, oval. Pale green, with oblong, dark green blotches and creamy-white feathering above, patterned red-purple beneath.
• NATIVE HABITAT Damp forests, E. Brazil.
• CULTIVATION Grow as a house or conservatory plant in cool climates. Keep just moist with soft water in winter. Needs high humidity, a constant temperature and draught-free conditions.
• PROPAGATION By division in spring.

Min. 15°C (59°F)

**HEIGHT** to 60cm (2ft)

**SPREAD** to 1.2m (4ft)

| Araceae | |
|---|---|

## AGLAONEMA PICTUM

**Habit** Upright, tufted. **Flowers** Creamy-white spathes, in summer. **Leaves** Evergreen, narrowly elliptic, to 15cm (6in) long. Lustrous, dark bluish-green, irregularly marked grey-green or grey-white.
• NATIVE HABITAT Sumatra.
• CULTIVATION Grow as a house or conservatory plant in cool climates. Grow in moist but well-drained soil, in bright, indirect light or part-shade. Water moderately and maintain humidity when in growth; keep drier in winter.
• PROPAGATION Division or stem cuttings in summer.

Min. 15°C (59°F)

**HEIGHT** to 60cm (24in)

**SPREAD** to 60cm (24in)

| Araceae | |
|---|---|

## AGLAONEMA COMMUTATUM 'Silver King'

**Habit** Upright, tufted. **Flowers** Greenish-white spathes, in summer. **Leaves** Evergreen, lance-shaped, to 30cm (12in) long. Mid-green, irregularly marked with dark green and pale silvery-green.
• NATIVE HABITAT Garden origin.
• CULTIVATION Grow as a house or conservatory plant in cool climates. Site in moist but well-drained soil. Needs moderate humidity. Keep moist in winter, but allow to become drier in winter.
• PROPAGATION By division or stem cuttings in summer.

Min. 15°C (59°F)

**HEIGHT** 45cm (18in)

**SPREAD** 45cm (18in)

| Marantaceae | RABBIT TRACKS |
|---|---|

## MARANTA LEUCONEURA var. KERCHOVEANA

**Habit** Low-growing, rhizomatous. **Flowers** Small, 3-petalled, borne intermittently, in an upright spike. White or mauve. **Leaves** Evergreen, oblong. Grey-green, with dark brown blotches fading with age.
• NATIVE HABITAT Damp, tropical forests, Brazil.
• CULTIVATION Grow as a house or conservatory plant in cool climates. Needs constant high humidity. Good for a terrarium.
• PROPAGATION By division in spring or summer, or stem cuttings in summer.

Min. 15°C (59°F)

**HEIGHT** to 30cm (12in)

**SPREAD** to 30cm (12in)

| Welwitschiaceae | |
|---|---|

## *WELWITSCHIA MIRABILIS*

**Habit** Long-lived, deep-rooting. **Flowers** Small, cone-like, seldom produced. Reddish-brown.
**Leaves** Evergreen; the 2 strap-shaped leaves continuously grow to 2.5m (8ft) or more, splitting and twisting at the tips with age. Pale grey-green.
• NATIVE HABITAT Coastal desert, S.W. Africa.
• CULTIVATION Grow as a house or conservatory plant in cool climates in a clay drainpipe. Difficult to grow.
• PROPAGATION By seed when ripe.
• OTHER NAMES *W. bainesii.*

☼ ◊
Min. 10°C
(50°F)
**HEIGHT**
30cm (12in)
or more
**SPREAD**
indefinite

| Lamiaceae/Labiatae | |
|---|---|

## *STACHYS BYZANTINA* 'Silver Carpet'

**Habit** Mat-forming. **Flowers** Seldom produced. **Leaves** Evergreen, thick, oblong to spoon-shaped or elliptic, mainly in basal rosettes. Densely white-woolly.
• NATIVE HABITAT Garden origin.
• CULTIVATION Grow in well-drained soil, preferably in a hot, sunny site. Tolerates poor soil. Good for ground cover and border edging and is especially useful in a silver border or for edging in a herb garden.
• PROPAGATION By division in spring.

☼ ◊
❋❋❋
**HEIGHT**
15cm (6in)
**SPREAD**
60cm (2ft)

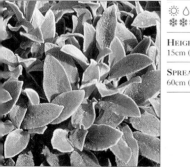

| Lamiaceae/Labiatae | BUNNIES' EARS, LAMB'S TONGUE |
|---|---|

## *STACHYS BYZANTINA*

**Habit** Mat-forming. **Flowers** Small, tubular, 2-lipped, in white-woolly, upright spikes, in summer. Pink. **Leaves** Evergreen, thick, oblong to spoon-shaped or elliptic, mainly in basal rosettes. Densely white-woolly.
• NATIVE HABITAT Rocky hills, Caucasus to Iran.
• CULTIVATION Grow in well-drained soil, ideally in a hot, sunny site. Good for ground cover and border edging, especially in a silver border.
• PROPAGATION By seed or division in spring.
• OTHER NAMES *S. lanata, S. olympica.*

☼ ◊
❋❋❋
**HEIGHT**
30–38cm
(12–15in)
**SPREAD**
60cm (2ft)

| Convallariaceae/ Liliaceae | |
|---|---|

## *OPHIOPOGON JAPONICUS*

**Habit** Spreading, clump-forming, stoloniferous. **Flowers** Small, tubular, in spike-like heads, in summer. Lilac. **Fruits** Berry-like, small. Blue. **Leaves** Evergreen, narrow-linear, grass-like, glossy. Dark green.
• NATIVE HABITAT Damp habitats, Japan.
• CULTIVATION Grow in fertile, humus-rich, moist but well-drained soil, in sun or light shade. Good for ground cover; may also be grown in the edge of a pond, but it will not flower.
• PROPAGATION By division in spring.

☼ ◊
❋❋❋
**HEIGHT**
30cm (12in)
**SPREAD**
indefinite

| Ranunculaceae | |
|---|---|

## *HELLEBORUS MULTIFIDUS*
## subsp. *HERCEGOVINUS*

*Habit* Clump-forming. *Flowers* Small, scented, nodding, cup-shaped, borne in clusters in winter and early spring. Green. *Leaves* Deciduous, very finely divided into 45–70 linear, leathery leaflets, hairy beneath. Green, tinted dull brown.
• NATIVE HABITAT Woods and scrub on the hillsides of the S. Balkans.
• CULTIVATION Grow in fertile, moist, well-drained soil, in a warm site sheltered from wind.
• PROPAGATION Fresh seed, or division in autumn.

☀ ◐
❄ ❄

HEIGHT
to 50cm
(20in)

SPREAD
30cm (12in)

| Ranunculaceae | |
|---|---|

## *HELLEBORUS ARGUTIFOLIUS* ♈

*Habit* Clump-forming. *Flowers* Nodding, cup-shaped, borne in large clusters, in winter and early spring. Pale green. *Leaves* Evergreen, divided into 3 elliptic, sharply toothed leaflets. Dark green.
• NATIVE HABITAT Maquis scrub in Corsica and Sardinia.
• CULTIVATION Grow in fertile, well-drained soil, in sun, with shelter from cold wind. May be short-lived but usually self-seeds.
• PROPAGATION Fresh seed, or division in autumn.
• OTHER NAMES *H. corsicus, H. lividus* subsp. *corsicus.*

☀ ◐
❄ ❄

HEIGHT
60cm (24in)
or more

SPREAD
45cm (18in)

| Urticaceae | BABYS TEARS, MIND-YOUR-OWN-BUSINESS |
|---|---|

## *SOLEIROLIA SOLEIROLII*

*Habit* Mat-forming, often vigorously invasive. *Flowers* Tiny, seldom produced. Yellow-white. *Leaves* Evergreen, small, thin, rounded, brilliant green, on delicate, translucent, rooting stems.
• NATIVE HABITAT Asia to Malaysia.
• CULTIVATION Grow in moist, well-drained soil in sun or part-shade. Good for ground cover beneath other, more robust plants, in paving crevices and very attractive grown indoors in pots.
• PROPAGATION Division from spring to summer.
• OTHER NAMES *Helxine soleirolii.*

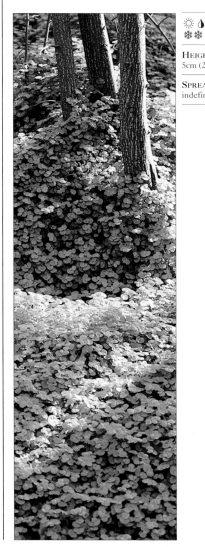

☀ ◐
❄ ❄

HEIGHT
5cm (2in)

SPREAD
indefinite

| Lamiaceae/Labiatae | |
|---|---|

## *BALLOTA PSEUDODICTAMNUS* 🏆

*Habit* Mound-forming, sub-shrubby. *Flowers* Small, tubular, 2-lipped, in summer. White or pale pink, borne within curious, pale green calyces. *Leaves* Evergreen, oval, woolly. Grey-green.
• NATIVE HABITAT Dry hills in the Greek Islands.
• CULTIVATION Grow in well-drained soil in a warm, sunny, sheltered site. Good for the front of a silver-leaved border. Cut back in spring before new growth begins.
• PROPAGATION By seed in spring or semi-ripe cuttings in summer.

☼ ◊
❄

HEIGHT
60cm (24in)

SPREAD
90cm (36in)

| Commelinaceae | |
|---|---|

## *CALLISIA REPENS*

*Habit* Creeping, dense, stem-rooting. *Flowers* Inconspicuous, 3-petalled, in winter, but seldom produced. White. *Leaves* Evergreen, small, rounded, slightly fleshy, heart-shaped at the base. Green above, purplish-green and sometimes banded white beneath.
• NATIVE HABITAT Texas and West Indies to Argentina.
• CULTIVATION Grow as a house or conservatory plant in cool climates. Shade from hot sun.
• PROPAGATION By tip cuttings in spring.

☼ ◊

Min. 15°C
(59°F)

HEIGHT
10cm (4in)

SPREAD
indefinite

| Droseraceae | SPOON-LEAF SUNDEW |
|---|---|

## *DROSERA SPATHULATA*

*Habit* Rosette-forming, insectivorous. *Flowers* Tiny, 5-petalled, borne in clusters of up to 15, on leafless stems, to 20cm (8in) high, in summer. White to pink. *Leaves* Evergreen, spoon-shaped. Mid-green, clothed in sensitive, glandular, red hairs.
• NATIVE HABITAT Bogs, S. Japan to E. China, south to New Zealand.
• CULTIVATION Grow as a house or conservatory plant in cool climates. Plant in a mix of peat and sphagnum moss, in sun. Keep moist with soft water.
• PROPAGATION By seed or division in spring.

☼ ◐

Min.
5–10°C
(41–50°F)

HEIGHT
8cm (3in)

SPREAD
8cm (3in)

| Piperaceae | WAX PRIVET |
|---|---|

## *PEPEROMIA GLABELLA*

*Habit* Upright or sprawling. *Flowers* Minute, insignificant, produced irregularly. *Leaves* Evergreen, softly fleshy, broadly oval, glossy. Bright green, on long red leaf stalks, on red stems.
• NATIVE HABITAT C. and S. America, West Indies.
• CULTIVATION Grow as a house or conservatory plant in cool climates. Plant in peaty soil or potting compost. Water moderately when in growth, less in winter.
• PROPAGATION By division, seed, or leaf or stem cuttings in spring or summer.

☼ ◊

Min. 10°C
(50°F)

HEIGHT
to 15cm
(6in)

SPREAD
30cm (12in)

| Ranunculaceae | GREEN HELLEBORE |
| --- | --- |

## *HELLEBORUS VIRIDIS*

**Habit** Clump-forming. **Flowers** Small, nodding, cup-shaped, borne in clusters of 2–4, in winter and early spring. Green, often blotched purple at the petal base. **Leaves** Deciduous, divided into 7–11 narrowly elliptic, toothed leaflets. Dark green.
• NATIVE HABITAT Woods, sunny banks, on limy soils, from C. France to Austria and N. Italy.
• CULTIVATION Grow in fertile, moist, well-drained, preferably alkaline soil, in semi-shade, with shelter from wind. A graceful specimen for a winter border.
• PROPAGATION Fresh seed, or division in autumn.

☼ ◊
❋❋❋

HEIGHT
30cm (12in)

SPREAD
30cm (12in)

| Piperaceae | VARIEGATED BABY RUBBER PLANT |
| --- | --- |

## *PEPEROMIA OBTUSIFOLIA* 'Variegata'

**Habit** Bushy, upright, stoloniferous. **Flowers** Minute, insignificant, produced irregularly. **Leaves** Evergreen, firm, fleshy, broadly oval. Mid-green and pale green, with irregular cream margins.
• NATIVE HABITAT Garden origin.
• CULTIVATION Grow as a house or conservatory plant in cool climates. Prefers peaty soil or compost and a bright position out of direct sunlight. Water moderately when in growth, less in winter.
• PROPAGATION By division, leaf or stem cuttings in spring or summer.

☼ ◊

Min. 10°C
(50°F)

HEIGHT
to 15cm
(6in)

SPREAD
to 15cm
(6in)

| Saxifragaceae | |
| --- | --- |

## *TOLMIEA MENZIESII* 'Taff's Gold'  ♥

**Habit** Spreading, mat-forming. **Flowers** Tiny, nodding, tubular to bell-shaped, borne in slender, upright spikes in spring. Green and chocolate brown. **Leaves** Semi-evergreen, 3-lobed, ivy-like. Pale lime-green, spotted and mottled with cream and gold.
• NATIVE HABITAT Garden origin.
• CULTIVATION Grow in moist but well-drained soil in shade or semi-shade. Good ground cover for woodland gardens. Also grown as a houseplant.
• PROPAGATION By division in spring or autumn.

☼ ◊
❋❋❋

HEIGHT
45–60cm
(18–24in)

SPREAD
30cm (12in)

| Amaranthaceae | |
| --- | --- |

## *IRESINE HERBSTII* 'Aureoreticulata'

**Habit** Bushy. **Flowers** Insignificant. White or greenish-white. **Leaves** Evergreen, oval, to 10cm (4in) long, waxy, borne on succulent red stems. Mid-green, with bright to pale yellow or red veins.
• NATIVE HABITAT Garden origin.
• CULTIVATION Grow as a house or conservatory plant in cool climates. Grow in well-drained, loam-based potting compost in bright light. Water freely when in growth, otherwise moderately. Pinch out young growing tips to encourage bushiness.
• PROPAGATION By stem cuttings in spring.

☼ ◊

Min.
10–15°C
(50–59°F)

HEIGHT
to 60cm
(24in)

SPREAD
45cm (18in)

| Droseraceae | VENUS FLYTRAP |
| --- | --- |

## DIONAEA MUSCIPULA

**Habit** Rosette-forming, insectivorous. **Flowers**
Small, 5-petalled, in clusters of 3–10, in summer.
White. **Leaves** Evergreen, 2-lobed, hinged at the
midrib, pink-flushed inside, fringed with stiff
bristles and with touch-sensitive hairs within.
• NATIVE HABITAT Bogs, N. and S. Carolina (USA).
• CULTIVATION Grow as a house or conservatory
plant in cool climates in a mix of vermiculite, peat
and sphagnum moss, in sun. Stand in a saucer filled
with soft water to a depth of about 1cm (½in).
• PROPAGATION By seed or division in spring.

Min. 5°C
(41°F)

HEIGHT
10cm (4in)

SPREAD
to 30cm
(12in)

| Dracaenaceae | |
| --- | --- |

## SANSEVIERIA TRIFASCIATA
### 'Golden Hahnii'

**Habit** Upright, stemless, rosette-forming and
rhizomatous. **Flowers** Small, seldom produced.
Pale green, **Leaves** Evergreen, stiff, erect, broadly
lance-shaped. Green, with broad yellow margins.
• NATIVE HABITAT Garden origin.
• CULTIVATION In cool climates, grow as a house
or conservatory plant in moderately fertile compost
or soil. Tolerates sun or shade. Water moderately
when in growth. A tough and adaptable plant.
• PROPAGATION By division in summer.

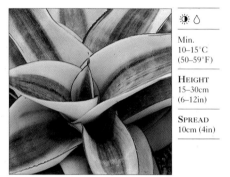

Min.
10–15°C
(50–59°F)

HEIGHT
15–30cm
(6–12in)

SPREAD
10cm (4in)

| Ranunculaceae | STINKING HELLEBORE |
| --- | --- |

## HELLEBORUS FOETIDUS

**Habit** Clump-forming. **Flowers** Small,
nodding, cup-shaped, borne in clusters of 2–4,
in winter and early spring. Green, with red petal
margins. **Leaves** Evergreen, divided into 7–10
narrow, elliptic, toothed, glossy leaflets. Very
dark green.
• NATIVE HABITAT Woods, rocky slopes, usually
on limy soils, in S.W. and Central Europe.
• CULTIVATION Grow in a sheltered site,
preferably in alkaline soil. Tolerant of dry shade.
• PROPAGATION Fresh seed, or division in autumn.

HEIGHT
45cm (18in)

SPREAD
45cm (18in)

| Gesneriaceae | |
| --- | --- |

## NAUTILOCALYX LYNCHII

**Habit** Robust, upright, bushy. **Flowers** Small,
tubular, borne in axillary clusters in summer. Pale
yellow, red-haired, purple-flecked within. **Leaves**
Evergreen, elliptic-lance-shaped, glossy, wrinkled.
Dark greenish-red above, red-tinted beneath.
• NATIVE HABITAT Tropical Colombia.
• CULTIVATION Grow as a house or conservatory
plant in cool climates. Needs high humidity.
Water moderately when in growth, less in winter.
• PROPAGATION By stem cuttings in summer or
by seed in spring.

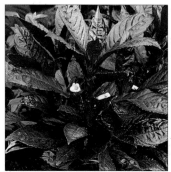

Min. 15°C
(59°F)

HEIGHT
to 60cm
(24in)

SPREAD
to 60cm
(24in)

# GRASSES, SEDGES AND RUSHES

Grasses (Gramineae), sedges (Cyperaceae) and rushes (Juncaceae) together form part of a group of generally trouble-free plants grown mainly for their foliage, which offers contrasts of form, colour and texture in borders and rock gardens. A number of grasses also have attractive flower heads some of which are useful for drying. Most grasses thrive in any well-drained soil and flourish in a range of light conditions. Rushes prefer moist or wet soil in sun or partial shade, although *Luzula* species often prefer drier conditions. Sedges grow in sun or partial shade, and although many occur naturally in water, most will grow well in moist, well-drained, moderately fertile soils.

Propagate species by seed in autumn, or division in autumn or spring.

*PHALARIS ARUNDINACEA* var. *PICTA*'
*Habit* Clump-forming.
*Flowers* Tiny, in narrow panicles in summer. Pale greenish-brown.
*Leaves* Evergreen, broadly linear. Green, striped white.
• TIPS Grow in damp, shady borders and by water. Invasive.
• HEIGHT 1m (3ft).
• SPREAD indefinite.

*Phalaris arundinacea* var. *picta*
Gardener's garters, Ribbon grass
☀ ◐ ❄❄❄ ⚱

*HOLCUS MOLLIS* 'Albovariegatus'
*Habit* Clump-forming, spreading.
*Flowers* Tiny, in purplish-white flower spikes, in summer.
*Leaves* Evergreen, linear, with hairy nodes. Green, striped white.
• OTHER NAMES *H. mollis* 'Variegatus'.
• HEIGHT 1m (3ft).
• SPREAD indefinite.

*Holcus mollis* 'Albovariegatus'
Variegated creeping soft grass
☀ ◐ ❄❄❄ ⚱

*CORTADERIA SELLOANA* 'Silver Comet'
*Habit* Clump-forming.
*Flowers* Tiny, borne in dense, silky, plume-like panicles in late summer. Silver.
*Leaves* Evergreen, narrow, sharp-edged, arching. Pale, silvery green.
• TIPS Protect young plants with a winter mulch. Avoid heavy soils. An excellent specimen plant. Propagate by division in spring.
• HEIGHT 1.2–1.5m (4–5ft).
• SPREAD 1m (3ft).

*Cortaderia selloana* 'Silver Comet'

☀ ◐ ❄❄

*ARUNDO DONAX* var. *VERSICOLOR*
*Habit* Clump-forming, rhizomatous.
*Flowers* Feathery, in dense, erect heads in late summer, but produced reliably only in hot summers. Creamy-white.
*Leaves* Broadly linear. Bluish-green, striped and edged creamy-white.
• TIPS Needs moist soil. Propagate by division in spring.
• OTHER NAMES *A. donax* 'Variegata'.
• HEIGHT 2.5–3m (8–10ft).
• SPREAD 60cm (2ft).

*Arundo donax* var. *versicolor*
Variegated giant reed

☀ ◐ ❄

## GLYCERIA MAXIMA var. VARIEGATA

**Habit** Clump-forming.
**Flowers** Tiny, in open heads in summer. Green, purple-tinted.
**Leaves** Broadly linear. Green, with cream stripes, pink-flushed when young.
• TIPS Ideally suited to waterside plantings. Propagate by division in spring.
• OTHER NAMES *G. aquatica variegata*.
• HEIGHT 80cm (32in).
• SPREAD indefinite.

*Glyceria maxima* var. *variegata*

☼ ◊ ❊ ❊ ❊

## CORTADERIA SELLOANA 'Sunningdale Silver'

**Habit** Sturdy, clump-forming.
**Flowers** Tiny, borne in long, dense, silky plumes in late summer. Silvery-cream.
**Leaves** Evergreen, narrow, very sharp-edged, arching. Pale olive-green.
• TIPS Protect young plants with a winter mulch. Avoid heavy soils. A robust and excellent specimen plant. Propagate by division in spring.
• HEIGHT 2.1m (7ft).
• SPREAD 1.2m (4ft).

*Cortaderia selloana* 'Sunningdale Silver'

☼ ◊ ❊ ❊    ♡

## LUZULA NIVEA

**Habit** Clump-forming.
**Flowers** Tiny, in early summer. Shining white.
**Leaves** Evergreen, linear, mostly basal. Dark green, fringed with white hairs.
• TIPS Grow in moist but well-drained soil. Suited to a woodland garden. Propagate by seed in autumn; division in spring.
• HEIGHT 60cm (24in).
• SPREAD 45–60cm (18–24in).

*Luzula nivea*
Snowy woodrush

☼ ◊ ❊ ❊ ❊

## SCHOENOPLECTUS LACUSTRIS subsp. TABERNAEMONTANI 'Zebrinus'

**Habit** Clump-forming.
**Flowers** Tiny, in spikelets in summer. Red-brown.
**Leaves** Almost leafless, stems banded with white.
• TIPS Grows well by water. Divide in spring.
• OTHER NAMES *Scirpus tabernaemontani* 'Zebrinus'.
• HEIGHT 1.5m (5ft).
• SPREAD indefinite.

*Schoenoplectus lacustris* subsp. *tabernaemontani* 'Zebrinus'

☼ ◖ ❊ ❊ ❊

## MISCANTHUS SINENSIS 'Zebrinus'

**Habit** Clump-forming.
**Flowers** Tiny, in silky-haired spikelets borne in fan-shaped heads in early autumn. White .
**Leaves** Long, arching, linear. Bluish-green, with transverse, creamy-white or yellow-gold banding.
• TIPS Well-suited for placing at the back of a border, but flowers reliably only in warm summers. Propagate by division in spring.
• HEIGHT 1.2m (4ft).
• SPREAD 45cm (18in).

*Miscanthus sinensis* 'Zebrinus'
Zebra grass

☼ ◊ ❊ ❊

*HORDEUM JUBATUM*
**Habit** Tufted.
**Flowers** Tiny, silky-bristled spikelets, borne in arching spikes from early to mid-summer. Pale green, flushed red, turning beige when mature.
**Leaves** Linear. Green.
• TIPS An annual or short-lived perennial grown for its flowers that dry well for winter arrangements. Propagate by seed in spring.
• HEIGHT 30–60cm (1–2ft)
• SPREAD 30cm (1ft)

**Hordeum jubatum**
Foxtail barley,
Squirreltail grass

☼ ◊ ✳ ✳ ✳

*CYPERUS PAPYRUS*
**Habit** Clump-forming.
**Flowers** Tiny, in large terminal umbels, in summer. Brownish-yellow.
**Leaves** Evergreen, insignificant, but with a whorl of short, linear, dark green, leaf-like bracts beneath the flowers.
• TIPS Grow as a house or conservatory plant in cooler climates. Suitable for planting in a large pot. Needs permanently wet soil and protection from direct sun. Propagate by division in spring.
• HEIGHT to 3–5m (10–15ft).
• SPREAD 1m (3ft).

**Cyperus papyrus**
Egyptian paper reed,
Papyrus

☼ ● ◊
Min. 7–10°C (45–50°F)

*PENNISETUM VILLOSUM*
**Habit** Tuft-forming.
**Flowers** Tiny, bearded spikelets, in plumes in late summer. Creamy-pink.
**Leaves** Flat, linear, on hairy stems. Mid-green.
• TIPS Flower heads cut and dry well. Propagate by seed in spring.
• OTHER NAMES
*P. longistylum*
• HEIGHT to 1m (3ft).
• SPREAD 50cm (20in).

**Pennisetum villosum**
Feather-top

☼ ◊ ✳ ✳

*HELICTOTRICHON SEMPERVIRENS*
**Habit** Tuft-forming.
**Flowers** Tiny, borne in spikes, in erect heads, in summer. Straw-colour.
**Leaves** Evergreen, narrowly linear, stiff. Silvery-blue, up to 30cm (12in) or more.
• OTHER NAMES *Avena candida* of gardens.
• HEIGHT 50cm (20in).
• SPREAD 20cm (8in).

**Helictotrichon sempervirens**

☼ ◊ ✳ ✳ ✳          ♗

*STIPA GIGANTEA*
**Habit** Tufted.
**Flowers** Tiny, in open, airy panicles in summer. Silvery, with golden anthers.
**Leaves** Evergreen, narrow, smooth or slightly rough. Dark green.
• TIPS An imposing specimen at the back of a border. Sow seed in spring or divide in autumn.
• HEIGHT 2.5cm (8ft).
• SPREAD 1m (3ft).

**Stipa gigantea**
Golden oats

☼ ◊ ✳ ✳          ♗

*CHONDROSUM GRACILE*
**Habit** Tuft-forming.
**Flowers** Tiny, in spikelets, in summer. Purple-brown.
**Leaves** Semi-evergreen, narrowly linear. Dark greyish-green.
• TIPS Must have good drainage. Divide or sow seed in spring.
• OTHER NAMES
*Bouteloua gracilis.*
• HEIGHT 50cm (20in).
• SPREAD 20cm (8in).

**Chondrosum gracile**
Blue grama
Mosquito grass

☼ ◊ ✳ ✳ ✳

## MELICA ALTISSIMA 'Atropurpurea'

**Habit** Tuft-forming.
**Flowers** Tiny spikelets, borne in narrow, terminal, arching heads in summer. Deep mauve.
**Leaves** Broadly linear, arching, roughly hairy beneath. Mid-green.
• TIPS Needs well-drained soil and sun. Propagate by division in spring.
• HEIGHT 60cm (2ft)
• SPREAD 60cm (2ft)

*Melica altissima* 'Atropurpurea'

☼ ◊ ❄❄❄

## JUNCUS EFFUSUS 'Spiralis'

**Habit** Tuft-forming.
**Flowers** Tiny, in short, dense heads in summer. Greenish-brown.
**Leaves** Leafless, but with spiralling, evergreen stems that are often prostrate.
• TIPS Plant by water or in a moist border. Divide in spring.
• HEIGHT 1m (3ft).
• SPREAD 60cm (2ft).

*Juncus effusus* 'Spiralis'
Corkscrew rush

☼ ◊ ❄❄❄

## MISCANTHUS SINENSIS 'Gracillimus'

**Habit** Clump-forming.
**Flowers** Tiny spikelets in fan-shaped heads in early autumn. Hairy, white.
**Leaves** Long, arching, narrow. Bluish-green, with a white midrib, often bronze-flushed.
• TIPS Ideal for the back of a border. Divide in spring.
• HEIGHT 1.2m (4ft).
• SPREAD 45cm (18in).

*Miscanthus sinensis* 'Gracillimus'

☼ ◊ ❄❄

## CYPERUS INVOLUCRATUS

**Habit** Tuft-forming.
**Flowers** Tiny, surrounded by green bracts, in summer. Creamy-yellow.
**Leaves** Evergreen, insignificant.
• TIPS Grow indoors in a big pot in cooler climates. Keep wet. Divide in spring.
• OTHER NAMES *C. alternifolius* (of gardens).
• HEIGHT to 1m (3ft).
• SPREAD 30cm (1ft).

*Cyperus involucratus*
Umbrella plant
Nile grass

☼ ◊ ◊
Min. 4–7°C (39–45°F) �器

*CAREX PENDULA*
**Habit** Densely tufted.
**Flowers** Tiny, in catkin-like spikes on long stems in summer. Brown.
**Leaves** Evergreen, narrow, rigid, keeled. Shining yellow-green, blue-green beneath.
• TIPS Suited to a woodland garden. Divide in spring or sow seed in autumn.
• HEIGHT 1m (3ft).
• SPREAD 30cm (1ft).

*Carex pendula*
Pendulous sedge

☼ ◊ ❊❊❊

*CAREX ELATA*
**'Aurea'**
**Habit** Tussock-forming.
**Flowers** Tiny, in small clusters, on triangular stems in spring and early summer. Dark brown.
**Leaves** Evergreen, linear. Golden-yellow.
• TIPS Suited to poolside plantings. Divide in spring.
• OTHER NAMES *C. stricta* 'Aurea'.
• HEIGHT to 40cm (16in).
• SPREAD 15–20cm (6–8in).

*Carex elata* 'Aurea'
Bowles' golden sedge

☼ ◖ ❊❊❊ ♒

*SPARTINA PECTINATA*
**'Aureomarginata'**
**Habit** Clump-forming, rhizomatous.
**Flowers** Tiny, in narrow spikes in late summer. Straw-coloured.
**Leaves** Tough, narrow, arching. Olive-green with yellow stripes and margin; orange-brown in autumn.
• TIPS Ideally suited to waterside plantings but will also thrive in a dry garden. Propagate by division in spring.
• OTHER NAMES *S. pectinata* 'Aureovariegata'.
• HEIGHT to 2m (6ft).
• SPREAD indefinite.

*Spartina pectinata*
'Aureomarginata'

☼ ◖ ❊❊❊

*HAKENOCHLOA MACRA* **'Aureola'**
**Habit** Mound-forming, rhizomatous.
**Flowers** Tiny spikelets, in open heads in late summer. Red-tinted.
**Leaves** Linear, arching. Bright yellow with narrow cream and green stripes, flushing red in autumn.
• TIPS Grow in moist but well-drained soil in partial shade or sun. Propagate by division in spring.
• HEIGHT 40cm (16in).
• SPREAD 45–60cm (18–24in).

*Hakenochloa macra*
'Aureola'

☼ ◊ ❊❊❊ ♒

*CAREX HACHIJOENSIS*
**'Evergold'**
**Habit** Densely tufted.
**Flowers** Tiny, in small clusters at the tips of solid triangular stems in mid- to late spring. Dark brown.
**Leaves** Evergreen, linear, Dark green, yellow striped.
• TIPS Needs good drainage. Divide in spring.
• OTHER NAMES *C. oshimensis* 'Evergold'.
• HEIGHT 30cm (12in).
• SPREAD 35cm (14in).

*Carex hachijoensis*
'Evergold'

☼ ◊ ❊❊❊ ♒

*ALOPECURUS PRATENSIS*
**'Aureovariegatus'**
**Habit** Tuft-forming.
**Flowers** Dense spikes, in summer. Pale green.
**Leaves** Flat, linear. Yellowish-green, striped and edged with gold.
• OTHER NAMES *A. pratensis* 'Aureomarginatus'.
• HEIGHT to 30cm (12in).
• SPREAD to 30cm (12in).

*Alopecurus pratensis*
'Aureovariegatus'
Golden foxtail

☼ ◊ ❊❊❊

# FERNS

Among the most popular of all foliage plants, ferns add texture and atmosphere to the house or garden, where they are particularly effective in settings by streams or in damp, shady corners.

Hardy ferns are suitable for growing in woodland gardens, or in the open garden where they benefit from moist, neutral to alkaline conditions. Many of the smaller types are excellent for a shady rock garden.

Tender tropical ferns are best cultivated indoors in a greenhouse or conservatory, or as house plants where they should be kept moist, but not waterlogged. Protection should be given from direct sunlight.

Ferns are raised mainly by spores but may be propagated by division, or, in some species, by bulbils.

*PTERIS CRETICA ALBOLINEATA*
**Habit** Clump-forming.
**Leaves** Evergreen or semi-evergreen, to 20cm (8in) long, forked or in linear segments. Pale green with a creamy-white central stripe.
• TIPS Grow indoors in cooler climates. Propagate by division in spring or spores in summer.
• HEIGHT 45cm (18in).
• SPREAD 30cm (12in).

*Pteris cretica albolineata*

☀ ◊
Min. 5°C (41°F)

*POLYPODIUM AUREUM* 'Mandaianum'
**Habit** Creeping.
**Leaves** Evergreen, to 1m (3ft) long, deeply lobed, with orange sporangia beneath. Blue-green.
• TIPS Grow indoors in cooler climates. Divide in spring.
• OTHER NAMES *Phlebodium aureum* 'Mandaianum'.
• HEIGHT 1–1.5m (3–5ft).
• SPREAD 60cm (2ft).

*Polypodium aureum* 'Mandaianum'

☀ ◊
Min. 5°C (41°F)

*DRYOPTERIS FILIX-MAS*
**Habit** Arching.
**Leaves** Deciduous or semi-evergreen, lance-shaped, arising like a shuttlecock from a crown of stout, brown-scaly rhizomes. Mid-green.
• TIPS Grow in humus-rich soil in a shady border. Sow spores in summer or divide in spring or autumn.
• HEIGHT 1.2m (4ft).
• SPREAD 1m (3ft).

*Dryopteris filix-mas*
Male fern

☀ ◊ ✳✳✳✳          ♛

*DICKSONIA ANTARCTICA*
**Habit** Slow-growing, trunk-forming.
**Leaves** Evergreen or semi-evergreen, to 3m (10ft) long, arching, divided into linear segments. Dark green, pale green when young.
• TIPS Needs fibrous, peaty soil and moderate humidity. Excellent for a cool conservatory. Propagate by spores in summer.
• HEIGHT 10m (30ft) or more.
• SPREAD 4m (12ft).

*Dicksonia antarctica*
Man fern, Soft tree fern

☀ ◊ ✳          ♛

*PLATYCERIUM BIFURCATUM*
**Habit** Epiphytic.
**Leaves** Evergreen, with round, papery sterile fronds, and arching, forked, fertile fronds with velvety-brown spores beneath. Grey-green.
TIPS Grow indoors in cooler climates, on bark attached to a wad of moss. Needs high humidity.
• HEIGHT 1m (3ft).
• SPREAD 1m (3ft).

*Platycerium bifurcatum*
Common stag's-horn fern

☀ ◊
Min. 5°C (41°F)

## *POLYSTICHUM ACULEATUM* 'Pulcherrimum'

*Habit* Arching, with woody, scaly rhizomes.
*Leaves* Evergreen or semi-evergreen, rigid, lance-shaped, to 90cm (36in) long, daintily cut into toothed segments. Bright green, maturing to dark green.
• TIPS Needs fibrous, moist but well-drained soil. Propagate by division in spring.
• HEIGHT 60cm (24in).
• SPREAD 75cm (30in).

*Polystichum aculeatum* 'Pulcherrimum'

☀ ◑ ❄ ❄ ❄

## *MICROLEPIA STRIGOSA*

*Habit* Creeping, rhizomatous.
*Leaves* Evergreen, irregularly lance-shaped, to 80cm (32in) long, finely divided into segments. Pale green.
• TIPS Grow indoors in cooler climates. Excellent for shallow pots or hanging baskets in the home or conservatory. Propagate by division in spring or spores in summer.
• HEIGHT 90cm (3ft).
• SPREAD 60cm (2ft).

*Microlepia strigosa*

☀ ◑
Min. 5°C (41°F)

## *POLYSTICHUM MUNITUM*

*Habit* Upright.
*Leaves* Evergreen, rigid, lance-shaped fronds, divided into leathery, spiny-margined segments. Dark green.
• TIPS Needs moist, fibrous soil. Propagate by division in spring or spores in summer.
• HEIGHT 1.2m (4ft).
• SPREAD 30cm (1ft).

*Polystichum munitum*
Giant holly fern

☀ ◑ ❄ ❄ ❄

## *BLECHNUM TABULARE*

*Habit* Upright.
*Leaves* Evergreen or semi-evergreen, with oval, sterile outer fronds, divided into paired, lance-shaped segments. Dark green. Inner fronds are upright, with linear segments.
• TIPS Needs neutral to acid soil. Sow spores in late summer.
• HEIGHT 30cm–1m (1–3ft).
• SPREAD 30–60cm (1–2ft).

*Blechnum tabulare*

☀ ◑ ❄ ❄    ♈

## *POLYPODIUM GLYCYRRHIZA*

*Habit* Upright, with a liquorice-scented rhizome.
*Leaves* Deciduous, narrowly oval, to 35cm (14in) long, cut into bright green segments.
• TIPS Needs fibrous, moist, well-drained soil. Divide in spring or sow spores in late summer.
• HEIGHT 45cm (18in).
• SPREAD 45cm (18in).

*Polypodium glycyrrhiza*
Liquorice fern

☀ ◑ ❄ ❄ ❄

## *POLYPODIUM SCOULERI*

*Habit* Creeping.
*Leaves* Evergreen, oval rigid, leathery, and divided into paired oblong segments. Dark green.
• TIPS Good for coastal gardens. Needs good drainage. Divide in spring or sow spores in summer.
• HEIGHT 30–40cm (12–16in).
• SPREAD 30–40cm (12–16in).

*Polypodium scouleri*
Coast polypody, Leathery polypody

☀ ◑ ❄ ❄

*RUMOHRA
ADIANTIFORMIS*
**Habit** Creeping, stoutly
rhizomatous, epiphytic.
**Leaves** Evergreen, to
60cm (24in) long, oval,
diamond- or lance-
shaped, leathery, with
pairs of stalked
segments. Dark green.
• TIPS Grow as a house
or conservatory plant in
cooler climates. Grow
epiphytically on bark
attached to a wad of
moss. Needs high
humidity. Propagate
by division in spring.
• HEIGHT 75–90cm
30–36in).
• SPREAD 75–90cm
30–36in).

*Rumohra adiantiformis*
Leather fern,
Leatherleaf fern
Min. 10°C (50°F)

*CYRTOMIUM
FALCATUM*
**Habit** Clump-forming,
with an erect rhizome.
**Leaves** Evergreen
(deciduous in cool
climates), to 60cm (2ft)
long, with holly-like
segments. Glossy,
bright green.
• TIPS An excellent
house plant. If grown
outdoors, protect with
a straw mulch in winter.
Needs a sheltered site.
Propagate by spores
in summer.
• HEIGHT 30–60cm
(1–2ft).
• SPREAD 30–45cm
(12–18in).

*Cyrtomium falcatum*
Fishtail fern,
Japanese holly fern

*SELAGINELLA
MARTENSII*
**Habit** Upright,
rhizomatous.
**Leaves** Evergreen,
tiny, scale-like, glossy,
in dense, much-
branched, frond-like
sprays. Rich green.
• TIPS Grow indoors in
cool climates. Needs
moist peaty soil. Separate
rooted stems at any time.
• HEIGHT 23cm (9in).
• SPREAD 23cm (9in).

*Selaginella martensii*
Min. 5°C (41°F)

*ASPLENIUM CETERACH*
**Habit** Rosette-forming.
**Leaves** Evergreen, with
lance-shaped fronds,
divided into alternate,
bluntly rounded lobes.
Dark green with silver
scales beneath that age
to red-brown.
TIPS Grow in moist,
well-drained, alkaline
soil. Sow spores in
summer; divide in spring.
• HEIGHT 15cm (6in).
• SPREAD 15cm (6in).

*Asplenium ceterach*
Rusty-back fern

*PTERIS CRETICA*
**Habit** Clump-forming.
**Leaves** Evergreen or
semi-evergreen, broadly
oval to triangular,
divided into finger-like
segments. Pale green.
• TIPS Needs high
humidity. Grow
indoors in cool
climates. By division
in spring or spores in
summer.
• HEIGHT 45cm (18in).
• SPREAD 30cm (12in).

*Pteris cretica*
Cretan brake
Min. 5°C (41°F)

*ASPLENIUM
TRICHOMANES*
**Habit** Rosette-forming.
**Leaves** Evergreen,
narrowly lance-shaped,
divided into leathery,
oblong to rounded
segments. Bright green.
• TIPS Needs moist, well-
drained, alkaline soil.
Good for rock crevices.
Sow spores in summer.
• HEIGHT 15cm (6in).
• SPREAD 15–30cm
(6–12in).

*Asplenium trichomanes*
Maidenhair spleenwort

## POLYPODIUM AUREUM
**Habit** Creeping.
**Leaves** Evergreen, arching, deeply lobed. Mid-green with orange-yellow sporangia beneath.
• TIPS Grow indoors in cool climates. Tolerates part-day sun. Propagate by division in spring; spores in summer.
OTHER NAMES *Phlebodium aureum.*
• HEIGHT 1–1.5m (3–5ft).
• SPREAD 60cm (2ft).

*Polypodium aureum*
Golden polypody

☀ ◑
Min. 5°C (41°F)

## THELYPTERIS PALUSTRIS
**Habit** Erect or gently arching, creeping.
**Leaves** Deciduous, lance-shaped, to 30–100cm (15–39in) long, with widely spaced, deeply cut pinnae. Pale green.
• TIPS Tolerates sun. Suited to waterside plantings. Propagate by division in spring.
• HEIGHT 75cm (30in).
• SPREAD 30cm (12in).

*Thelypteris palustris*
Marsh buckler fern, Marsh fern

☀ ● ❄❄❄

## POLYSTICHUM SETIFERUM 'Divisilobum'
**Habit** Arching.
**Leaves** Evergreen or semi-evergreen, narrowly oval, finely divided into soft-textured segments. Fresh green, covered with white scales as they unfurl.
• TIPS Needs fibrous, moist, well-drained soil. Divide in spring.
• HEIGHT 60cm (2ft).
• SPREAD 30cm (1ft).

*Polystichum setiferum*
'Divisilobum'

☀ ◑ ❄❄❄

## CRYPTOGRAMMA CRISPA
**Habit** Tuft-forming.
**Leaves** Deciduous, with oval outer, sterile fronds, divided into toothed segments. Bright green.
• TIPS Grow in a sheltered, damp site in well- drained, gritty, humus-rich soil. Sow spores in late summer.
• HEIGHT 15–23cm (6–9in).
• SPREAD 15–30cm (6–12in).

*Cryptogramma crispa*
European parsley fern

☀ ◑ ❄❄❄

## ADIANTUM PEDATUM
**Habit** Clump-forming with a stout, creeping rootstock.
**Leaves** Deciduous, with linear-lance-shaped fronds, to 30cm (12in) long, divided into triangular to oblong segments, on a slender dark brown stem. Fresh green.
• TIPS Needs moist, humus-rich, acid soil. Propagate by dividing very carefully in early spring or by sowing spores in summer.
• HEIGHT 45cm (18in).
• SPREAD 45cm (18in).

*Adiantum pedatum*
Northern maidenhair fern

☀ ◑ ❄❄❄   ▽

## DAVALLIA FEJEENSIS
**Habit** Arching, with scaly rhizomes, clothed in curly brown hair.
**Leaves** Evergreen, to 45cm (18in) long, finely divided into lance-shaped segments. Mid-green.
• TIPS Needs fibrous, peaty soil and high humidity. Grow indoors in cool climates. Excellent for hanging baskets. Propagate by division or spores in summer.
• HEIGHT 20–100cm (8in–3ft).
• SPREAD 20–100cm (8in–3ft).

*Davallia fejeensis*

☀ ◑
Min. 10°C (50°F)

## POLYPODIUM VULGARE 'Cornubiense'

**Habit** Upright, creeping.
**Leaves** Evergreen, lance-shaped, finely divided into lacy segments. Fresh green.
• TIPS Needs fibrous, moist but well-drained soil. Divide in spring or sow spores in summer.
• HEIGHT 25–30cm (10–12in).
• SPREAD 25–30cm (10–12in).

*Polypodium vulgare* 'Cornubiense'

☀ ◊ ❄❄❄

## ONOCLEA SENSIBILIS

**Habit** Arching, creeping, rhizomatous.
**Leaves** Deciduous, broadly triangular, finely divided into segments. Pale green, flushed pink when young.
• TIPS Good for waterside plantings in humus-rich soil. Divide in autumn or winter.
• HEIGHT 45cm (18in).
• SPREAD 45cm (18in) or more.

*Onoclea sensibilis*
Bead fern, Sensitive fern

☀ ◊ ❄❄❄            ♕

## SELAGINELLA KRAUSSIANA

**Habit** Prostrate, trailing.
**Leaves** Evergreen, tiny, scale-like and overlapping along jointed stems, with a moss-like appearance. Bright green.
• TIPS Needs moist peaty soil. An excellent foliage plant for the home or conservatory. Separate rooted stems at any time.
• HEIGHT 1cm (½in).
• SPREAD indefinite.

*Selaginella kraussiana*
Spreading club moss, Trailing spike moss

☀ ◊
Min. 5°C (41°F)

## ADIANTUM PEDATUM var. ALEUTICUM

**Habit** Clump-forming.
**Leaves** Deciduous, with finger-like fronds, divided into triangular segments, densely arranged on dark brown stems. Bluish-green.
• TIPS Needs moist, humus-rich, alkaline soil. Divide carefully in early spring or sow spores in summer.
• HEIGHT 45cm (18in).
• SPREAD 45cm (18in).

*Adiantum pedatum* var. *aleuticum*
Aleutian maidenhair

☀ ◊ ❄❄❄

## TODEA BARBARA

**Habit** Slow-growing, trunk-forming with a massive rhizome.
**Leaves** Evergreen, with erect, fronds to 120cm (4ft) long, with lance-shaped segments. Bright glossy green.
• TIPS Grow indoors in cool climates. Needs fibrous, peaty soil and moderate humidity. Suitable for a warm greenhouse. Propagate by sowing ripe spores.
• HEIGHT to 2m (6ft) or more.
• SPREAD 2m (6ft).

*Todea barbara*
Crepe fern, King fern

☀ ◊
Min. 10–13°C (50–55°F)

## OSMUNDA REGALIS
**Habit** Clump-forming, with fibrous rootstock.
**Leaves** Deciduous, broadly oval to oblong, to 1.8m (6ft) long. Bright green, bearing tassel-like, rusty-brown, fertile segments, at tips of mature fronds.
• TIPS Excellent for waterside plantings. Propagate by spores sown immediately they ripen or by division in autumn or winter.
• HEIGHT 2m (6ft).
• SPREAD 1m (3ft).

**Osmunda regalis**
Royal fern

## ASPLENIUM SCOLOPENDRIUM
**Crispum Group**
**Habit** Upright.
**Leaves** Evergreen, strap-shaped, in an irregular rosette, with waved and ruffled margins. Glossy bright green.
• TIPS Needs moist, humus-rich, alkaline soil. Propagate by root leaf bases in summer.
• HEIGHT 45cm (18in).
• SPREAD 75cm (30in).

**Asplenium scolopendrium**
**Crispum Group**

## MATTEUCCIA STRUTHIOPTERIS
**Habit** Upright or gently arching, rhizomatous.
**Leaves** Deciduous, lance-shaped. Fresh green. Dark brown inner, fertile fronds are winter-persistent.
• TIPS Excellent for waterside plantings. Tolerates part-day sun. Divide in autumn or winter.
• HEIGHT 1m (3ft)
• SPREAD 45cm (18in).

**Matteuccia struthiopteris**
Ostrich-feather fern, Ostrich fern

## ASPLENIUM SCOLOPENDRIUM
**Habit** Upright.
**Leaves** Evergreen, strap-shaped, to 40cm (16in) long, in an irregular rosette. Bright green.
• TIPS Needs moist, humus-rich, alkaline soil. Sow spores in summer.
• OTHER NAMES *Phyllitis scolopendrium.*
• HEIGHT 45–75cm (18–30in).
• SPREAD to 45cm (18in).

**Asplenium scolopendrium**
Hart's-tongue fern

## POLYSTICHUM SETIFERUM PROLIFERUM
**Habit** Slightly arching.
**Leaves** Evergreen or semi-evergreen, oval, finely divided into soft, moss-like segments. Fresh green, covered with white scales as they unfurl.
• TIPS Needs well-drained soil. Divide or plant bulbils in spring.
• HEIGHT 60cm (24in).
• SPREAD 45cm (18in).

**Polystichum setiferum proliferum**

## POLYPODIUM VULGARE
**Habit** Upright, creeping.
**Leaves** Evergreen, narrowly lance-shaped, with thin-textured segments. Mid-green.
• TIPS Needs fibrous, moist but well-drained soil. Divide in spring or sow spores in late summer.
• HEIGHT 25–30cm (10–12in).
• SPREAD 25–30cm (10–12in).

**Polypodium vulgare**
Common polypody, Polypody

## ASPLENIUM COLOPENDRIUM Marginatum Group
**Habit** Upright, stoutly rhizomatous.
**Leaves** Evergreen, strap-shaped, leathery, with frilled margins, often "winged" beneath; arranged in an irregular rosette. Bright green.
• TIPS Needs moist, humus-rich, alkaline soil. Propagate by root leaf bases in early summer.
• OTHER NAMES *Phyllitis colopendrium* 'Marginatum'.
• HEIGHT 30cm (12in) or more.
• SPREAD 30cm (12in) or more.

*Asplenium scolopendrium*
**Marginatum Group**

## ADIANTUM VENUSTUM
**Habit** Spreading, with creeping rhizomes.
**Leaves** Semi-evergreen, with black stipes and triangular fronds, to 80cm (32in) long, divided into fan-shaped pinnules. Pale green, pink-tinted on emergence.
• TIPS Grow in moist, humus-rich, acid soil. Propagate by carefully dividing in early spring or sow spores in summer.
• HEIGHT 15cm (6in).
• SPREAD indefinite.

*Adiantum venustum*
Himalayan maidenhair

## ASPLENIUM NIDUS
**Habit** Stiffly upright.
**Leaves** Evergreen, almost stemless, broadly lance-shaped, in a shuttlecock-like rosette. Glossy bright green.
• TIPS Grow indoors in cool climates, in coarse potting compost with added sphagnum moss. Sow spores in late summer.
• HEIGHT 60cm–1.2m (2–4ft).
• SPREAD 30–60cm (1–2ft).

*Asplenium nidus*
Bird's-nest fern

Min. 5°C (41°F)

## NEPHROLEPIS EXALTATA
**Habit** Vigorous, erect.
**Leaves** Evergreen, linear, on wiry stalks. Bright green segments.
• TIPS Prefers damp and shade, but stands drought and waterlogging. Divide in summer or autumn. An excellent house plant.
• HEIGHT 90cm (3ft) or more.
• SPREAD 90cm (3ft) or more.

*Nephrolepis exaltata*
Boston fern, Sword fern

Min. 5°C (41°F)

## ATHYRIUM NIPONICUM
**Habit** Clump-forming.
**Leaves** Deciduous, oval, divided into oblong segments. Grey-green, purple-tinged, with dark purple stalks and midribs.
• TIPS Needs a sheltered site, in neutral to acid soil. Sow spores in summer or divide in spring.
• OTHER NAMES *A. goeringianum*
• HEIGHT 30cm (12in).
• SPREAD 30cm (12in).

*Athyrium niponicum*
Painted fern

## PSILOTUM NUDUM
**Habit** Branched, erect, or pendulous if epiphytic.
**Leaves** Tiny, triangular, evergreen, with triangular, branching, pale green stems. Leaves bear yellow sporangia.
• TIPS Grow indoors in cool climates in warm, humid conditions. Sow ripe spores or divide in early spring.
• HEIGHT 60cm (24in).
• SPREAD 45cm (18in).

*Psilotum nudum*
Skeleton fork fern

Min. 13–15°C (55–59°F)

# CARING FOR PERENNIALS

IF HERBACEOUS PERENNIALS are to give of their ornamental best, it is essential to match the plants' individual needs with the growing conditions that exist in the garden. Perennials originate in many areas of the world, from a range of climates, habitats and soil types, so whether the site is sheltered or exposed, sunny or shaded, damp or dry, or on poor or fertile soil, there is always a number of plants that will thrive in a given set of conditions. A thorough site survey to assess soil type, aspect and local microclimate may reveal that different areas of the garden provide a variety of growing conditions. A south-facing border, for example, is perfect for sun-loving plants, while a site beneath shrubs or trees, or a north-facing wall, suits shade-lovers. Damp, low-lying areas of the garden, provided that they are not sited in a frost pocket, may prove ideal for bog plants and natives of other moist habitats. Borders at the base of a wall are usually fairly dry, due to rain-shadow effects, and since they are also usually warm and sheltered, they can provide a perfect niche for plants that are not fully hardy or that require good drainage.

## SELECTING PERENNIALS

GOOD EXAMPLE

POOR EXAMPLES

LUPIN

Weak, woody
top-growth

Strong, healthy
top-growth

Under-
developed
root system

Moist
compost

Moss and
weeds grow-
ing on top of
compost

Established,
vigorous roots

Pot-bound
roots

# SOIL PREPARATION AND PLANTING

Few gardens are blessed with the ideal fertile, moisture-retentive, and well-drained loam that suits the majority of herbaceous perennials. However, the drainage, aeration, fertility and moisture-holding properties of most soil types can be improved by the incorporation of well-rotted organic matter. This is best done in the season before planting, to allow the soil to settle. Very wet soils can be improved by the installation of drainage systems or soakaways, and soil acidity or alkalinity can be modified to a degree by either liming acid soils or by adding well-rotted organic matter to alkaline soils.

Pre-planting clearance of all weeds is essential, since they compete for light, moisture and nutrients. Where the ground is infested with perennial weeds spray off in the season before planting with a systemic herbicide that also kills their roots. This is most effective when the weeds are growing strongly, usually in early summer. Although this may mean delaying planting, patience at this stage will be amply rewarded later. Repeated applications may be needed to remove persistent weeds like ground elder, couch grass, or nettles. A few perennial weeds can be forked out carefully. Annual weeds may be hoed or sprayed off immediately before planting.

## Selecting plants

Most perennials are now sold container-grown. Look for healthy, vigorous top-growth with no sign of pests, die-back, or abnormally coloured leaves which may indicate nutrient deficiencies. If buying early in the season, select plants with strong emerging shoots or few fat healthy buds in preference to those with many small, weak buds or shoots. Check the roots and look for a strong system of healthy roots that almost fills the pot. Avoid plants with a mass of tightly coiled roots or those with large roots pushing through the drainage holes. Examine the compost surface for perennial weeds, or mats of mosses or liverworts. This may indicate that the plant has been in the container too long, and may have suffered nutrient deficiency or waterlogged conditions, in which case the roots may have rotted or died back.

## DIVIDING LARGE PLANTS

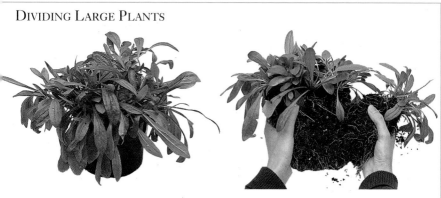

1 *When buying easily divided perennials like this Michaelmas daisy (Aster), choose large plants with several strong shoots. They prove good value since they will yield several plants for the price of one.*

2 *Gently tease the roots apart to make several small sections, each with its own roots. These can be planted immediately in groups or, if the divisions are small, potted up and grown on until well-established.*

## HOW TO PLANT A CONTAINER-GROWN PERENNIAL

1 *In a prepared bed, dig a hole 1½ times wider and deeper than the plant's root ball. If necessary, break up the soil at the bottom of the hole so that it is friable and permits free drainage.*

2 *Water the potted plant well to ensure that the compost is evenly moist, and allow to drain thoroughly. Then slide the plant gently out of the pot, taking care not to damage the roots or disturb the root ball.*

3 *Gently scrape off the top 3cm (1½in) of compost to remove weeds and weed seeds. Gently tease out the roots at the sides and base of the root ball, taking care not to break or damage them.*

4 *Set the plant in the hole, and adjust the depth by backfilling, so that the plant crown is at the correct depth. Backfill gradually, firming gently as you go, then water in thoroughly.*

## When to plant

Container-grown perennials may be planted at any time of the year provided that the soil is workable. In the drier months, however, they will need conscientious aftercare until they are well-established, especially with regard to watering. The best seasons for planting are autumn and spring. Autumn planting allows plants to establish quickly before the onset of winter, since the soil is still warm enough to permit good root growth, and is likely to remain moist, without the need for additional watering, until they are well-established. In cold areas, spring planting is better for perennials that are not fully hardy or for those that dislike wet winter conditions, such as cultivars of *Schizostylis coccinea* or *Cosmos atrosanguineus*. They then have a full growing season to become established before their first winter.

Bare-rooted plants should be replanted as soon as possible after receipt. Although occasionally offered by nurseries during the dormant season, the most common source of bare-root plants will be friends carrying out routine lifting and dividing of established clumps, usually during spring or autumn. A few perennials, such as hostas, may be transplanted during the growing season.

## How to plant

Always plant into well-cultivated, weed-free soil and, if necessary, remove any weeds that have escaped the herbicide spray with a hand or border fork. Take care to position plants at the correct depth (see below). Most perennials should be planted with the crown at ground level, at the same depth as it was in the pot. Those that are prone to rotting at the base, or with variegated foliage that may revert should be planted with the crown slightly proud of the soil. Some plants, such as those with a tuberous root system, are planted deeply, about 10cm (4in) below the soil surface.

To plant container-grown plants, first water the plant well to ensure that the

## PLANTING DEPTHS

*Most perennials are best planted with their crown at the same level as it was in the pot. A number grow better if planted higher or deeper, depending on their individual needs.*

HOSTA     POLYGONATUM     MICHAELMAS DAISY     SISYRINCHIUM

**Shallow**
*For plants needing moist soil, set the crown 2.5cm (1in) below soil level*

**Deep**
*Plant the crown of tuberous-rooted species 10cm (4in) below soil level.*

**Ground level**
*Plant most perennials with the crown level with the soil surface.*

**Raised**
*If plants are prone to rot at the base, set the crown just above ground level.*

## TRANSPLANTING SEEDLINGS

*Lift self-sown seedlings carefully when still small. Retain the soil around their roots so as not to break up the root ball. Transfer to the flowering site or nursery bed, firm in and water thoroughly.*

conditions suit them. These may be transplanted directly to a new flowering site, or grown on in nursery beds. Before lifting, prepare the new planting site and dig a small hole to receive the young plants, allowing plenty of space for both the roots and top growth to develop. Lift gently with a hand or border fork, taking care to not to break up the root ball and to retain as much soil around it as possible. Replant immediately, firm in and water thoroughly. Shade the plants in sunny weather and water regularly until well-established.

### Planting in containers

Growing perennials in containers can be a versatile and very attractive way of displaying a range of plants. It also offers the opportunity for growing plants that would not thrive in the open garden, either because the soil type is unsuitable, or because they are not sufficiently hardy. When planting containers with more than one type of perennial, it is important to select those with similar cultural requirements. Consider also the eventual size and shape of the selected plants to ensure that their top growth forms a balanced composition that is in proportion with the dimensions of the pot.

The range of containers is diverse, from terracotta or plastic pots to wooden tubs and ceramic urns. Whatever the style of container, it is essential that it has drainage holes to permit free flow of water and prevent waterlogging. It must also be sufficiently deep and wide to accommodate the plant roots. If the container is to be sited permanently outdoors, it must be made of frost-resistant materials, and even then may need additional insulation in winter, both to preserve the pot and to prevent soil from freezing around the root ball. Suitable materials include hessian sacking (burlap), old blankets, bubble wrap or horticultural fleece.

If planting up a large container such as a stone urn, lead trough or heavy

compost is evenly moist and leave it to drain thoroughly. This is especially important for plants in a peat-based compost. Once peat dries out only re-absorbs moisture very slowly, even when surrounded by moist soil, and this often results in the loss of the plant through lack of water at the roots.

Dig a planting hole one-and-a-half times the width of the pot, and adjust the depth so that the crown of the plant is at the appropriate level. Remove the plant carefully from its pot and loosen the potting compost at the base and sides of the root ball by gently teasing out the roots with your fingers. Take care not to damage the roots. Set the plant at the appropriate depth and replace the backfill gently but firmly. Loosen the soil surface lightly with a hand fork and water in thoroughly. For bare-root plants, the planting technique is essentially the same, but it is vital that the roots never dry out before re-planting. If necessary, store them in moist sand or garden compost until ready to plant.

Many perennials will produce large numbers of self-sown seedlings where terracotta pot, set it in position before planting, since it will be cumbersome to move when filled with potting compost. Stand the container on bricks or proprietary "pot feet" to ensure unimpeded drainage from the bottom. Bear in mind that containers need frequent and regular watering during the summer months, so, if possible, site with easy access to a water source. Terracotta pots, although nearly always more attractive, dry out more quickly and need more frequent watering than plastic ones.

Most modern potting composts, which are usually formulated to include a slow-release fertilizer, are suitable for container planting. Ericaceous and acid-loving plants need a lime-free or ericaceous potting compost. For plants that need sharp drainage, incorporate additional grit (up to one-third by volume). Loam-based potting composts have the advantage of being heavier than those with a peat or coir base, lending additional stability to the pot. They also tend to hold nutrients better and are more easily moistened again, if accidentally allowed to dry out.

Cover the drainage holes with a 5–8cm (2–3in) layer of broken crocks or stones and cap with a layer of fibrous material, such as upside-down turves, to prevent the compost being washed down to block the drainage holes. Fill the pot so that the compost surface is at least 2.5–4cm (1–1½in) below the pot rim, to permit thorough watering. Plant as for perennials in open ground and keep well-watered, especially during the establishment period. Top-dressing with a 2.5cm (1in) layer of gravel looks attractive, keeps the foliage free of soil splash and helps conserve moisture.

## PLANTING IN CONTAINERS

Heuchera

Penstemon

Artemisia

Geranium

1 When planting in a container, group the plants on the compost surface when still in their pots to determine their spacing and arrangement. Then plant, firm in and water thoroughly.

2 A few months later, the plants have grown and developed to form an attractive display, with a well-balanced graduation of height and form, and good contrasts of colour and texture.

# ROUTINE CARE

Most perennials grow well with very little maintenance, but certain routine tasks, such as weeding, or dead-heading , will help to keep them looking attractive and in good health throughout the growing season.

The amount of water that plants require depends on the soil type, climate and seasonal weather variations, as well as the individual plant's tolerance of dry conditions. The majority of perennials need regular watering while they are establishing themselves, but once they are established, provided that they are grown in appropriate conditions, they generally only need additional irrigation during prolonged periods of warm, dry weather. This is best applied in the evening, when water evaporates more slowly and wet leaves are unlikely to be scorched by strong sun. Bear in mind that such irrigation must be copious,

and sufficient to wet the soil well below the natural root zone. If only the soil surface is wetted, roots will grow upwards to seek moisture making them more vulnerable to damage by heat and drought. If established plants do wilt, they usually recover fully after prolonged rainfall, or may go dormant until the following growing season.

In some areas, there may be legal restrictions on irrigation at certain times of the year, and, in this case, other means of conserving soil water must be used. The most effective way of doing this is by incorporating plentiful well-rotted organic matter when preparing the bed, followed by regular mulching. On established beds, apply an annual mulch of organic matter, 5–7.5cm (2–3in) thick, onto the surface of moist soil in early spring, avoiding the area immediately around the plant crown. Suitable materials include spent mushroom compost, garden compost, well-rotted manure or proprietary mulches such as cocoa-shells or bark chips. All help to conserve soil moisture by reducing surface evaporation and by improving humus levels in the soil, since they will be incorporated into the soil when they eventually break down.

Mulching also helps to keep down weeds in the border, which is essential if plants are to grow and thrive. It prevents most weed seeds from germinating by depriving them of light, and any wind-blown seedlings are easily removed from the loose surface of the mulch with a hand fork. Any perennial weeds that occur must be dug out carefully with a hand or border fork. If established clumps become infested with perennial weeds, lift the whole plant, wash the soil off the roots and tease out the weed species. Replant immediately, ensuring that no trace of weed roots remains in the planting site. It is usually impractical to spot-treat weeds with a spray of translocated herbicide without risk of damage to surrounding perennials. An

## MULCHING

*Clear any weeds and apply a 2.5–5cm (1–2in) layer of mulch, such as spent garden compost or bark chips, to moist soil. Take care not to damage the young shoots of the plant (here a peony).*

alternative is to use a "weed wiper" or "weeding glove" according to the manufacturers' instructions.

Organic mulches also provide some nutrients and are very important in maintaining the health and fertility of the soil. When planted into well-prepared and well-mulched soil, most perennials need little additional feeding, other than an annual top-dressing of bonemeal or a balanced slow-release fertilizer in spring. This is best applied after rain to the surface of moist soil. In dry conditions, water thoroughly first, then work the fertilizer gently into the soil surface with a hand or border fork. Do not let the fertilizer come into contact with the leaves, as it may scorch them. Plants such as *Rheum* or *Hosta*, which are grown mainly for their foliage, benefit from the occasional application of a high-nitrogen liquid fertilizer during the growing season to help produce large, lush leaves.

## Improving flowering

There are several ways of improving the number or size of flowers borne by perennials. Although most perennials produce many vigorous shoots in spring, some may be weak and spindly. If weak shoots are thinned at an early stage of development, the remaining shoots will be sturdier and usually produce larger flowers. When the shoots reach about one-quarter to one-third of their eventual height, pinch out or cut back the weak shoots at the base. This technique may be used with plants like delphiniums, phlox and Michaelmas daisies (*Aster*). Stopping is a similar technique that involves pinching out the growing tip of each stem, to produce sturdier growth and to prevent the plant from becoming tall and leggy. It also encourages the development of buds in the upper leaf axils, and is usually used on plants like *Rudbeckia* and *Helenium*, that readily produce sideshoots.

## HOW TO THIN PERENNIALS

**Thinning**
*Thin young shoots (phlox) when no more than a third of their final height. Remove one shoot in three by cutting or pinching out the weakest shoots at their base.*

## HOW TO STOP PERENNIALS

**Stopping**
*Stop shoots (here a Michaelmas daisy) by pinching out the top 2.5–5cm (1–2in) of the stem tip, when plants reach about one-third of their final height.*

## DEAD-HEADING TO PROLONG FLOWERING

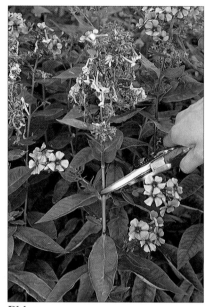

### Delphinium
*After flowering, when new basal shoots are visible, cut back the flowered stems to ground level. Delphiniums must be fed and watered well to produce a second crop of flowers later in the season.*

### Phlox
*Remove the terminal flower head as the flower begins to fade, cutting back to where sideshoots are produced from the leaf axils lower down the stem. This will encourage further sideshoots to flower.*

### Dead-heading
Unless a plant produces decorative seedheads, or seed is needed to raise further plants, most perennials are best dead-headed as the flowers fade. This prevents the plant from expending energy in the production of seed, and it then puts on new vegetative growth instead, giving rise to strong plants that bloom well the following year. In many cases, dead-heading also encourages a second crop of flowers on sideshoots, thus prolonging the flowering season. For some plants, such as *Centaurea* and delphiniums, the flowered stems are cut back right to the base when the first flowers have faded. The new shoots that develop may then produce another, lesser crop of flowers later in the season.

### Cutting back
A number of evergreen or semi-evergreen, sub-shrubby perennials, such as the marguerites (*Argyranthemum frutescens*), should be pruned annually in early spring. If left unpruned, they tend to produce bare, woody stems with a tuft of foliage at the top, creating a leggy and unattractive habit. Using secateurs, cut back the main stems by about half of their length to remove any twiggy, semi-woody and untidy growth. This will help maintain a dense mound of attractive foliage and encourage the production of strong new shoots that will then produce a succession of flowers throughout summer and autumn.

## Autumn clearance

In autumn, once the perennials have finished flowering, cut down all top-growth to the base and remove all dead or faded leaves and stems. Clear any residual weed growth to leave the beds and borders neat and tidy. In very cold areas, or if plants are not fully hardy, the top-growth may be left in place until early spring, since it offers the dormant crown some protection against winter frosts. Some perennial plants, such as *Sedum spectabile*, some astilbes and many grasses, have foliage or flower heads that remain attractive even when brown and dry in winter. These may be left in place during the winter months, but they are best removed in late autumn or just as new growth begins in spring.

A number of plants, such as *Cosmos atrosanguineus*, that may not be fully hardy in areas with cold wet winters, may be lifted in autumn and stored in frost-free conditions overwinter, to be replanted when the soil warms up in spring. This technique may also be used if autumn planting has been delayed by prolonged spells of wet weather, and is especially useful if transplanting perennials to a new garden, for example, when moving. Lift the plants when dormant and pack into boxes or crates of damp compost or bark so that the roots do not dry out. Store in a cool, dry, frost-free place.

## Spring operations

Just before new growth resumes in early spring, cut back any dead material that has been left *in situ* overwinter. Protect emerging new growth from slugs and snails; this is especially important for species with fleshy shoots like *Veratrum* or *Hosta*. Tall or fragile perennials need staking, and this is most easily done in early spring before the new growth is well-developed. Most forms of staking, although initially obtrusive, will be masked by foliage as the plants reach their final dimensions. Match the type of support used to the plant's habit of growth (see p.316).

## CUTTING DOWN IN AUTUMN

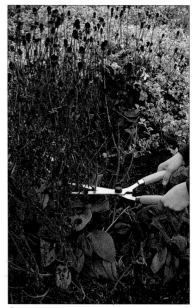

*In autumn or early winter, at the end of the flowering period, cut down all top-growth to ground level (here* Rudbeckia*) and remove all faded leaves and stems. Clear any weeds from the surrounding soil and leave the beds and borders neat and clean.*

## STORING PLANTS

*Lift dormant plants in winter and place them in a dry, frost-free place in boxes half-filled with moist bark or compost. Cover the roots with more bark or compost to keep them from drying out.*

## STAKING TALL AND FRAGILE PERENNIALS

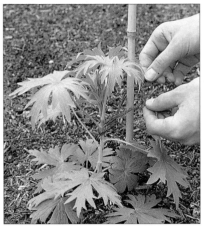

**Single cane**
*For tall, single-stemmed plants, such as this delphinium, as growth reaches 20cm (8in) insert a cane, two-thirds of the plant's height. Tie in the stem loosely with soft twine.*

**Link stakes**
*For tall, clump-forming plants, such as the* Aster *shown here, push link stakes deep into the soil, and raise them gradually as growth proceeds.*

**Ring stake**
*For low to medium-sized clump-formers, like peonies, use a grow-through ring stake. Set in position early in the season and, if necessary, raise the stake as the plant grows.*

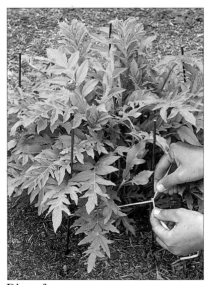

**Ring of canes**
*For weak-stemmed plants that are inclined to flop, here* Centaurea, *encircle the clump with split canes, and loop soft twine around and between the canes and stems.*

## Perennials in containers

Plants grown in containers need more care than those in open ground since they have limited supplies of food and water. During the growing season, keep the compost evenly moist, but never waterlogged. In periods of warm, dry weather, plants will need daily watering. Once they are well-established and in full growth, apply a balanced liquid fertilizer every two to three weeks. Lift and divide the plants every year or two in spring or autumn, and replant into fresh compost. If the container is to be re-used, wash it well before replanting, or pot up into a larger container. Trim the roots of shrubby perennials by about a quarter before repotting. In cold areas, move half-hardy and tender plants into the greenhouse in autumn. Keep them protected until the spring, and set out again when all danger of frost has passed.

## MAINTAINING PERENNIALS IN CONTAINERS

1 *Rejuvenate container-grown perennials in spring or autumn. Lift out and separate the plants carefully and shake the compost from their roots.*

2 *Discard the old compost and refill the container with fresh compost to within 10cm (4in) of the rim. Divide overgrown plants.*

3 *Plant up the container, fill with more fresh compost around the plants, to within 2.5–4cm (1–1½in) of the pot rim. Firm in with your fingers.*

4 *Finally, top-dress with a balanced slow-release fertilizer and mulch with gravel or bark chips. Water thoroughly, so that the compost is evenly moist and water runs through the drainage holes at the base. The plants shown here are bergenias, a* Pachysandra *and a hosta (now dormant) all of which are ideal for a shady patio or terrace.*

# PROPAGATION

There are several ways of propagating herbaceous perennials. Growing from seed is ideal where large numbers of new plants are required, although it is usually only suitable for species, since most cultivars will not come true from seed. For most perennials, division is the easiest and most frequent means of increase. This, and the other vegetative methods described here, should be used for increasing almost all cultivars.

### Seed
Raising plants from seed is a simple and inexpensive means of raising large numbers of plants. If collecting seed from the garden, bear in mind that most species will show natural variation in habit, vigour and flower colour, so only collect from strong plants with good flower form and colour. The seed of early flowering species usually ripens by mid-summer, and is best sown as soon as it is ripe, as this is when it germinates best. The young plants can be overwintered in a nursery bed or cold frame, depending on hardiness. Sow seed of later-flowering species when it

ripens in autumn; a few may germinate immediately, but most will sprout in the following spring. Alternatively, store ripe seed in a cool, dry place and sow in spring. The seed of some genera, notably *Paeonia*, and *Helleborus*, may remain dormant for long periods unless suitable conditions are provided, or occur naturally, to break dormancy.

Other seeds need a period of exposure to cold or to light to break dormancy, while those of many in the pea family have a hard seed coat that needs soaking or scarifying to allow it to imbibe the water necessary for germination.

### Pre-germination treatments
Seeds that need exposure to cold to break dormancy may be sown in autumn or winter. It is usually most convenient to sow them in containers placed outdoors in a cold frame or open frame, where they will germinate in spring. Alternatively, mix seed with damp seed compost in a plastic bag, and place it in a domestic refrigerator at 1–5°C (34–41°F) for 4–12 weeks. Check regularly for signs of germination (usually the appearance of the white root tip), then sow immediately.

Peony and *Trillium* seeds usually need two periods of cold to break dormancy. After the first winter the roots appear and, following the second winter, the shoot growth emerges. Seed is sown in autumn in the normal way, but is left in the cold frame for two winters.

Scarify seeds with hard coats either by rubbing them gently between two sheets of sandpaper (for small seeds) or by nicking the seed coat with a sharp blade (for larger ones). Alternatively, hard seed coats may be softened by soaking for up to 24 hours in hot, not boiling, water. As the seed imbibes water, it swells slightly but visibly. It is then sown immediately in the normal way. Seeds of *Baptisia* and other legumes, *Arum* and *Euphorbia* are treated in this way.

## COLLECTING SEED

*Collect ripened seedheads and shake seed out directly onto a piece of paper, or enclose the pods upside-down in a paper bag so that seeds fall into it. Store in a cool, dry place until ready to sow.*

Sowing seed in containers is the most convenient technique; a plastic half-tray, or 13cm (5in) pot, will accommodate sufficient plants for even the largest garden. Most proprietary seed composts are suitable, but if seedlings are to be kept in containers for any length of time after germination, use a good-quality loam-based one. Fill the container with compost, level off, then firm with a presser so that the compost surface is about 1cm (½in) below the container rim. Sow seed thinly (about 0.5cm/¼in apart); sowing too thickly results in spindly seedlings that are prone to damping off.

In general, seed needs to be covered to its own depth with sieved compost; leave those that need light to germinate uncovered (e.g. gentians). Label clearly with the plant name and sowing date, and water well, either using a can with a fine rose, or by standing in a tray of water until the surface is moist. Cover with a sheet of glass and place in a cold frame. Shade from hot sun with newspaper or shade netting. Remove the cover and reduce shading once seeds have germinated. If seeds need chilling, top-dress containers with fine grit and plunge them in an open frame.

## RAISING PLANTS FROM SEED

1 *Fill a 13cm (5in) pot with damp seed compost and firm gently with a presser, to about 1cm (½in) below the pot rim.*

2 *Using a clean, folded piece of paper, sprinkle seed thinly and evenly onto the soil surface (shown here are chrysanthemum seeds).*

3 *Cover with a shallow layer of finely sieved seed compost. Label and water from below until the surface is moist.*

4 *Cover with glass or clear plastic to retain moisture. Place in a cold frame until seeds develop 2 pairs of leaves.*

5 *Prick out seedlings into pots, trays or degradable pots (see inset). Handle only by the seed leaves; the stems are easily damaged.*

6 *When seedlings have developed into young plants with a good root system, plant out or pot on as appropriate.*

## Dividing perennials

Propagating by division, as described here, is the most usual means of increasing perennials that have a spreading rootstock and produce many shoots from the crown. By removing any old or unproductive parts, division can also be used to rejuvenate plants that lose vigour with age, become over-crowded, or die out at the centre of the clump.

Most plants should be divided during their dormant phase, between late autumn and early spring, but not in very cold, wet or dry weather, since the divisions will not re-establish well in

## HOW TO PROPAGATE PERENNIALS BY DIVISION

1 *Lift the plant to be divided gently, taking care to insert the fork beyond the immediate root zone, to reduce the risk of damaging fine roots. Shake off the surplus soil. The plant shown here is a helianthus.*

2 *Plants with a tough, woody rootstock are separated into sections by chopping through the crown with a spade. For very tough plants, set the spade in position and stand on it to apply your full body weight .*

3 *If possible, divide the plant into sections by teasing the roots apart gently by hand. Retain only the healthiest and most vigorous sections, each with several new shoots or growth buds and discard the remainder.*

4 *Cut back any old or dead top-growth, and replant the divisions at the same depth as the original parent plant. Firm in gently and water thoroughly. Continue to water regularly until re-established.*

these conditions. Division of fleshy-rooted perennials is best left until the end of their dormant season. In early spring, the new buds will have begun to sprout, thus giving a good indication of the most vigorous, and therefore most suitable, material for replanting.

First lift the plant to be divided, levering it up gently with a fork, taking care not to damage the roots. Shake off any loose soil and remove dead leaves or stems to reveal the next season's growth buds. Discard any old, unproductive or damaged sections of the clump. For fleshy-rooted plants, it is advisable to wash off the soil from the roots and crown so that all buds are clearly visible; they are then less likely to be damaged inadvertently when they are divided.

Many fibrous-rooted perennials are easily divided by teasing apart sections of the clump by hand (see left), and this is preferable wherever possible. Where the fibrous roots are tough and congested, insert two garden forks back-to-back near the centre of the clump with the tines close together. Separate the roots into sections by levering the fork handles backwards and forwards.

## ALTERNATIVE METHOD

*The technique of dividing fibrous-rooted, herbaceous perennials with garden forks, as shown here, is an old and traditional one. It can seem awkward at first, but is an invaluable technique once mastered. Set the forks back-to-back, so that they touch where the top of the tines meet the shaft. This acts as a leverage point, as the fork handles are moved backwards and forwards to prise the roots apart.*

## DIVIDING HOSTAS

1 *Divide large hostas with tough rootstocks in early spring, using a spade. Aim to produce sections with several buds. A section with six or more buds will produce a moderate-sized clump in its first year.*

2 *Smaller hostas that have looser, fleshy rootstocks may be separated by hand, or prised apart using forks back-to-back. Divide in early spring. Each section should have at least one eye, preferably more.*

Plants that form woody clumps or that have thick solid roots, like hostas, are cut into sections with a spade or knife. Trim each division cleanly with a sharp knife, to remove any damaged or rotting roots. Make sure that each section has at least two growth buds. Dust all cut surfaces with an appropriate fungicide and replant divisions as soon as possible. Large divisions should be replanted directly into their final flowering site, and will usually re-establish quickly. Smaller divisions may be grown on in a nursery bed, or potted up until they begin to grow vigorously. In general, divisions are best planted at the same depth as the original plant, but any that are prone to rotting at the base are best set slightly proud of the soil surface (see Planting Depths, p.309). After planting, water the plant in thoroughly, taking care not to wash away any soil from around the roots.

If replanting is delayed for any reason, it is vital to keep the roots moist. Dip them briefly in water and store the divisions in a plastic sack in a cool, shady

## DIVISION OF RHIZOMATOUS PLANTS

1 *Lift the plant to be divided (here an iris), inserting the fork well away from the rhizomes to avoid damaging them. Shake loose soil from the roots and separate the rhizomes into manageable pieces by hand.*

2 *Cut out any old or diseased rhizomes and discard them, then, using a sharp knife, slice off the newer, more vigorous rhizomes from the clump and trim off their ends neatly.*

3 *Dust the cut surfaces with fungicide. Trim long roots by about one-third of their length. For irises, cut the leaves to a mitre, no more than about 15cm (6in) long, to reduce wind rock.*

4 *Plant the rhizomes about 12–15cm (5–6in) apart. For irises, the rhizomes should be only half buried, with leaves and buds upright, and preferably with the rhizomes facing the sun.*

place until you are ready to replant. If the delay is likely to be longer than a few days, it is a good idea to store plants in a box of moist bark or compost (see p.315).

The technique for plants with thick rhizomes, such as bergenias or rhizomatous irises, is slightly different (see left). Split the clump into pieces by hand, then cut the rhizomes into individual sections, each with one or more growing points. Plants with long, narrow, upright leaves, such as irises, are susceptible to being blown about by the wind during the time they are becoming re-established. To reduce the risk of this happening and knocking over the new plants at such a critical time, the leaves are trimmed to a mitre, about 15cm (6in) long; they will be replaced by new leaves once the young roots have become established and growth resumes.

## Dividing peonies

Herbaceous peonies must be divided with special care, since they resent root disturbance and dislike being transplanted. Divisions re-establish very slowly and may take several growing seasons before they are large enough to resume flowering. They are, nevertheless, well worth a patient wait, as once established they continue to bloom for many years in the same site. For best results, lift and divide the plants towards the end of their dormant season in early spring, when the new buds are beginning to swell and are clearly visible. Cut the crown into sections, each with several buds, with a clean sharp knife, taking care not to damage the thick, fleshy roots. Dust the cut surfaces with fungicide and replant immediately. Prepare the new planting hole by digging deeply, incorporating bone meal and very well-rotted manure or garden compost to the bottom of the planting hole. Replant the divisions at the same depth as the original parent plant.

## DIVIDING PEONIES

1 *Lift the plant in early spring, when healthy growth buds are visible on the crown. Cut the crown into sections, each one with several buds.*

2 *Dust the cut surfaces of the divided sections with fungicide to discourage fungal infections and rot, which could cause the young, newly divided peony plants to perish.*

3 *Plant out the divided sections approximately 20cm (8in) apart. The buds should be just visible at the surface of the soil. Firm in gently and water thoroughly.*

324 • GUIDE TO PERENNIAL CARE

## Stem tip cuttings

Herbaceous perennials that are difficult to divide successfully, such as *Argyranthemum* and *Erysimum*, can be increased by taking stem tip cuttings. Cuttings can be taken at any time during the growing season, provided that suitable shoots are available.

Select the strongly growing tips of non-flowering shoots and reject any that are thin, weak, leggy or damaged. They should be inserted as soon as possible, and must not be allowed to wilt. They are best taken in the early morning, when plants are at their most turgid, and placed into a sealed, opaque plastic bag until insertion.

Take cuttings 7.5–12cm (3–5in) long, with secateurs or a clean, sharp knife, cutting just above a leaf joint. Trim the cuttings to just below a node and remove the leaves from the lowest third of the stem. Insert the cuttings, almost to the lowest leaves, into prepared pots of proprietary propagating compost, firming in gently with the fingers. Ensure that the leaves do not touch each other and that air can circulate freely.

Water in using a can with a fine rose, and treat with liquid fungicide. If possible, place the pot in a mist unit or propagator to maintain high humidity. Alternatively, cover the cuttings with a plastic bag or tent, supported by wire hoops or canes, to keep the plastic well clear of the leaves. Any condensation that forms on the foliage may lead to fungal infection and the loss of the cuttings. Shade the cuttings in hot weather to prevent the leaves from scorching or wilting, but remove shading as soon as possible to admit maximum light. Cuttings will become drawn and leggy in poor light. Inspect them daily and remove any fallen or dead leaves to reduce the risk of fungal infections. Keep the compost moist but not wet.

The cuttings should root within about three weeks. Admit air gradually to wean them from their humid environment, then pot up singly and grow on before planting out into their flowering site.

## STEM TIP CUTTINGS

1 *Select short lengths of soft, non-flowering shoots, about 7.5–12cm (3–5in) long. Use only the tips of strong healthy shoots, and cut them just above a node. The plant shown is a penstemon.*

2 *Trim the lower end of the cutting just below a node, with a straight cut, reducing the length to about 5–7.5cm (2–3in). Remove the leaves from the lowest third of the cutting.*

3 *Insert the cuttings around the edge of the pot. Space so that the leaves do not touch. Cover with a plastic bag supported by hoops or canes to keep it clear of the leaves.*

## Basal stem cuttings

Propagating from basal stem cuttings is a technique used for plants with pithy or hollow stems, such as lupins (*Lupinus*) and delphiniums, and those such as chrysanthemums and cultivars of *Anthemis tinctoria* that produce soft new shoots from the base in spring. This type of cutting is usually taken in mid-spring, from the base of the plant at or just below soil level. To produce cutting material earlier in the season, plants may be lifted and planted in boxes of potting compost and forced into growth in a heated greenhouse. When cuttings have been removed, the plant may be returned to the open garden.

Select strong healthy shoots of which the first leaves have just unfolded, and remove them with a sharp knife, cutting as close to the base as possible, so that part of the firmer, semi-woody basal tissue is also included. Trim off the lowest leaves, treat the base of the cutting with hormone rooting preparation and insert in a proprietary cutting compost, either singly in individual pots, or several to a tray or pot. Firm in and water well, then transfer the containers to a cold frame or propagator. Alternatively, enclose them in a clear plastic bag, kept clear of the cuttings with canes or wire hoops. Shade the cuttings from direct sun to prevent scorching or wilting of the leaves.

Check the cuttings every few days, and remove any faded or fallen leaves to reduce the risk of fungal infections. Keep the compost evenly moist, but not wet, and wipe the glass or plastic covers clean to remove condensation.

Basal cuttings should root within a month. Once rooted, tip them gently out of the pot and separate them carefully. retaining as much soil around the new roots as possible. Pot them up into individual pots using a suitable loam-based potting compost. Grow on until large enough to set out into their final flowering site. Plants that are not fully hardy must be hardened off and planted out when all danger of frost has passed.

## BASAL STEM CUTTINGS

1 Take cuttings (here a chrysanthemum) when the shoots reach about 3.5–5cm (1½–2in). Remove close to the base with a small portion of basal wood. Delphinium cuttings should be 7.5–10cm (3–4in) long.

2 Remove all the basal leaves and trim the base of the cutting, making a straight cut with a sharp knife. Treat the cut end with hormone rooting preparation.

3 Insert the cuttings into a prepared pot of damp propagating compost. Water well. Place in a propagator or use a plastic bag supported by hoops or canes to keep the plastic clear of the leaves.

## Root cuttings

This method is used for perennials such as *Acanthus* and *Papaver orientale* that have thick fleshy roots. It is also useful for the non-variegated cultivars of border phlox that are susceptible to an eelworm that affects the top-growth, but not the roots. Variegated cultivars produce only green foliage plants from root cuttings.

Root cuttings are best taken when the plant is dormant, usually in winter.

The technique for thin-rooted plants, like *Anemone hupehensis*, *Campanula*, *Phlox*, and *Primula denticulata*, differs slightly from that shown below. Make cuttings 7–12cm (3–5in) long, so that there is sufficient food storage for the developing cuttings. Lay them horizontally on the surface of damp compost in a tray, and cover to at least their own depth. Then treat as for standard root cuttings.

## PROPAGATING PERENNIALS BY ROOT CUTTINGS

1 *Lift the parent plant (here an acanthus) when dormant and wash the soil from the roots. Select roots of pencil thickness and cut them off with a sharp knife close to the crown. Trim off any fibrous roots.*

2 *Cut the roots into sections, 5–10cm (2–4in) long, with a straight cut at the top of the root, and an angled cut at the bottom. New shoots appear from the top of the cutting; be sure to insert the right way up.*

3 *Insert cuttings vertically into pots of damp cutting compost, with the top end of the cutting flush with the surface. Firm in, water well, and top-dress with coarse grit. Label and place in a cold frame.*

4 *When the cuttings have developed young shoots, pot them up into individual pots filled with loam-based potting compost. Label each pot clearly and grow on the new plants until large enough to plant out.*

## Grafting

A few perennials, such as *Gypsophila paniculata* 'Bristol Fairy', do not root readily from cuttings and are increased by grafting onto seedling understock of the species. Lift plants of the cultivar to be propagated in autumn, pot up and grow on in a cool greenhouse. They will then produce new shoots in mid-to late winter, the optimal time for grafting.

Lift 1–2 year old stock plants of the species in mid- to late winter. The principle is to graft strong healthy shoots of the scion (the cultivar) onto strong roots of the rootstock (*Gypsophila paniculata* species). In ideal conditions, the graft union should form within six weeks. The grafted plants can then be potted up and grown on in frost-free conditions, to be planted out in early summer when danger of frost has passed.

## PROPAGATION BY GRAFTING

1 Select and prepare the rootstock. Cut a straight piece of strong, healthy root, 1cm (½in) thick, and 9cm (3½in) long.

2 Remove fibrous roots, shorten lateral roots to 1cm (½in), and cut a 1cm (½in) incision into the straight-cut top of the stock.

3 Select a vigorous shoot from the scion, 3–4mm (⅛in) thick, 3–7cm (1½–3in) long. Trim the lower end to a wedge shape.

4 Insert the stock into a 6cm (3in) pot of damp cutting compost. Place the scion into the vertical incision in the stock.

5 Bind the graft union with plastic tape or raffia to hold the scion firmly in position. Label and water well.

6 Cover with a plastic bag supported by canes. Place in light, warm conditions until new shoots appear above the union.

# GLOSSARY OF TERMS

Italicized words have their own entry.

**ACID** (of soil). With a pH value of less than 7, or lacking in lime; see also *alkaline* and *neutral*.

**ALKALINE** (of soil). With a pH value of more than 7, or lime-rich; see also *acid* and *neutral*.

**ALPINE HOUSE.** An unheated, well-ventilated greenhouse used for cultivating alpine and bulbous plants.

**ALTERNATE** (of leaves). Occurring successively at different levels on opposite sides of a stem. (Cf *Opposite*).

**ANEMONE CENTRED** (of flowers). Flowers or flower heads in which the central petals or flowers (modified *stamens*) form a cushion-like mound and the outer rim or petals or ray florets are flat and spreading, as in some chrysanthemums.

**ANTHER.** The part of a *stamen* that produces pollen.

**AWN.** A sharp point or bristle, commonly found on grass seed and flower heads.

**AXIL.** The angle between a leaf and stem where an axillary bud develops.

**BACKFILL.** To fill in a planting hole around a plant's roots with a soil mix.

**BRACT.** A modified leaf at the base of a flower or flower cluster. It may resemble a normal leaf or be reduced and scale-like in appearance. It may also be large and brightly coloured.

**BULBIL.** A small bulb-like organ, often borne in a leaf axil, occasionally on a stem or in a flower head.

**CALYX.** The outer part of a flower, usually small and green but sometimes showy and brightly coloured; it is formed from the sepals and encloses the petals in a bud.

**COMPOUND LEAF.** A leaf that is divided into two or more leaflets.

**COROLLA.** The part of a flower formed by the petals.

**CROCKS.** Broken pieces of clay pot, used to cover drainage holes of pots in order to provide free drainage and air circulation to the root system and to stop the growing medium from escaping, or blocking, the holes.

**CROWN.** The basal part at soil level of a *herbaceous* plant where roots and stem join and from where new shoots are produced.

**CULTIVAR.** A contraction of "cultivated variety" (abbreviated to "cv"); a group (or one among such a group) of cultivated plants clearly distinguished by one or more characteristics and which retains these characteristics when propagated.

**CUTTING.** A section of a plant which is removed and used for propagation. For the various methods see *Guide to Perennial Care*, pp.324–327.

**DEAD-HEADING.** The removal of spent flowers or *flower heads*.

**DECIDUOUS.** Losing its leaves annually at the end of the growing season; semi-deciduous plants lose only some leaves.

**DIEBACK.** The death of tips or shoots due to damage or disease.

**DISBUDDING.** The removal of surplus buds to encourage production of high-quality flowers or fruits. See also *stopping*.

**DIVISION.** A method of propagation by which a plant clump is divided into separate parts during dormancy. See *Guide to Perennial Care*, pp.320–323.

**DORMANCY.** The state of temporary cessation of growth and slowing down of other activities in whole plants, usually during winter.

**ELLIPTIC** (of leaves). Broadening at the centre and narrowing towards each end.

**EPIPHYTE.** A plant which grows on another without being parasitic, obtaining nutrients and moisture from the air without rooting in soil.

**EVERGREEN.** Retaining its leaves all year round, although losing some older leaves regularly throughout the year. Semi-evergreen plants retain only some leaves or lose older leaves only when new growth is produced.

**EYE.** The centre of a flower, of particular note if different in colour from the petals.

**FALLS.** The drooping, or horizontal petals of irises.

**FLOWER.** The part of the plant containing the reproductive organs usually surrounded by *sepals* and *petals*.

**FLOWER HEAD.** A mass of small flowers or florets that together appear to form a single flower e.g. daisy.

**FLORET.** A single flower in a head of many flowers.

**FRIABLE.** Soil of a crumbly texture, able to be worked easily.

**GENUS** (pl. genera). A category in plant classification, consisting of a group of related *species*.

**GLAUCOUS.** Blue-green, blue-grey, grey, or with a bluish, greyish, or whitish bloom.

**GLOBOSE.** Spherical.

**GRAFTING.** Method of propagation by which an artificial union is made between different parts of individual plants. See *Guide to Perennial Care*, p.327.

**HABIT.** The characteristic growth or general appearance of a plant.

**HERB.** A plant grown for its medicinal or flavouring properties or for its scented foliage.

HERBACEOUS. Non-woody plant of which the upper parts die back to the rootstock at the end of the growing season.

HUMUS. The organic residue of decayed vegetable matter in soil. Also often used to describe partly decayed matter such as leafmould or compost.

HYBRID. The offspring of genetically different parents, usually produced accidentally or artificially in cultivation, but occasionally arising in the wild.

INCURVED. Applied to *petals* and *florets* that curve inwards to form a compact, rounded shape.

INFLORESCENCE. A group of flowers borne on a single axis (stem) e.g. *umbel.*

LATERAL. A side growth that emerges from a shoot or root.

LEAFLET. A subdivision of a compound leaf.

LINEAR (of leaves). Very narrow with parallel sides.

LIME. Compounds of calcium; the amount of lime in soil determines whether it is *acid, neutral* or *alkaline.*

LOBE. A rounded projecting segment or part, forming part of a larger structure.

MICROCLIMATE. A small, local climate within a larger climate area, such as a greenhouse or a protected area of a garden.

MULCH. A layer of *organic* material applied to the soil over or around a plant to conserve moisture, protect the roots from frost, reduce the growth of weeds, and enrich the soil e.g. chipped bark, rotted manure, garden compost, black polythene, gravel.

NEUTRAL (of soil). With a pH value of 7, the point at which soil is neither acid nor alkaline.

ORGANIC. 1. Compounds containing carbon derived from decomposed plant or animal organisms. 2. Used loosely of mulches, composts, etc. derived from plant materials.

PALMATE (of leaves). Having four or more leaflets growing from a single point, as in horse chestnut (*Aesculus hippocastanum*).

PERENNIAL. Living for at least three seasons; commonly used of *herbaceous* plants, and *woody* perennials, i.e. trees and shrubs.

PETAL. One portion of the often bright and coloured part of the *corolla.*

PETIOLE. The stalk of a leaf.

PHYLLODE. An expanded leaf stalk, which functions as, and resembles, a leaf blade e.g. asparagus.

PINCH OUT. Remove the growing tip of a plant, with finger and thumb, to induce the production of sideshoots or the formation of flower buds.

PINNATE (of leaves). A compound leaf in which the leaflets grow in two rows on each side of the midrib.

PROPAGATOR. A structure that provides a humid atmosphere for seedlings, cuttings, or other plants being propagated.

PROSTRATE. With stems growing along the ground.

RECURVED. Of petals or leaves, curved backwards.

REVERT. To return to an original state, as when plain green leaves are produced on a variegated plant.

RHIZOME. Underground, creeping stem, that acts as a storage organ and produces leafy shoots.

ROOT. The part of a plant, normally underground, that functions as an anchorage and through which nutrients are absorbed.

ROOT BALL. The roots and accompanying soil or compost visible when a plant is removed from a container or lifted from the open ground.

RUNNER. A horizontally spreading stem that runs above ground and roots at the nodes to form new plants. Often confused with *stolon.*

SEPAL. Part of a *calyx.* Though usually green and insignificant, they may sometimes be showy.

SPATHE. One, or sometimes two, large *bracts,* that surround a flower cluster or individual bud.

SPECIES. A category in plant classification, the rank below *genus,* containing closely related, very similar individual plants.

STAMEN. The male floral organ, bearing an *anther* that produces pollen.

STIGMA. The area of the female part of the flower which receives pollen.

STOLON. A horizontally spreading or arching stem, usually above ground, which roots at its tip to produce a new plant. Often confused with *runner.*

STRATIFICATION. The storage of seeds in warm or cold conditions to break dormancy and aid germination.

STOPPING. The removal of the growing tip of a plant (by finger and thumb) to induce the production of sideshoots or the formation of flower heads. Also known as "pinching out".

STYLE. The part of the flower on which the *stigma* is carried.

SUB-SHRUB. A plant that is *woody* at the base, but whose shoots die back in winter.

TUBER. Thickened, usually underground, food storage organ, derived from a stem or root.

UMBEL. A usually flat-topped or rounded flower cluster, in which the individual flower stalks rise from a central point. In a compound umbel each primary stalk ends in an umbel.

VEGETATIVE GROWTH. Non-flowering, usually leafy growth.

WHORL. Where three or more organs, e.g. leaves, arise from the same point.

WIND-ROCK. The destabilizing of a plant's roots by wind.

WOODY. With branches of hard, woody fibres, that persist, unlike soft-stemmed herbaceous plants. A semi-woody stem contains some softer tissue and may be only partially persistent.

# INDEX

Each genus name is shown in **bold type**, followed by a brief description. Species, varieties and subspecies are given in *italics*; cultivars are in Roman type with single quotes. Common names appear in brackets.

## A

Abyssinian banana see *Ensete ventricosum*

**Acanthus (Bear's breeches)**
Hardy perennials, some of which are semi-evergreen, grown for their large, deeply cut leaves and their spikes of flowers.
*balcanicus* see *A. hungaricus*
*hungaricus* 113
*longifolius* see *A. hungaricus* 114

**Achillea**
Hardy, mainly upright perennials, some of which are semi-evergreen, suited to borders and rock gardens. Have fern-like foliage and large, usually plate-like flower heads mainly in summer.
*ageratum*
'W.B. Childs' (Sweet Nancy) 71
'Coronation Gold' 142
'Fanal' 112
*filipendulina* 'Goldplate' 144
'Forncett Candy' 85
'Lachsschönheit' 107
*millefolium* 'Cerise Queen' 91
'Moonshine' 257
*ptarmica*
'Boule de Neige' see 'The Pearl'
'The Pearl' 71
'Salmon Beauty' see 'Lachsschönheit'
'Schwellenburg' 257
'Taygetea' 256
'The Beacon' see 'Fanal'
'Wesersandstein' 78

**Achimenes (Hot-water plant)**
Frost-tender, erect or trailing perennials with small rhizomes and showy flowers.
'Little Beauty' 217

**Aciphylla**
Hardy, evergreen perennials grown for the architectural value of their spiky foliage but also for their flowers, which are produced more freely on male plants.
*aurea* (Golden Spaniard) 68

*Aciphylla continued*
*squarrosa* (Bayonet plant, Common Spaniard) 168

**Aconitum (Monkshood, Wolf's bane)**
Hardy perennials with toxic, tuberous or fibrous roots, rounded leaves and upright stems, bearing hooded flowers in summer. Good for rock gardens and borders.
'Bressingham Spire' 118
x *cammarum* 'Bicolor' 120
*lycoctonum* subsp. *vulparia* 131
'Spark's Variety' 28
*vulparia* see *A. lycoctonum* subsp. *vulparia*

**Actaea (Baneberry)**
Hardy perennials grown for their colourful, toxic berries.
*alba* (Doll's eyes, White baneberry) 146
*pachypoda* see *A. alba*

**Adiantum**
Fully hardy to frost-tender, semi-evergreen, evergreen or deciduous ferns.
*pedatum* 302
var. *aleuticum* 303
*venustum* 305

**Adonis**
Hardy, spring-flowering perennials grown for their foliage and flowers.
*amurensis* 199
*brevistyla* 173
*vernalis* 198

**Aegopodium (Bishop's weed, Gout weed, Ground elder)**
Hardy, invasive, rhizomatous perennials, many of which are weeds. Grown as ground cover.
*podagraria* 'Variegatum' (Variegated ground elder) 203

African violet see *Saintpaulia*

**Agapanthus**
Clump-forming perennials (some of which are evergreen) with upright stems carrying large heads of usually blue flowers, often ageing to purple. Narrow leaved forms are frost hardy, broad-leaved ones half hardy.
'Blue Giant' 124
'Dorothy Palmer' 124
*praecox* subsp. *orientalis* 126

**Aglaonema (Chinese evergreen)**
Frost-tender, evergreen, erect,

*Aglaonema continued*
tufted perennials grown mainly for their foliage.
*commutatum* 'Silver King' 288
*picta* 288

**Ajuga**
Hardy annuals and perennials, of which some are semi-evergreen or evergreen. Good ground cover.
*reptans*
'Atropurpurea' 285
'Multicolor' 286
'Rainbow' see 'Multicolor'

**Alchemilla (Lady's mantle)**
Hardy perennials bearing sprays of tiny, greenish-yellow flowers, with conspicuous outer calyces, in summer. Good ground cover.
*conjuncta* 247
*mollis* 247

**Alocasia**
Frost-tender, evergreen perennials with underground rhizomes, grown for their attractive foliage. Tiny flowers are produced on a spadix enclosed in a leaf-like spathe.
*cuprea* 167

Alpine catchfly see *Lychnis viscaria*

**Alopecurus** see **Grasses**
*pratensis*
'Aureomarginatus' see 'Aureovariegatus'
'Aureovariegatus' (Golden foxtail) 298

**Alpinia**
Frost-tender, mainly evergreen perennials with fleshy rhizomes, grown for their flowers.
*nutans* see *A. zerumbet*
*speciosa* see *A. zerumbet*
*zerumbet* (Shellflower, Shell ginger) 22

**Alsobia** see **Episcia**

**Alstroemeria (Peruvian lily)**
Hardy, mostly summer-flowering, tuberous perennials with showy, multicoloured flowers. The cut flowers last well in water.
Ligtu Hybrids 145

Alum root see *Heuchera*

**Amsonia (Blue star)**
Hardy, slow-growing, clump-forming, summer-flowering perennials.
*orientalis* 243

*Asperula odoratum* see *Galium odoratum*

**Asphodeline**
Frost to half-hardy perennials with thick, fleshy roots.
*lutea* (King's spear, Yellow asphodel) 69

**Asphodelus**
Frost to half-hardy, spring- or summer-flowering perennials. The genus also includes annuals.
*albus* (White asphodel) 73
*luteus* see *Asphodeline lutea*

**Aspidistra**
Frost-tender, evergreen, rhizomatous perennials that spread slowly, grown mainly for their glossy foliage.
*elatior* 'Variegata' 278

**Asplenium**
Fully hardy to frost-tender, semi-evergreen or evergreen ferns.
*ceterach* (Rusty-back fern) 301
*nidus* (Bird's nest fern) 305
*scolopendrium* (Hart's tongue fern) 304
  Crispum Group 304
*trichomanes* (Maidenhair spleenwort) 301

**Aster (Michaelmas daisy)**
Fully to half-hardy perennials and deciduous or evergreen sub-shrubs with daisy-like flower heads borne in summer-autumn.
*amellus* 'King George' 160
*cordifolius* 'Silver Spray' 157
*ericoides* 'White Heather' 156
× *frikartii*
  'Mönch' 158
  'Wunder von Stäfa' 159
  'Goldilocks' see *A. linosyris*
*lateriflorus*
  'Delight' 156
  'Horizontalis' 157
*linosyris* (Goldilocks) 160
*novae-angliae*
  'Alma Pötschke' see 'Andenken an Alma Pötschke'
  'Andenken an Alma Pötschke' 158
  'Autumn Snow' see 'Herbstschnee'
  'Barr's Pink' 157
  'Harrington's Pink' 157
  'Herbstschnee' 157
*novi-belgii*
  'Apple Blossom' 157
  'Carnival' 157
  'Chequers' 160
  'Fellowship' 158

*Aster novi-belgii* continued
  'Freda Ballard' 158
  'Jenny' 158
  'Lassie' 157
  'Marie Ballard' 159
  'Orlando' 158
  'Patricia Ballard' 158
  'Peace' 160
  'Professor Anton Kippenburg' 159
  'Royal Ruby' 158
  'Royal Velvet' 160
  'White Swan' 156
*thomsonii* 'Nanus' 159
*turbinellus* 159

**Astilbe**
Hardy, summer-flowering perennials grown for their sprays of flowers that remain handsome even when dried brown in winter. Suited to borders and rock gardens.
× *arendsii* 'Venus' see 'Venus'
  'Deutschland' 204
  'Fanal' 228
  'Irrlicht' 204
  'Montgomery' 108
  'Ostrich Plume' see 'Straussenfeder'
  'Straussenfeder' 90
  'Venus' 89

**Astrantia (Masterwort)**
Hardy perennials widely used in flower arrangements.
*major* 208
  subsp. *involucrata* 208
  'Sunningdale Variegated' 128
*maxima* 210

**Athyrium**
Fully hardy to frost-tender deciduous or, occasionally, semi-evergreen ferns.
*goeringianum* see *A. niponicum*
*niponicum* (Painted fern) 305

*Avena candida* of gardens see *Helictrotrichon sempervirens*
Avens see *Geum*

## B

Baby's tears see *Soleirolia*
Balloon flower see *Platycodon grandiflorus*

**Ballota**
Frost-hardy perennials and evergreen or deciduous sub-shrubs grown for their foliage and flowers.
*pseudodictamnus* 291

Banana see *Musa*

Baneberry see *Actaea*

**Baptisia**
Hardy summer-flowering perennials grown for their flowers.
*australis* (Blue false indigo) 120

**Barbarea**
Hardy summer-flowering perennials, biennials and annuals of which most species are weeds or winter salad plants. The variegated form of *B. vulgaris* is grown for decorative purposes.
*vulgaris* 'Variegata' (Variegated winter cress) 257

Barberton daisy see *Gerbera jamesonii*
Bastard balm see *Melittis*
Bayonet plant see *Aciphylla squarrosa*
Bead fern see *Onoclea sensibilis*
Bear's breeches see *Acanthus*
Bedstraw see *Galium*

**Begonia**
Frost-tender, deciduous shrubs, small tree-like plants, perennials and annuals grown for their colourful flowers and/or ornamental leaves.
*albopicta* (Guinea-wing begonia) 269
  'Apricot Cascade' 273
  'Billie Langdon' 269
*bowerae* (Eyelash begonia) 272
  'Can-Can' 273
× *corallina* 'Lucerna' 271
  'Duartei' 271
  'Flamboyant' 271
*foliosa* (Fern begonia) 269
*haageana* see *B. scharffii*
  'Helen Lewis' 271
  'Ingramii' 270
  'Iron Cross' see *B. masoniana*
  'Lucerna' see *B.* × *corallina* 'Lucerna'
*manicata* 270
  'Crispa' 272
*masoniana* (Iron-cross begonia) 272
  'Merry Christmas' 270
*metallica* (Metallic-leaf begonia) 270
*nelumbiifolia* (Lily-pad begonia) 273
  'Norah Bedson' 273
  'Oliver Twist' 273
  'Orange Rubra' 273
  'Organdy' 271
  'Orpha C. Fox' 272
*olsoniae* 269
*prismatocarpa* 273
*pustulata* 'Argentea' 272

Cape dandelion see *Arctotheca
calendula*

**Cardamine (Bitter cress)**
Hardy spring-flowering annuals and
perennials. Some are weeds, but
others are suitable for informal and
woodland gardens.
  *enneaphyllos* 198
  *pentaphyllos* 181

Cardoon see *Cynara cardunculus*

**Carex see Sedges**
  *elata* 'Aurea' (Bowles' golden
    sedge) 298
  *hachijoensis* 'Evergold' 298
  *oshimensis* 'Evergold' see *C.
    hachijoensis* 'Evergold'
  *pendula* (Pendulous sedge) 298
  *stricta* 'Aurea' see *C. elata*
    'Aurea'

**Catananche (Blue cupidone)**
Hardy perennials with daisy-like
flower heads that dry well.
  *caerulea* 'Major' 240

Cat's valerian see *Valeriana
officinalis*
Cathedral windows see *Calathea
makoyana*
Catmint see *Nepeta*

**Cautleya**
Frost-hardy summer- and autumn-
flowering perennials.
  *spicata* 267

Celandine see *Chelidonium*

**Centaurea (Knapweed)**
Hardy annuals and perennials
grown for their flower heads of
slender ray petals around a thistle-
like centre.
  *hypoleuca* 'John Coutts' 214
  *macrocephala* 134
  *montana* (Perennial cornflower)
    236
  *pulcherrima* 89

**Centranthus**
Hardy late spring- to autumn-
flowering perennials.
  *ruber* (Red valerian) 107

**Cephalaria**
Hardy coarse, summer-flowering
perennials, best suited to large
borders and wild gardens.
  *gigantea* (Giant scabious, Yellow
    scabious) 31
  *tatarica* see *Cephalaria
    gigantea*

**Chaerophyllum**
Fully hardy perennials with finely
divided foliage and heads of tiny
white or pink flowers. Most are
suitable only for wild gardens;
ornamental species are grown for
their foliage and flowers.
  *hirsutum* 'Roseum' 90

*Chamaenerion* see *Epilobium*
Chamomile see *Anthemis*
Chatham Island forget-me-not see
  *Myosotidium hortensia*
Checkerbloom see *Sidalcea
  malviflora*

**Cheiranthus see Erysimum**

**Chelidonium
(Celandine, Greater celandine)**
A genus of only one species of
hardy perennial that rapidly forms
ground cover.
  *majus* 'Flore Pleno' 69

**Chelone (Turtle-head)**
Hardy summer- and autumn-
flowering perennials.
  *barbata* see *Penstemon barbata*
  *obliqua* 146

Chicory see *Cichorium*
Chinese evergreen see *Aglaonema*

**Chirita**
Frost-tender evergreen perennials or
sub-shrubs grown for their flowers.
  *lavandulacea* 268

**Chlorophytum**
Frost-tender, evergreen, stemless
perennials with short rhizomes,
grown for their foliage.
  *comosum* 'Vittatum' (Spider plant)
    277

Chocolate cosmos see *Cosmos
  atrosanguineus*

**Chondrosum see Grasses**
  *gracile* (Blue grama, Mosquito
    grass) 296

Christmas rose see *Helleborus
  niger*

**Chrysanthemum**
Genus of hardy annuals grown for
their flowers. The genus used to
include deciduous and evergreen
perennials and evergreen sub-shrubs
that are now botanically reclassified
into various genera; the florists'
chrysanthemums (now considered to
belong to the genus *Dendranthema*)

*Chrysanthemum* continued
listed here are classified according to
flower form and flowering season.
  'Alison Kirk' 149
  'Autumn Days' 155
  'Brietner' 151
  'Bronze Fairie' 154
  'Bronze Hedgerow' 155
  'Bronze Yvonne Arnaud' 154
  'Buff Margaret' 155
  'Cherry Chintz' 150
  'Chippendale' 151
  'Clara Curtis' 147
  'Cloudbank' 149
  'Dawn Mist' 149
  'Discovery' 152
  'Dorridge Dream' 150
  'Duke of Kent' 149
  'Edwin Painter' 153
  *frutescens* see *Argyranthemum
    frutescens*
  'Jamaica Primrose' see
    *Argyranthemum* 'Jamaica
    Primrose'
  'Mary Wootton' see
    *Argyranthemum* 'Mary Wootton'
  'George Griffiths' 152
  'Golden Woolman's Glory' 154
  'Green Satin' 152
  'Madeleine' 150
  'Maria' 151
  'Marian Gosling' 150
  'Marion' 152
  'Marlene Jones' 153
  'Michael Fish' 149
  'Oracle' 155
  'Pavilion' 149
  'Peach Brietner' 155
  'Peach Margaret' 155
  'Pennine Alfie' 154
  'Pennine Flute' 151
  'Pennine Jewel' 153
  'Pennine Oriel' 149
  'Primrose West Bromwich' 153
  'Purple Pennine Wine' 151
  'Redwing' 150
  'Ringdove' 150
  'Roblush' 150
  'Rose Yvonne Arnaud' 152
  *rubellum* 'Clara Curtis' see 'Clara
    Curtis'
  'Rytorch' 155
  'Sally Ball' 154
  'Salmon Fairie' 154
  'Salmon Fairweather' 149
  'Salmon Margaret' 155
  'Sentry' 152
  'Skater's Waltz' 151
  x *superbum*
    'Elizabeth' see *Leucanthemum* x
      *superbum* 'Elizabeth'
    'Esther Read' see *Leucanthemum*
      x *superbum* 'Esther Read'
  'Talbot Jo' 151
  'Wendy' 154

Fishtail fern see *Cyrtomium falcatum*

**Fittonia**
Frost-tender, evergreen, creeping perennials grown mainly for their foliage. Useful as ground cover.
*argyroneura* see *F. verschaffeltii* var.
*argyroneura*
*verschaffeltii* (Mosaic plant, Painted net-leaf) 284
var. *argyroneura* (Silver net-leaf) 277

Flame violet see *Episcia cupreata*
Flamingo flower see *Anthurium andreanum*
Flax lily see *Dianella*
Fleabane see *Erigeron*
Flower of Jove see *Lychnis flos-jovis*
Flowering banana see *Musa ornata*
Flowering tobacco see *Nicotiana sylvestris*
Foamflower see *Tiarella*

**Foeniculum**
Fully to frost-hardy summer-flowering perennials, some of which are grown for their umbels of yellow flowers. Also grown for the decorative leaves, which can be used for culinary flavouring. The genus also includes biennials.
*vulgare*
'Bronze' see 'Purpureum'
'Purpureum' (Purple fennel) 27

Four o'clock flower see *Mirabilis*
Foxglove see *Digitalis*
Foxtail barley see *Hordeum jubatum*
Foxtail lily see *Eremurus*

**Francoa**
Frost-hardy, summer- and early autumn-flowering perennials.
*sonchifolia* (Bridal wreath) 87

Freckle face see *Hypoestes phyllostachya*
French honeysuckle see *Hedysarum coronarium*
Funkia see *Hosta*

--------- G ---------

Garden loosestrife see *Lysimachia punctata*

**Gaillardia (Blanket flower)**
Fully to frost-hardy, summer-flowering annuals and perennials that tend to be short-lived.
*aristata* 258
'Dazzler' 232

*Gaillardia continued*
x *grandiflora* 'Dazzler' see 'Dazzler'

**Galega (Goat's rue)**
Hardy summer-flowering perennials.
*orientalis* 120
x *hartlandii* 'Lady Wilson' 30

**Galium (Bedstraw)**
Hardy spring- and summer-flowering perennials, many of which are weeds. *G. odoratum* is cultivated as ground cover.
*odoratum* (Sweet woodruff, Woodruff) 201

Garden myrrh see *Myrrhis odorata*
Gardener's garters see *Phalaris arundinacea* var. *picta*
Garland flower see *Hedychium*
Gay feathers see *Liatris*

**Gazania**
Half-hardy perennials often grown as annuals, useful for summer bedding, pots and tubs.
*rigens* var. *uniflora* 261

Gentian see *Gentiana*

**Gentiana (Gentian)**
Hardy perennials, some of which are semi-evergreen or evergreen, grown for their usually blue flowers. Excellent for rock gardens and peat beds. The genus also includes annuals and biennials.
*asclepiadea* (Willow gentian) 161
*lutea* (Great yellow gentian) 131

**Geranium (Cranesbill)**
Fully to half-hardy perennials, some of which are semi-evergreen, grown for their attractive flowers and often as ground cover. Compact species are suitable for rock gardens.
'Ann Folkard' 217
*armenum* see *G. psilostemon*
*asphodeloides* 212
'Buxton's Blue' see *G. wallichianum* 'Buxton's Variety'
*clarkei* 'Kashmir White' 205
*endressii* 212
*erianthum* 240
*grandiflorum* var. *alpinum* see *G. himalayense* 'Gravetye'
*himalayense* 239
'Gravetye' 236
'Johnson's Blue' 238
*macrorrhizum* 214
'Ingwersen's Variety' 174
x *magnificum* 238
*nodosum* 180
x *oxonianum* 87
'Southcombe Star' 87

'Wargrave Pink' 212
'Winscombe' 85
*phaeum* (Mourning widow) 53
'Album' 72
*pratense*
'Kashmir White' see *G. clarkei* 'Kashmir White'
'Mrs Kendall Clark' 122
*psilostemon* 94
*renardii* 206
*sylvaticum* 'Mayflower' 116
*wallichianum* 'Buxton's Variety' 246

**Gerbera**
Half-hardy perennials flowering from summer to winter, depending on growing conditions.
*jamesonii* (Barberton daisy) 281

**Geum (Avens)**
Hardy perennials grown for their flowers in summer.
x *borisii* 265
'Lady Stratheden' 260

Giant butterbur see *Petasites japonicus*
Giant fennel see *Ferula*
Giant Himalayan cowslip see *Primula florindae*
Giant holly fern see *Polystichum munitum*
Giant rhubarb see *Gunnera manicata*
Giant scabious see *Cephalaria gigantea*

**Gillenia**
Hardy perennials grown for their flowers in summer.
*trifoliata* (Bowman's root, Indian physic) 84

Ginger lily see *Hedychium*

**Glaucidium**
A genus of only one species of hardy, spring-flowering perennial. Excellent in woodland gardens.
*palmatum* 180

**Glechoma**
Hardy, evergreen, summer-flowering perennials. Good ground cover, but may be invasive.
*hederacea* 'Variegata' (Variegated ground ivy) 275

**Globba**
Frost-tender, evergreen, aromatic, clump-forming perennials grown for their flowers.
*winitii* 169

Globe thistle see *Echinops*

Globeflower see *Trollius*

**Glyceria see Grasses**
*maxima* var. *variegata* 295

**Glycyrrhiza
(Liquorice)**
Hardy, summer-flowering
perennials.
*glabra* 113

Goat's beard see *Aruncus dioicus*
Goat's rue see *Galega*
Golden foxtail see *Alopecurus
pratensis* 'Aureovariegatus'
Golden marjoram see *Origanum
vulgare* 'Aureum'
Golden oats see *Stipa gigantea*
Golden polypody see *Polypodium
aureum*
Golden rod see *Solidago*
Golden spaniard see *Aciphylla aurea*
Goldilocks see *Aster linosyris*

**Gomphocarpus (Swan plant)**
Half-hardy to frost-tender perennials
and sub-shrubs, sometimes included
in *Asclepias*, grown for their often
fragrant and colourful flowers.
*physocarpus* 43

Gooseneck loosestrife see *Lysimachia
clethroides*
Gout weed see *Aegopodium*
Grapevine begonia see *Begonia*
'Weltoniensis'

**Grasses (Gramineae)**
A family of fully hardy to frost-
tender, evergreen, semi-evergreen,
or herbaceous, sometimes creeping
perennials, annuals and marginal
water plants, usually with rhizomes
or stolons, that form tufts, clumps or
carpets. All have basal leaves and
rounded flower stems that bear
alternate, long, narrow leaves.
Flowers are bisexual (males and
females in same spikelet). Each
flower head comprises spikelets,
with one or more florets, that are
covered with scales from which awns
(long, slender bristles) may arise.
See also *Alopecurus, Arundo,
Chondrosum, Cortaderia, Glyceria,
Hakonechloa, Helictotrichon, Holcus,
Hordeum, Miscanthus, Oplismenus,
Pennisetum, Phalaris, Spartina* and
*Stipa.*

**Gunnera**
Frost-hardy, summer-flowering
perennials grown mainly for their
foliage. Some are clump-forming
with very large leaves; others are

*Gunnera continued*
mat-forming with smaller leaves.
*manicata* (Giant rhubarb) 30

Great yellow gentian see *Gentiana
lutea*
Greater celandine see *Chelidonium*
Green hellebore see *Helleborus
viridis*
Ground elder see *Aegopodium*
Guinea-wing begonia see *Begonia
albopicta*

**Gypsophila**
Hardy spring- to autumn-flowering
perennials, some of which are semi-
evergreen. The genus also includes
annuals.
*paniculata* 'Bristol Fairy' 70
'Rosenschleier' 205
'Rosy Veil' see 'Rosenschleier'
'Veil of Roses' see 'Rosenschleier'

---

# H

**Hakonechloa see Grasses**
*macra* 'Aureola' 298

Harebell poppy see *Meconopsis
quintuplinervia*
Hawkweed see *Hieracium*

**Hedychium
(Garland flower, Ginger lily)**
Frost-hardy to frost-tender
perennials with stout, fleshy
rhizomes. Fragrant, showy flowers
are short-lived, but borne profusely.
Ideal for sheltered borders and
conservatories.
*densiflorum* 35
*gardnerianum* (Kahili ginger) 43

**Hedysarum**
Hardy perennials, biennials and
deciduous sub-shrubs.
*coronarium* (French honeysuckle)
110

**Helenium (Sneezeweed)**
Hardy, late summer- and autumn-
flowering perennials grown for their
sprays of daisy-like flower heads,
each with a prominent, central disc.
'Butterpat' 137
'Moerheim Beauty' 163
'Riverton Gem' 47
'Sonnenwunder' 45
'Wyndley' 162

**Helianthus (Sunflower)**
Hardy, summer- and autumn-
flowering annuals and perennials
grown for their large, daisy-like,

*Helianthus continued*
usually yellow flower heads. May
be invasive.
'Capenoch Star' 44
*decapetalus*
'Morning Sun' 46
'Soleil d'Or' 47
x *laetiflorus* 'Morning Sun' see
'Morning Sun'
'Loddon Gold' 46
'Monarch' 47
'Triomphe de Gand' 46

**Helichrysum**
Fully hardy to frost-tender, summer-
and autumn-flowering perennials.
Dried flower heads are
"everlasting". The genus also
includes, annuals, and evergreen
sub-shrubs and shrubs.
'Schwefellicht' 257
'Sulphur Light' see
'Schwefellicht'

**Heliconia (Lobster claws)**
Frost-tender, tufted perennials,
evergreen in warm climates, grown
for their spikes of colourful flowers
and for the attractive foliage on
younger plants.
*psittacorum* (Parrot's flower,
Parrot's plantain) 35

**Helictotrichon see Grasses**
*sempervirens* 296

**Heliopsis**
Hardy summer-flowering perennials.
'Ballet Dancer' 143
*helianthoides* var. *scabra*
'Light of Loddon' 35
'Sommersonne' 136
'Summer Sun' see *H. helianthoides*
var. *scabra* 'Sommersonne'

**Helleborus**
Fully to half-hardy perennials, some
of which are evergreen, grown for
their winter and spring flowers. Most
deciduous species retain their old
leaves over winter. These should be
cut off in early spring as flower buds
develop. Excellent in woodlands.
*argutifolius* 290
*corsicus* see *H. argutifolius*
*cyclophyllus* 193
*foetidus* (Stinking hellebore) 293
*lividus* subsp. *corsicus* see *H.
argutifolius*
*multifidus* subsp. *hercegovinus* 290
*niger* (Christmas rose) 278
'Potter's Wheel' 278
*orientalis* (Lenten rose)
pink 280
purple 284

# I

Ice-plant see *Sedum spectabile*
'Brilliant'

**Impatiens**
Frost-hardy to frost-tender, mainly
evergreen perennials and sub-
shrubs, often with succulent but
brittle stems. In cold climates some
may be herbaceous. The genus also
includes annuals.
 *repens* 264

**Incarvillea**
Fully to frost-hardy, spring-or
summer-flowering perennials, suited
to rock gardens and borders.
 *delavayi* 225
 *mairei* 216

Indian physic see *Gillenia trifoliata*

**Inula**
Hardy, summer-flowering, clump-
forming, sometimes rhizomatous
perennials.
 *ensifolia* 265
 *hookeri* 134
 *magnifica* 34

**Iresine**
Frost-tender perennials grown
for their colourful leaves.
 *herbstii* 'Aureoreticulata' 292

**Iris**
Genus of upright, rhizomatous or
bulbous (occasionally fleshy-rooted)
perennials, some of which are
evergreen, grown for their
distinctive and colourful flowers.
 *afghanica* 55
 'Anniversary' 54
 'Arnold Sunrise' 55
 'Blue-Eyed Brunette' 60
 'Bold Print' 57
 *chrysographes* 58
 *confusa* 54
 *cristata* 56
 *douglasiana* 58
 'Dreaming Yellow' 55
 'Early Light' 57
 'Eyebright' 60
 'Flamenco' 60
 *forrestii* 59
 *fulva* 60
 x *fulvala* 57
 'Fulvala' see *I.* x *fulvala*
 'Geisha Gown' 55
 *hoogiana* 58
 *iberica* 55
 *innominata* 60
 'Joette' 56

*Iris continued*
 *kerneriana* 55
 'Krasnia' 57
 *lacustris* 58
 *laevigata* 58
 'Mary Frances' 58
 'Matinata' 58
 *missouriensis* 56
 'Mountain Lake' 58
 *pallida* 'Aurea Variegata' 56
 'Paradise Bird' 56
 'Peach Frost' 60
 *pseudacorus* (Yellow flag) 59
 'Rippling Rose' 56
 *setosa* (Bristle-pointed iris) 59
 'Shepherd's Delight' 60
 'Sun Miracle' 60
 *tectorum* 57
 *tenax* 56
 *unguicularis* (Algerian iris,
   Winter iris)
 'Mary Barnard' 57
 *variegata* (Variegated iris) 59
 *versicolor* (Blue flag, Wild iris) 56
 'Wisley White' 54

Iron-cross begonia see *Begonia
masoniana*

# J

Jacob's ladder see *Polemonium*
Japanese anemone see *Anemone
hupehensis*
Japanese banana see *Musa basjoo*
Japanese burnet see *Sanguisorba
obtusa*
Japanese holly fern see *Cyrtomium
falcatum*
Jasmine tobacco see *Nicotiana alata*
Jerusalem cross see *Lychnis
chalcedonica*
Joe Pye weed see *Eupatorium
purpureum*

**Juncus see Reeds**
 *effusus* 'Spiralis' (Corkscrew rush)
 297

# K

**Kaempferia**
Frost-tender, tufted, rhizomatous
perennials grown for their flowers
and aromatic leaves.
 *pulchra* 233

Kaffir lily see *Schizostylis*
Kahili ginger see *Hedychium
gardnerianum*
Kangaroo paw see *Anigozanthos*
King fern see *Todea barbara*
King's spear see *Asphodeline lutea*

King's spear see *Eremurus*
Kingcup see *Caltha palustris*

**Kirengeshoma**
Hardy late summer- and autumn-
flowering perennials.
 *palmata* 162

Knapweed see *Centaurea*

**Knautia**
Hardy summer-flowering annuals
and perennials.
 *macedonica* 108

**Kniphofia
(Red-hot poker, Torch lily)**
Fully to half-hardy perennials, some
of which are evergreen. Grown for
their colourful poker-like flower
spikes in summer and autumn.
 'Atlanta' 162
 *caulescens* 162
 'Ice Queen' 43
 'Little Maid' 255
 'Percy's Pride' 161
 'Royal Standard' 144
 'Strawberries and Cream' 232
 *thomsonii* var. *snowdenii* 144
 *triangularis* 163
 'Wrexham Buttercup' 33

Knotweed see *Persicaria*

**Kohleria**
Frost-tender, erect perennials with
scaly rhizomes, grown for their
showy, tubular flowers.
 *digitaliflora* see *K. warscewiczii*
 *eriantha* 112
 *warscewiczii* 92

# L

Lace flower see *Episcia dianthiflora*
Lady's mantle see *Alchemilla*
Lamb's tongue see *Stachys byzantina*

**Lamium (Deadnettle)**
Hardy, spring- or summer-flowering
perennials, most of which are semi-
evergreen. Many species are weeds,
but some make useful ground cover.
 *maculatum* 177
 *album* 171
 'White Nancy' 170
 *orvala* 182

Lampshade poppy see *Meconopsis
integrifolia*

**Lathraea**
Hardy, spreading perennials that
grow as parasites on tree roots – in

# M

## Macleaya (Plume poppy)
Hardy, summer-flowering perennials grown for their overall appearance.
*cordata* (Tree celandine) 21
*microcarpa* 'Coral Plume' 22

Maidenhair spleenwort see *Asplenium scolopendrium*
Male fern see *Dryopteris filix-mas*
Mallow see *Malva*
Maltese cross see *Lychnis chalcedonica*

## Malva (Mallow)
Hardy, free-flowering but short-lived perennials grown for their abundant displays of flowers.
*moschata* (Musk mallow) 86

Man fern see *Dicksonia antarctica*

## Maranta
Frost-tender, evergreen perennials grown for their coloured and patterned foliage.
*leuconeura*
'Erythroneura' (Herringbone plant) 287
var. *kerchoveana* (Rabbit tracks) 288

Marble leaf see *Peristrophe hyssopifolia* 'Aureovariegata'
Marguerite see *Argyranthemum frutescens*
Marsh buckler fern see *Thelypteris palustris*
Marsh fern see *Thelypteris palustris*
Marsh marigold see *Caltha palustris*
Marvel of Peru see *Mirabilis*
Masterwort see *Astrantia*
Matilija poppy see *Romneya*

## Matteuccia
Hardy, deciduous rhizomatous ferns grown for their foliage.
*struthiopteris* 304

Meadow rue see *Thalictrum*
Meadowsweet see *Filipendula*

## Meconopsis (Blue poppy)
Hardy perennials, some short-lived, others monocarpic (die after flowering), grown for their flowers.
*betonicifolia* 125
*cambrica* (Welsh poppy) 200
*grandis* 'Branklyn' 125
*integrifolia* (Lampshade poppy) 260
*napaulensis* (Satin poppy) 26
*quintuplinervia* (Harebell poppy) 184

## Melianthus
Half-hardy to frost-tender, evergreen perennials and shrubs grown primarily for their foliage.
*major* (Honeybush) 26

## Melica see Grasses
*altissima* 'Atropurpurea' 297

## Melittis (Bastard balm)
A genus of only one species of hardy perennial grown for its flowers in summer.
*melissophyllum* 208

## Mentha (Mint)
Fully to frost-hardy perennials, some of which are semi-evergreen, grown for their aromatic foliage, which is used both for decoration and as a culinary herb. Plants are invasive.
*suaveolens* 'Variegata' (Variegated apple mint) 203

Merry-bells see *Uvularia grandiflora*

## Mertensia
Hardy perennials grown for their funnel-shaped flowers.
*asiatica* see *M. simplicissima*
*maritima* subsp. *asiatica* see *M. simplicissima*
*pulmonarioides* (Blue bells, Virginia cowslip) 184
*simplicissima* 243
*virginica* see *M. pulmonarioides*

Metallic-leaf begonia see *Begonia metallica*
Mexican foxglove see *Tetranema roseum*
Mexican violet see *Tetranema roseum*
Michaelmas daisy see *Aster*

## Microlepia
Frost-tender, deciduous, semi-evergreen or evergreen ferns, best grown in pans or hanging baskets.
*strigosa* 300

Milkweed see *Euphorbia*

## Mimulus (Monkey musk)
Fully to half-hardy perennials popular for their attractive summer flowers. Small species suit damp pockets in rock gardens. The genus includes evergreen shrubs.
'Andean Nymph' 209
*lewisii* 217
*luteus* (Yellow musk) 260
'Royal Velvet' 232

Mind-your-own-business see *Soleirolia*

Mint see *Mentha*

## Mirabilis (Four o'clock flower, Marvel of Peru)
Half-hardy, summer-flowering tuberous perennials. The genus also includes annuals.
*jalapa* 95

## Miscanthus see Grasses
*sinensis*
'Gracillimus' 297
'Zebrinus' (Zebra grass) 295

## Moltkia
Fully, to frost-hardy, deciduous, semi-evergreen or evergreen perennials and sub-shrubs grown for their funnel-shaped flowers in summer.
*doerfleri* 236

## Monarda (Bergamot)
Hardy perennials grown for their flowers and aromatic foliage. The genus also includes annuals.
'Beauty of Cobham' 115
'Cambridge Scarlet' 110
*didyma*
'Cambridge Scarlet' see 'Cambridge Scarlet'
'Croftway Pink' see 'Croftway Pink'
'Croftway Pink' 87
*fistulosa* (Wild bergamot) 116

Monkey musk see *Mimulus*
Monkshood see *Aconitum*

## Morina (Whorl flower)
Frost-hardy, evergreen perennials, of which only one species is in general cultivation for its thistle-like foliage and its flowers.
*longifolia* 84

Mosaic plant see *Fittonia verschaffeltii*
Mosquito grass see *Chondrosum gracile*
Mother of thousands see *Soleirolia*
Mother-in-law's tongue see *Sansevieria trifasciata*
Mourning widow see *Geranium phaeum*
Mullein see *Verbascum*

## Musa (Banana)
Frost-hardy to frost-tender, evergreen, palm-like suckering perennials with false stems formed by overlapping leaf sheaths, grown for their foliage, flowers and fruits (bananas), not all of which are edible.
*arnoldiana* see *Ensete ventricosum*

**Selaginella**
Frost-tender, evergreen, moss-like
perennials grown for their foliage.
  *kraussiana* (Spreading club
  moss, Trailing spike moss) 303
  *martensii* 301

**Senecio**
Fully hardy to frost-tender,
succulent, and non-succulent
perennials grown for their foliage
and usually daisy-like flower heads.
The genus also includes annuals,
shrubs, sub-shrubs and climbers.
  'Gregynog Gold' see *Ligularia*
  'Gregynog Gold'
  *przewalskii* see *Ligularia przewalskii*
  *pulcher* 268

Sensitive fern see *Onoclea sensibilis*
Setcreasea purpurea see *Tradescantia
pallida* 'Purple Heart'

Shell ginger see *Alpinia zerumbet*
Shell flower see *Alpinia zerumbet*

**Sidalcea**
Hardy, summer-flowering
perennials grown for their
hollyhock-like flowers.
  'Elsie Heugh' 93
  'Jimmy Whitelet' see 'Jimmy
  Whittet'
  'Jimmy Whittet' 88
  *malviflora* (Checkerbloom) 86

Silk weed see *Asclepias*
Silver inch plant see *Tradescantia
zebrina*
Silver king see *Artemisia ludoviciana*
var. *albula*
Silver net-leaf see *Fittonia
verschaffeltii* var. *argyroneura*

**Sinningia**
Frost-tender, usually summer-
flowering, tuberous perennials with
showy flowers.The genus includes
deciduous sub-shrubs.
  'Red Flicker' 225
  'Switzerland' 229

**Sisyrinchium**
Fully to half-hardy perennials, some
of which are semi-evergreen, grown
for foliage and spring flowers.
  *striatum* 254

Skeleton fork fern see *Psilotum
nudum*

**Smilacina**
Hardy perennials grown for their
graceful appearance.
  *racemosa* (False spikenard) 52

**Smithiantha**
Frost-tender, bushy, erect
perennials with tuber-like rhizomes,
grown for their flowers.
  'Orange King' 230

Snake plant see *Sansevieria trifasciata*
Sneezeweed see *Helenium*
Snowdrop windflower see *Anemone
sylvestris*
Snowflower see *Spathiphyllum
floribundum* 'Mauna Loa'
Snowy woodrush see *Luzula nivea*
Soft tree fern see *Dicksonia antarctica*

**Soleirolia**
(Baby's tears, Mind-your-own-
business, Mother of thousands)
A genus of only one species of,
usually, evergreen, prostrate
perennial that forms a dense carpet
of foliage. Frost hardy, but leaves are
killed by winter frost.
  *soleirolii* 290

**Solidago (Golden rod)**
Hardy, summer- and autumn-
flowering perennials, some species
of which are vigorous plants that
tend to crowd out others in borders.
  'Golden Wings' 44
  'Goldenmosa' 133
  'Laurin' 136

x **Solidaster**
Hybrid genus (*Solidago* x *Aster*) of
one hardy, summer-flowering
perennial.
  *hybridus* see x *S. luteus*
  *luteus* 256

Solomon's seal see *Polygonatum*
Spanish shawl see *Heterocentron
elegans*

**Spartina** see **Grasses**
  *pectinata*
  'Aureomarginata' 298
  'Aureovariegata' see
  'Aureomarginata'

Spear lily see *Doryanthes palmeri*

**Spathiphyllum**
Frost-tender, evergreen perennials
with rhizomes, grown for their
foliage and flowers.
  *floribundum* 'Mauna Loa'
  (Snowflower) 274

**Sphaeralcea**
Half-hardy perennials grown for
their flowers. The genus also
includes deciduous sub-shrubs.
  *ambigua* (Desert mallow) 144

Spider plant see *Chlorophytum
comosum* 'Vittatum'
Spiderwort see *Tradescantia*
*Spiraea aruncus* see *Aruncus dioicus*
Spoon-leaf sundew see *Drosera
spathulata*
Spreading club moss see
  *Selaginella kraussiana*
Spring vetch see *Lathyrus vernus*
Spurge see *Euphorbia*
Squawroot see *Trillium erectum*
Squirreltail grass see *Hordeum
jubatum*
St. Bernard's lily see *Anthericum
liliago*

**Stachys**
Fully hardy to frost-tender, late
spring- or summer-flowering
perennials, some of which are
evergreen. The genus also includes
shrubs, and sub-shrubs.
  *byzantina* (Bunnies' ears,
  Lamb's tongue) 289
  'Primrose Heron' 254
  'Silver Carpet' 289
  *lanata* see *S. byzantina*
  *macrantha* 'Superba' 237
  *olympica* see *Stachys byzantina*

Stinking hellebore see *Helleborus
foetidus*

**Stipa** see **Grasses**
  *gigantea* (Golden oats) 296

Stoke's aster see *Stokesia laevis*

**Stokesia**
A genus of only one species of
hardy, evergreen, summer-flowering
perennial.
  *laevis* (Stoke's aster) 239

Stonecrop see *Sedum*
Stork's bill see *Erodium*

**Strelitzia**
(Bird-of-paradise flower)
Frost-tender, large, evergreen,
tufted, clump-forming, palm-like
perennials grown for their showy
flowers.
  *nicolai* 48
  *reginae* 169

**Streptocarpus**
Frost-tender perennials (some are
evergreen) with showy flowers.
  *caulescens* 205
  'Constant Nymph' 287
  *saxorum* (False African violet) 233

**Strobilanthes**
Frost-hardy to frost-tender

# Acknowledgments

Key: t=top; b=bottom; r=right; l=left; c=centre; cra=centre right above

The publishers would like to thank the following for their kind permission to reproduce the photographs:

**A-Z Botanical Collection Ltd**/Neil Joy 300cr
**Gillian Beckett** 301tl
**Deni Bown** 303b, 305br
**Pat Brindley** 299tl
**Derek Gould** 21cr, 86bl, 199t, 251cra, 261cr
**Mike Ireland** 216bl
**Marc King** 138b
**Andrew Lawson** 57tr, 107br, 117tl, 124bl
**Photos Horticultural Picture Library** 26br, 82b,96cl, 197tr, 266br
**Harry Smith Collection** 34r, 83cl, 97cr, 202br, 208tr,213tr, 221cr, 273cra, /Polunin Collection 302br

**Special photography:** Eric Crichton, John Glover, Jerry Harpur, Andrew Lawson, Andrew de Lory, Howard Rice

**Index:** James J. Parker

**Design assistance:** Mark Tattam

In addition to the above, the publishers would also like to thank the staff of the Royal Horticultural Society Publications

## Abbreviations

| | | | |
|---|---|---|---|
| C | centrigrade | in | inch, inches |
| cm | centimetre | m | metre |
| cv. | cultivar | mm | millimetre |
| F | fahrenheit | oz | ounce |
| f. | forma | sp. | species |
| ft | foot, feet | subsp. | subspecies |
| g | gramme | var. | variant |